Best Wishes

Jim

1978 2003

growing with the community

Stephen tells me you
are feeling on a new
adventure — good luck.

310

Michael Collins and Harry Boland, taken in Croke Park c.1921-1922.

Hibernia London team 1903 – Sam Maguire was born in Maulabracka, Dunmanway, Co. Cork. He died a young man, 6th February 1927 and is buried in St Marys Church of Ireland Cemetery, Dunmanway. He captained the London teams who played in the All Ireland finals in 1902 and 1903 and played with the 1900 and 1902 finalists. The 1900 final was played in October 1902 and was won by Tipperary (Clonmel Shamrocks). The victors of 1902 final, played August 1903, were Dublin. The All Ireland final of 1902 was played for the official opening of the Cork Athletic Grounds (now Pairc Ui Chaoimh) in November 1904. Dublin (Bray Emmets) were victorious. Kerry (Mitchels) won the 1903 final, which was played November 1905.

The picture shows Sam Maguire with the ball. On his left are his brothers Dick and Bill. On his right, 3rd from left of picture is Andy O'Leary, (played in the 1902 and 1903 finals), granduncle, on her father's side of Eileen Breheny, St Judes. She is grandniece, on her mother's side of Jack Hooper, (played in the 1900 and 1901 finals), who is on extreme right of back row. His brother Patsy is in the row in front of him, 4th from left of picture.

"In one's life, one is, if one is lucky, permitted once or twice to make a difference, to touch the hem of history. Together we have had that chance. Together we have taken it. We should all be proud of that."

Valéry Giscard d'Estaing

ACKNOWLEDGEMENTS

This project commenced in October 2002 and has taken almost 12 months to complete. The early months were taken up in gathering data and records. In practice most of the intense work commenced in March 2003. Whilst there are many articles containing details of teams, performances and results for adult and juvenile games, it is not intended to be a comprehensive history but rather a 25 year Commemorative Book.

We wish to acknowledge the huge effort of all contributors. To those who produced old minute books, press cuttings, match reports and photographs, our thanks.

A big debt of gratitude is owed to each member of the Editorial Committee: Declan Feore Chairperson, Don Lehane, Declan Doyle Club PRO and Charles Moran.

Others who deserve special mention for their research work, articles and/or invaluable assistance to the Editorial Committee are: Neil Doyle, Seán Breheny, Bobby Carty, Garrett Edge, Nick Finnerty, Michael Fortune, Tommy Hartnett,Peter Lucey, Seán McBride, Paul McGann, Finbarr Murphy, Marie O'Brien,Jimmy O'Dwyer, and the many others who contributed so willingly from time to time.

A sincere word of gratitude must go to Shay Lynch of Irish Rubies who designed our St Judes 25 logo. To the Irish Press Group, Evening Herald and The Echo our thanks for allowing us use the various newspaper extracts. We must also thank Tina Lawlor of Kilkenny People Printing Ltd for all her hard work, advice and patience throughout the project.

Finally, our thanks to Kay McKinney and Deirdre Feore for their considerable input in assisting with the formatting, editing and proof reading of the various articles and submissions.

Executive Committee
St Judes GAA Club

Published by:
St Judes GAA Club, 2003

Print & Design by:
Kilkenny People Printing Limited
056 7763366

Contents

Fáilte

Is mór an onóir agus brodúlacht dom bheith im Chathaoirleach ag an am stairuil seo, fiche cuigiú bliain den Chumann.

Is fearr fósta an pribhléid dom focal fháilte a sholáthar daoibh go léir a léann an foilseachán seo.

Is cuntas fairsing, eagsúil é, a léirionn agus a nochtann smaointí, tuairimí agus cuimhnithí na scribhneoirí difriúla atá le sonnrú ann. Is scríbhneoirí iad a bhfuil gné comónta speisialta amháin acu, is é sin gur thug siad uilig cuid mhór da saol chun Cumann Naomh Jude a bhun, a leathnú agus a chothú.

Molaim go hárd iad, agus an Coiste Eagrúchain a chur le céile an leabhar.

Tá súil agam go mbainfidh sibh taithneamh agus eolas as, agus go mb'fheidir go spreagfadh sé cuimhne ionat ar shaol an Chlub agus an Pharóiste, san am atá imithe tharainn.

Gabhaimis buíochas leis na bunaitheoirí a raibh an t-amharc, fadradharc agus fiontar acu cun an Cumann a chur ar bun. Tá an Cumann ag dul cun cinn agus an forbairt ag leanúint.

Tá aidhmeanna an Cumann socraithe don na todhchaí agus mar sin táim muiníneach faoin bóthar atá romhainn.

Buíochas do chách

I am honoured and privileged to be Chairman of Saint Judes GAA Club as we celebrate its 25th anniversary.

I invite you to read this splendid account of our activities over the past 25 years. The many and diverse contributors to this volume have much in common, especially a love for and loyalty to Saint Judes that stretches back over years of dedicated service to the Club as members, players, mentors, staff or officers.

I am sure you will join me in thanking them and the Editorial Committee for their commitment and painstaking work. I am confident that wonderful memories will flood back as you read. I trust that these pages will evoke in you a warm appreciation of the heroic and varied accomplishments of this club and the extraordinary contribution ordinary people can make in shaping the lives around them.

Praise, gratitude and awe are our responses to the foresight, enterprise and determination of the Club's founder members. We must take forward their ideals and vision to make our club even more successful in the years ahead.

Since 1978 the Club has had unparalleled development and expansion. We now have over 50 teams representing us in football, hurling, camogie and ladies football. Our Clubhouse is second to none in facilities and we have recently entered into joint partnership in the development of an all-weather pitch.

While every club aspires to win a senior championship it must never neglect the equally important aims of community development and the furthering of the social activities of all our members.

At a recent planning seminar for the Club, a vision for the future was set out and major objectives for the Club over the next 3 to 5 years agreed. Our various committees are presently working on the implementation of these aims.

It is appropriate at this juncture to express gratitude to all our many sponsors and advertisers over the years. Their generosity has contributed significantly to the promotion and development of the club.

I would also like to take this opportunity to thank all officers and committee members for their immense contributions down the years. Also, I would like to offer to all players, managers, coaches, patrons, volunteers, bar management and staff the Executive's sincere gratitude for all their efforts in promoting and developing the ideals of St Judes. Thank you all for your hard work and dedication.

In our celebrations let us not forget our deceased members and friends, who made such a significant contribution to the development of our Club.

Go ndéana Dia trócaire ar a n-anamacha.

Yours in sport,

John Brady
Chairman

Teachtaireacht an Uachtaráin

Is mór an onóir domsa an deis seo a fháil cupla focal a scrí ar fhoilsiú an leabhair seo.

I am honoured to be presented with the opportunity to extend this message to everyone involved with St Judes as you celebrate the 25th Anniversary of your club.

The foresight and calculation of those who recognised the need for a GAA presence in the Templeogue area in the 1970s have been justified repeatedly in the last quarter of a century, and from humble beginnings, St Judes has become one of the better known clubs in Dublin, providing a social and sporting outlet for the community that it serves with such enthusiasm and dedication.

The GAA, and indeed the broader community, owe the likes of St Judes a huge debt of gratitude. The contribution of our GAA clubs to Irish society over the past 120 years is much more significant than merely the legacy of our National Games. Our clubs have served to create a more integrated society and have helped to create a sense of community that is seldom found anywhere else in the world.

Having visited your wonderful facilities in Templeogue, it leaves one in no doubt as to the ambition of this club. Further evidence of this lies in the appointment of your own full time coaching director in 2001 and indeed the establishment of the All Ireland Junior sevens as a permanent feature on the GAA calendar brought the club to national attention. Anyone who has visited this event will know of the exceptional organisational ability of all at St Judes. I know that your club caters for hurling, football, camogie and ladies football with equal emphasis and with over 50 teams being fielded, this is clearly a club on the rise.

As the population of your catchment area increases, it is immensely important that you are prepared to meet the challenges that this will bring. I have no doubt that you are prepared and I salute your proactive approach, in affording a wonderful service to Templeogue and the surrounding areas. I take this opportunity to wish your club continued success, both on and off the field and extend my congratulations on this historic publication.

Gabhaim buíochas libh uile,

Seán Ó Ceallaigh
Uachtarán C.L.G

Overview - An exciting odyssey

Michael Fortune

THE 1970S represented a golden era in the history of the GAA in Dublin. Heffo's Army was on the march and the battalions of supporters rowed in behind them. Young and old were converted to the Dubs' ideal and Croke Park became a sea of blue.

In the midst of this great reformation, interest in the games was growing at a tremendous rate. The suburbs of Dublin were also growing, new villages and parishes were being established and the need for new clubs to cater for the mushrooming population was urgent.

Willington, Templeogue was one such area, houses were sprouting everywhere and in 1975 Bishop Galvin National School was opened. In that first year the school catered for just 110 pupils and the demand for a GAA club in the area became intense.

The Summer Project of 1977 saw football introduced for the first time and it was at these evening games that the seeds were sown. St Judes GAA Club was conceived. The birth finally took place on the night of Saturday, 9th September, 1978 when a meeting was held in Bishop Galvin School and a committee was appointed to look after the affairs of the new Cumann Peil Naomh Jude.

Fr John Greene cc was the first Chairman with Cyril Bates as Secretary and John Gallen as Treasurer. Ernest Kenny was the Vice Chairman.

Things happened fast. Within weeks two teams were contesting the South East Leagues, the Under 10 football side under Donnchadh Ó Liatháin, Ernest Kenny, Seamus Durkan and Jimmy O'Dwyer and the Under 14 team under Ernest Kenny, Fr Greene and Charles Moran. Pitches were scarce and most of the home games took place in Bushy Park and later in Bancroft Park.

The growth was steady and the successes soon began to flow. The Under 11A side became the first team to win a league when taking the 1980 South East League. This coincided with the permanent move of St Judes to Tymon Park and suddenly the club went into overdrive.

Now there were teams in all age categories, more than one in some. The Under 10s won the South East League in both 1981 and 1982.

But the year 1982 was an historic one when a new hurling and camogie section was inaugurated and the club's name was officially changed to Cumann Luthcleas Gael Naomh Jude.

The first official meeting of the Hurling and Camogie section took place on 24th March, 1982 with Finbarr Murphy the first Chairman, Jimmy O'Dwyer as Secretary and Jack Boland Treasurer. Two teams were entered at Under 10 and Under 12 levels.

The young club was making huge strides and there was the first sign of adult success with the junior footballers finishing second in Division 4 in 1983. But 1984 was even more significant, a first Camogie side represented the club and the Under 11 hurlers were runners-up in their league.

We didn't have long to wait for a first hurling success, the Under 10 side taking their league in 1985. The club was now fully established in all codes and people were beginning to sit up and take notice.

But with the success and the influx of young members, the need for a clubhouse had become an absolute priority. The AGM of 1984 had discussed the matter and an EGM, held in the spring of 1985, resulted in a decision to proceed with a major development.

The actual process of the building of the Clubhouse is dealt with elsewhere and outlines how a combination of a members' draw and various grants resulted in a magnificent new Clubhouse being opened by GAA President, Dr Mick Loftus on Sunday, 11th October, 1987.

The new Members' Lounge became an instant success and John Gallen became the first manager. However he retired within a year to run his own business and Tommy Hickey took over as manager on 1st May, 1988 and is still going strong, with the assistance, now, of Patsy Tyrell.

The demands on the club became even greater. More successes on the field, Seamus Durkan's team was now on the march and they swept everything before them. A magnificent six years reached a zenith in 1989 when they beat Erins Isle in O'Toole Park to clinch the Under 16 Dublin Football Championship.

A red letter year for the club was completed with the Junior A Hurlers winning the Dublin Championship.

It was now a case of going from one peak to another. The All Ireland Junior Sevens competition was introduced in 1990 and the same year saw the Under 11 Camogie side achieve the League and Championship double.

Our young players were also making their mark with regular recognition from the county selectors, and Enda Sheehy claimed a special place in the club's history when he was a member of the 1995 Dublin All Ireland winning side. It was a signal occasion in the club's history when Enda brought Sam to the Clubhouse for all to admire. Another massive achievement was just around the corner. In 1996 the Senior Footballers gained promotion from Division 2 to Division 1, the club had finally arrived!

The same year the Executive decided to proceed with the building of a major extension to the Clubhouse and this provided much needed extra changing facilities as well as a new Lounge, Committee Room and an enhanced Hall.

Then came 1998 and in August we celebrated in style when the hurlers earned Senior status by beating Naomh Olaf in Tymon Park to win the Intermediate Premier Championship. Suddenly St Judes were senior in football and hurling and in that same year, 1998 the camogie girls also gained promotion to senior. Great days.

There have been other tremendous developments since then, particularly our Senior footballers heading up Division 1 League in 2000 and none bigger than the completion of the magnificent All Weather Pitch, a joint development with our neighbours Templeogue Utd. These have all provided an extremely solid foundation for the future when the youth of today will become the leaders of the club as the 21st Century evolves.

This is just an appetiser, a very brief summary of what has been a quite incredible 25 year odyssey that has seen a club grow from a nomadic outfit to one of the strongholds of the GAA in the capital. It has been an exciting trip but one sincerely hopes that the next 25 will be even more thrilling and rewarding for all concerned.

The Boothmen – Elsie and Achill Bothman, with Jack in St Judes, 1996. Achill played for Dublin in their last All-Ireland hurling final, 1961.

Ar an Ócáid Seo

Donnchadh Ó Liatháin

AG CEILIÚRADH cúig bliain is fiche ó bhunú an Chlub seo againne is tairbheach dúinn ár n-aire a dhíriú ar na rudaí a chabhraigh le forbairt, neartú, agus dul chun chinn an Chlub. Orthu siúd tá leanúnachas, díograis agus dílseacht. Is deacair Traidisiún a mhíniú.

An féidir le clubanna ar có-aois leis an Club againne a rá go bfhuil traidisiún acu? An gá dúinn caoga bliain, no fiú amháin an céad, a chur isteach sar bheith cinnte go bhfuil traidisiún againn? Ní fheadar. Ach is cinnte go bhfuil baint ag traidisiún le leanúnachas.

Tá tosach maith déanta againn agus tig linn bheith bródúil as. Ach bímis aireach. Caithfimíd leanúint gan staonadh chun an Club a neartú agus a fhorbairt. Beidh sé naireach dúinn an éacht atá tosnaithe againn dul le faillí. Caithfidh glún eile an brat a iompar. Caithfidh stiúrthoiri an lae inniu tacaíocht agus diriú a thabhairt don glún sin go bheadfaidh siad leanúint leis an obair. "Mol an óige agus tiochfaidh sé". Bun-ábhar an Chlub amárach is ea óige an Chlub inniu.

Is soiléir freisin go mbraitheann an gnáth-chlub ar obair deonach na mball. San lá atá inniu ann ta brú úfasach ar daoine aire a thabhairt dá gnó pearsanta féin. Ina dteannta sin tá an sochaí, go mór-mhor, tógtha le cúrsaí rachmais agus maoin. Tá baol, mar sin, nach mbeidh daoine díograiseacha ar fáil chun an mór-obair deonach – a chuir tús leis an Club seo - a leanúint 'sna glúnta ata romhainn. Tá, fos, agus beidh, riamh, gá le daoine díograiseacha i saol an Club.

Mar sin bímis uile – idir imreoirí, traenáilithe, baill-choiste, gnath-bhaill agus leanúnai – díograiseach gnóthach agus dírithe ar aidhm amhain .i. dul chun chinn ár gClub.

Cad as dúinn? Taimíd lonnaithe anseo i dTeach Mealóg agus Clubtheach breá mór fairsing tógtha againn agus áiseanna de'n céad scoth againn. Ta dlúth-bhaint againn le cúrsaí imeartha i mBaile Atha Cliath agus bíonn, mar is ceart, tacaíocht fé leith á thabhairt againn leis Na Dubs.

Ach is cóir freisin ar an ocáid seo aitheantas a thabhairt dos na fir agus mná, as beagnach gach áird in Éirinn, a thug agus a thugann fós dílseacht agus inspioráid do'n Club seo nuair a bhí se á bhunú agus tríd an treimhse ó 1978 go dtí an lá inniu.

Mar creidigí seo: is cuma cad as dúinn nuair a bhíonn culaith an Chlub á chaitheamh againn nó dathanna an Chlub á n-iompar againn. Seasaimís lena chéile. Ní cóir dúinn mar baill an Chlub deighilt a bheith eadrainn bunaithe ar Cúige ná ar Chontae; ar peil, iomáint nó ar camógaíócht. Uaireannta beimíd san uachtar. Uaireannta eile beimid síos agus an sruth ag dul in ár gcoinne. 'Sna h-amanna sin seasaimíd le cheile. Ar scáth a cheile a mhaireas na daoine. Is amhlaidh don Chlub seo againne. Go maire sé céad.

Donnchadh Ó Liatháin ag caint le Micheál Ó Muirchearthigh, Céilí House, Naomh Jude, 1992.

A trip down memory Lane

Seamus Durkan

WHEN my family and I moved from London to Templeogue in the mid 1970s, St Judes parish was in its infancy and various clubs and organisations were formed. At Mass one Sunday morning in the summer of 1977, the then parish priest, Fr Boland, read out a letter at the request of Pat O'Grady from Robert Emmets Club in Perrystown. He was looking for interested players to enter a street league at Under 10 level.

Shortly after hearing this, I got into my VW Variant car with my son James and literally drove around the neighbourhood rounding up young recruits. (Can you imagine anyone getting away with that today!?) I entered this very first team in the league at Robert Emmets Club. They played three matches, won one, lost one and drew one. Incidentally, it was at one of these matches that I first met Donnchadh Lehane whose son Conor was on the team.

That summer of 1977, a Summer Project was organised in the parish by local residents. Gaelic teams for boys Under 10 and Under 14 were formed as well as men's teams from the different estates in the parish. At one of the committee meetings, my wife May met with Ernest Kenny and Cyril Bates R.I.P. Ernest expressed an interest in forming an under 10 team in the parish and May suggested introducing him to me. Subsequently, in 1978, a committee was set up consisting of Charles Moran, Ernest Kenny, Donnchadh Lehane, Cyril Bates, Carl Page, myself and others. Under 10 and under 14 teams were registered in the Dublin Leagues under the name of St Judes Club.

The Club at this stage had no facilities, finances or resources. Bancroft Park in Tallaght and Bushy Park in Terenure were used as home pitches. The Club owned just one football. Jimmy O'Dwyer lent us Bishop Galvin school jerseys for matches. Davy Griffin of Thomas Davis Club also supplied us with jerseys.

Funds were raised for the Club in those early days through cake sales in Bradys Butchers in Orwell shopping Centre and quizzes held in the local schools. The 25 card games were commenced and still continue to this day. At the centre of all these fundraising events were the following GAA wives: Rita Moran, Maureen Lehane, Tina Kenny, Bernie O'Boyle, Marie O'Dwyer (RIP), Marie Malone, Helen Page and May Durkan.

To cut costs all team jerseys were taken home after matches and washed by team managers' wives.

The very first Under 10 team was managed by Donnchadh Lehane, Ernest Kenny, Jimmy O'Dwyer and myself. In our first year, we came third in the South East Division 1 League. In our second year (Under 11) in 1979 we won the first ever League for the Club.

Conor Lehane and Gerard McSweeney later went on to play at Senior level for the Club. Paul Curran went on to play for the Dublin Senior team. To reward the team for doing so well, we organised trips to Belturbet in Co Cavan, Killasser in Co Mayo and to Liverpool where they played against local teams.

Back row (left to right): Ciaran O'Reilly, Damian O'Reilly, Eamonn O'Reilly, Ernest Kenny, Joe Morrin, Dessie Brannigan, Seamus Durkan, Frank McSweeney. Middle Row: Peter Kieran, Paul Curran, Alan Page, Michael Kavanagh, Willie Murphy, Niall Robinson, James Durkan, Conor Lehane, John Carroll, Stephen Masterson, Colm Mooney, Jim Dolan. Front row: Stuart Cahill, Eoin Darcy, Kevin Hogan, Ray Whelan, Gerard McSweeney, Eamonn O'Reilly, Graham McHugh, Billy Brannigan, Gavin Kavanagh and Pat Heslin. Managers: Seamus Durkan, Ernest Kenny, Donnchadh Lehane and Jimmy O'Dwyer.

It was at this stage in 1983, that Michael O'Boyle and I managed the Under 10 team. During their first year, they ended up as runners up in the South East Division 1 League. This team went unbeaten for the next 5 years in Division 1 Leagues. Unfortunately, they were beaten in the under 15 Championship final by St Vincents. We also won the Centenary cup in 1984. In 1989 they won the Under 16 All-Dublin League and the Championship as well.

During these years, to reward the boys' achievements, we took them to Killasser, Co Mayo, Beaufort Co Kerry and to London where they played local teams. Plaques and medals for these events were sponsored by Dermot Byrne.

From this Under 16 team, the following players went on to play at Senior level for the Club - Declan O'Boyle, Kieran Durkan, Dara Murphy, Peter Keohane and John O'Riordan.

Kieran Durkan played at Minor level for the Dublin team and Declan O'Boyle at Senior level for the Dublin team. In later years, I became selector for the St Judes Intermediate and Senior teams. I hope that they will enjoy continued success.

Over the past 25 years, May and myself have enjoyed watching St Judes Club grow from its very humble beginnings and have witnessed it go from strength to strength. We are proud to have been part of that.

U10 Division 1 winners 1981/82 – Back row (l-r): Dara Heraty, John Malone, Alan Gallagher, Alan Whelan, Keith Donnelly, Dara Murphy, H. Smith, Darren Donnelly, Paul Lavelle. Front: Billy Brannigan, Kieran Durkan, Fergal McCarthy, Kenneth Smith, Shane Gallen, Declan O'Boyle, Cathal Conway, Joe Denvir, Liam Dunne.

A walk in alien corn

Danny Lynch

FOLLOWING several years of organic existence in the flatland community that is Rathmines, I eventually headed for far off Templeogue. At that time we considered Bushy Park the outer limits of civilisation and we were never too sure of the ultimate destination of the various varieties of the 15 bus. It was a dank and dark November evening and with all my worldly possessions in a black plastic bag the 15A brought me to the top of Whitehall Road and I attempted to find the house that I had mortgaged my life to several months previously.

It was 1977 and the area was still in the throes of development, treeless and with many of the road arteries and facilities now in place yet to be provided. In many ways it was a forbidding place, a walk through alien corn.

After some time I discovered the odd face from the past who had also stumbled into this area and discussion on the common denominator, football, began to fuse some of us culchies together. It had to. Dublin, the then kingpins, masters of the Gaelic world, had suppressed the Kingdom's efforts in 1976 and 1977. Jim Coghlan tried to make me feel at home. He tried to persuade me that in the midst of the cauldron of triumphalist Dublin voices and the blue and white standards, existed an apparent dormant culchie presence. Jim reckoned that insurrection was nigh and that it was only a matter of time before we emerged from the catacombs with Sam again nestling under the shadows of the McGillicuddys.

He was right. In 1978 we had the five goals in the rain, Sheehy's miracle goal and Cullen's famous retreat. The culchie sound grew to a crescendo to be met by the Dubs' unique analysis, which amongst other things questioned the parentage of referee, Seamus Aldridge. But, it threw us together and from the seeds of acrimony grew the tree of unity, culminating in the establishment of a fledgling St Judes.

I had heard about these apostles of Gaelic Games setting about sowing the seeds of a new Club in the midst of people of disparate origins and with a playing population not yet matured. I doubted that it could be done and felt that the challenge of focusing and welding a new population together would prove insurmountable. I thought that the seed might come to flower but that the bloom would be brief, shortly dying on the vine. I was wrong.

As always, visionaries ask not "why" but "why not" and I learned of small and faltering progress being made under the stewardship of the late Joe Morrin. A tiny Club was born.

After years of traversing the various grounds of Dublin, from Beann Eadair to Cuala and from Stars of Erin to O'Dwyers I had little enthusiasm for becoming involved. However, in one moment of weakness Jim Coghlan persuaded me to become about the fifth supporter of a motley crew that appeared more suited to rape and pillage than the skills and subtleties of sport. My worst fears were confirmed when I ended up playing in goal, resplendent in a pair of wellingtons and a multi colour jersey. It is no wonder that a wag from the opposing team was heard remark, "where's the circus".

From humble beginnings the Club grew before our eyes, galvanising and uniting a community in a common cause. We were very proud indeed when in 1987 the magnificent new Clubhouse was built and even more proud when our representatives appeared in various grades in the sky blue jersey of Dublin for the first time.

St Judes is now indelibly imprinted in the urban tapestry that is South Dublin. In a short space of time it has created a sense of unity, identity and pride of place in a community. It has become the sporting and social focus, an entity of the community by the community and for the community. For this we owe an inestimable debt to the founding fathers and to those who nurtured it through its formative years. The torch has been handed down to new generations. Long may the Club prosper to illuminate the lives of so many. There is no longer a sense of walking in alien corn.

Danny Lynch, Martin Breheny and Jack Boothman.

25 years a-growing

Charles Moran

IT IS celebration time. St Judes proudly looks back at its achievements over the past twenty five years of promoting and fostering the objectives of Cumann Luthchleas Gael. It is a testament to the success of St Judes that its sporting achievements and development have become part of the fabric of GAA activities in the city and County of Dublin. St Judes club is synonymous with a continuous proactive enactment and promotion of our games, heritage and our culture.

It is indeed a pleasure and a privilege to outline and detail in this article the bricks and mortar development of St Judes. Firstly, I will briefly outline the initial conception and birth of our club. In the early 1970s several estates were being developed in the Templeogue area to cater for the many people who wished to settle and raise families in the area. We were all strangers. However, many were true GAA disciples, with a common purpose and mission to foster and promote GAA in our adoptive parish.

As a result of a very successful Summer Project and numerous after Mass discussions it was agreed to call a public meeting for 9th September 1978. This meeting was attended by Séamus Durkan, Ernest Kenny, Cyril Bates, (RIP) Donnchadh Ó Liatháin, Joe Morrin,(RIP) John Gallen, Matt Healy, Pat Farrelly, Eamonn O'Reilly, Des Cullen, Fr. John Greene and myself. It was the unanimous decision of the meeting that we start a new club for the youth of our parish. Thus "Cumann Peil Naomh Jude" was born. Two teams were entered into the football leagues, one at Under 10, and one at Under 14. The seeds of success were firmly sown. The number of teams multiplied as the years progressed despite the fact that we had no facilities at all. The time for togging out on the sides of a football pitch in all kinds of weather had to come to an end.

I will now focus on the development of our Clubhouse and Centre. When I was elected Chairman in 1982, I was very conscious of a potentially major problem facing the club. Because of the lack of an identifiable home base I could envisage our promising young players being lured to more established clubs. I had come from a background of playing for my local club, St Michaels, in County Roscommon, where players and members were intensely loyal regardless of success. Here in the city it became painfully clear that loyalty to one's club was more fickle, and that players were in fact being lured to the bigger clubs where better facilities were available.

When I put my concerns and proposal for the building of a clubhouse before the Executive it was their considered opinion that this would certainly create a sense of identity and a base for future generations. This was a monumental challenge for a very young and small club. We had no funds, just barely enough to cover day to day expenses. Many team managers paid referees fees and other expenses out of their own pockets. An extract from our first financial statement will show the meagre finances of the club at the time (see page 28). However, we ploughed ahead with our dream.

A feasibility study was carried out by Eoin Heraty, on behalf of the Executive. This recommended that it was essential that we proceed with the building of a clubhouse and centre on our own initiative. Prior to this an attempt was made to undertake a joint venture with St Judes Soccer Club. This did not prove successful.

A specially selected development committee, under the chairmanship of Joe McDonnell, was put in place. The members of the Committee were Seán Conway, Declan Feore, Mick Hartnett, Eoin Heraty(Treasurer) Mick O'Brien (Secretary) Donnchadh O'Liatháin, John Gallen, Bob Carty, Danny Lynch, Jim Coghlan and myself. Our first task was to undertake a major fundraising campaign. Details of the fund raising required to finance the building ,and of the proposed draw were presented to a specially convened executive meeting on 16th July 1986 for sanction and approval .This report was unanimously adopted. The first event was a draw. Our aim was to sell two thousand £100 tickets. This event was launched on the 28th July 1986 in the Spawell. To our delight it was over subscribed.

We had made a decision to await the outcome of this draw before proceeding to seek planning permission. In August 1986, the then Minister of State for Local Government and the Environment, Fergus O'Brien, contacted me while I was on holiday in Kerry, promising us a grant of £50,000 provided we could start building before the 31st December that year. On the day in question Rita and myself were having an enjoyable pint in Kate Kearney's Cottage with Dermot and Ann Byrne, who were also very involved at the time. We could hardly believe our luck when we got this momentous news, but all that worried me was that we might have difficulty meeting the time limit. Needless to say I was anxious to return to Dublin to set the ball rolling. I immediately contacted Eoin Heraty and Mick Hartnett and asked them to set up a meeting for the night of my return to make sure that we were able to collect this grant.

The committee was ecstatic when given this latest piece of information and it was their unanimous decision that we should strive to meet this time limit and secure this very welcome grant. Plans were agreed and planning permission sought. This was granted on the 30th November 1986.

In anticipation we had selected a contractor and were ready to proceed. Everything was in place and on schedule until a local Residents Association lodged a spurious objection to the planning permission. This objection eventually delayed commencement of the building by some four months and had the potential to cause the loss of the promised grant. With the co-operation of the Dublin County Council, in particular, Mr Dan O'Sullivan, and Fergus O'Brien, Minister of State it was agreed that the grant would be drawn down by the Co. Council and placed in a suspense account and paid out as the development proceeded. At this time a small number of persons in the parish felt that our clubhouse and centre should be managed by a community based management committee. They felt that this grant was being made available for a community centre. This was the gist of their objection to our planning permission. A Community Council, with representatives of all the organisations and groups in the parish, was later established. After a number of meetings, and with the assistance of the Community Council, the objection was formally withdrawn and the building was allowed to proceed.

The cost of building, fit out and equipping this first phase was approximately £360,000. It was financed by £130,000 from the first draw, £50,000 Government grant (referred to above) and a £30,000 grant from Dublin County Council. This left a balance of £130,000 which had to be borrowed from the bank. £50,000 was advanced on the personal guarantees of some fifty members to reduce this borrowing to a manageable amount. It was therefore necessary to hold a further draw, selling two thousand tickets at £100 each. This netted approximately £110,000.

We were fortunate to have many professional and business members on our development committee who guided us successfully through uncharted waters. All members of both the executive and development committees gave willingly and freely of their time and expertise and without this we wouldn't be where we are today. Number 82 Orwell Park was the venue for the majority of these meetings. Weekly, Rita vacated the sitting room to make way for these meetings and regularly provided tea and sandwiches, while we planned and monitored the progress of our planning application and our fundraising draw.

The co-ordination of this first draw was a major task. It was a learning process as we progressed. We did not have computers to record or trace the hundreds of monthly cash collections. Every entry had to be manually recorded and checked each month. This task would have been almost impossible but for the dedication and commitment of my good friend, Eoin Heraty. Many times we toiled into the early hours of the morning recording the up to date position of each monthly draw.

When subsequent draws were planned he was the first person I turned to, to be part of the organising committee.

As chairman I was indeed extremely privileged, proud and honoured to welcome Dr Michael Loftus, Uachtarán Cumann Luthchleas Gael to officially open our new Clubhouse on the 11th October 1987. This achievement was due to an unstoppable resolve on the part of all the committees and members who were determined to succeed. The result of all their hard work generated a community feel good factor, silencing the critics and knockers.

We were originally offered a site just inside the present entrance. Faughs were much more advanced with their plans and were granted permission to build along the roadway. We were then given our present site. This move created additional expenses as it was necessary to build a roadway and a pumping station and all other services were further from the road. After much negotiation, the Co. Council met most of these additional expenses. The majority of our members will have no knowledge of what the site originally looked like. It was some four feet lower than it is now. It was the base of an old quarry. The foundations were poured and the steel frame erected and the blockwork was about to start in earnest when an engineer arrived from the County Council. He directed that all work would have to cease unless the entire floor area and structure was raised by a further 18 inches. The reason the Council so directed was that the site and surrounding area was liable to flooding. We did have the right to appeal this direction from the Co. Council but there was no guarantee that on appeal we would have succeeded. We would then have had to face a disruption claim from the contractor, plus expert fees and still have to raise the building. Having considered all the legal and engineering advice we accepted the direction and raised the entire structure. This unexpected development increased the cost by approximately £20,000 The car park around the Clubhouse was raised up to four or five feet in places.

With all the above problems solved one more hurdle had to be overcome. The Licensed Vintners Association objected in court to a licence being granted. Thankfully, their attempt failed on a technical point and we had secured our greatest financial asset. The lounge was fitted out with top of the range fittings as it was essential that we establish a steady clientele. At the end of August 1987 we pulled our first pints. I still can picture Mick Hartnett serving me the first pint. It was a very proud moment indeed and every time I look at the photograph of that occasion it brings back very happy memories.

As time went on it became obvious that the area around the clubhouse needed to be further raised to its present level. This work was completed about four years after the opening at a cost of approximately £40,000.

At this stage the entire original debt was paid back. As the club expanded with more teams, including Camogie and Ladies Football it became necessary to provide additional dressing rooms and other facilities such as a gym, a games room, meeting rooms, a shop and a kitchen. The then Chairman, Mr Seán Breheny asked me to undertake the task of organising and chairing a development/finance committee with this in mind. I was more than happy to oblige and gathered together a finance committee comprising Eoin Heraty, Pat Kennedy, Colum Grogan, Johnnie O'Gara, Tom Ryan, Jack Lernihan, Frank Mahon, and Ann Ryan (Secretary).

Having established the requirements of the club, architects were retained, planning permission was obtained and the development committee (Eoin Heraty, Jack Lernihan, John Brady, Martin Molamphy, Seán Mc Bride, Bobby Carty and myself) were off once again on the building express. After a very competitive tendering process Tolmac Construction was selected as the contractor to carry out this work. The new extension and re-vamped original is a credit to the workmanship of Mick Hartnett and his men.

Finance for this new phase was once again raised by a Major Draw, selling three thousand tickets at £100 each and bank borrowing. We also received a lottery grant of £60,000. The new extension was opened on 3rd May 1998 by Joe McDonagh, Uachtarán Cumann Luthchleas Gael, who was warmly welcomed to St Judes by our then Chairman Martin Molamphy.

The Club was granted a first pitch in Tymon Park in 1982 at the Rushbrook end. Over the early years our pitch allocation was moved on a number of occasions. In the late eighties we were forced to take a major stand when once again the Co. Council sought to reallocate our prime pitch. After many meetings, petitions and lobbying our pitch was restored. I must state that St Judes is grateful to South Dublin Co. Council and its staff in Tymon Park for their help and co-operation over the years.

Finally, it was a pleasure to have contributed, with many others, to the foundation and building of St Judes over the past twenty five years and to have played an active part in the promotion of our national games and culture in this urban setting. Over this time I have made several very good permanent friends and have spent many long hours cheering on one of the best clubs in Dublin. Roll on the next twenty five years.

Official opening of clubhouse on 11th October 1987 – President of GAA Dr Michael Loftus and Chairman Charles Moran.

Development Committee 1987 – Front row (l-r): D. Lynch, S. Conway, J. McDonnell (Chairman), Mick O'Brien (Secretary), C. Moran, D. Lehane. Back row: D. Feore, J. Coghlan, M. Hartnett, E. Heraty (Treasurer), J. Gallen, B. Carty.

Official opening of club extension, May 1998 – (l-r): Joan Molamphy (Secretary), Betty Collard, Cáit Keane (MCC), Charles Moran (Dev. Committee), Martin Molamphy (Chairman), Mary Harney (Táiniste), Joe McDonagh (President), Eamonn Walsh (MCC), John Egan (Chairman Dublin Co. Board), Stanley Laing (MCC).

Draw in progress – Mick O'Brien, Mick Hartnett, Eoin Heraty with Declan Feore and Charles Moran in background.

Celebrating in St Judes – Seamus and May Durkan with their football team, Rita Moran, Eileen Lyons, Peggy Smyth (RIP) and Marie Russell.

St Judes Sevens Team, runners-up 1995 – Back row (l-r): Brendan Coughlan, Declan O'Reilly, Enda Crennan, Ciaran McSherry, Peter Ryan, Christy Kilcoyne (manager). Front: Gavin Russell, Damien Carroll, Colm Gough, Peter Harlow, Jeff Kane.

2000 Junior A Football team – Back row (l-r): Ernest Kenny (selector), David Campbell, Eamonn Hartnett, Gerard Hartnett, Phil McGlynn, Stephen Van Loon, Dermot Barry, Kevin Hayes, Paul Crennan, Damien McGlynn, Ciaran Cash, Tommy Hartnett (manager). Front: Donal Evoy, Greg Kane, Paul Costello, Eoghan Mangan, Paul Goodall, Michael Hartnett, John Purcell, Stephen Dunne.

1990 U11 Camogie League and Championship winners – Back row (l-r): Frank Carty, Lorraine Carty, Barbara O'Connor, Ellen Bone, Roisin Fitzpatrick, Sheila Loughman, Emer Ryan, Joanne Hartnett, Gillian Barry, Ruth Carty. Front: Niamh Farrell, Helen McGrath, Keira Skelly, Isobel Russell, Denise McGough, Andrea Hartnett, Fiona Guckian, Claire Walsh.

First Financial Statement

[Handwritten document — page 2]

Cumann Peil Naomh Jude
V.E.C. Sports Grant
Application
79/80

Balance Sheet at 1 October 1980

Capital 16/1/80	281 58	Football gear	334- 83	
Less Excess	129- 37	Less Items not bought	93- 50	
Capital 1/10/80	152- 21		241 33	
		Added Juvenile Team	150- 00	
			391 33	
Creditor - Jerseys	150 00	Depreciation 2 yrs	100 00	
			291 33	
		Cash in Hand	10 88	
	302 21		302 21	

We the undersigned certify that these accounts represent a fair and true statement of the affairs of Cumann Peil Naomh Jude in the period 16/1/79 to 1/10/80.

Signed _____ TREASURER

Signed _____ SECRETARY

DATED THIS DAY 10th OCTOBER 1980.

[Handwritten document — page 1]

Cumann Peil Naomh Jude
V.E.C. Sports Grant
Application
79/80

Receipts and Payments Account

Receipts		Payments	
Balance 16/1/79	105 25	Affiliations Levy etc	56 50
V.E.C. Grant	150 00	Trav. Exps. U.14 Liverpool	116 43
Subs 80/81	27 00	Referees fees +	
		Mentors expenses	66 44
		Charitable Donation	25 00
		Sundry	7 00
		Balance 1/10/80	10 88
	282 25		282 25

Income and Expenditure Account

Expenditure		Income	
Affiliations etc	56 50	V.E.C. Grant	150 00
Liverpool	116 43	Subs 80/81	27 00
Referees and Mentors	51 44		
Charitable Donation	25 00		
Sundry	7 00	Excess of Expenditure	
Depreciation - Year	50 00	over Income	129 37
	3 06 37		3 06 37

Notes:

1) New set of jerseys + new balls bought for extra Juvenile team taken on this year. Amount due £150 - 00

2) Mens set of gear not proceeded with

A tribute to my favourite (Dublin) club

Jack Boothman

THE LANDSCAPE of Cumann Luthchleas Gael has changed as dramatically as the landscape of South Dublin since St Judes first pulled those jerseys over their heads 25 years ago. Our Association has seen a dramatic change. It has been through some very challenging times.

Happily, it has risen to those challenges, as anyone who witnessed the spellbinding championship encounters of recent weeks or the gleaming showcase of the Special Olympics Opening Ceremony at Croke Park can testify. Our games are stronger and have a higher profile than ever before in our history.

The small urban village of Templeogue has had equally rigorous challenges, as it was transformed into a thriving conurbation. The spirit of the club shows that it too has risen to the challenge. A sense of pride in the community, of patriotism in the best sense of the word, and sense of identity has been maintained despite the rapid change.

An entire generation have this club to thank for something that means far more than medals won on hurling or football fields. That is in no small way due to the spirit of the club and the positive way it has played its role in the local community.

It wasn't easy. The people who planned the massive housing estates in these parts had no idea of the task they left behind. The job of preserving a sense of community in the new urban developments was left for someone else to do.

It is the GAA, and the go-ahead spirit of clubs like St Judes, that managed to preserve that sense of place, sense of pride and sense of identity. Where there is no sense of community, of pride and identity, a whole range of other problems are sure to follow.

The army of volunteers who gave up their spare time for the services of others, often with no thanks or recognition, are owed a huge debt by society.

These are the heroes of the GAA and of society in general whose exploits won't feature in any history, but without whom the organisation would have seized up long ago.

Their legacy is in the faces of the young people in the community nowadays, their sense of place and their sense of pride in what this club has to offer.

The GAA was founded as a rural, community based organisation. It lived and breathed as the community did.

And as the population moved out of rural homesteads into urban housing estates, so the GAA followed.

It was a difficult task. Sometimes the pressures on personnel and finance were great. But the organisation has risen to the challenge. Because the community of Templeogue, and the 2,000 plus other communities that make up the GAA, all rose to the challenge. For no other reason.

Sad to relate, the landscape I remember, the leafy lanes where myself and my wife, Nuala, first courted over 40 years ago, have long disappeared. Thankfully, the loving memories are still fresh today.

Thankfully the spirit which sustained the community has not faded. Then as now, it lives as proudly and as strong as ever.

This adventure is only beginning. The years ahead will bring more changes, new challenges. May there be many many more to join you in that adventure.

Jack Boothman and friends at Judes Sevens.

Executive Committee 2003 – Back row (l-r) Della Grogan, Kevin Coghlan, Neil Doyle, Joey Donnelly, Stephen Joyce, Garrett Evans, Nick Finnerty, Jack Lernihan (President), Mick O'Brien, Marie O'Brien. Front: Declan Doyle (PRO), Paul McGann (Vice-Chairman), John Brady (Chairman), Colum Grogan (Secretary), Frank Mahon (Treasurer).

St Judes founding members 1978 – Front row: Donnchada Ó Liatháin, Patrick Finn, Joe Morrin (RIP), Ernest Kenny, Seamus Durkan. Back: Charles Moran, Des Cullen, Matt Healy, John Gallen, Cyril Bates (RIP), Eamonn O'Reilly, Jimmy O'Dwyer. Absent: Fr John Greene and Pat Farrelly.

Juvenile Committee 2003 – Back row (l-r): John Healy, Martin Hayes, Martin Donnelly, Declan Doyle, John Brady (Club Chairman), Paddy Reid, Seán Ward. Middle: Paul McGann, Philip Breen, Adrienne Weston, Mary Joyce, Dave O'Flaherty, Liam McMahon, Seán O'Loughlin, Peter Ryan, Hugo Devine. Front: Brendan McLoughlin, Della Grogan, Niamh Leahy, Mary Monaghan (Secretary), Nick Finnerty (Chairman), Irene Dunne, Mick Brown, Ann Whitmore, John Gilmore, Padraig McManus.

2002 opening of all weather pitch in Tymon North, (l-r): Jim Daly (Mayor South Dublin), Seán McBride, (Chairman St Judes 2002), Bertie Ahern (Taoiseach), Colum Grogan (Secretary St Judes); John Brady, (Vice-chairman, St Judes); Declan Doyle (PRO, St Judes)

May 1998, the opening of the newly developed extension to St Judes clubhouse, Templeogue. From left: Declan Feore (Press Officer); Martin Molamphy (Chairman); Joe McDonagh (President of GAA) and Joan Molamphy (Secretary). Joe McDonagh is holding an Elm wood carving presented to him by Martin Molamphy on behalf of St Judes.   (The Echo)

Launch of plans for extension and third draw – back row: Michael Stokes, Joan Molamphy (Secretary), Conor Lenihan TD, Chris Flood (Minister of State), Seán Ardagh TD, Brian Hayes TD, Pat Upton TD (RIP), Cáit Keane MCC, Martin Molamphy (Vice-Chairman), Michael Fortune (PRO). Front: Seán Breheny (Chairman), Charles Moran (Development Committee), Jack Boothman, Gay Mitchell TD, Colum Grogan (Secretary).

2003 Summer Camp with Niamh Leahy and colleagues.

The mountaineers in 2002 – Declan Doyle with Declan Feore, Donie Cummins, Garrett Edge and President Jack Lernihan on expedition with Under 21 hurlers.

St Judes Golf Society 2003 handover €8,000 cheque raised at Golf Classic 2003 – (l-r): John Brady (Chairman, St Judes), Frank Mahon (Treasurer, St Judes), Michael Hartnett (Golf Society), Martin McCabe (Captain Golf Society), Declan Doyle (PRO, St Judes).

2002 All Forms of Humanity at U21 football final – how many can you identify? Gardai are keen to interview a number of these individuals!

1988 Millennium Culchie winners versus the Dubs – Back row: Finbarr Murphy, Neil Doyle, Don Lehane, Seamus Durkan, Tom Lyons, Michael Ryan, Jim Coghlan, Jimmy O'Dwyer, Ernest Kenny, Liam MacMathuna. Front: John McGovern, Seán Conway, Charles Moran, Frank Carty, Billy O'Frighil, Joe Keane, Declan Feore, Jim O'Hare. Note: There is unfortunately no photo of the Dubs due to photographic and reporting restrictions in the casualty dept. of Mater Hospital.

Club Trustees, (l-r): Mick Hartnett, Seán Conway, Jim Coghlan.

Susan Hughes with recruits at Summer Camp 2003.

Green graduates – Back row (l-r): Joe McDonnell (coach), –, Enda Maher, Eoin Larkin, –, –, Paul Kiernan, Alan O'Beirne, Seán O'Loughlin, –, Brian Bateman, Cathal Farrell. Front: Conor O'Toole, Killian Barden, Joseph McMahon, Michael O'Shea, Stephen Higgins, Oisin –, –, Bobby Moran, Chris Peggs.

The early years at the Summer Project. Who are those young people in the background?

Now boys, now boys – Joe Morrin snr gives instructions at the Summer Project on The Green 1978, second from left, standing, Marie Beil.

The doyen of Irish sports journalists, Paddy Downey (The Irish Times) with President, Frank McSweeney (St Judes) in the Clubhouse, 1994. The club made a presentation to Paddy on his imminent retirement at the press launch for the All Ireland Sevens.

Presidents at the Sevens (1999) – (l-r): Jack Boothman, Colum Grogan (secretary), Pat Farrell (EBS), Joe McDonagh, Seán McCague

Hall committee for Sevens 1998 – Celine Daly, Catherine Edge, Geraldine Mangan, Ans Lehane, Bernadette O'Malley, Mary Joyce, Mary McDonnell.

Junior Sevens winners 1993 (Football) – Back row (l-r): Seamus Lynch, James O'Dowd, Enda Sheehy, Ciaran Gallagher, John O'Riordan. Front: Shane Gallen, Ciaran Durkan, Colm O'Brien, Declan O'Boyle, Ciaran McGovern.

Winners of 1997 Junior Sevens Hurling Shield – Back row: (l-r): Denis Ryan, Kieran Quigley, David Roche, Fiachra Feore, Seán Fallon, Martin McGivergan, Joe Maloney, Peter Lucey (manager). Front: Colm Ryan, Kevin O'Dwyer, Padraig Kennedy, Neil Guinen, Bryan Duggan, Shay Collins, Kevin Roche.

1995 Sam Maguire Cup visits St Judes – (l-r): Donnchadh Ó Liatháin, Enda Sheehy (St Judes/Dublin), Tommy Hartnett.

Presentation night, 2001 – (l-r): Colum Grogan (PRO), John Bailey (Chairman Dublin County Board), Charles Moran, Danny Lynch (PRO CLG), Brian Talty (Senior Manager), John Costelloe (Secretary, County Board), Joe McDonagh (former President CLG), Sean McBride (Chairman).

Kay McKinney and friends at Senior Citizens Christmas Party.

Ethel and Jimmy Lee (RIP), early Judes supporters.

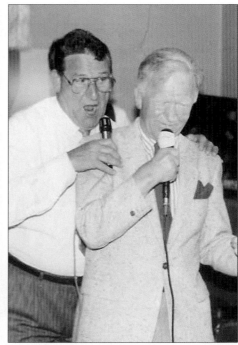

Frank McSweeney and Bill Tisdall (RIP).

First Bishop Galvin NS winners Frank Cahill, Croke Park, 1989 – Rear: Jimmy O'Dwyer (manager). Back row: Donagh O'Dwyer (mascot!!), Ciaran Lenihan, Stephen Brady, Alan McGreal, Aidan Lawlor, David Edge, Stevie Joyce, Kevin O'Dwyer, Michael Glover, Patrick Brien, Gareth Roche, Gary Downes, Gerard Orr. Front: Enda Crennan, Ian Fortune, Brendan Carty, David Mallon, Martin Sherkle, David McGovern, Ken Molloy, Richad Keenan, Karl O'Malley.

All the mens' President – Jack Boothman, President GAA, being conferred with Honorary Life Membership of St Judes, 14th September 1996, (l-r): Jack Lernihan, Charlie Hennessy, Declan Feore, Jack Boothman, Seán Breheny, Jim Coghlan, Colum Grogan and Danny Lynch.

Spawell sponsorship 1996 – Back: John Kennedy (Spawell), John Fogarty (Spawell), Declan O'Boyle (football captain), Tommy Basset, Peter Lucey. Front: Seán Breheny, Eugene Murray (hurling captain).

Sam at Summer Camp, 2002.

The yeaʀ Thaт was 1978

Deirdre Feore

THE YEAR 1978 has gone down in the history books in the parish of St Judes as the year when its GAA Club was founded. So, we know what we did in 1978 but what was the rest of the country and the world up to in the year that saw the birth of St Judes GAA Club?

To start with, Kerry beat the previous year's champions, Dublin, in the All-Ireland Senior Football Final. This started them on the road to their famous four-in-a-row victories. In 1982, Offaly shattered Kerry's chances of a first ever five-in-a-row by beating them by one point in the All-Ireland Final. This probably wasn't as bad as being beaten by seven points by Tyrone in 2003, but let's not digress.

The Rebel County brought the Liam McCarthy home to Cork, having beaten Kilkenny by four points. Kilkenny got revenge in 2003, beating Cork by three points.

One person who was happy with the All-Ireland Senior Hurling result of 1978 was our Taoiseach of the day, Jack Lynch, a man who had won both All-Ireland hurling and football medals for Cork. Staying with politics, the Irish President at the time was Patrick Hillery, and James Callaghan was British Prime Minister.

When they wanted to get away from politics, what did the people of 1978 do for a bit of entertainment? If you went to the cinema in 1978, you would have seen films such as The Deer Hunter (which won the Oscar for best film that year), Midnight Express (if you're still afraid of going to Turkey, you took this film far too seriously) and Grease (am I the only one who dreamt of being a Pink Lady?). Of course, there's one more film that deserves to be mentioned. If the words 'just when you thought it was safe to go back in the water' still sends a shiver down your spine, you remember the movie Jaws 2.

If you were happier to sit at home and watch the television, what would you have seen on the box in 1978? Think ten-gallon hats, oil wells and a sprawling ranch in Braddock County – 1978 was the year when Dallas first graced our screens. If you can still remember who shot JR, you were a real Dallas fan. For those of you who don't know, the answer is Kristen Shepherd.

Some of us would have been too caught up in a long-time favourite RTE programme to worry about new ones such as Dallas. This programme was Wanderly Wagon, which had characters such as O'Brien, Judge, Godmother, Mr

Crow and Sneaky Snake. Judge sometimes did work outside Wanderly Wagon. One of his famous 'nixers' was his involvement in the 'Safe Cross Code' (Remember 1, look for a safe place, 2 don't hurry, stop and wait...).

Talking about RTE, 1978 was the year when it launched a second television channel. RTE 2 was first beamed into our homes in November. Some of the Irish stars involved in the line-up were Terry Wogan, Val Doonican, Gemma Craven and Maureen Potter. Some of these would be considered to have musical talent but who was really popular in 1978?

The Boomtown Rats reached the No 1 spot in the UK charts with 'Rat Trap'. Some other big hits of the year were The Undertones' 'Teenage Kicks', Gloria's 'One Day at a Time' and some of the songs from Grease such as 'Summer Nights' and 'You're the One that I Want'. The big Christmas hit was 'Mary's Boy Child' by Boney M.

As I have mentioned music, I'd better not forget the Eurovision which was held in Paris. Colm CT Wilkinson represented Ireland with 'Born to Sing.' He came fifth. The winners were Israeli band, Izhar Cohen and the Alphabeta, who sang 'A-Ba-Ni-Ba'. (I bet you don't remember that tune!)

Of course, 1978 wasn't all laughter and entertainment. Beirut was divided by civil war, and Palestinian forces used Lebanon as a training base for attacks against Israel. Irish peace keeping troops were sent into the region for the first time. It was also the year when the Corporation decided to build offices over a Viking site at Wood Quay. Despite protests from the general public, the Corporation built their offices.

1978 has also gone down in history as the year when the Catholic Church had no less than three popes. Pope Paul VI died in August and was replaced by Pope John Paul I. He died after only 33 days in office. John Paul II was elected after this. This year, in 2003, he is celebrating the silver jubilee of his pontificate.

With all that happened in 1978, it's worth looking at what we didn't have. Locally, there was no St MacDara's Community College, which didn't open until 1982. There were no cars flying through Tymon North on the M50 motorway. In general, the CD hadn't been invented. If you're of the CD generation, the phrase 'you sound like a broken record' probably doesn't make too much sense to you. Nevertheless, music was played on vinyl records then. The Walkman hadn't been introduced either.

I think that's all I've left to say about 1978. If there's anything left out, I'll paraphrase one of the Jacksons' big hits of the year, 'don't blame it on the writer, blame it on the boogie'...

Adult Football history (1979-2003)

Don Lehane

THIS INTERIM history of adult football in St Judes covers the period from the establishment of the first junior team in 1979 to the start of the year 2003 season. The history has been split into the following four separate sections in this publication:

Adult Football Part 1: The Early Years Junior Football (1979-1986)

Adult Football Part 2: The Growing Years Junior to Intermediate (1986-1989)

Adult Football Part 3: The Push to Senior 1 (1989-1996)

Adult Football Part 4: The Senior 1 Years (1996-2003)

The timescale to pull together this history has been very short so apologies in advance for any inaccuracies or omissions in the text. I hope that no one will be disappointed by the coverage or lack of coverage of events but this is very much a personal and sometimes light hearted review of the period and I hope everyone will treat it in that light. I have however tried to ensure the accuracy of the factual aspects of the history and the progress of teams from year to year.

Please excuse the changes from past to present tense throughout these articles as some were written up in the dim distant past and others are more current. Commentary and opinions have no doubt changed with the passage of time and views expressed have to be taken in context with the period they were written in.

The focus of the history has been the progress of the initial 1979 St Judes junior football team from Division Junior 4B to Senior 1 level and as such concentrates mainly on the first team but it also includes information on other adult teams including junior and U21. If there appears to be an imbalance between the amount of information for different periods in the club's history then this is entirely due to the amount of information available at time of going to press. I am grateful for the help and assistance I received from numerous people both inside and outside St Judes who helped in getting this information together. My solicitor has advised me to include the following caveat: Any resemblance to actual individuals, institutions or events in this text is purely a coincidence or the product of a devious or vivid imagination. All rights reserved. No part of this publication may be reproduced or transmitted in any form or by any means, electronic, mechanical, photocopying, recording, or otherwise without prior written permission of the author. © Don Lehane October 2003

ADULT FOOTBALL HISTORY
ADULT FOOTBALL PART 1 – THE EARLY YEARS JUNIOR FOOTBALL
(1979-1986)
Don Lehane

1979/80 SEASON

The first St Judes adult team officially took the field at 11.30 am on the 7th October 1979 when a junior football team played Round Towers at Clondalkin in a Murphy Cup game refereed by Eamonn Moffat. This was the year the Pope came to Ireland, a great Kerry team beat Dublin in the All-Ireland football final and house price increases were running at 25% in Dublin. Michael Fortune was writing about squash in the Evening Press and cruciate and hamstring injuries were as rare as hens' teeth. The first adult football team was actually registered with the Dublin Junior Football Board on the 27th July 1979 with a view to competing in junior football league, cup and championship for the 1979/80 season. The team appeared to be run by a consortium headed up by Ernest Kenny whose ability to coerce the most unlikely recruits into donning a pair of football boots became legendary as the years progressed. They played their initial home matches at Bancroft in Tallaght and played in Thomas Davis jerseys thanks to the welcome assistance of Davy Griffin and the Thomas Davis GAA club.

The initial St Judes adult team developed out of a seven a side football competition run on Orwell Green as a recruiting exercise to test the waters regarding the potential availability of players in the area. Teams were made up of a loose amalgam of teachers, Gardai, barmen, civil servants, shopkeepers, students, Cara computer staff and other local residents. The competition was extremely competitive to put it mildly and on occasions deteriorated into a form of faction fighting. My own recollection of the events is diminished by concussion having been sent off in the first match together with my Rossmore neighbour John Fitzpatrick after a bout of fisticuffs. The event was eventually won by the teachers who at the time were being weaned off corporal punishment and seemed to find the physical aspects of junior football very much to their liking as an alternative form of hand to hand combat.

For the record the following was the first list of players registered with the Junior Football Board for the 1979/80 season. It is not apparent that many of these players actually played on the first junior football team and in some cases it would be extremely doubtful if they had as a few of them had never played Gaelic football up to that point in their lives. It is unlikely that they would have initially sampled the joys of Gaelic games by togging out in Saggart on a frosty December morning unless holders of a large life insurance policy.

A lifelong participation in lawn bowling or tennis was no preparation for the skills necessary to return home from Rolestown or Glencullen without the requirement of an intermediary visit to the casualty department of the Mater hospital. The initial team was certainly strengthened by the addition of a couple of mercenaries, whose refusal to put their signature to a transfer form was more conditioned by the fear of a public flogging in Crossmolina or Cahirciveen the following weekend rather than an inability to write their names. First list of players registered with Dublin Junior Football Board on 27th July 1979:

Brazil C.	Orwell Pk.
Cavanagh Michael	Templeogue Woods
Cremin Con	168 Orwell Pk.
Curran Noel	
Currin P.J	170 Domville Temple.
Devine Hugo	88 Orwell Pk.
Doherty Neil	Carricklea, Firhouse Rd.
Donohoe Robert	7 Arran Quay Terrace
Durkan Seamus	93 Templeogue Woods
Farrelly, Pat	Orwell Park
Farrell	Rossmore
Farrell	Rossmore
Fitzgerald Gus	450 Orwell Pk.
Fitzpatrick John	11 Rossmore Lawn
Fitzpatrick Sean	124 Orwell Pk.
Gallen John	60 Orwell Pk.
Hamill T.	39 Rossmore Lawn
Healy Maurice	Firhouse Rd.
Kilgarrif Jim	18 Rushbrook Av.
Lehane Don	23 Rossmore Lawn
Lehane Donnchadh	275 Orwell Pk.
McDonnell Joe	273 Orwell Pk.
McKeown Tom	183 Whitehall Rd. West
Mooney Hugh	62 Orwell Pk.
Moran Charles	87 Orwell Pk
O'Connell Gerry	16 Rushbrook Av.
O'Grady Frank	174 Whitehall Rd.
O'Reilly P.J.	421 Orwell Pk.
O'Sullivan Michael	28a Benburb St
Russell Pat	27 Orwell Pk.
Travers Cathal	21 Mountdown Estate

Information regarding the exploits, successes and failures of the first St Judes adult football team put on the field is fairly sketchy but by all accounts they did not go on to win the junior championship or the league despite the presence of a number of useful footballers. The team competed in Junior Division 4B South, which was the lowest division in South Dublin at that time – there was a corresponding group of four junior divisions in North Dublin and of course the Fingal league had its own competitions.

The first official fixture fulfilled by a St Judes adult team was a Murphy Cup game against Round Towers at Clondalkin on the 7th October 1979 at 11.30 refereed by E. Moffat and it resulted in a defeat. Teams in this cup group included Clan Colaiste Mhuire, Kilmacud Crokes, St Patrick's, Bank of Ireland, Ballyboden, Postal Gaels, St Endas, St Annes, Portobello, Stars of Erin, Thomas Davis, Robert Emmets, St Mark's, Round Towers and St Judes.

The first league fixture for St Judes was at 11am on 28th October 1979 at Benildus, when they were defeated by Kilmacud Crokes. The teams making up Division 4B included Ballyboden, Portobello, St Marks, Kilmacud Crokes, Stars of Erin, St Endas, Bank of Ireland, Round Towers and St Judes. St Judes had two wins from their first eight league matches. As expected the first year competing at junior football level was quite difficult with the team registering three wins from the first twelve games, two league wins and one cup win. The only reassuring aspect of our performances was that we had both Ballyboden and St Endas teams pinned in a headlock to the bottom of the table in both league and Murphy Cup in the days when they operated as separate teams at this level.

The first round of the Junior Football Championship was scheduled for the 9th December 1979 with St Judes down to play Geraldine Morans at Cornelscourt. St Judes failed to show up for the game at the designated time. Apparently a team did travel late to the game in Cornelscourt but got lost in transit and arrived well after the game was due to start. To the embarrassment of all concerned a photographer and reporter from the Evening Press did turn up together of course with the referee and a full contingent of Geraldine Moran's players. The Evening Press sported the banner headline "It's the GAA game that didn't take place" in the following week's Gaelic sports section together with three photographs covering the referee and Geraldine Morans team. The first photograph showed the referee G. McCarton (Kilmacud Crokes) with outstretched hands indicating the game was all over. Another photograph showed the Geraldine Moran's team with the referee tucked into the back row to rub salt in the wounds. The coverage of the non-event took up over half a page of the old broadsheet Evening Press and in all honesty was a bit over the top on what must have been a quiet weekend in the sports department.

So here we were out of our first adult championship before Christmas without having kicked a ball! Additional championship fixtures took place on 13th January and 2nd February. We roll the clock on to 24th February 1980 for the continuation of the 1979/80 junior football championship and who do we have here at the bottom of the fixture list! St Judes versus Geraldine Morans at Cornelscourt at 3pm to be refereed by our old friend G. McCarton (Kilmacud Crokes). We are back in the championship after no doubt extensive negotiations at the Junior Board. Unfortunately the long delay had apparently thrown the St Judes altitude training program into chronic disarray and the team was defeated by Geraldine Morans after a tense battle. St Judes apparently voiced their objection to the result on the basis that Geraldine Morans had played some of their senior team but our argument was considerably weakened when it was established that Geraldine Morans did not have a senior team at the time. The objection was thrown out and now we were definitely out of the 1979/80 championship. Little did we know at the time that we would not compete in the junior football championship again until the 1983/84 season.

St Judes played Bank of Ireland in a Murphy Cup game on 16th July 1980. That was one of the last games noted for the 1979/80 season. The newspaper copy was pretty faded and one school of thought is that the team robbed (as distinct from played) the Bank of Ireland on the 16th July 1980 and headed for the Carribean with their ill-gotten gains until the money ran out in 1983 !. The next time St Judes junior footballers graced the fields of Dublin in serious competition was in a Division 4 junior football league game against Ballinteer St Johns on the 16th October 1983 at Marlay Park. The presence of a number of players sporting serious suntans and pot bellies added credence to the Carribean rumour. However speculation that the team had spent the intervening years in an intensive training camp were immediately discounted with a poor performance against Ballinteer. However we were back in business with Jim Coghlan at the helm and this time we were determined to make a lasting impression in Dublin football.

The first junior team included a number of players who went on to play an active part in running teams and club development and included Joe McDonnell, Jim Coghlan, Don Lehane, John Gallen, Charles Moran, Danny Lynch, Luke Mooney, Gerry Quinn, Hugo Devine and Frank O'Grady. The Garda Siochana and the Post Office played an important role in ensuring early St Judes junior teams took to the pitch with a full complement of players. The Gardai contributed players like Hugo Devine (Donegal), Vincent O'Donnell (Tipperary), Mick Mellon, Tom McKeown, John Fahy and John Kane in the early years. Players from the Post Office included Gerry Quinn (Longford), Paddy O'Donnell (Longford), Peadar

McGlinchey (Donegal), Peadar Carbery (Longford), Frank Jordan, Kevin Synon (Clare) and Eddie Egan (Kerry). Many will remember waiting around at the shops at a quarter past eleven with nine or ten players, one football, and time running out for the 11.30 start. It brought back memories of earlier years in the countdown to Christmas when all the expectations were geared around getting the big parcel from America. We would eagerly await the arrival of the postman on his bike but of course more often than not we would be disappointed and we would have to postpone our lookout duties until the following morning.

Anyway back to St Judes with time and hope running out on Sunday morning when around the corner would arrive either a Hugo Devine sponsored Garda hit squad in a Black Maria or an Ernest Kenny arranged delivery from the Post Office. On an odd morning both would arrive and we might be lucky enough to actually have a selection meeting and a couple of subs. The first greeting the lads would get was "How many do ye have" and any number less than five would be greeted with a shower of obscenities and a heated discussion on the inefficiencies of state bodies. Of course we were very grateful for the great contribution of both the Gardai and the Post Office to early St Judes teams. With a Black Maria arrival we were at least assured that we were going to have a bit of physical presence, with more than likely a Biffo or a Buffalo or two on board. If you were vertically challenged in those days then the Gardai was not a career option. The physical requirements of the Post Office on the other hand was confined to an ability to lift a telephone handset or to run the 100 yards in under twelve seconds with a bag on your back and a Doberman Pincer in hot pursuit. It is a form of training which has some attractions to liven up coaching sessions in the middle of winter. Post Office lads were usually nippy corner forwards whilst the boys in blue usually manned midfield or defensive positions.

Of course there were occasions when neither delivery arrived and we were sometimes confronted with what was known as the "Last Resort" which was a visit to 11 o'clock Mass for a quick scan and a beck and call to any likely looking lad. This was not as soul destroying an exercise as it seems in the cold light of day twenty five years later because our interventions were usually timed to take place during the collections or after the Gospel and protocol insisted that no one should be interrupted while on their knees. In addition all players were given the option of continuing with a decade of the rosary in the car on the way to the game and being dropped back at the church after the game to finish their devotions. The offers were rarely taken up in my experience even though I am sure there were occasions when some of the younger lads recited a small novena as we made our way to venues like Glencullen or Saggart for the inevitable painful experience.

The intercessions in the church were not always gratefully received, particularly when someone made the long walk from his pew in the front of the Church in an agitated state expecting grave news of a serious domestic situation, like the house being burned to the ground or the father after "taking bad" only to be asked if he would get his boots for a game against Kilmacud Crokes. In defence of team mentors and players it should be said that the "Last Resort" was a card which we were very reluctant to play even though some club officers maintained it was in the same league as grave robbing and should be discontinued forthwith. Others felt that grave robbing might be a better option as in all honesty sticking a jersey on a few residents of the graveyard at Spawell could not have resulted in a worse performance than what we received from some of our Sunday Mass recruits. A lifetime of prayer was a great preparation for the consequences of playing in Glencullen but was of little apparent benefit in preparing you to take part in the actual match itself.

For the history books the following is a list of senior football teams in Dublin in June 1980. There were three senior football divisions with a total of 27 teams in total with senior division 1 comprising: Thomas Davis, St Vincents, O'Dwyers, Na Fianna, Parnell's, St Oliver Plunketts, Scoil Uí Chonaill, Civil Service and Synge Street. Senior division 2 comprised Raheny, St Margaret's. Kilmacud Crokes, Ballymun Kickhams, Whitehall CC, O'Toole's, Crumlin, Fingallians and Good Counsel. Senior division 3 consisted of Round Towers, Craobh Chiarain, Ballyboden St Endas, St Vincents B, Garda, St Annes, St Mary's (Saggart), Clanna Gael and Clontarf. A comparison with the senior football leagues (SFL1 & SFL2) in the year 2003 gives an indication of the transformation of the face of senior football in Dublin over the past 20 years. There are no less than fourteen new teams competing at senior level in 2003 and most of these teams were either not in existence in 1979/80 or were not competing at adult level. The new teams at senior level in 2003 include St Judes, St Brigids, Lucan Sarsfields, St Olafs, Ballinteer St Johns, Erins Isle, Naomh Mearnog, Trinity Gaels, Naomh Barrog, St Marks, St Sylvesters, Naomh Fionbarra, St Finnians (Swords) and St James Emmet's.

With the exception of a few teams like St James Emmets (amalgamation of Caislean, Guinness and Robert Emmets) most of these were teams built up around new areas of population growth in suburban Dublin in the seventies and eighties. In many ways they were a new type of club in Dublin coming from mainly sprawling suburban areas. Many of them however managed to develop a "parish" ethic from a potentially explosive cocktail of "culchies" and "jackeens". The massive developments in clubhouses with associated social facilities helped of course to cement the parish culture.

First Junior Hurling team for St Judes played Faughs in friendly 5th September 1988 – Back row (l-r): Frank Gallagher (selector), Liam Larkin, John Dwane, Dave O'Connell, Sean Doherty, Eamonn Moloney, Jerry Maguire, Peter Ryan, Davy Mahon, Joe Clavin (manager). Front: Christy Reidy, Colum Grogan, Frank Carty, John Boyce, John Kerins, Michael Ryan and Martin Molamphy(selector). Missing from picture is Martin Hayes.

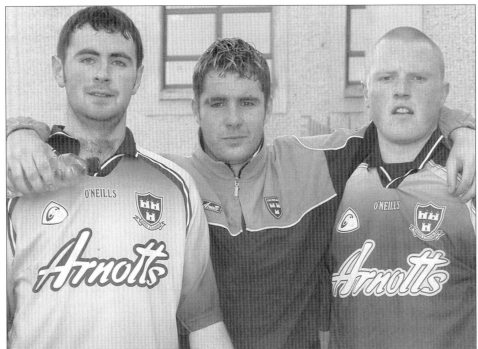

St Judes players who won All-Ireland U21 Football final winners medals in 2003 – (l-r): Michael Lyons, Brendan McManamon, Paul Copeland.

St Judes Decies members (l-r): Neil Doyle, Don Lehane, John Halpin, Jim Power.

St Judes mentors through the decades – (l-r): John Waldron ('90s), Gerry Quinn ('80s), Padraic Monaghan ('00s), John Foley ('70s rock and roll!).

Left - right: Con O'Brien and Fonsie McNamara.

Adult teams, which have departed senior level during this period, include Civil Service, Scoil Ui Chonaill, O'Dwyer's, Synge Street, Clanna Gael, O'Toole's, Crumlin, Good Counsel and St Vincents B.

1980/81 SEASON

St Judes entered a junior team for the 1980/81 league but the team appeared to have been withdrawn from competitions at an early stage of the season. They were down to play St Endas in a Division 4B league game on 23rd November 1980 but there is no record of this match having taken place and there were no apparent league or cup fixtures after this date. A Division 4B league table from 7th October 1981 showed the St Judes team as having being withdrawn at the bottom of the table:

Date: 1981/10/07 Division 4B Football League Table

Team	Played	Won	Drew	Lost	Points
Robert Emmets	9	7	0	2	14
Portobello	9	5	1	3	11
Caislean	8	5	0	3	10
St Endas	8	5	0	3	10
St Marks	7	4	1	2	9
Kilmacud Crokes	9	4	1	4	9
Stars of Erin	9	4	1	4	9
Round Towers	9	3	0	6	6
St Judes(Withdrawn)	9	0	0	9	0

1981/82 AND 1982/83 SEASONS

St Judes apparently did not compete at adult football level in those seasons.

1983/84 SEASON

Jim Coghlan, a native of Beaufort in Kerry, took over the management of the junior football team around 1983/84 and brought the team up to the end of the 1985/86 season. Jim had played minor championship for Kerry for three years in the 1966-68 period and I had the distinction of keeping him scoreless in a Waterford v Kerry Munster minor football championship semi-final in the Fraher Field in 1966. I would have to accept that I was helped in this feat by the positioning of Jim at full-back on the Kerry team on the day in question. Jim picked up a couple of Kerry senior championships with Mid Kerry and also played junior championship on a Kerry team which was beaten by Wicklow in the All-Ireland final and was a substitute on the 1968 Kerry senior team. Jim was captain of the UCC team in the early 1970s, which won two Sigersons and also won the

Cork senior football championship. The team went on to be beaten by Bellaghy in the All-Ireland club final of 1972 and by all reports gave a good account of themselves in social circles with Blackie Keane and Moss Keane in the vanguard.

This was all a far cry from St Judes in late 1983 with the appalling vista of trying to cobble a team together in the rugby and lawn tennis heartland of Tempelogue to play in the lowest Junior Division 4 South in Dublin. This was the year that the twelve man Dublin team beat fourteen man Galway in a bitter All-Ireland Senior Football Final played in poor weather conditions. Brian Talty played at midfield for Galway but did not appear for the second half after an "incident" in the tunnel as the teams departed from the field at half time.

At this point in St Judes underage players had still not worked their way up to adult level and the junior team was largely dependant on country players residing in Dublin. Players who togged out for St Judes during the period from 1983/84 to 1985/86 included Hugo Devine, Joe McDonnell, Don Lehane, Charles Moran, Mick O'Brien, Jim Coghlan, Danny Lynch, Luke Mooney, Frank O'Grady, Cyril and Eugene Loughlin, O'Malley brothers, Con Cronin, Liam Reilly, Tom McKeown, John and Denis O'Leary, Moss Keane, Denis Reid, Patsy Tyrrell, Tommy Quinn, Brian McSweeney, Seamus McCartin, Frank Jordan, Richard Jordan, Vincent O'Donnell, Eddie Egan, Peadar McGlinchey, Paddy O'Donnell, Noel Curran, Dessie Coyle, Donal Brennan and Jimmy Hanniffy to name a few. The first home fixtures for St Judes to be played in Tymon North took place in the Autumn of 1983 as they had played their home games in Bancroft up to this point.

The first official adult football league match after a three year break took place on 16th October 1983 against Ballinteer St Johns at Marlay Park. Teams in Division 4 junior included St Judes, Churchtown, PO Telephones, Bank of Ireland, Cuala, Kilmacud Crokes, Round Towers, Naomh Eanna, Portobello. The first Murphy Cup game took place on 23rd October 1983 at Bushy Park against Naomh Eanna. Teams in this Murphy Cup group included St Judes, Naomh Eanna, Bank of Ireland, Round Towers, Stars of Erin, Clanna Gael, St Patricks, St Annes, Kilmacud Crokes, St Johns Ballinteer, St Martins and Thomas Davis. The Junior A team had a good year finishing well up in the league and the Murphy Cup.

On 23rd February 1984 at Russell Park St Judes inflicted a twelve point defeat on St Brigids in the first round of the junior championship, coming away with a 3.06 to 0.03 win in one of the shocks of the first round. St Judes were defeated by Na Fianna in the second round in Tymon North on the 25th April 1984 in a match refereed by P O'Grady.

1984/85 SEASON

The first match of the 1984/85 season was a Junior Division 3A game against Clanna Gael in Ringsend Park on 7th October 1984. Jim Coghlan was manager of the St Judes team for the 1984/85 season. League teams in JFL3 included St Judes, St Patricks, Kilmacud Crokes, Liffey Gaels, Robert Emmets, AIB, Stars of Erin, Ballinteer St Johns, Clanna Gael, Cuala, St Mary's (Saggart) and Round Towers. St Judes finished up around mid table in the league and did not figure in the final stages of the Parsons Cup.

On 24th February 1985 St Judes were beaten by Churchtown in the first round of the Junior Football Championship at Tymon in a game refereed by K. Mulvey.

St Judes U21 footballers were defeated by St Monicas in the first round of the championship on 25th November 1984. St McDara's CC won the Donegan Cup in February 1985 – photo and full report in the Evening Press on 13th Feb 1985.

1985/1986 SEASON

In 1985/86 St Judes again competed in Junior Division 3A and Parsons Cup with a team again managed by Jim Coghlan.Teams competing in JFL3A included Bank of Ireland, Cuala, St Judes, Churchtown, AIB, Liffey Gaels, Robert Emmets, St Marys, Clan na Gael, Caislean and Fr. Murphys. Teams competing in Parsons Cup included Ballinteer St Johns, St Annes, Kilmacud Crokes, Churchtown, Bank of Ireland, St Marys, Stars of Erin, Round Towers, Thomas Davis and St Judes.

The first round of the junior championship against Postal Gaels took place on 16th March 1986 in the Phoenix Park and St Judes were knocked after a very fussy refereeing performance.

The game was played on St Patricks Day weekend, which meant that St Judes were inevitably short a few players.

The match was interrupted at one point by a bunch of horses careering across the pitch, seemingly as irate as the Judes supporters with the performance of the referee.

SUMMARY OF 1983/86 PERIOD

This was an important period in the history of football in St Judes as it finally established our credentials in junior football. We had not come away with any trophies but the team had performed creditably against all the odds and with a couple of additional league wins would have been in contention for promotion on a couple of occasions. Great credit was due to Jim Coghlan in particular for keeping the show on the road in a period where there were very few native parish players to call on.

Getting a team on the pitch on Sunday mornings was always a battle and often involved personal visits to houses to rouse people from their slumbers. Not all the players lived locally or had their own transport, which added to the difficulty of getting a side together. A number of players lived in flats with an often faulty public phone in the hall so communication was a real problem. One of Jim's regular Sunday morning visits was to Con Cronin's residence in Tallaght where anything from small pebbles to bricks had to be thrown at Con's upstairs bedroom window to get him out of the leaba after a heavy social night.

Of course there was no clubhouse in Tymon North or indeed in most clubs in those days and togging out in ditches or in portacabins was the usual. Leaving your clothes and valuables in a neat pile behind the goal was no guarantee of their safety or well-being and all players will remember occasions when they returned to a rain-sodden trousers or an ant-infested pair of socks. The above mentioned Con Cronin usually hid his hard earned Gardai wages in a rock behind the goals. Of course on one occasion he could not remember the precise rock he had chosen and it necessitated a search party the following evening when literally no stone was left unturned in the ditch that bordered the pitch.

In the early years St Judes got great support from Thomas Davis in finding their feet in Dublin football and the early Judes teams played in borrowed Thomas Davis jerseys as well as playing their games in the Thomas Davis pitch at Bancroft. Davy Griffin in particular will always be remembered in St Judes for his tremendous support in those early years. His generosity understandably did not extend to the matter of player availability as was proven when Luke Mooney was due to turn out for his first game for St Judes in Bancroft.

He had been given precise instructions from Joe McDonnell regarding the location of the Bancroft pitch and the colour of the Judes jerseys. Luke nevertheless turned up at the Graveyard pitch, which was another Thomas Davis pitch in those days, and where Davy Griffin was managing a Thomas Davis team who were togging out for a league game but were short a few players. Davy Griffin subsequently maintained that he never heard Luke's enquiry to confirm that this was the St Judes team and promptly tossed him a jersey before instructing him to line up at corner back. Luke was pleased with his performance and was quite unprepared for the berating he received from Joe McDonnell at work the following morning regarding his failure to turn out for his debut with St Judes.

Moss Keane made a few guest appearances for St Judes during this period. Moss of course had played Gaelic football before he took up rugby in UCC in the late sixties and indeed had played in a full-back line with Jim Coghlan on successful UCC Sigerson and Cork senior championship teams teams.

He had won an All-Ireland Junior Football runners-up medal with Kerry on a team, which included Jim Coghlan and Brendan Lynch. Expectations that Moss would have a revolutionary effect on the team performance failed to materialise partly because of wear and tear in the intervening years since his Sigerson days but mainly due to the quality of the surrounding personnell. In addition Moss had spent a considerable period of his adult life with his arms around a flag waving unionist whilst being "interfered with" from behind by a mad Kilkenny man and a couple of lads from Dublin 4. This seemed to have a psychological effect on Moss who seemed reluctant to stand in front of or beside anyone wearing a pair of white shorts when playing in his customary full-forward role for St Judes. He nevertheless had a great pair of hands and any high balls into the square were gobbled up with consummate ease, as were the subsequent pints in the Blue Haven.

One of the enduring memories of the period was the substitution of Moss Keane for the fiery Frank O'Grady in a junior championship match against Churchtown in Tymon in the 1984/85 season. Frank did not take too kindly to being replaced by the former Triple Crown winning Irish second row forward who had failed to put in an appearance at our altitude training sessions. He stormed off the pitch and having thrown his jersey in the general direction of Jim Coghlan declared that "I don't give a *&@k how many triple crowns he has - that's my last game in a Judes jersey" (expletives deleted) or words to that effect. Frank was true to his word and as it happens I don't think Moss Keane played for St Judes after that game either – the end of an era !!

Jimmy Hanniffy (Longford) was a regular player for St Judes in the mid to late eighties although nearing the end of his career at that point. Jimmy hailed from Drumlish in Longford and won a couple of All-Ireland senior colleges medals with St Mel's in successive All-Irelands finals against St Jarlath's (Tuam) and St Brendan's (Killarney) in 1962 and 1963 respectively. He won a National League medal wiith Longford in 1966 and a Leinster championship medal on a very good Longford team in 1968.

He always maintained a good level of fitness, which enabled him to play well into his forties and indeed into his fifties with the Dublin over fifties team. Jimmy usually lined out at centre forward or full forward and played some tremendous games for St Judes in a forward line which included players like Declan and Brian McSweeney, Christy Kilcoyne, Ger Tannam, Michael Barrett, Ger Treacy and Ciaran McGovern.

Danny Lynch was another Kerryman who turned out for St Judes in the early eighties before going on to bigger and better things as PRO for Cumann Luthcleas Gael.

Danny had played his early football with junior club Dingle before moving to Dublin where he played for Erins Hope, Clanna Gael and Civil Service before joining St Judes in the early eighties. He played his earlier games for St Judes in goals before moving to full-forward with Jim Coghlan moving temporarily to goals.

Danny and Frank O'Grady (Dublin) were regular full-forward line partners in a number of St Judes junior football games in the early eighties. The partnership however seemed to be confined to their presence on the same team as they rarely passed the ball to each other following some unwritten rule that a Kerryman should never pass a ball to a Dub and vice versa. Come to think of it they rarely passed the ball to anyone else either but sin sceil eile. Matters came to a head in a game against Round Towers when Danny, though surrounded by about three Towers men, failed to get a pass away to Frank who was standing unmarked on the edge of the square. Towers cleared the danger and "words were exchanged" between Danny and Frank and the heat had not dissipated by half time. Jim Coghlan was in the middle of his half time talk when the ever persistent Frank enquired from Danny as to why he never passed the ball to him. Danny being in the PR business thought briefly about a diplomatic answer before eventually settling on the reply "Because you are no *$#&ing good ". Ah – the teamwork and camaraderie in those early days!.

Pitch marking was a major undertaking in the early days. A team would assemble in Tymon at nine o'clock on a Saturday morning wearing an assortment of gear reminiscent of actors in John B Keane's The Field. The first item on the agenda was a stock check, to ensure that all the expertise and ingredients were available. Main requirements were qualified personnel, pitch marking machines, lime, water, flags, rolls of string, GAA rulebook with pitch dimensions, tape measures and of course a small bag of weedkiller or "stuff" to ensure that the pitch markings would not disappear with the first shower. There were a couple of unwritten rules regarding allocation of duties which usually meant that Dubs, (with a few exceptions like Frank McSweeney) should be kept far away from handling any of the equipment. Any farmer will tell you there is nothing worse than a fellow who is awkward around "gear" as you would be at your wits end with broken plough shares or harrow springs. The Dubs were steered as much as possible into areas like water transport, pitch measurement or traffic management.

A "good eye" is an essential for a top class pitch marker as it enables the marker to draw a straight white line from A to B in one attempt, without the presence of balls of string and marker flags – no mean feat when we are talking about a sideline of over 100 metres.

Jack Crennan is a noted proponent of this particular skill but it has been known to end in disaster particularly on a day when your "eye" might not be in or you suffered a crisis in confidence when half way across the pitch.

This once resulted in a line that resembled a ski slope in St Moritz being laid down on the camogie pitch – rumour had it that Jack got distracted by the sight of the camogie team warming up on the side of the pitch and temporarily lost his bearings. Early pitch crews included Frank McSweeney as foreman, Don Lehane, Ernest Kenny, Joe McDonnell and Donnchadh Lehane. In later years a number of other club members including Tommy Bassett, Mick O'Brien, Jack Crennan, Seán Breheny and Bernie Gallagher graduated up to the top level of senior pitch marker.

1986/87 U-21 Football team, Division 2 winners – back row (l-r): Donnchadh Lehane (mentor), Joe McDonnell (mentor), Ger Keaty, Ger Kenny, James Durkan, Conor Lehane, Dara Murphy, Ciaran Cribbs, Ray Whelan, Patsy Kenneally, Ernest Kenny (mentor). Front: Philip Doyle, Seán Dunne, Seamus Clifford, Killian McCaffrey, Derek McGuckin, Stephen O'Brien.

Juvenile Football – The early years
Tommy Hartnett and Garrett Edge

IN THE BEGINNING

1978 was one of those almost forgettable years. With few exceptions, a glance at the history books reveals but a few extraordinary developments. In July, European Union member states agreed to study a proposal linking together EU currencies. Catholicism witnessed the rare phenomenon of three Popes in virtually as many weeks. On the national stage, the government of the day was busy imploring the masses to invest heavily in hair shirts in anticipation of cool times in the forthcoming 1980s. Dublin, however, was four years into the football renaissance of Heffo and his army. The men in blue added a distinctive glow to the gloom of the Capital's grey skies and the children of her burgeoning suburbs emulated their heroes on green spaces and tarmac roads. Willington Parish was no exception to this delightful trend. Bishop Galvin Primary School had opened its doors in 1975, and internal school Leagues were played there from the beginning.

In the first Parish Summer Project in 1977, Ernest Kenny provided Gaelic football activities at the request of Fr Greene. It was decided to organise two competitions at Under 10 and Under 14 using the four areas of the parish as the basis for organising the teams. So the first Gaelic teams in St Judes parish were Templeogue Wood, Glendown, Orwell Park and Willington. The community spirit in St Judes parish came to the fore with Seamus O'Connor providing soccer goal posts on the Green for the competitions. The Under 10 competition was won by the Orwell team led by Mick Kavanagh and the Under 14 competition was won by the Glendown team led by Kieran O'Reilly who beat Orwell in the final. After this project people were sought who would be interested in Gaelic games with a view to starting a club in the parish. Ernest Kenny and others set about talking to and encouraging people into attending a meeting to discuss the possibilities of the above. With the enthusiasm shown in the 1978 Parish Summer Project it was right that we should form our own GAA club. The first meeting held on the 9th September 1978 it was agreed the name of the club would be "St Judes Gaelic Football Club" "Cumann Peil Naomh Jude" The first Officers elected at this meeting were Chairman Fr John Greene cc, Vice Chairman Ernest Kenny, Secretary and Registrar Cyril Bates, Assistant Secretary Eamon O'Reilly and Treasurer John Gallen.

After this inaugural meeting it was decided to enter teams in the South East League at Under 10 and Under 14 in the South Dublin League. The first match for the under 10s was played in Bushy park against Templeogue and the under 14s played their first match in Bancroft against Robert Emmetts both on the 23rd September 1978. In their first year of existence St Judes Under 10s finished a creditable third in their League.

In that first season the mentors who bravely took St Judes to the field for the first time were, at Under 10, Seamus Durkan, Donnachadh Lehane, Ernest Kenny and Jimmy O'Dwyer. The Under 14 team was managed by Erenest Kenny, Cyril Bates, Charles Moran, John Gallen and Pat Farrelly. This team played its first match (a friendly) against a strong Thomas Davis Under 12 team in Orwell Green. Jim Turner and Dave Kinsella managed the Thomas Davis team. Charles Moran became the first referee for St Judes when he agreed to referee Under 14 matches for the coming season in the South Dublin League.

It was also in 1978 that the club applied to the Co Dublin VEC for funds from their new scheme for Youth and Sport organisations. To the great delight of the club the VEC granted us £200. It was agreed immediately that the club should go wild and they bought two footballs which were badly needed. In those early days there was major fund raising to keep the club afloat. This took the form of cake sales in Brady's Butchers, and in a lot of instances, the bakers bought cakes themselves after already donating the ingredients, the time and their cookers. This was true club spirit. From these fundraisers two sets of jerseys were bought from Mick Dowling. One set purchased was too small and Mick Dowling agreed to allow credit for twelve jerseys and the club sold the jerseys to the players for £2 each to finance a new set.

In those pre-Tymon Park days, League games were played in Bushy Park, Watergate and later in Bancroft. While the juvenile footballers represented their new club with pride, their unfortunate mentors grappled with myriad difficulties. It is noted in Executive Minutes that jerseys were borrowed from Thomas Davis GAA Club, Bishop Galvin School and the South City Board. As ever, the juvenile mentors swung into action and house to house collections were considered. What with the enthusiasm peculiar to juveniles and the courage and determination of the mentors, St Judes were level on points with Ballyboden and required a win against Ballyboden to reach a final spot with St Annes. So on a cold May night in Bancroft, the stars of St Judes played a strong Ballyboden team. It was point for point in a very exciting hard fought match and with five minutes to go Ballyboden were leading by a point. In the last few minutes a great move linking Hogan, Lehane and Whelan made the opening for Brannigan to crash home the winning goal.

After beating Ballyboden we were now set for the final pairing of St Judes and St Annes. St. Judes won their first honours by defeating St Annes in an exciting game, even the gallant St Annes could not hold out against the rampaging forwards of St Judes who ran out winners by 4-5 to 0-5.

Paul Curran, who played at Under 10, Under 11 and Under 12 for St Judes, went on to play with Thomas Davis GAA Club at Under 13. He later won honours at club and senior intercounty levels, finally retiring from top flight inter-county football in 2002. It is a credit to Curran that for a number of years he served as a Development Officer for Dublin County Board .

This season saw Jimmy O'Dwyer, Carl Page and Finbarr Murphy lead the Under 10s and from reports to the executive by Jimmy, they did very well in their League and held their own. The Under 14 mentors were reduced in their ranks to Ernest Kenny and Charles Moran.

In April 1980 Jimmy O'Dwyer and Charles Moran were put in charge of the organisation of a trip to Liverpool and it was also agreed to invite Davy Griffin (Thomas Davis) from the board to travel with the group. However, he was unable to travel. The club made its first application for the use of pitches in Tymon North to the County Council. In October 1979, the club agreed to sponsor Niall Stokes and Bernard Molloy on a trip to Manchester, which was organised by the Board.

The 1980/81 season saw an increase in teams due to the organised Gaelic in the Parish Summer Project. The organisers, Fr John Greene, Ernest Kenny and resident referee Joe Morrin, were joined by Charles Moran and the musical Gerry Quinn, who led the parade with his accordion. This season also spelled the end of the first Under 14s, some of whom were under age and moved to their proper age group. The numbers of mentors however remained the same and were starting to be stretched. We entered two Under 10 teams, the A team under Charles Moran and Ernest Kenny and the Bs under Frank O'Grady, Frank McSweeney and John Gallen. The Under 11s and Under 12s remained with their mentors from the previous season and all teams held their respective divisions.

1980 seemed to be the year of trips. In May 1980, thirty-two boys and six adults travelled to St Patricks, Ellesmere Port, Liverpool. Later on in the year teams travelled to Wicklow and to Killasser.

The plaques for the Under 11 SW League winners for the 1979/80 season were presented in September 1980 by Tony Hanahoe, one of the greats of "Heffo's Army". In October 1980 all jerseys were called in and it was agreed that the washing would be shared by the committee. In November 1980 the club agreed to purchase materials to make flags and to purchase another set of jerseys.

For the 1981/82 season four teams were entered under the same management.

To the delight of the club we were granted the use of pitches in Tymon North. We now had a home ground. The Under 10A team under John Gallen, Frank O'Grady and Frank McSweeney had a marvellous season, winning all their matches to be crowned Division 1 League winners. Declan Feore, Michael O'Boyle and Tom Fitzpatrick were new mentors this year. Michael O'Boyle helped out with the As and Declan Feore, Joe Morrison and Tom Fitzpatrick worked with the 10Bs.

This League win saw the start of an illustrious career for one Declan O'Boyle who became the first club player to represent the club at Senior Inter-county level, having to retire early due to serious knee injuries. Declan still serves the club today as part of the Senior Football management team.

In 1981 the close links with Bishop Galvin National School were to be fostered and the school classed as a training ground for St Judes while the Parish Summer Project was to continue as the recruiting ground. In the Community Games St Judes Under 13s finished runners up. This community spirit continued when we were presented with a set of jerseys by our neighbours Faugh's Hurling Club.

The Parish Summer Project of 1982 saw tremendous activity on the Gaelic football front with a full competition being run. At the end of the project trials were held for those interested, in Tymon North. The king of recruiters Ernest Kenny took over as the trials ended and the club had new mentors in their ranks. While watching the trial at which his son was playing, Tommy Hartnett was approached by Ernest Kenny and Joe Morrin and asked what he thought of the players. He made the mistake of stating that they all tried their best and they could turn into a nice little team. He was handed a set of jerseys, a list book, and a ball and was told he had a match the following Saturday.

There was no escape once you were snared and the other parents there on the day were roped in also. Thus, the Under 10C team under Tommy Hartnett, Pat Campbell, Matt Naughton, Jack Lernihan and Pat Quigley was born. That panel contained many members, some of whom are still playing in the club today. With names such as Enda Sheehy, Kieran Quigley, Michael Hartnett, Anthony Gilleran, Stephen Willoughby, David Campbell, Colin Campbell, Paul Moran this team took to the field with enthusiasm. The unusual thing about this panel was that the ages ranged from the youngest at six years of age to the oldest at eight years of age. As a result, this team did not win a match in their first season.

In the final match of the season we played St Marys of Saggart in Tymon North and nearly recorded our first win. With a large number of parents in attendance, St Judes seemed to have gained a new level of skill. As is usual with children of this age, the outfield players followed the ball as one from the first to the final whistle.

ACC Football Festival 1989 – U12, back row (l-r): Alan Murphy, Paul Bannoll, Michael Murphy, Ken Molloy, Padraig Shaughnessy, Niall Carty, Derek Fitzgerald, Gavin Russel, Barry McGann, Paul Brennan. Front: Gareth Roche, Donal Evoy, David Lawlor, David Raymond, Warren Linney, McDonald, Enda Brenna, Martin Shankle.

1993 U12 presentation night (l-r): Enda Sheehy, Caoimhin Joyce (U12 Hurling Captain), Andrew Glover (U12 Football Captain), Paul Bealin (Dublin).

St Judes had a secret weapon in Enda Sheehy who had improved vastly over the season. Despite this we ended up with the most possession but not enough scores. This team was the start of the career of Enda Sheehy who represented the club at county level in all age groups up to Senior in football and Minor in Hurling. Enda was the second player to represent the club at Senior Inter-county level and is also the only player to receive an All Ireland Medal. Enda returned to the club after the 1995 All Ireland and toured the parish with the Sam Maguire. This was indeed a proud day for the club.

While our Under 10Cs were trying to come to terms with not winning a match our Under 10Bs were holding their own in their League but the stars were the Under 10As under Seamus Durkan, Joe Morrin, Ernest Kenny, who were joined this season by Michael O'Boyle, Declan Feore and Tom Fitzpatrick who won their Division 1 League. To add to this win we had our first South Dublin Under 10 representatives in Declan O'Boyle, Seán Sweeney and Brendan Byrne.

Our Under 11s finished runners up in their League and had three representatives on the South Dublin Under 11 Panel namely Shane Gallen, Dara Heraty and Adrian O'Grady. Our Under 12s and Under 13s finished well in their Leagues with our Under 12s having three representatives on the South Dublin Panel, namely, Mick Fallon, Leonard Fitzpatrick and Kieran McDonnell.

In the 1983/84 season while Dublin had "Heffo's Army" in the 1970s, St Judes had "Durkan's Army" in the 1980s. After winning their League the previous season this team went on to win the Under 11 Division 1 League and the Under 11 Centenary Cup. The Centenary Cup caused quite a stir at the end of 1984 when the board demanded the cup back even though this was a once off competition. One can only presume that this cup is now in the vaults of some bank awaiting another century to pass when it can be resurrected and called the second Centenary Cup.

It was in the 1983/84 season that the club increased its mentors and teams with the addition of Gus Barry, Paddy Russell, Bob Carty and the first lady Manager Marie Bell. The introduction of Marie Bell was a milestone twenty years ago but St Judes never let anything get in the way of progress.

"Mol an óige agus tiocfaidh sí", was certainly the watch word and this was reflected in the 1984/85 season when St Judes fielded no fewer than ten teams from Under 10 to Under 15. With three teams at Under 10, the A team being in Division 2 and two teams at Under 11 all holding their own in their respective Leagues, St Judes was guaranteed that there was going to be a good supply of players for the future.

There were two teams at Under 12, the A team being "Durkan's Army" now taken care of by Seamus Durkan and Michael O'Boyle. This team continued its successful march through the Leagues by winning Division 1. Tommy Mulready, Bob Carty and Joe Morrin kept the flag flying with the Under 12Bs.

At Under 13 we were winners of Division 2 under the guidance of John Gallen, Don Lehane and Frank McSweeney. This win showed that St Judes mentors were making every effort to get their teams into the top football Leagues in Dublin. At Under 14 and Under 15 we were still keeping our heads above water.

The 1985/86 season continued with the Saturday morning nursery on the Green run by Jimmy O'Dwyer, Jim Coghlan, Gerry Wright and Finbarr Murphy. The club fielded six teams from Under 10 to Under 12, all of whom did well in their respective Leagues. But once again the glory for St Judes football came in the form of Durkan's Under 13s who won Division 1 with ease. The Under 14s finished midway in Division 1 and the Under 15s under Charles Moran finished in the top half of Division 2 and were beaten in the quarter final of the championship. It was towards the end of this season that mentors had to really put their shoulders to the wheel. While still ensuring that their teams were competing well, they had to ensure that tickets were sold for the monster draw after the plans for the development of the clubhouse were announced. This was done with enthusiasm as it would mean no more togging out on the side of the pitch in all weathers.

Juvenile football was beginning to make inroads into competitions in the 1986/87 season and the nursery continued with great success under Jimmy O'Dwyer with Garrett Edge and Joe McDonnell joining those already working hard on the Green. At Under 10 the A team were runners up in the Corrigan Cup and the Bs won Division 4 of the South East League comfortably. The Under 11As finished fourth in their League while the Under 12Bs were runners up in their League. Again this year Durkan's heroes won Division 1 and were an inspiration to all those who were following them. The Under 15s finished well in Division 1 but were beaten in the first round of the championship.

After the forward movement of the last season the 1987/88 season continued this move for honours. Again the Green continued its hard work and at Under 10 we fielded three teams with the Under 10Cs being all eligible for Under 10 next season. The Under 10Bs under Jim Coghlan and Pat Brien finished runners up in their League after much encouragement from both Jim and Pat. But the stars were the Under 10As with Seán McBride, Neil Doyle and John Carroll who succeeded in winning Division 1 in the League and also winning the Corrigan Cup. The Under 11s finished third in the League and were runners up in the Millennium Cup and the Under 12s also finished third in their League after a ruling by Coiste na nÓg. This ruling gave second place to An Caisleán even though St Judes could prove from the referee's report that he had totalled the scores incorrectly. St Judes then became the first team to finish in third place and still be promoted to Division 1 in the South City League. Perhaps this was the Board's acknowledgement of an earlier error? Kieran Quigley and Michael Hartnett from this team represented the club on the South East Dublin team that season. This Under 12 team was beaten in the quarter final of the Millennium Cup and also received the Evening Herald's Team of the Month award for November 1987.

Our Under 13As finished in the top half of Division 1 while the Under 13Bs were runners up in Division 4 and the Under 14s finished in the top half of their League. Durkan's army was really on the march this year winning Division 1 and beaten narrowly in the clubs first Championship final. The excitement in the club in reaching the first championship final was unbridled and added to the fact that the new clubhouse was opened in 1987.

The 1988/89 season got off to a great start with the thoughts of last year's successes in its League and memories of our first championship final still in mind. With this to spur them on our teams did not shirk their duty. The Green being the starter pack was busier than ever with players as young as five years of age being coached, a daunting task to say the least. The same group of people were still unselfishly putting their shoulders to the wheel. Our three Under 10 teams all finished midway in their respective Leagues while Seán McBride and Neil Doyle's Under 11As continued their previous season's success by winning Division 1 to follow in Durkan's army's steps and our Under 11Bs finished third in their League. The Under 11s also travelled to Rhode and a great trip was had by all. Our Under 12s finished third and our Under 13s finished midway in their Leagues and the Under 12s also travelled to Ardee with the Minors for a day trip to play a friendly match. One of the highlights of the day for the players was when on the journey up someone pulled a mooner out the back window of the bus. This would have been easy to handle except the car travelling behind happened to be a Garda car, however we got away with a stern warning. This year also saw the inaugural Dublin Juvenile Football Festival sponsored by ACC Bank being held in Tymon North and St Judes clubhouse was used as the headquarters for the weekend. Teams from all over Leinster including St Judes took part and an excellent weekend of football was had by all.

Success was the order of the day for our Under 14s the A team under Gus Barry and Tony Maguire winning their League and the Under 14Bs under Paddy Russell, Jack Lernihan and Stephen Willoughby finishing runners up in their League.

The Under 15s under Máire McSherry, Pat Brien and Bobby Carty finished third in the League and were beaten in the quarter final of the championship.

In the 1989/90 season the Green nursery was in the charge of Joe McDonnell ably assisted by Pat Brady, Noel Lyons, Aidan Brosnan, Michael Coleman and John Browne. The Under 10As under Billy Ó Frighil and Michael O'Boyle finished in the top half of their League and were runners up in the Corrigan Cup. They also had a great day out in Mosney this year with a well-deserved break. The rest of the Under 10s and the Under 11s held their own in their Leagues. Seán McBride and Neil Doyle's Under 12s went marching on to win Division 1. They also won the Under 12 Special League and were runners up in the Dublin Juvenile Football Festival. The Under 13s under Charles Moran were runners up in Division 1, and in late May they also travelled to Thomas McCurtin's GAA Club in London.

Inspired by the success of Seamus Durkan's heroes and the new kids on the block Seán McBride's Under 12s, the Under 14s under Tommy Hartnett, Pat Quigley and Gary Kane became under 14 Division 1 winners after a thrilling final against Ballyboden with Kieran Quigley slotting over a point in extra time to seal the victory. This team also won the McCarthy Cup. This team went on to win Division 1 Under 15 after a second outstanding final against Ballyboden.

The victorious Under 14s travelled to both ends of Ireland during this year. Early in the spring they visited Mungret in Limerick where they played both Football and Hurling, winning the football and just losing out in the hurling. However, new friends were made and both players and mentors had a great time. The second trip was to St Marys of Banagher in the north glens of Derry. We were the first southern team ever to travel to St Marys and as such we were treated like lords. The players could not believe the reception they received when they got there and this continued throughout the weekend.

A four team tournament was played with St Judes finishing runners up. The mentors who travelled were Tommy Hartnett, Gary Kane and Noel O'Reilly (RIP) and this weekend will never be forgotten. Tommy Hartnett managed the South Dublin Under 14 team and the players who represented the club were Michael Hartnett, Jeff Kane, Kieran Quigley and Anthony Gilleran. The South Dublin team was beaten by two points in the Garda Tournament. Tommy Hartnett went on to manage the South Dublin Under 14 and All Dublin Under 14s and 15s. He also became the second South Dublin Under 14 manager to win the Garda Tournament in 1996. Fintan O'Brien and Shane Lynch represented the club. The Under 15s finished in the top half of their League and were beaten in the second round of the championship.

During this season Enda Crennan (Hurling), Ian Fortune and David McGovern (Football), and Catriona Dennehy (Camogie), all St Judes players were selected from Bishop Galvin National School to play on the Dublin Primary Schools teams.

The vision of the men who nurtured the club from the early years was for their club to attain senior status and a glance at the progress and growth of juvenile football throughout the 1980s and 1990s is testament to their grit, foresight and sheer determination. The juvenile section is seen as the lifeblood of every club and St Judes was no exception. It is through the dedication of its members, the local teachers and the Green nursery that St Judes will continue to breed success. Long serving clubman Tommy Hartnett once remarked that it was not that he wished our club to be the St Vincents of the southside, but he wanted St Vincents to want to be the St Judes of the northside!

The start of the 1990s saw St Judes continue to maintain a huge juvenile section with eleven teams entered in Leagues for the 1990/91 season. At Under 10A Bob Carty and Don Lehane's team finished third in Division 1 while the Under 10Bs raced through the League to come out winners led by Bill Sheehy, Donal Duggan and a new name to the mentor list but not new to the players, a young Enda Sheehy. The Under 11s and Under 12s continued to make steady progress in their respective Leagues. The Under 13s continued their march through the Division 1 Leagues by again taking the title at this age group and Seán McBride, Neil Doyle and John Carroll's team giving everybody great hope for the future. They also competed in and won a tournament in Portlaoise on St Patricks weekend. The spoils of victory were not confined to the A team, as the Under 13Bs won their League to show that they too were going to be a force to be reckoned with.

The Under 14s, fresh from their trip to Thomas McCurtin's Club in London, finished in the top half of their League. Tommy Hartnett, Pat Quigley and Gary Kane were determined not to let the Division 1 title won at Under 14 go at Under 15. The team did not let them down with brilliant performances from Ross Mac Mathuna, Jeff Kane, Michael Hartnett scoring, Kieran Quigley, Derek McGrath and a star goalkeeper Michael (The Mouth) Mahon. We beat Ballyboden in a most thrilling final in Cherryfield. In the championship in a great quarterfinal display, St Judes went down by a single point to St Vincents in their home venue Marino. The team was busy this year travelling to Longford after being invited to play an exhibition match for the opening of their clubhouse. A great day was had by all and we were well catered for by Tony Gilleran's home club.

The 1991/92 season saw our Under 10 teams performing well under the stewardship of Bobby (The Kid) Carty and Marie Bell. At Under 11 we saw the start of the next great juvenile team of St Judes under Don Lehane and Michael Glover. This team won Division 1 only losing one match along the way but this was just the start for this superb team as will be seen from their trip through the different age groups. Our Under 12s, 13s, 14s and 15s acquitted themselves well in their Leagues without taking any honours. The Under 14s won the McCarthy Cup. Again this year, St Judes was used as headquarters for the Dublin Juvenile Football Festival.

The 1992/93 season saw a slowdown in honours for the juveniles. Of note that year were the Under 10A players who were runners up in both League and Shield. Don Lehane and Michael Glover's team continued their winning ways by again winning Division 1 at Under 12. They then went on to win the Shield. Don Lehane was appointed South Dublin Under 12 Manager and St Judes representatives on the team were Anthony O'Reilly, Andrew Glover, Mark O'Brien and Seán McLoughlin. The rest of the teams performed well again without any degree of success. Tommy Hartnett was appointed South Dublin Under 14 Manager while Keith Kelleher and Greg Lehane represented the club on the pitch.

There was no significant improvement in the 1993/94 season. At Under 10 we finished in the bottom half of the Leagues and were beaten in the quarterfinals of the cup and the shield. The Under 11As finished in the bottom half of the League and were beaten in the semi-final of the championship while the Under 11Bs were runners up in their League. Seán Breheny's team was the team of the year winning the Division 1 title, but was defeated in the final of the championship. They were also runners up in the Féile and went on to win the Lucan Bank of Ireland Tournament at which Seán Breheny was named player of the tournament. The Under 13As finished third in the premier division and were runners up in the Féile. They also travelled to Lake Muckno for the weekend of the 4th and 5th of June 1994, playing a match against St Marys of Castleblaney. The Under 14s finished fourth in Division 2 and were beaten in the quarterfinal of the Féile. Tommy Hartnett was again South Dublin Manager but there were no representative players this year. The Under 15s under Martin McCabe and Bernie Gallagher were runners up in Division 3 but were beaten in the first round of the championship.

The 1994/95 season was not a very good season for the juveniles. Of note that season were the Under 12As finishing third in Division 1 and second in the Lucan Bank of Ireland Tournament. They also had South Dublin Under 12 representatives in Conor Foley, Shane Lynch, Mark Molloy and Stephen Early. The Under 12Bs were runners up in their League and the Under 14As finished third in the premier division and were beaten in the final of the McCarthy Cup. Tommy Hartnett continued as South Dublin Manager and was now leading the All Dublin Under 14s. Representative players on the South Dublin team were Gerard Hartnett, Kevin Hayes and Fergal Daly and on the All Dublin Under 14s were Gerard Hartnett and Kevin Hayes.

Dublin Representatives

South Dublin: Declan O'Boyle, Seán Sweeney, Brendan Byrne
South Dublin: Shane Gallen, Dara Heraty, Adrian O'Grady
South Dublin: Mick Fallon, Lenny Fitzpatrick, Keith McDonnell
South Dublin Mgr: Seamus Durkan
Dublin South East: Kieran Quigley, Michael Hartnett
Dublin: Karl Coleman, Brendan Byrne, Joe Moran, John O'Riordan, James Weldon, Chris Cullen and Niall Bowe
Dublin Under 16 Mgr: Seamus Durkan
South Dublin: Michael Hartnett, Anthony Gilleran, Jeff Kane, Kieran Quigley.
South Dublin Mgr: Tommy Hartnett
South Dublin Under 12 Mgr: Don Lehane
South Dublin Under 12: Anthony O'Reilly, Andy Glover, Mark O'Brien, Seán McLoughlin, Fergal Daly
South Dublin: Greg Lehane, Keith Kelleher
South Dublin Mgr: Tommy Hartnett. Won Lucan BOI Tournament Seán Breheny Player of Tournament.
South Dublin Mgr: Tommy Hartnett
Dublin Under 16: Enda Crennan
South Dublin Under 12: Conor Foley, Shane Lynch, Stephen Earley
South Dublin Under 14: Gerard Hartnett, Kevin Hayes, Fergal Daly.
Dublin Under 14: Gerard Hartnett, Kevin Hayes
South Dublin and Dublin Mgr: Tommy Hartnett
South Dublin Under 14: Seán Breheny, Stephen Lynch, Mícheál Lyons, John Waldron.
South Dublin and Dublin Mgr: Tommy Hartnett
Dublin: Gerard Hartnett, Andy Glover, Kevin Hayes
Dublin Under 15 Mgr: Tommy Hartnett
South Dublin: Shane Lynch, Fintan O'Brien
South Dublin and Dublin Under 14 Mgr: Tommy Hartnett
Dublin Under 15: Seán Breheny, Stephen Lynch, Mícheál Lyons, John Waldron
Dublin Under 15 Mgr: Tommy Hartnett
Dublin Under 16: Gerard Hartnett, Andy Glover, Kevin Hayes
Dublin Under 16: Seán Breheny, Stephen Lynch, Mícheál Lyons, John Waldron, Ciaran O'Brien
South Dublin Under 14: Stephen Hyland
South Dublin Under 14 Mgr: Tommy Hartnett
South Dublin Under 12: Martin Hartnett, Chris Guckian, Stephen Larkin, Gerard Fehily
Dublin Under 14: Kris Greene, Chris Guckian
South Dublin Schools: Martin Hartnett

Social and personal

Declan Feore

If I may be so bold as to paraphrase Paddy Kavanagh:
If ever you go to Temple Ogue
In a hundred years or so
Enquire from those who knew them
What kind they were to know
They'll say they were a quare bunch
Rye fol de dol di do!

AND, I suppose, we were a quare bunch, coming from diverse backgrounds, united not only in our determination to promote and develop the games and culture we so dearly loved and cherished in as convivial an atmosphere as possible, but also in our determination to build and foster a community. Prior to St Judes GAA Club being founded, with the exception of the schools, the Church was the only institution capable of gathering so many people together in common cause. When we held our Draws for the Clubhouse building project, the Development Committee suggested that these occasions should be truly social events. There may, indeed, have been the odd row at some of the committee meetings. What else could you expect, you might say, with Joe McDonnell as Chairman! The truth is Joe was a brilliant chairman of this committee and it is acknowledged that the Clubhouse would never have been built if everybody agreed on everything. The social events for the monthly Draws, where we filled The Templeogue Inn and The Spawell by supplying the Bands and usually a personality, ranging from the likes of Ciaran Duff to Mick Lally, were truly memorable occasions. It was here that differences were forgotten and friendships forged with colleagues and supporters, which have blossomed over the years and still flourish to this day.

Each person views his/her contribution to the Club differently. I am reminded of the story of the two stonemasons who, when asked what were they doing, one modestly replied "I am cutting stones", the other proudly proclaimed "I am building a Cathedral". This story, perhaps, best epitomises the divergent views of St Judes members over the last twenty five years. Those who have joined over the last five years are just as important as those who joined in the first five or subsequent years. All are making a contribution and nobody denies its vital importance in nurturing a great club and shaping a vibrant community.

Since the idea of this book to commemorate our first "fiche cuig bliain ag fás" was mooted, I have been amazed, but not surprised at the number of people who claim to have been founding members and at others who are quite adamant as to who was not. I suppose this is not too surprising, given the evolutionary history of the "Club".

The minute book of the first meeting of Cumann Peil Naomh Jude held in Bishop Galvin National School on Saturday 9th September 1978 records, ironically, that on a proposal by Joe Morrin and seconded by Eamonn O'Reilly, it was agreed that the name of the club should be "St Judes Gaelic Football Club". These minutes were proposed by C. Moran, seconded by O. Connolly and signed by E. Kenny 14/9/78. The following officers were elected at that inaugural meeting: Fr John Greene cc Chairman; Ernest Kenny Vice Chairman; Cyril Bates Secretary and Registrar; Eamonn O'Reilly Assistant Secretary; John Gallen Treasurer. Committee: Seamus Durkan, Charles Moran, Matt Healy, Joe Morrin, Des Cullen, Pat Farrelly, Donnchadh Lehane. Also elected to the committee, although not present, were Mr O. Connolly and Paddy Finn. For the record Jimmy O'Dwyer was co-opted the following month. He was seen to be an experienced mentor in the locality, as Bishop Galvin had already started football in the school and had entered teams the previous year in Cumann na mBunscol Leagues. He was also, of course, involved with Joe Morrin and Ernest Kenny in the Summer Project. They had had a very successful season prior to the Club's inaugural meeting. John Gallen, incidentally, has the record of being the longest serving officer in one position, having held the post of Treasurer from 1978 up to 1988 (the three year rule was not introduced until AGM 1991).

In 1981, the outcome of a protracted dispute over another matter led to the club being officially known as Cumann Peil Naomh Jude.

Gradually members with hurling orientation began to "infiltrate" the football scene. Carl Page was there almost from the beginning and Finbarr Murphy officially joined in 1979/1980. Jimmy O'Dwyer introduced hurling to the Summer Project of 1981 and this probably was what prompted others of us to join the Club and attend the public meetings in BGNS to propose the setting up of a Hurling/Camogie section for the parish. It was around this time that I first met Mick Hartnett, Eddie Walsh, Peter Lucey and Michael Ryan. This led to a separate Hurling and Camogie Committee being set up with the Chairman (Finbarr Murphy) and Secretary (Jimmy O'Dwyer) as delegates to Cumann Peil Naomh Jude. Eventually, following restructuring proposals by these two officers "Cumann Luthchleas Gael Naomh Jude", otherwise known as "St Judes GAA Club" was approved on a proposal by Donnchadh Ó Liatháin and seconded by Charles Moran at the 18th November 1982 AGM.

The Football and Hurling/Camogie would now be two separate sub-committees with delegates to the 11 man Executive of CLGNJ.

On a personal note, I am recorded as having joined in 1981. I was somewhat surprised, being afraid of a football, to be put in charge of the U10B team with Joe Morrin ("now boys, now boys" – when about ten young lads were trying to get into his white mini) and Tom Fitzpatrick (Tipperary). I had come from Ballyhea, a hurling stronghold in North Cork and had played minor hurling with Na Fianna in Dublin. I had also played adult hurling with Commercials, when their headquarters was Tom Dawson's pub in upper Rathmines. For the record I was the first of two players to play for both Ballyhea and Na Fianna. The other, of course, was a guy called Jason Sherlock.

MEMORIES

I have many happy and proud memories of my involvement with St Judes. I remember being presented with Man of the Match medal by Ernest Kenny in a Mentors v Juvenile match on The Green in the early years. Perhaps it was that man's cunning gesture to keep me on board for having the temerity to play football in a pair of sandals. I remember being presented with a brandy flask and a half dozen golf balls by Michael Fortune following one of Frank McSweeney's retirement pitch and putt classics.

Maybe it was Mick Hartnett's exclamation "'tis alright, we can still see it", whenever I managed not to drive one out of bounds that helped to secure that prize.

Free, free at last

I am very proud to have been the manager with Finbarr Murphy, Willie Nolan and Michael Ryan of the very first U10 hurling team fielded by St Judes and have been involved with juvenile hurling teams at all age levels up to U16 and with minor teams in different eras and U21 through junior up to senior. I was lucky enough to have been on away trips with senior and not so senior hurlers and have very happy memories of same.

But the most vivid recollection I have is of a weekend trip to Athboy, Co Meath on the weekend of 6th/7th June 1987. The Leinster Festival of Hurling was being held there that weekend.

We qualified for participation by virtue of being runners up in the Dublin Féile na nGael competition the previous month. Garrett Edge and I were the mentors travelling. Mick Hartnett claimed he was not available, but we knew he just wanted to stay and watch the World Cup Rugby match being relayed from Down Under.

We arrived by coach to a tea and biscuit reception in the local hall in Athboy at around 7.30p.m. on the Friday evening. A melodeon and a few girls were produced to entertain the visiting troops and we watched proudly as our team quickly adapted to this rustic environment. It wasn't long before the players were quickly assigned to their hosts. We looked at one another in great surprise. There we were free, free at last, but then our own host said "We'll just drop your gear out to the house". "Where's the house?" "Oh, just a few miles out the road". Our protestation that we only had a tooth brush and a razor fell on deaf ears, as we were ushered into the back of a fairly rough looking Ford Cortina Estate. We were driven out of town, further and further out into the country. The further we went the darker it got and the quieter we became.

After about three quarters of an hour – you can cover a lot of ground in three quarters of an hour in the country - we pulled into a farmhouse bungalow. The wife gave us a towel apiece and showed us to our twin-bedded room. We sat on our beds – towels neatly folded on our laps. We looked across at one another, each recognising the agony etched on the other's face. It was gone 10 o'clock at this stage. We peered out the window – miles and miles of what appeared to be boggy marshland, not a sign or light of a pub in any direction. We were marooned. Instinctively we made our way out to the sitting-room. A tentative knock. "Come in". After an uncomfortable silence, one of us just to be sociable enquired of a team photo prominently displayed – bad move this. We were given a full history of the team's achievements and an analysis of individual players' performances. This was supplemented by reference to other albums. During this appraisal tea and sandwiches were produced. No getting out now. I saw Garrett growing paler and paler. It was getting dangerously close to closing time. Suddenly our host closed the album, stretched himself and then, as if driven by some telepathic power, asked "Would yis like to go for a drink?" The harmony of the response "yes, yes please" would have done justice to any Negro spiritual leader's proclamation, "Free, free at last".

We drove all the way back to Athboy in no time at all. They were still open. We went into one that was fairly full. After two quick rounds we discovered, sure there was no need to worry. The night was only just beginning. We felt sorry for Mick Hartnett. We were up early the following morning to watch the Rugby International between Ireland and Australia.

We played Athboy in the morning and Leixlip in the afternoon – great but tough games of hurling. We told the wife we didn't want to be any trouble and would stay in town after the game. They collected us later and gave us a mighty feed. Off to Trim the following morning for the finals. I forget how we did. There was an inter-county match between Roscommon and Down in the afternoon and in the middle of the confusion we didn't notice that our coach, as it was later claimed, had come and gone without us. Desperate phone calls were made. By this stage the driver was back in Dublin. We had to use all our powers of persuasion to get the coach back at no extra charge. The team members were very happy to get home. Perhaps we should have paid greater attention to the note in the Féile na nGael programme sponsored by Coca Cola "Each club will return with memories of the hospitality of their hosts, exciting hurling and a very different way of life to what they are used to".

CLUB FIRSTS

At first meeting (9th September 1978) it was agreed to ask parents to subscribe £1 to the club. Colour of jerseys agreed sky blue at meeting, 21st September 1978. These were to be financed by house to house collection. Cake sale proposed for Brady's Butcher shop, 22nd October 1978. Agreed to write to Fr John Greene cc – whether this was in his capacity as club chairman or local curate I was unable to establish.

First recorded vote was at meeting 26th October 1978. "Following a long discussion on the purchasing of jerseys Mr E. Kenny proposed, seconded by E.O'Reilly that we buy a set of jerseys each with numbers for the Under 10 and Under 14 teams.

Mr D. Lehane proposed an amendment, seconded by J. Kirwin, that we purchase jerseys with numbers for the Under 14 team and plain jerseys for the Under 10 team. The amendment was carried by 5 votes to 4". (Note: 10 persons are minuted as being in attendance. Obviously, one person bottled it, thereby, possibly denying Ernest Kenny the opportunity to go down in history as the first pro-tem Chairman to exercise his casting vote in St Judes.)

When the jerseys did arrive, Seamus Durkan reported one set was too small. M. Dowling, the supplier, agreed to give a credit in respect of 12 jerseys and the committee agreed to sell the remainder to club members at £2 each and further agreed to purchase a new set of size 36 inch for the Under 14 team.

Charlie Moran and Jimmy O'Dwyer organised the first away trip to Ellsmere Port in Liverpool. Davy Griffin (Thomas Davis) in appreciation of the tremendous help he had given the new club was invited but could not travel. Thirty-two boys and six adults travelled, including Ernest Kenny, Seamus Durkan and Brian Hogan (father of Rugby international, Niall), May 1980.

Famous Dublin footballer, Tony Hanahoe was the first person to present medals to St Judes players. This was to the Under 11 league winners and Under 12 runners up. This was in BGNS, 1981.

Killasser, Mayo Under 14 footballers were the first non-Dublin visiting team to St Judes. They were beaten by hosts. Medals were presented by the great Roscommon player and future Kildare Manager, Dermot Earley. He also presented medals at the party in BGNS that evening to Under 10A team, October 1981.

Faughs was the first club to present St Judes with a set of jerseys.

Marie Bell was the first female in the club to be trained as a coach (and from what we can establish, the first in Dublin and Leinster) and to manage a boys' football team (U10) in St Judes. At the AGM 7th March 1984, it was reported that "women can be just as good as men" (and slowly the females were encouraged to participate).

The *Dublin VEC* is acknowledged in January 1979 as being the first benefactors of the Club with a grant of £200. The club agreed to buy two footballs.

Ernest Kenny was the first to propose a Céilí. He said he could get a band if the club could get the women to organise it. (And from such humble beginnings were females allowed into the club). Jimmy O'Dwyer claims he sang "Spancil Hill" and not "Tipperary so far away" that night. It was held in Bishop Galvin National School on the 15th November 1980.

Dinner Dances

First mentioned in the minutes 24th January 1979. Carl Page would make enquiries re availability of hotel and price. Estimated that about 200 would go. This did not materialise – the first dinner dance was held on 11th November 1983 in Stackstown Golf Club. Following publicity for this Mick O'Brien rang Charlie and enquired about joining the Club. The first Dinner Dance that was held in the Clubhouse took place on Friday 12th February 1988. This was a tremendously enjoyable and successful night. We felt we had 'arrived' when the press attended. Photographs appeared in evening papers.

At St Judes dinner, Seán McBride, Marie McBride, Elish and Neil Doyle, February 1988.

Evening Press, Wednesday 21st October, 1987 – St. Judes (Templeogue) – A well organised presentation took place in the clubhouse last Saturday night. Mr. Bill McCarthy, formerly of Arravale Rovers in Tipperary and a 1934 Tipperary minor, fulfilled his father's wishes by donating the cup to a club for juvenile competitions. Bill's father had bought the cup two days before he died in 1952. St. Judes are honoured to be the recipients of such a fine historic trophy. Our sincere thanks to David Carroll, Joe McNally and Declan Bolger for attending our juvenile function on Sunday to honour the extended official opening. The executive were delighted to make available the hall for the senior citizens concert last Monday night. The Dubliners, prior to their Austrialian Embassy engagement, headed the bill, which was well supported by folk groups, ballad groups, bands, traditional musicians and choir from local communities. Hurling training continues on Saturday afternoon.

It happened in Osprey

Tomás Joyce from Inis Oirr was the first person to bring in £100 without selling a ticket. It happened during our development draw in 1986. Tomás was one of our top ticket sellers. One Chinese man was so impressed by Tomás's enthusiasm that he ran upstairs and came down with £100 in cash. Tomás was so shocked that he forgot to give him the ticket. It was only at a sales review meeting that the discrepancy was noticed. The Chinese man got his ticket the following morning. Fuair Tomás bás Samhain 1993, eighteen months after his brother Pádraic, who was also a great supporter of the Club. Tomás's wife, Mary, has been in charge of An Siopa since it opened in October 1995.

Fr John Greene cc was the first chairman. He was succeeded by Donnchadh Ó Liathain. The first President was also Fr Greene and was succeeded by Joe Morrin. Cyril Bates was the first secretary of the Football Club. He was succeeded by Charles Moran. The first PRO was Declan Feore. Get the spelling right. Remember there's only one "F" in Feore. In the 1989/90 season Tommy Bassett became the first Dub to manage a top adult team in St Judes. Deirdre O'Riordan was the first female referee from St Judes in juvenile football.

1989 WAS A GOOD YEAR

Peter Ryan was the first county player to represent St Judes in either code, when he played centre back for Dublin against Kilkenny in the Leinster minor hulring championship in May 1989.

The first St Judes hurler to represent us internationally was Kieran Quigley, when he played in Luxenbourgh for Cumann na mBunscol, following Bishop Galvin's first hurling trophy victory in Croke Park in June 1989.

Our Under 16 footballers are honoured with bringing the first championship success to St Judes, when they won division 1 against Erins Isle, in the summer of 1989. Later on in the year our Junior hurlers became the first adult team to win a championship cup, when they defeated St Vincents in the final.

Mick Hartnett was the first sponsor of this Junior hurling team, when he supplied them with a fine set of jerseys.

MINUTE SNIPPETS

Golf Society – A letter received from Tommy Hickey requesting permission to form a Golf Society for St Jude,s members. Agreed on condition it did not interfere with the playing side of the club – Executive Meeting 29th Sept 1993. At the same meeting, Aodhán McSuibhne was approved for membership. Cost of running playing side of club was £19,000 last year – AGM 1st Dec 1993. Cost of running adult teams up £11,000 from previous year to £44,000 – AGM 1999.

Trapper Dalton Appeal – Request from St Vincents to buy tickets for this. Fund raising match between Dublin and Meath being organised. Declan O'Boyle and Enda Sheehy selected to play their first senior football match for Dublin in this event – Executive Meeting 27th Oct 1993. Match played on 13th November 1993.

And you too pal ... Tommy Bassett makes a point or two.

Changing Rooms for Camogie and All Weather Pitch – Don Lehane suggested that changing rooms for camogie teams was a major priority (presumably, because as his sons were getting older now, it would be unfair on them watching the girls change outside the dressing rooms). He also stated that an All Weather Pitch was essential for training during the winter – Executive Meeting 12th Dec 1993. Letter received from Councillor Stanley Laing re All Weather Pitch – Executive Meeting 26th Jan 1994. That was quick Don!

The Bassett Hound – Trip for Senior Football team to Killarney approved on the basis of a grant of £1,500 and what subsequently appears to have been a non refundable loan of £2,000 – Executive Meeting Jan 1994. Bassett, you were some negotiator!!!

The Big Screen – Management Committee reported a profit of £184 on hire of Big Screen in hall for World Cup – Executive Meeting 1994. "That Gaelic Games on RTE will be shown on the big screen irrespective of time" following letter of complaint from Charlie Moran – Executive Meeting 27th April 1994.

Girls Football – Girls football is to be started with an Under 14 team being run by Marie Bell – Executive Meeting 23rd Feb 1994. Áine Byrne from Wexford is interested in starting Ladies Football team. Players' meeting arranged for 20th Nov 1995 by Gillian Gilleran and Maire McSherry – Executive Meeting 12th Oct 1995.

Youth Delegate – Seán Fallon is congratulated on his selection as Dublin Youth Delegate to the GAA Annual Congress. (He gets his photograph with a line of GAA presidents in The Irish Times) – Executive Meeting 31st Mar 1994.

Scór – The Quiz Team of Seán Breheny, Gerry Hurley and Tony O'Dowd were beaten by one point after Tie Break question – Executive Meeting 27th Feb 1989. Mary Hurley comes first in the Dublin scór. Bill Tisdall and Eileen Lyons come second and the Set Dancers did very well, getting to the final. The dancers were: Liam and Áine MacMathuna; Tod and Jo Culhane; Seán and Francis Ward; Billy O'Frighil and Rita Moran – Executive Meeting 24th Jan 1990. Mary Hurley is congratulated on getting to the Leinster Final – Executive Meeting 28th Feb 1990.

The Ban – Under AOB Finbarr Murphy asked that the Club should support any moves to do away with the ban on British Security forces joining the Association. Agreed to forward this as club recommendation to Dublin County Board AGM – Club AGM 1997. Tommy Bassett raised matter of a letter from St Michaels Roscommon requesting support for fund raising. Secretary admits to having mislaid letter. Club agrees to £75 support – Executive Meeting 1st Dec 1993. Whose club is St Michaels anyway?

A Hole Lot of Trouble – "At a recent function, a woman fell into an unfilled hole outside fire door." It was agreed to fill in the hole – Executive Meeting 23rd Feb 1994. Presumably after the woman was removed.

New Structure – A motion was passed that as and from start of season 1990/91 there would be two committees: Adult to cater for Hurling, Football and Camogie from U16 to Senior and Juvenile to cater for Hurling, Football and Camogie from Green to Under 15 – AGM 1989.

McVicker and his Dog – The Club agrees to give Mr McVicker Social Membership in appreciation of his dog retrieving £120 worth of sliothars – Executive Meeting 26th Sept 1990. There is no mention of a gesture to the dog.

The Old Folks – Frank McSweeney, in his capacity as chairman of the General Purposes Committee, requests permission for Jack Tierney to run Christmas Raffle in aid of the Old Folks Party – Executive Meeting 28th Nov 1990.

And with a politically more correct name it is still going strong. Raffle for Old Folks raises £300, to be divided between St Vincent de Paul and the Old Folks – Executive Meeting 30th Jan 1991.

There's a whole lot of culture going on – Tommy Hartnett reports that he has set up the cultural side of the club. Music classes starting 8th April. Set Dancing being set up and Irish club for youth being investigated – Executive Meeting 20th Mar 1991.

A Hurling Football – Finbarr Murphy is elected Chairman of the Hurling and Camogie committee in 1982 and one of his first gestures, as he reports to Cumann Peil Naomh Jude, is to present a football and a notice board to Bishop Galvin NS. Finbarr progresses from here to arrange the first Tug o' War, featuring Eoin Heraty and Steve Bearpark as the main stays with support from Charlie Moran and Tony Gilleran. He also organised the first Barbecue and Mystery Tour in November 1988. And of course his table quiz in 1984 was a first. It was also minuted that he was starting Bridge classes on 6th March 1989. (Did anyone turn up for these?)

Looking after Number One – "It was proposed by Mr Jimmy O'Dwyer and unanimously agreed that the mentor in charge of each team be given £2 for each match. £1 for referee and £1 to buy minerals for the team" "It was also agreed that Mr C Moran be paid the amount due to him" – Football Meeting 17th April 1980.

When the U16 Football Championship final was fixed for 4th March 1989, Seamus Durkan requested video (£40), professional photographer, socks and nicks. He also requested tracksuits for his team – Executive Meeting 27th Feb 1989.

All Ireland Tickets – Distribution of match tickets, especially All Ireland tickets, is always a contentious issue in any club. Naturally, we in St Judes have always tried to be fair. When Dublin were playing in the championship it was particularly difficult. At one stage certain members cocooned themselves in the office, where they held an "equitable" private members' draw. It was amazing how fortunate some family members had been in those draws.

The Executive was seen to be above board always as evidenced by this extract from the minutes of September 1985.

"It was disclosed that the club had received 4 x Hogan Stand, 4 x Cusack Stand and 90 x Hill 16 (50 of which had been originally allocated and a further 40 of which had just that night been collected by the Secy (sic). On the proposal of J. O'Dwyer seconded by D. Feore it was proposed that Executive (11 in number) and team mentors be put into hat (sic) for a Special Limited Draw for Stand Tickets (8). It was agreed. It was further agreed and understood (without a formal proposition being put) that those members of Executive and mentors who had been unsuccessful in the Limited Draw should have priority on the Ground (ie Hill 16 Tickets). Provisional allocations of Ground Tickets made there and then. The Secretary pointed out that players or rather the older ones from say 14 upwards would have to be accommodated in the chase for tickets as otherwise they would be very disaffected and might not play for the coming season. A provisional list of players was drawn up which took account of their age, their subscription being paid and the span of the teams they represented. It was agreed (without a formal proposition being put) that persons be they Executive members or mentors who felt that they did not want to be included in the Limited Draw should indicate so now. Messrs J O'Dwyer and J Morrin so indicated."

Present at meeting were: J Morrin, C Moran, E Walsh, J Gallen, J O'Dwyer, D Lehane (Donnchadh), M O'Brien, S Durkan and E Kenny (representing Football Section); M Hartnett and D Feore (representing Hurling Section).

Set Dancing – In 1984, Mick and Marie O'Brien decided to start up Set Dancing in the area. They gathered together a group of Club members, including Michael and Bernie O'Boyle, Seán and Frances Ward and Mick's brother Muiris and his wife Marie. Early classes were held on Friday nights in the kitchens of various houses. Mick (from Ballinskelligs) and his brother were the 'tutors'.

When the group had mastered the Kerry set and the Sliabh Luachra set, the tutors decided that the group could go public. Classes were advertised for Friday nights in Bishop Galvin National School, with Muiris as tutor. Very soon there were up to 30 people attending every week and the repertoire was extended to include the Clare set and the Conamara set. The dancing was so energetic that the shine was continuously removed from the wooden floor in the school hall. Every six months the set dancers had the floor resealed and polished.

After the opening of the Naomh Jude Clubhouse, the venue was switched to there. Mick Hartnett supplied a wooden floor for the Lounge and several sessions were held. After a few years, Naomh Jude entered a set dancing team in the GAA Scór Competition.

The team consisted of Mick and Marie O'Brien, Seán and Bridie Bradshaw, Seán and Frances Ward, Margaret Coghlan and Muiris O'Brien. They achieved third place in Dublin.

And there's more

When the Clubhouse opened in 1987 most of us who were involved in its development were in our mid thirties to early forties. We were energetic, enthusiastic and had a great zest for life. We felt justifiably proud of our achievement and wished to share that with others. In appreciating the support we received for our development from within the community, we held an open house and gave everyone who attended a few drinks. It was a cold night and as a consequence we ran out of brandy. We had to raid Charlie Moran's private stock to resolve the dilemma.

There was always a great buzz in St Judes and everyone loved it as they still do. We had found a communal home and had many a formal and informal party here. We had the Dubliners here one night for a Senior Citizens party the year after the opening. We didn't have enough microphones for them so we had to borrow from the Church and School. Often John Carroll from Willington Cottages, who was a former County Board delegate, would drop in a regale us with his vast repertoire of stories and songs. His friend Chris Casey often entertained us with jokes while standing on a stool.

St Judes is not just a GAA Club. It is a vital focal point for the community. We have catered for Arts and Crafts, Senior Citizens, Active Retirement, Set Dancing, 25 Card and Bridge Players, Fun Quizzes, Nights at the Dogs, Badminton, Golf and Hill Walking as well as Barbecues.

Senior Citizens Committee, 1995 – Included are Frank McSweeney, Jack Tierney, Tommy Hickey, Sr Patricia, Patti Finn, Angela Parkinson and Marie Kelly. Mary (RIP) and Tom Horan were also prominent.

St Judes attracts a great calibre of people.

GEORGE WRIGHT :
Give me the Moonlight!

George Wright was born within, what is now, the curtilage of The Beggars Bush Public House. Is it any wonder he feels so at home here in our Clubhouse. He was in fact born in Landsowne Park, in the house which was then nearest to

Haddington Road. The house has since been knocked down and is now part of the Beggars Bush Pub complex. He was an enterprising young lad and together with the son of the proprietor Jack Ryan always managed to have enough money for clothes and the flicks, by retrieving empties, arranged by the son and selling them back to the father.

George is, of course, already immortalised in the book "Stealing Sunlight" by Angeline Kearns Blain, wherein he is reputed to have taken a fancy to Granny Doyle's late husband's train engine. Even then George had a husky voice.

George, in my own father's words, is a man who "enjoys a drink". He,s a dapper dresser and always looks healthy, despite life not being kind to him in that regard. He and his father spent long spells in hospital together. He was a heavy smoker in his youth and had one of his lungs removed several years ago. He has to go back regularly for check ups. On one such visit, the doctor while examining the X-Rays enquired if George had given up the cigarettes. "Oh, yes Doctor", replied George. "Haven't touched one for years". "But, I see", said the doctor, "you still take a drink". George was intrigued and staring at the X-Ray, blurted out "How can you tell that by looking at the X-Ray?" "Because", exclaimed the doctor "I can smell it off you".

FRANK MCSWEENEY

"There's a young person here tonight..."

On the social front Frank McSweeney is famous for his "There's a young person here tonight celebrating his/her birthday", always apparently to the great surprise of the birthday boy or girl and then Frank will sing birthday wishes "from old friends and new"

Hardly a week goes bye without a birthday or two and Frank always obliges. In the unlikely event of he not being there, the honours are done by Paddy Russell. Frank has been involved with St Judes since its foundation. Firstly as supporter and parent of Brian, Declan and Ger, the latter being one of the toughest cornerbacks in the club's football history. It's not for nothing they call him "Whacker". Subsequently, Frank was mentor-selector with several juvenile teams and served on the Club Executive as well as other committees.

As chairman of the Social and General Purposes committee he was responsible for initiating the Senior Citizen's Christmas Party, with Jack Tierney as the main fundraiser.

Frank played his early football with Rialto Gaels, before emigrating to the USA, where he played very lucratively for Monaghan in New York and Connecticut. He married his Cavan girl in the States and his son Brian was born there. He returned to Dublin in 1962 and joined the ESB. In 1968 Frank and his colleagues were involved in a manning/pay dispute. It was illegal for ESB power station employees to go on strike, but strike they did and ended up "doing time" in Mountjoy. Shan Mohangi, the infamous Green Tureen murderer was an inmate there at the time.

On the Saturday morning a union meeting was organised in the prison. It must have been the only time inmates had such a meeting. Following a Government meeting that afternoon in Wexford all ESB strikers were mysteriously released late on the Saturday night. Taxis were surreptitiously provided. When Frank's brother Fred heard of his release he drove from Dalkey to Rialto with a bottle of whiskey.

The first thing they did on opening the bottle was to throw away the cap. As a result of the strike, conditions were not only greatly improved for the ESB workers but indeed for all. Subsequently the law banning strikes by ESB power workers and other such employees was rescinded.

Frank McSweeney is highly regarded in St Judes. He was conferred with Honorary Life Membership in January 2002 on reaching his 75th birthday. He is only one of three people accorded such an honour. The others being Joe Morrin, Snr 1991 and Jack Boothman 1996.

Frank was Club President from 1992 to 1994 and was very proud of this. Long may we continue to enjoy his company and friendship.

BILL TISDALL

Bill was involved in amateur dramatics for many years before joining St Judes. He still spoke in the clipped tones of the stage actor. He suffered from severe Rheumatoid arthritis and whenever you'd ask him how he was, he replied "Lousy thank God, lousy" before letting out one his famous chuckles. He was married to Anne. They were a delightful couple, each very dependent on the other.

Bill was also, like George Wright, a dapper dresser. One night he arrived in the Clubhouse looking particularly spruce, complete with button hole and handkerchief. Frank McSweeney, who enjoyed his company approached him as he entered. "Are you coming from the theatre?" enquired Frank. "Well actually" declaimed Bill, in his best theatrical accent , "I was on my way to Faughs, but my driver left me here by mistake. Hard to get good staff these days." And then casting his eyes over Frank's shoulder "Barman ! Whiskey please." Then he fixes Frank with one of those looks and emphatically says "You hardly think I dressed up like this to come in here do you?" One time Bill neglected to pay his membership fee. He was "incensed" on receipt of a demand notice from the Club. He got a great "ribbing" about it from the bar staff.

But Bill used his theatrical and Bardic knowledge when he replied in his verse.

Upperscross Manor, Today

Respected Sir
Your letter of a recent date
Reminding me my sub is late
At this moment is close to hand
It seems so like a final demand.
And now no matter however hard
I'll endeavour to emulate the Bard
Knowing that however terse
You'll appreciate my reply in verse!
Bar Management tease me as very rude
To the noble Club named after St. Jude
You'd think that my not renewing my sub
Was as worrying to them as Hamlet's 'Rub'
The whole position can get very tricky
When I have to deal with the Hon. T. Hickey.
And then who better to further rub it in
That his consort Seán surnamed after a brand of Gin.
They cry to all and sundry to remember
That William T. is no longer a member.
And so I pray to Saints that are Latter day
That this odd couple feature on Scrap Saturday!
Enough! And to a halt let this farce grind
And like Gillian Bowler leave it all behind.
My renewal of membership fee I now enclose
For my name in your register to repose.
My fee is at the appropriate rate,
The years seeming to have sealed my fate.
For they are growing on apace.
A gypsy asked to read my face!!
And now my regards to you who signs in erse
From this genius who writes in verse.
Respectfully,
Baron Uppercross, Bill Tisdall

Bill died quietly and suddenly in late December 1996. His beloved Anne predeceased him by only a few weeks. We miss their gaiety and great company.

Corrigan Cup – nostalgia

Seán McBride and Neil Doyle

C AN YOU just picture it! Twenty young boys all geared up for a day trip away with the Club and this time with a slight difference. It was a Feast Day, the 8th December and as the boys were off school, the mentors were taking them on a day trip to Wales by boat.

This was the panel that had swept all before them from under 10 upwards, winning their division 1 leagues for a number of years in succession in the competitions that were then organized by the South East and South City Boards. Those involved will surely recall a number of thrilling encounters for final honours with clubs such as Round Towers, Clondalkin, Ballyboden St Endas and Lucan Sarsfields.

A few years previously, this team had won the Corrigan Cup (first time for the club) in the final that was played on the 12th. June 1988, a beautiful Sunday evening in Bushy Park. This was a match that was a huge one for the Club at that time, so much so that it was videoed with commentary by Declan Feore who conducted interviews at half and full time with all and sundry. Any copy of that video still extant is of course a collectors item!

St Judes beat Lucan Sarsfields comfortably in the end with the following line up: In goal, Padraig O Shaughnessy and from right to left, Ken Molloy, Enda Crennan, Thomas Quinn, Dermot O Reilly, Ian Fortune, Karl O' Boyle. Midfield was Owen Mc Bride and Paul Carroll. In the forwards were Aidan Lawlor, David Mc Govern, David Barry, Trevor Percy, Alan Bowe and Antoin Doyle. The subs included Trevor Mc Donald, Shane Lynch, Jim Mulready, Philip Kearns, Patrick Mc Loughlin and Niall Tierney.

The trip to Holyhead took place a few years later during which time we had lost some players and had been joined by others including Thomas Quinn, Garrett Roche, David Edge, Alan Tierney, Mark Naughton, Niall Tierney, Kevin O Dwyer, Gary Downes, Ross Kinsella, Pat Brien, Eamonn Dunne, Neil Fitzpatrick, James Kelly, Greg Lehane, Ciaran Fitzpatrick, Michael Glover, Rory O'Connell, Eamon Coghlan, Philip McGlynn, Ronan O'Brien and Ciaran Voyles.

It must have been one of the worst days of the year for the wind was at gale force. Against our better judgement we decided to make a go for it as we just could not disappoint the lads. We got to Wales all right and spent a few hours shopping in Holyhead and then left at about 3pm in atrocious conditions to travel back to Dun Laoghaire. Green does not adequately describe the colour of some of us!!! Boy was it rough although our charges seemed to manage all right.

We were just glad to see the lights of Dublin Bay only to be informed by the captain on the tannoy that he could not make it into Dun Laoghaire Harbour. We spent the next 12 hours bobbing up and down on the Irish Sea, eventually reaching safe haven at six the following morning. No wonder the boys, now men, still talk about this trip as an experience not to be easily forgotten.

The managers and supporters who travelled everywhere with the team during those years and washed the jerseys included Jack & Mary Crennan, Michael and Rita Fortune, Neil and Elish Doyle, Seán & Marie Mc Bride, John Carroll and others. (If I have left off someone who should have been mentioned, please forgive me).

Those were wonderful years and we all got terrific enjoyment from just watching the boys compete and enjoy themselves as they grew up. It is great to see that a number of them are still enjoying their sport and lining out for the Club at different levels and those who are not playing are still very supportive of St Judes.

It was in the late 1980s also that the Club started to encourage the mentors to take the Foundation level coaching course and a number of hopefuls spent a hard week-end over at St Vincents being put through our paces by the likes of Brian Mullins who was helping to run the programme.

Paddy Russell, Marie Bell, Pat Brien and Tommy Hartnett were others I can remember who participated in the course. It was far from straight forward, however, as I and others received official letters from the Board advising that, as we had not attained the required standard, we would not be getting the certificates. Little, however, did we know that we had a prankster in our midst who had managed to get his hands (for it was a he) on some official stationery and had written the letters.

We all had a good laugh when the truth unfolded and we got the official certs deeming us to be fully qualified to coach at juvenile level. Hey, when you think about it, maybe the prankster was right after all!!

Good times!

Bishop Galvin/Shanahan School

Jimmy O'Dwyer

O N THE last Thursday of term, a third class boy and girl summoned me from my office to the school pitch. "Come quickly" they said "It's starting any minute". They were referring to the annual clash in Gaelic Football between the veterans from third class Bishop Galvin and the aspiring scouts from second class Bishop Shanahan. Both teams were immaculately kitted out, the pitch was lined and flagged, fifth class pupils were released from the chores of lessons to act as umpires, ball-boys, water carriers and security personnel.

The sun was beaming down as Seán Breheny and Alan Dodd replicated the gesturing of Tommy Lyons and Larry Tompkins on the sideline. Lá dár saol – a day to dream about. The result was of no importance; the symbolism however was immense. All this was happening because dedicated teachers in both parish schools have throughout the years ensured that our traditions would prosper and that children would enjoy the benefits of sport through our own Gaelic Games.

In Bishop Galvin NS we have indeed come a long way. When the school opened in July 1975, finding a place to train teams often proved difficult. Many exciting inter-class games took place where the Osprey houses now stand, sometimes to the displeasure of builders who saw us as trespassers on occasion. Telling them that we were from St Pius X or Joseph's Terenure didn't cut much ice especially when we had to beat a hasty retreat down Osprey Road followed by an irate JCB driver ... in the JCB.

Massive expansion came to the school within a very short time and the development of the games needed a wider setting. By 1977 we made our first venture into the Cumann na mBunscol leagues. The Cumann was to become a major catalyst in the promotion of games in the school. As a delegate to the Monday night meetings, I soon learned the geography of greater Dublin and my Gaeilge certainly improved as to this day all Cumann meetings are conducted through Irish.

Opportunely, Eamonn Treacy and Peter Lucey had joined the staff early on and we had moved to Orwell Green for our coaching sessions. Our games on the Green attracted many onlookers, including Ernest Kenny who was to become a major link between the school and the new emerging club – St Judes. By the way, Eamonn and Peter were to form the backbone of the "Primary Aces" team, winners of the club football seven-a-side in 1980.

Other members were Tom Sweeney, Eamonn Scully, Robbie O'Leary, Robbie O'Connor, Cormac Egan, Richard Delaney, Jimmy O'Dwyer and Jim Coghlan. Jim, the only non-practising teacher among us, was allowed on the team as his intellectual and football ability matched the combined talents of all the rest us – some man for one man. All the team resided in one house in Rushbrook for the duration of the tournament!

Indeed when the first competitive Club league match was played in Bushy Park, the school provided most of the team and all of the jerseys for the occasion. For many years, until the splendid clubhouse was built, the school was the centre of many club activities including meetings and fundraising functions.

The school's efforts in Cumann na mBunscol competitions was to bear fruit in the early eighties when practically every child was playing gaelic football to some level. When the school reached its first football final in Croke Park in 1980 against the mighty force of St Mary's Haddington Road the game got a mighty boost, despite losing. It was now cool to play gaelic football and even the old Croker was alluring to all young players. That game was played on 8th December 1980 the same day that Charles Haughey and Margaret Thatcher were discussing affairs of the nation in Dublin Castle. When we lost again to the same opposition in the senior final of 1981, the loss didn't seem to matter, as we had established the school as a force in Gaelic football.

For many years we have been in Division One of both junior and senior football competitions, giving hundreds of boys and girls a programme of games where they can be proud to represent the school.

One very notable feature of our involvement in Gaelic games has been the equitable approach adopted as policy in the school, where the involvement of both boys and girls is fostered and encouraged. Indeed a healthy rivalry exists between the boys and girls. When the girls won the Division One final in 2000, Kathryn O'Connell, who for a season played for St Judes when managed by Tommy Bassett, expertly coached the team. Along with the boys many girls from the school have represented Dublin in inter county competitions and many have remained with the game and are indeed involved in coaching throughout the country and abroad.

It was only a matter of time before Hurling and Camogie became part of the school's activities and in 1980 the games were introduced and consolidated through courses at Summer Projects in the parish. In 1982 a Hurling and Camogie Committee was formed in the club with major influence from the school. The now famous fundraiser "Run for Hurling", the brainchild of Jack Boland, raised over £1000 for the purchase of hurleys and helmets and by 1984 both school and club teams were entered in competitions.

In 1984 another inspired decision that was to have a monumental effect on Gaelic Games in the parish was made when Seán Breheny was appointed to the staff. Seán was then secretary to Cumann na mBunscol and his superb vitality was a huge boost to our work. Sean's first task in the school was to take charge of Camogie teams, reaching finals against Donard in Bohernabreena and St Mark's in Bushy Park before winning in the Phoenix Park in 1989 against Loreto, Rathfarnham.

The school reached its first hurling final in 1986 losing out by one score to Scoil Naithí. Peter Lucey was the manager of that team and years later many of the team was to star for him on Senior, Intermediate and Junior Hurling Club teams. In 1987 we lost to Holy Family Rathcoole and in 1988 to Scoil Cholmcille, Knocklyon. It seemed as if we could never be winners in finals but the best was yet to come.

As sport builds self esteem, so too does it reveal character, and the image recurs of countless great matches at schools level through the years. The best match - and what a host of games from which to choose - will always be a matter of personal choice, decreed perhaps by evocative memories of idyllic times with the sun on our backs, freshly cut grass and the pride of the parish at stake. For my own part, one match, and I have been involved in hundreds over the years, will always stand high on my list. The events at Croke Park on the evening of June 8th 1989, are embedded in my memory.

The school junior hurling team defeated James's St CBS that evening by 3 Goals to nil to win the Corn Frank Cahill and the first cup for the school after 14 years of trying. The win was the product of truly magnificent performances that embraced all the best elements of the schools' game : skill, courage, pride and total commitment. It was also the best possible promotion of the games in the school as every pupil roared on their team from the stand.

The panel that performed that feat is worth noting: Ian Fortune, David McGovern, Gerard Orr, Patrick Brien, Michael Glover, Kevin O'Dwyer, David Edge, Aidan Lalor, Stevie Joyce, Richard Keenan, David Mallon, Ciaran Lenihan, Alan McGreal, Martin Sherkle, Ken Molloy, Enda Crennan, Gareth Roche, Declan Brady, Carl O'Malley, Brendan Carty and Gary Downes. The dream double was achieved the same year when the Camogie team beat off all opposition to win the final of the Corn Chuchulainn against a strong Loreto Rathfarnham side in the Phoenix Park.

Those successes ensured widespread participation in games in the school and the only limit to our progress was time and human resources. This is where the club was of great assistance catering for all players from nursery to sixth class and beyond. The amount of reminders to children to "meet at the shops" for training and games was testament to the solid links between club and school. The club's support for the development of two pitches at the school was of immense benefit to all the children.

We have been back to Croke Park many times since, winning the Corn Bean Ui Phuirseail (Camogie) in 1993; the Corn Marino (Senior Hurling) in 1994; the Corn Herald Special (Senior Hurling) in 1996; the Corn Royal Breffni Girls' Division One Football in 2000 and of course the pinnacle of our achievements – winning the Corn Oideachais this year in Division One Junior Hurling. The last minute of that game was heart-stopping with the ball flying from end to end, but BGNS finished well and claimed the trophy for the first time against superb opposition from Scoil Mobhi. Two weeks later the "B" team was to equal that performance winning the Corn Irish Permanent with style.

It is certain that the amount of coaching of the basic skills by Seán Breheny was a major factor in these victories, but two inputs by St Judes must be acknowledged. The appointment of Niamh Leahy as club coach has been the best decision made by the club and the generous availability of the all-weather pitch to the school has given us another fantastic resource in promoting the games.

Team: Gerard McManus, Darragh O'Connor, Alan O'Beirne, Michael Scanlon, Niall Conroy, Emmet McKenna, Paul Maguire, Danny Devine, Evan Griffin, Ciaran Mangan, Robert Hardy, Eoin Larkin, Niall Murray, Mark Hannon, Cillian O'Hora, Robert Martina, Stephen Elliott, Conor McMahon, Carl Dunne, Oisin O'Donnell, Paul Kiernan, Keith Dunne, Killian Morgan, Ross Murphy, Danny Riordan.

The schools' leagues are about glory, honour and pride in a noble cause. Many players speak with fond enthusiasm about the pleasure gained in the schools' arena, particularly if they have been fortunate enough to play in Croke Park finals. At no level of the game is zeal and family involvement so pronounced.

Schools have always been absolutely crucial to the development and promotion of the game in the city and their importance is no less today. However, schools working closely with clubs are the model to which many aspire. It would be difficult to better the relationship between club and school in this parish, with five of the teachers, Seán Breheny, Eamonn Treacy, Kathryn O'Connell, Peter Lucey, Dónal Ó Loingsigh and myself acting as mentors on juvenile and adult teams in the club from time to time. Both Bishop Galvin NS and St Judes GAA Club are fortunate to have achieved this ideal. Long may it remain so.

THANKS, JIMMY

Church & General
Cumann na mBunscol

*(Cathaoirleach Cumann na mBunscol
1995–1997)*

Jimmy O'Dwyer (centre) with Cumann na mBunscol Chairman, Gerry O'Meara, who also hails from Templemore, and Nicky English at the Cumann na mBunscol finals in Croke Park.

Jimmy O'Dwyer has just stepped down as Cathaoirleach of Cumann na mBunscol. The Tipp man has completed an eventful two years in which he motivated and inspired colleagues and children. His chairmanship was positive, facilitative and dynamic.

An historic first during his stewardship was the meetings with an Coiste Iarbhunscoileanna. Together a "Dublin Hurlng Development Plan" was submitted to eager and earnest Coaching and Games Development Committee in Parnell Park with Jimmy as accomplished speaker and skilful presenter of the case for such a plan.

The Bishop Galvin N.S. Principal has always lauded the County Board Officers – John F. Bailey, John Costello and Donal O hIceadha – for their help in promoting games among the schoolchildren of the Capital. The affable Templemore man had regular contact with Coiste Oiliúna and Coaching Director Cyril Duggan and lost no time, with the Laois dual player, in recommending refinements to the coaching programme.

Jimmy had a justifiable leaning towards the game of hurling. He found time, outside the constant ordinary demand, to help out with Coaching for U-10's for Coiste na nÓg; to organise and deliver Foundation and Level One Hurling Coaching courses in Dublin and beyond; to address the Shinty Association in Inverness on motivation, team spirit and planning a yearly programme. He witnessed an increase

in the number of schools participating in hurling and camogie and rejoiced at the record of 8,400 hurleys distributed. This represents an increase of more than 100% on the 92/93 figure of 4,050 camán. He continued to encourage his own boys – Kevin, Donagh and Barry – who are mad into hurling with local club, St. Jude's. All the while he pioneered the introduction of computers to aid Cumann na mBuncscol.

Eagraí den scoth a bhí ann. Ní dhearna se dhá leath na dhiogras riamh. Bhí súil leis an árd-chaighdean iompar agus dea-mhúinte ar an bpáirc agus mar a bhí ar scoil. Thuig sé go raibh brú mór a chur ar mhúinteoirí ó thaobh cúraimí oideachais de. Da bharr mhol se go hard na múinteoirí a thógann daltaí in dhiaidh ama scoile, a chothaionn grá dár gcluichi gaelacha iontu agus a dhiríonn na paistí clarú le club aitiúil.

Of the 38 Cathaoirligh of Cumann na mBunscol since 1928, 20 have hailed from Cuige Mumhan, Jimmy, however, is the first from the Premier County and we shall allow the former chairman the last word: "Rud a thugann ardú chroí go léir ná na focail molta agus buíochas a chloistear ó dhaoine a thuigeann gur ar mhaithe na bpáistí a spregtar sinn chun bheith i bhfeighil spóirt."

84

The ʄun Quiz

Seán Breheny

THE SECOND Tuesday of the month some years ago: Question: (as Danny Lynch comes through the door of the Members' Lounge): "What is deer meat known as?" Without breaking stride, Danny bellows "DEAR MEAT?" DEAR MEAT"? CONWAY'S meat is DEAR MEAT!!"

This encapsulates the whole meaning of the monthly Quiz – fun. Although the Quiz is not an endless round of banter and wit, there is a great willingness on the part of the participants to lighten the atmosphere and make the most of any opportunity offered to get a laugh at the expense of the Quizmaster or each other. Indeed, the Quizmaster has rarely been known to pass up any chance to highlight perceived deficiencies in certain teams' performances. Over the years, the quiz has evolved to the stage where all participants are comfortable with one another, where there is always a welcome for new people and regulars are missed if they fail to turn up on a particular night. Indeed, Martin and Gary can read the audience so well that they more often that not say "wait five more minutes, so-an-so will be on their way". And so it happens. A major part of the enjoyment of any quiz is the ability to answer the questions, and the record of answering at the Fun Quiz is excellent. Usually, the vast majority of teams come within 10 points of the winning score. Then there is the phenomenon of the playoff rounds, which are required when teams finish on equal points. It is a rare quiz night indeed when there is no need of a playoff round. Playoff questions are difficult to gauge - too hard, and they're no fun, too easy and they have no point. Sometimes the easy option is taken and the Quizmaster asks for a "list" – not always the most popular with the participants, it must be said, but it does allow all members of a team to throw in their shovelful. The "list" can be a great source of fun and argument about how accurate certain film titles or book titles are. The Fun Quiz attempts to be just that - an enjoyable series of practical questions that aren't too specialised, and are, theoretically, "answerable". There are some certainties about the monthly Quiz: The participants take the Quiz seriously. Inaccuracy on the part of the Quizmaster, (a rare occurrence!) is not tolerated, but is always dealt with by means of a thunderous, but good-humoured howl from the floor. This is followed by the Quizmaster sucking in a deep breath, pulling himself together and repeating the inaccuracy, in the vain hope that the mob will accept his version as being the expert one. Not a hope.

Up comes Gary or Martin to say, "It's no good. They're right. You're wrong". This results in a swift readjustment of the relevant scores and yet one more fact added to the small store of knowledge accumulated by the Quizmaster! Another certainty is that trick questions are not that popular, even though they raise a sort of laugh.

Q. What creature has a beak like a duck, has webbed feet and lays eggs?

The answer we get from nearly everybody is "The Platypus". But if the Quizmaster, when calling out the answers, says that the answer is "a duck", there is a moment of stunned silence, then a laugh, but he had better say "also the platypus", very quickly or things could turn seriously ugly. Actually, this is an exaggeration. Over the last ten years or so since the Quiz started, there has never been an unpleasant incident or serious disagreement. Challenges have always been conducted in a good-humoured, patient manner, with both parties agreeing to differ, but acknowledging that further checking of facts may be needed.

For those of you reading this who are unfamiliar with the monthly quiz, the participants pay €2 a head to answer 50 questions in teams of any size and make-up, with the money collected being returned as prizes for first, second and third. Once or twice during the year we have a fund-raising quiz for some worthy cause. We have raised funds in the past for a missionary priest, to support athletics training for Olympic athlete Ciara Sheehy, for a young French athlete in the Special Olympics and for the local branch of the St Vincent de Paul. On these occasions the generosity of our regular Quiz participants never fails to surprise. Indeed, it has been known for winning teams to donate their cash prize to the particular cause being supported.

The experience of the St Judes monthly Fun Quiz has been a positive, very enjoyable one from the start, full of good humour and a very high standard of answering. It is enhanced by the participation of all ages. It is a compliment to the Quiz that young people attend as regularly as the more senior among us, and have competed successfully. In finishing, it is very gratifying to have the opportunity, on behalf of all the quiz people, to thank Martin McCabe and Gary Kane for the hard work and good humour they apply to correcting and scoring each team's efforts. Their great contribution should be acknowledged and on more than one occasion the answer provided by the Quizmaster has been hastily changed for the correct one on the advice of Martin and Gary. Question: Name the only mammal that can't jump? Answer: Peter "Hippo" Ryan, (one time mid-fielder on the Senior Football Team). Sadly, not awarded a point, "elephant" being the correct answer. We look forward to many more quizzes with our regulars and some new members, who are always welcome. Incidentally, Whitney Houston and Diana Ross ARE cousins, not aunt and niece, so yiz were wrong!

Juvenile hurling and camogie
– The early years
Jimmy O'Dwyer

1975 TO 1982

In the late 1970s and early 1980s, hurling and camogie were played in Bishop Galvin NS and in 1981 coaching was undertaken in the first week of July as part of the Summer Project. In the winter of 1981 and the spring of 1982, hurling and camogie followers in St Judes called meetings for fellow minded hurling and camogie followers in the parish with a view to setting up a hurling and camogie section of the club. Many Faughs members attended those meetings and indeed some of them remained to participate in the first committee. However, the idea of a merger did not happen.

1982

The first hurling and camogie meeting was held in Bishop Galvin NS on 24th March 1982. The meeting was attended by Carl Page, Jack Boland, Michael Ryan, Eddie Walsh, Paddy O'Brien, Peter Lucey, Tom Fitzpatrick, Finbarr Murphy, Carmel Reen, Charles Moran, John Gallen, Donnchadh Ó Liatháin and Jimmy O'Dwyer. Kay Hughes sent her apologies.

The following officers were agreed: Finbarr Murphy as Chairman; Jack Boland as Treasurer and Jimmy O'Dwyer as Secretary. The Chairman and Secretary to act as delegates to Cumann Peil Naomh Jude.

Two main items dominated the first meeting – the need for insurance and a decision to take part formally in the Summer Project.

Finbarr Murphy met Donal Hickey of the Dublin County Board and matters concerning insurance and affiliation were cleared up. As the hurling and camogie section was part of Cumann Peil Naomh Jude, players were covered under the insurance scheme which was £1 at the time.

Coaching sessions began in May 1982 on Thursday nights when all hurling and camogie enthusiasts descended on Tymon Park from 7.15pm to 8.15pm. This immediately raised the issue of training coaches and Fintan Walsh was invited to the club to talk with the members about hurling and camogie coaching. (He received an £11.19 bottle of whiskey for his efforts.) Money matters had to be addressed and it was agreed to have a sponsored "Run for Hurling and Camogie" in Tymon. This was extremely well supported due mainly to the hard work of the committee, particularly Jack Boland who was adept at getting money from all quarters. Declan Feore, Nora Farrell and Michael Glover had joined the committee by this stage.

Hurling and camogie in the Summer Project took place in the first two weeks in July and all the participants were taken on a tour of the Feile na nGael museum in Merrion Row.

As a direct result of the coaching nights and the Summer Project, internal club leagues were organised to begin in September. The leagues were held on Tuesdays and Thursdays at 6.30 pm. Under 10 and Under 12 hurling and camogie leagues were set up. While this was a very worthwhile undertaking, it also highlighted the need for better coaching of the basic skills and this became a fundamental objective of the committee. Training times were changed to Saturday at 3.00 pm for camogie and Sunday at 11.00 for hurling and camogie.

The purchasing of hurleys and helmets was ongoing at this stage and Hurling and Camogie sticks were made available through Bishop Galvin NS at £2 each, while helmets were on sale at £3 each (heavily subsidised). Two notice boards were also purchased – one for BGNS and the other for the shops.

By this stage it was necessary for the committee to open a dedicated bank account for hurling and camogie transactions. The bank manager generously gave a starting contribution of £25 to the account.

The club was also undertaking a re-structuring and a report from the recent club AGM was discussed at length. A strong case was put forward to the reconvened AGM that money raised for the promotion of hurling and camogie would be specifically used for that purpose.

1983

This year began with a decision by the committee to enter teams in the Dublin juvenile hurling leagues. Numbers suggested that we begin with Under 10 and Under 12 teams. Meetings for club delegates take place in the North Star Hotel and Finbarr Murphy, Declan Feore, Jack Boland, Eddie Walsh and Michael Glover expressed an interest in attending these meetings. It was decided that Eddie Walsh would take charge of the Under 12 team, with Michael Hartnett, Jack Boland and Tom Fitzpatrick assisting. Declan Feore would manage the Under 10 team with Finbarr Murphy, Michael Ryan and Willie Nolan as assistants.

The Under 10 team was selected from the following panel of players: Alan Boyce, Conor Burns, Gary Brannigan, Brendan Byrne, Noel Byrne, David Duggan, Liam Dunne, Kieran Durkan, Brian Farrell, Paul Farrell, Fiachra Feore, Barry Jeffries, Gary Kirwan, Paul Kirwan, Fergal McCarthy, Ciaran McFeeney, Dara Murphy, Declan O'Boyle, Darren Orr, Ted Russell and Eoghan Ryan. They finished in third position in the league.

Only two players Kieran Durkan and Fiachra Feore from that inaugural panel are still playing at the highest level in the Club. Kieran, a natural and talented hurler concentrated on football from Under 16/Minor onwards and is now a regular member of the senior football team. Fiachra, after dabbling as well in football at juvenile level, concentrated on his hurling and is a regular player with the senior team. He is still one of the fastest runners in the squad. Dara Murphy also concentrated on football from Under 16/Minor up and he played at senior level up to three years ago. Declan O'Boyle, who represented the Club at inter-county football level, had to retire prematurely due to injury a few years ago and is now involved at management level with the senior footballers. Eoghan Ryan also played adult hurling with the Club and is currently involved at management level with our third junior team.

Kieran Durkan and Fiachra Feore deserve great credit for their loyalty and consistent service to the Club for in excess of 20 years playing activity. Mick Fallon affectionately known as the Bull, and a member of the inaugural Under 12 hurling team, is unique in that as a dual player he has given sterling service to the Club in both codes up to and including senior. He caught the last puck of the ball in our famous victory over St Vincents in our first junior hurling championship victory in 1989 in Parnell Park. Mick, a strong, but not a dirty player was the victim of an ungentlemanly attack from an opponent in an intermediate hurling match one afternoon in Tymon Park. Mick's late father John became a little agitated on the sideline. He raised his fist and as he brought it down forcibly, he was heard to shout "flatten him Michael". You could almost see the stake being driven into the ground. Other hurlers from subsequent years such as Bryan Duggan, Seán Fallon, Kieran Quigley, Ciaran McLoughlin, Gareth Roche and Terence Orr (who was equally adept as a back or a forward, and who is now the senior football goalkeeper) have been equally loyal and consistent in their service to the Club over as many years.

The question of length of pitches in Tymon was of concern as no proper juvenile pitch was marked out. Michael Hartnett to enquire about this with the Parks Department.

The club re-structuring was in effect from 1st January – necessitating a name change to Cumann Luthchleas Gael Naomh Jude. Carmel Reen and Jack Boland were nominated as delegates from the hurling and camogie section to the Club Executive.

It was decided to hold a public meeting on 24th March 1983 to outline our intentions and to report on progress to date. About ten new faces were present at the meeting despite massive publicity. By April the teams entered had played in the juvenile leagues with the following record:

	Played	Won	Lost	Drew	Points
Under 10	5	3	2	0	6
Under 12	2	0	2	0	0

(I believe the very first representative game was at Under 12, against Shankill Hurling Club in Quinns Road, Shankill. Shankill club no longer exists and is now part of Cuala.)

Many games had to be postponed because of weather conditions. Up to 30 girls were training for camogie and more adult help was needed.

A training programme for the club was drawn up as follows:

Under 8	Carl Page and Seán Ward
Under 10	Declan Feore
Under 12	Eddie Walsh
Under 14	Finbarr Murphy
Camogie Novices	Carmel Reen, Nora Farrell
Camogie	Kay Hughes

A trip to Killenaule, Co Tipperary was organised by Willie Nolan. The Under 10 and Under 12 teams made the trip. Both games were described as hard with the Under 10's game being a very close win for Killenaule by 2 – 0 to 1 – 1, while the Tipp boys were far superior at Under 12. All enjoyed the trip and thanks were expressed to Willie Nolan, Declan Feore, Michael Hartnett and Tom Fitzpatrick for looking after the teams.

Jimmy O'Dwyer was in charge of the Summer Project hurling and camogie which took place from 4th to 15th July in Tymon. Members enjoyed a great occasion in Croke Park when Galway played the Rest of Ireland in the Feile na nGael exhibition game. Internal club leagues took place again in September and October.

Contact was made with St MacDara's CC with a view to assisting in coaching in the school.

Killenaule 1983 trophy

1984

Regular meetings did not take place in early 1984. The secretary lamented the fact that attendance at two planned meetings did not have a quorum and it was decided that the committee should revert to regular monthly meetings in future.

The first camogie team took part in the Community Games.

Three teams – Under 10, Under 11 and Under 12 were entered in Saturday morning juvenile hurling leagues with three mentors per team.

An Under 13 team under the management of Eddie Walsh was entered in the juvenile leagues and was placed in Division B South with eleven other teams.

The committee appreciated the fact that Thursday night was set aside by the club for juvenile hurling and camogie training. Over 150 children attend this training on a regular basis.

Declan Feore and Michael Harnett replaced Jack Boland and Carmel Reen on the Executive.

The first hurling medals won for St Judes were won this year by the Under 11 team who were runners-up in the South Dublin League. Obviously, the experience gained at Under 10 the previous season, where they won 60/70 per cent of their games, together with their trip to Killenaule, as well as the organised coaching on Thursday evenings, was a factor in their progress. The panel was as for the inaugural Under 10s.

St Judes U12 hurling team, League winners 1987 – Back (l-r): Seán Ward (mentor), Stephen Willoughby, John Reen, Stewart O'Neill, Enda Sheehy (captain), Robert Hyland, Niall Ryan, Barry Heraty, Ciaran Quigley, Andrew Moore, Terence Orr, Paul McGovern, Gus Barry (mentor). Front: Mark O'Reilly, Colm Rooney, Ronan Colgan, Brian Ward, John Lenihan, Brendan Culhane, Fergal Griffin, Barry Corrigan, Alan Byrne, Conor Lyons, Graham Allen.

The historic Under 11 team was presented with medals on Friday 21st September in Bishop Galvin NS Hall. A video of the Munster final of that year was shown to the audience. This was the game where a certain point saved by John Doyle, for Tipperary, resulted in an opportunist goal for Cork by Seanie O'Leary.

The Under 13 team won both their opening league games and the committee sent a letter of concern to the County Board regarding incidents connected with the game against Good Counsel.

Training continued at 6.00 pm for all players on Thursdays until the clock changed and then on Sunday mornings at 10.30. Catherine Kelleher registered eighteen Under 14 camogie players with the board. They would need proper playing outfits and a regulation pitch before being sanctioned to play in leagues.

1985

Michael Hartnett took over as Chairman of the committee, Seán Ward as Treasurer and Jimmy O'Dwyer remained as Secretary. Declan Feore and Michael Hartnett remained as delegates to the Executive. Meetings at this time took place in St MacDara's Community College.

By the end of 1985, the camogie teams at Under 11 and Under 13 were well established. Several beginners were also being coached and a junior team was also formed for adults. Catherine Moore and Mary Devins joined the club this year and gave great help to the other mentors. A team took part in the Feile competition and also in the Community Games.

Hurling Mentors for the season were as follows:

Beginners	Jimmy O'Dwyer.
Under 10	Seán Ward, Pat Quigley, Michael Ryan, Gus Barry
Under 11	Eddie Walsh, Michael Hartnett, Willie Nolan
Under 12	Declan Feore, Finbarr Murphy, Garrett Edge

The prices of hurleys on sale in the club were as follows: 36inch: £5; 34inch: £4; 32inch: £3; 30inch: £2.50; 28inch: £2.50; 26inch: £2.

In hurling the highlight of the season was the great success of the Under 10 team. They won the first league title for the club in the junior juvenile section (Under 10 to Under 12) and were only narrowly beaten in the county final against St Monica's in September, having won the South Dublin section.

The Under 12 team performed well and finished third in their league. It was a fourteen team league and included the following clubs: St Mark's; St Patricks, Palmerstown; Clanna Gael/Fontenoy's; St Kevins; Crumlin; Commercials; St Olafs; Round Towers; Donore Iosagáin; Kilmacud Crokes; Thomas Davis; Ballyboden St Endas A and Lucan Sarsfields.

The Under 13 team was unbeaten in all league games played in 1985. The season ran from September to the following June. The team was picked from the following panel: Fergal McCarthy, Dara Murphy, Fiachra Feore, Barry Jeffries, Paul Farrell, Ciaran McFeeney, Eoghan Ryan, Conor Burns, Noel Byrne, David Duggan, Gary Kirwan, Darren Orr, Brian Farrell, John Nolan, Ted Russell, A. Banks, Gary Brannigan, Declan O'Boyle, Liam Dunne, John Finlay, Turlough Doyle, Kieran Durkan, John Farrell and Alan Boyce.

It was a ten-team league involving St Judes; Liffey Gaels; St Kevins; Clanna Gael/Fontenoys; Ballyboden St Endas; Good Counsel; St Annes; Kilmacud Crokes; Commercials and St Olafs.

The results of the 1985 portion of the league are as follows:

HOME/AWAY	V	DATE	WON/LOST	SCORE
H	Liffey Gaels	14/9/85	Won	3-2/1-0
A	Kevins	28/9/85	Won	4-6/1-5
A	St. Annes	12/10/85	Won	6-4/2-2
H	Commercials	2/11/85	Won	3-0/1-1
A	Ballyboden S.E.	16/11/85	Won	3-2/0-2

The manager of the Under 13 Kevins team at that time was a guy called Eugene Murray who later joined Judes and has given 100 per cent commitment to us as player, mentor and coach. He is currently manager of our senior hurling team. His daughter Roisin is on the 2003 Under 14 Dublin camogie team.

Coaching of the younger and less able hurlers was a remarkable feature of the Club. The Club presented cups and medals for class leagues in Bishop Galvin NS and this further strengthened the bond between club and school.

Pat Cleary of Offaly twice visited the Club to present awards and to help with coaching teams.

1986

The Under 13 team continued to be unbeaten in their campaign and went on to record the Club's first league victory in the senior juvenile section (Under 13 to Under 15), while interest in the Under 11 team was thriving.

The committee welcomed the provision of the camogie pitch in Tymon, but were a little concerned at the citing of the posts so near the ditches. The camogie board did not pass the pitch, as it did not comply precisely with the dimensions required. The mentors in hurling for the coming season were:

Beginners	Jimmy O'Dwyer, Finbarr Murphy
Under 10	Pat Quigley, Eddie Walsh, Tommy Hartnett
Under 11	Seán Ward, Gus Barry, Michael Ryan
Under 12	Garrett Edge, Michael Hartnett, Willie Nolan.

Peter Ryan and John O'Riordan had joined the Club from St Kevins, Kilnamanagh at this stage. The desirability of an equitable hurling/camogie and football season was a matter of priority for the committee.

Declan Feore outlined the timetable for our involvement in our first Feile na nGael competition which would take place in Silver Park on 17th May.

The Club supported the involvement of a team from the parish in the Community Games and Tom Fitzpatrick, teacher in St Joseph's School, Terenure agreed to help in the preparation.

The panel of 20 players was Brendan Byrne, Bryan Duggan, Kieran Durkan, Seán Fallon, Colin Farrell, Gerard and Paul Farrell, Fiachra Feore, John Finlay, Barry Jeffries, Dara Murphy, John Nolan, Declan O'Boyle, Darren and Terence Orr, John Reen, Ted Russell, Eoghan Ryan, Enda Sheehy, and Jim Treacy. They succeeded in winning the Dublin County Board Hurling Trophy. Previous winners of this trophy were: Ballyfermot, 1971; Donnycarney 1972; Marino 1973; Maryfield 1974; Iona 1975; Palmerstown 1979; Maryfield 1980; Butterfield 1981 and 1982; Marino 1983; Portmarnock 1984; Trinity 1985 and St Judes 1986.

Rita Moran took charge of the camogie team. Congratulations were extended to Bishop Galvin N.S. on reaching the Under 11 final in Croke Park and the camogie final in Bohernabreena. A £50 donation was made to the school to offset expenses incurred. The junior B camogie team won their first game in May. The Under 9 internal league had almost 50 boys taking part, while our involvement in the Feile lead to us being paired with Moorefield of Kildare in the Leinster Feile.

(Legend has it that the shout "Low, hard and savage" was first heard from Jack Crennan when St Judes were given a penalty in the dying minutes of the game against Kevins in the Feile.) The group draw was Ballinteers/St Johns v Duffy Rovers, (Wexford); St Marks v Clara (Kilkenny); Kevins v Carrickshock (Kilkenny); Lucan Sarsfields v Shinrone (Offaly); St Judes v Moorefield (Kildare); Dundrum Churchtown v Shelmaliers (Wexford); Cuala v Dainsfort (Kilkenny); Clanna Gael/Fontenoys v Blackwater (Wexford).

The Under 13 team was also invited to play in an eleven-a-side blitz by Commercials with the following panel: Brendan Culhane, Brendan and Alan Byrne, Paul and Gerard Farrell, Darren and Terence Orr, John O'Riordan, Dara Murphy, Fiachra Feore, Kieran Durkan, Bryan Duggan and Aidan Quigley.

A trip to Ballingarry in Tipperary was organised by Willie Nolan.

1986 was a very busy year for the successful Under 13 team. As a result of winning their league, we were invited to represent Dublin in an inter-county tournament against Tipperary represented by Ballybacon/Grange in Bushy Park. Liberty Gaels having won the Under 11 league were invited to play them in that age group. Our team lined out as follows:

Barry Jeffries
Gerard Farrell   Brendan Byrne   Paul Farrell
John Nolan   John O'Riordan   Martin Carty
Dara Murphy   Ted Russell
Fiachra Feore   Kieran Durkan   Seán Fallon
Eoghan Ryan   Darren Orr   Bryan Duggan
Subs: Peter Murray, Enda Sheehy, Colin Farrell, Alan Byrne, Brendan Culhane.
Mentors: Declan Feore, Finbarr Murphy, Garrett Edge, Michael Hartnett

It was a high scoring game. We matched the opposition on points, but whereas they could score goals, we couldn't. A contributory factor in our failure may have been that the current All-Star Tipperary Goalkeeper, Brendan Cummins was the Ballybacon/Grange custodian. Time and time again he countered our assaults on the goalmouth.

We played skilfully and manfully, but our spirited display was as nothing compared to the "kangaroo dance" performed by Darren Orr in a lap of Bushy Park following a belt of a sliothar in the "goolies". Dara Murphy collected a puck out from Barry Jeffries, sent it to Fiachra Feore who went on a solo run, passed it inside to Kieran Durkan, who took a bullet of a shot - goal written all over it. Unfortunately for him, the team and Darren Orr's anatomy, the effort was in vain.

In September, the following teams were entered in camogie competitions:
Under 11A   Michael Reynolds
Under 11B   Ann Dennehy
Under 12   Bob Carty
Under 14   Rita Moran
Junior B   Catherine Kelliher

In hurling, an Under 14 team under the charge of Declan Feore, Willie Nolan, Garrett Edge and Michael Hartnett was entered. An Under 13 team was not viable. However, Charles Moran said that several of his football team were interested in playing hurling and John Gallen and himself were prepared to manage the team. This team was also entered.

At the committee's AGM, Michael Hartnett stepped down as Chairman and was replaced by Garrett Edge, while Seán Ward and Jimmy O'Dwyer remained as treasurer and secretary. There was a motion from Charles Moran that the camogie affairs be dealt with by a separate committee. It was decided that all camogie mentors should meet to discuss this as only three were present at the AGM. When they did meet, the decision was to remain with the same committee for the time being. The clubhouse development was a major item on the agenda with all present being eagerly urged to support the project.

1987

The mentors for the hurling season were appointed at the February meeting:

Under 10   Declan Feore, Michael Hartnett
Under 11   Tommy Hartnett, Pat Quigley, Eddie Walsh
Under 12   Seán Ward, Gus Barry
Under 14   Garrett Edge, Declan Feore, Michael Hartnett and Willie Nolan
Under 16   Charles Moran, John Gallen, Finbarr Murphy (this was the Club's first entry at this age level)

Betty Collard was elected as delegate to replace Michael Hartnett on the Executive.

Richard Stakelum presented medals to the Under 13 team, winners of the Under 13B South league, at a function in Bishop Galvin N.S.

The Under 16 team won the first four of their five league games.

In camogie the Junior B team beat Thomas Davis in their first league game despite having a depleted panel.

Feile na nGael was hosted by the club in May. We were beaten by two points by Good Counsel in the semi-final. The groups were Na Fianna v Good Counsel; St Monicas v Dundrum, Churchtown; Naomh Fionbarra v St Judes; St Kevins v Kilmacud. Our team lined out as follows:

Barry Jeffries

Gerard Farrell   Brendan Byrne   Derek Fitzpatrick

Terence Orr   John Nolan   Ted Russell

John O'Riordan   Seán Fallon

Fiachra Feore   Kieran Durkan   Eoghan Ryan

Enda Sheehy   Ciaran McLoughlin   Paul Farrell

Subs: Bryan Duggan, Paul Kirwan, Martin Carty, Colin Farrell

The U12 hurlers with Seán Ward and Gus Barry as mentors had a very successful season, culminating with victory in the South Dublin League.

The Clubhouse was officially opened on Sunday 11th October 1987 by Mick Loftus, President of the GAA.

The official opening was marked by a senior football game between Dublin and Longford, a camogie game between Judes and St Patricks, Wicklow and a juvenile hurling game between Judes and Durlas Óg, Tipperary. The juvenile hurling team was a representative selection of the Under 13 and Under 14 panels. They lined out as per match programme below.

The No. 7 for Durlas Óg was Eddie Enright, the current Senior Inter-County Hurler with Tipperary.

cumann luthchleas gael
naomh jude

OFFICIAL OPENING

MATCH PROGRAMME

Sunday 11th October 1987

JUVENILE HURLING

NAOMH JUDE	DÚRLAS ÓG
1. Barry Jeffries	1. M Campion
2. Terence Orr	2. G. Grogan
3. Brendan Byrne	3. J Curry
4. Brian Duggan	4. J. Doyle
5. John Nolan	5. T. Tierney
6. John O'Riordan	6. E. Mc Aree
7. Ted Russell	7. E. Enright
8. Darren Orr	8. T. Dwyer
9. Seán Fallon	9. D. Keher
10. Fiachra Feore	10. M. Murphy
11. Ciarán Durkan	11. L. Barrett
12. Eoghan Ryan	12. S. Ryan
13. Paul Farrell	13. D. Kenny
14. Declan O'Boyle	14. T. O'Connor
15. Fergal Mc Carthy	15. K. Hegney
16. Enda Sheehy	16. J. Purcell
17. Gerard Farrell	17. T. Max
18. Dara Murphy	18. T. Kennedy
19. Paul Kirwan	19. D. Burke
20. Ciarán Mc Loughlin	20. M. Larkin
21. Martin Carty	21. M. Bowe
22. John Reen	22. N. Hanrahan
23. Joe Denvir	23. N. Dundon
24. Colin Farrell	

Referee: Peadar O'Neill

Game Commences at 2.15 P.M.

Club notes from Tipperary Star

Durlas Óg – On Sunday we were invited to open the new St Judes pavilion in Dublin. Our Under 14 hurlers played an exhibition game and were presented with beautiful medals to commemorate this great occasion. We hope to have this great club as our guests in the near future.

We are still awaiting their invitation.

The visiting teams received commemorative medals. The Judes camogie girls and the juvenile hurlers did not receive any.

The first meeting of the committee in the new Clubhouse took place on 30th September.

The Under 12 team reached the final, but lost to St Monicas. A coffee morning held by the camogie mentors raised £80 for equipment. All hurling teams were well supported and the first minor team would represent the club this season.

Joe Clavin joined the club as trainer to the Under 15 team.

Richard Stakelum held a coaching session for players from 12 to 15 and also presented medals to last season's Under 12 team winners of the Division 2 south league.

In 1985 Coiste na nOg um Iomaint, The Juvenile Hurling Board, was restructured with the appointment of two Assistant Secretaries to look after the Under 10 to 12 leagues North and South. The St Judes delegate, Declan Feore, was elected with responsibility for the Southside and Danny O'Connor of St Sylvesters, Malahide taking care of the Northside. Following the opening of our clubhouse, the Juvenile Board honoured us by holding one of its meetings on our premises in December 1987.

It was a dreadful night. There was torrential rain. Unfortunately, they neglected to advise Faughs of the change of venue. Their delegate, Padraig Purcell, cycled into Belvedere Place where the meetings were normally held, only to be told that he should be in Judes Clubhouse, which is separated from that of Faughs by a Lake and a Car Park. Padraig cycled back out to Templeogue in the continuous downpour. When he arrived in the Meeting Room...late, tired and dripping wet, everyone stopped and stared at him. The Judes delegate was heard to enquire of him "Did you swim across?" Relations between the two neighbouring clubs could only improve after that!

1988

The elected officers for the coming year were Chairman: Garrett Edge; Secretary: Jimmy O'Dwyer; Treasurer: Seán Ward; Garrett Edge and Betty Collard as delegates to Club Executives. A problem with camogie insurance despite efforts by the camogie board during the year to get cover for the players.

Hurling Report 1988

This was a year of significant progress in many aspects of our hurling development. It is best to record the events in chronological order to avoid highlighting any single item. In May Peter Ryan was selected at centre back on the Dublin Minor team. This was the Club's first county representative in any code and we were very proud of Peter's achievement. Although Kilkenny won the game Peter's selection will mean a great deal to us in years to come.

The Under 14 team made history also by winning the Féile na nGael Competition. This was a prestigious tournament to win and as a result the boys competed in the Leinster Féile in Wexford. The team was as follows: Bryan Duggan, Brian Ward, Colin Farrell, Mark O'Reilly, Alan Kennedy, John Nolan, Gerard Farrell, Seán Fallon, Terence Orr, Enda Sheehy, Ronan Colgan, John Reen, Alan Byrne, John McGovern, Ciaran McLoughlin, Niall Ryan, Brendan Culhane, Andrew Moore, Marcus Mallon, Colin Lyons, Jonathan Duffy and Ciaran Quigley.

The Millennium weekend saw fine hurling activity at all grades. Our thanks to Celbridge, Templemore, Liffey Gaels, Kilmacud Crokes for competing against us that weekend. We also took part in the Leinster Hurling Festival in a section with Kilmacud Crokes, Sarsfields Kildare, Kilduff and Lucan Sarsfields. We emerged as the only Dublin winners of the Festival.

During the summer a group of mentors in the Club looked at the possibility of entering a junior team in competition. Having researched the project, the Club decided to give the go-ahead to Joe Clavin, Frank Gallagher, Martin Molamphy and Michael Ryan. The team has been placed in Division 1 of the league and looks resplendent in their new jerseys and very skilful in their hurling approach. Our thanks to Michael Hartnett for sponsoring the jerseys.

Our appreciation is also due to the local schools for their hurling and camogie endeavours during the year. St. MacDaras won their division of the Leinster Juvenile Competition. Bishop Galvin reached their finals in both camogie and hurling, losing to Donard and Knocklyon respectively. Bishop Shanahan N.S. are also to be commended in their coaching of the games to the under eights.

1989

The first meeting of 1989 was held on 1st February. The committee was Garret Edge, Jimmy O'Dwyer, Seán Ward, Joe Clavin, Ruth Carty, Tommy Hartnett Bob Carty, Mary Farrell, John O'Gara, Frank Gallagher, Declan Feore, Ann Dennehy, Martin Molamphy, Charles Moran and Kay Hughes. The meeting regretted the decision of Betty Collard and Ann Moore who resigned as mentors.

Teenage hurling teams were going through a difficult time at this stage and a more concentrated approach to St MacDara's Community College was approved.

This year saw the change in age structure for teams entering in competition – from now on it would be as of calendar year. Due to the upsurge of boys playing hurling in Bishop Galvin N.S., it was decided to enter:

One Under 10 - managed by Seán Breheny and Seán McBride

Under 11A – Jimmy O'Dwyer

Under 11B – Garrett Edge, Declan Feore

Under 12 – Charles Moran, John Keating, Peter Kennedy

On 4th February Nicky English was the guest of honour at the club for the presentation of medals to successful teams.

By March 1989, Donal O'Gorman and Seán Breheny had joined the committee. Seán Ward, as treasurer, reported that £346 had already been spent so far this year on hurleys, sliotars and general equipment.

The Under 11 camogie team had a great win over Rathcoole by 8 goals to nil, while the Under 14 hurlers beat Clontarf by 6-3 to 3-0.

Frank Gallagher reported from the Junior Board. 27 teams had entered in the Junior A hurling championship. St Judes had a bye in the first round.

Feile na nGael took place on the weekend of 20th and 21st May.

A set of one dozen hurleys was presented to St. Peter's NS Limekiln Road.

The May meeting was poorly attended as many members were involved in other meetings concerning the on-going difficulties regarding the allocation of pitches.

Twenty-one new camogie players were recruited by Seán Breheny from Bishop Galvin N.S. Club member Kieran Quigley was selected for Dublin Primary Schools to visit Luxembourg to play against EEC ex-pats.

On 26th July St Judes won the County Junior hurling championship defeating St Vincents. The treasurer reported that £1081 had been spent on hurleys, while only £100 had been collected.

Five camogie teams were entered in the leagues:

Under 11 Ruth Carty, Mary O'Toole

Under 12 Ann Dennehy, Mary Crennan, Kathleen McCabe

Under 13 Kay Hughes, Joan Molamphy

Under 14 Seán Breheny Joe Scanlon

Junior B Mary Farrell, Catherine Kelliher, Tadhg Dennehy

The mentors for the new season in hurling was as follows:

Under 13   Charles Moran, Jim Coghlan, Jack Crennan, John Boyce

Under 14   Pat Quigley, Tommy Hartnett, Finbarr Murphy

Under 16   Seán Ward, Willie Nolan

Minor   Declan Feore, Garrett Edge, Michael Hartnett
Under 21   Padraig Riordan
Intermediate Joe Clavin, Frank Gallagher, Martin Molamphy

A coaching night was held for all mentors in October and was very well attended. A benefit dance for the injured players' fund was held on 2nd December.

At the AGM the following officers were elected: Chairman – Colum Grogan; Secretary – Jimmy O'Dwyer; Treasurer – Bobby Carty.

At this time hurling was on the rise in St Judes as the new Junior A adult hurling team were powering their way to the club's first adult championship trophy. Colum Grogan had recently been appointed Chairman of the Hurling Committee, and hurling mentors for the young juveniles rapidly entering our club ranks were, to put it mildly as scarce as hens' teeth.

Having secured the 'guaranteed' assistance of fellow junior hurling team mates Liam Larkin and Denis Ryan, Colum undertook to manage the Under 11 hurlers. As he recalls, we were in a Southside League Group involving Clann na Gael/Fontenoys, Kilmacud Crokes and St Marks with six matches to be played by each team on a home and away basis. I can remember defeating 'Crokes' both at home and away (where he also refereed the away game) as well as a home victory over Clann na Gael and a draw with St Marks.

Don Lehane, whose eldest son Greg was a member of the team, helped out whenever he could as did some other parents who were interested in the game of hurling as well as the hurling progress of 'their budding young Christy Ring' or at that time their 'budding Joe Cooney'. (Other members of that squad still with the club are Tadgh O'Connor, Paul Molamphy, Tadhg O'Brien, Tomás O'Brien, Ali McGurn and Paraic Joyce.)

Our season wound up with an away trip to Wexford and a challenge match with Faythe Harriers which introduced the team to outside hurling competition and developed friendships and memories to be cherished for years to come.

1990

In camogie, hurleys were presented to St MacDara's College and help is ongoing for their internal leagues etc.

No games had been played in any grade of hurling since November 1989.

A trip to the Mungret club in Limerick was organised for February and plans were drawn up for the Night of Champions which the club would host to mark the occasion of all county hurling championships being won by southside clubs.

The weather in the first half of 1990 was atrocious and very little activity took place. Plans for entries into the leagues were made with two Under 10 teams – to be known as 10 Blue and 10 Gold; one Under 11 team; one Under 12 team competing. Buses of juvenile players to Croke Park were a regular feature of club activities at this time for League and Leinster championship games.

The camogie mentors were given the go-ahead to buy skirts in Ebbs sports shop. This was important, as officials had called off some games because players were not uniformly togged out. Promoting camogie the hard way!!

The search for a member to represent the club at the Juvenile Board meetings continued. At the May meeting the agenda was amended to allow Martin Hayes to bring forward an idea that the club should consider hosting and organising a Junior Hurling All Ireland 7 a side tournament. The proposal was strongly supported. By June, 16 teams had been selected and the initial response to the invitations was positive.

In camogie, Ruth Carty's team won the Under 11 championship. Ann Dennehy and Joan Molamphy were nominated to go on a coaching course to Gormanstown.

Pat Quigley's Feile team won all their Saturday matches, but lost the semi final mainly due to exhaustion as the opposition had only one game on Saturday.

The last meeting of the Hurling and Camogie Committee took place on 5th September 1990.

Willie Nolan with 1987 Under 14 Hurling team.

The Song of a Hurl

Oh! cut me a hurl from the mountain ash,
That weathered many a gale,
And my stroke will be lithe as the lightning flash
That leaps from the thunder's flail
Oh! my feet shall be swift as the white spin-drift
On the bay, in wintry weather,
As we run in line through the glad sunshine
On the trail of the whirling leather.

Oh! to dart to the wing, and twist again
With a puck that is swift and burning
Or to swing out the line in attack, and strain
Every nerve till the tide is turning—
To weaken the swirl of a Wicklow hurl
With a good ash bred in Kerry,
And press for the goal with all your soul
Or lose with a heart as merry.

I have seen the children of other lands
At games of down and feather
Applauded by dames with delicate hands
In the mild, midsummer weather—
But such poor sport is a weary sort,
With never a thrill to quicken
Like the flash and flame of the Gaelic game
When the hot strokes swarm and thicken.

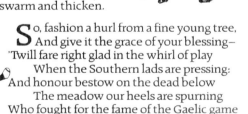

So, fashion a hurl from a fine young tree,
And give it the grace of your blessing—
'Twill fare right glad in the whirl of play
When the Southern lads are pressing:
And honour bestow on the dead below
The meadow our heels are spurning
Who fought for the fame of the Gaelic game
When the fire of their youth was burning!

CRAWFORD NEIL

Adult football history (1979-2003)
Don Lehane

PART 2 – THE GROWING YEARS (1986-1989)

THE FOLLOWING is a review of St Judes adult football in the period from 1985 to 1989. It covers a short but in retrospect an important period in the club's history as it endeavoured to progress upwards from the lowest junior division in Dublin. It coincided with important milestones in the club's history including building of the clubhouse in 1987, our first underage football and junior hurling championship successes in 1989, underage teams now competing at all age levels from U10 upwards, the ongoing development of hurling and camogie as well as football.

In 1985/86 season the junior team was still plying its trade in Junior Division 4 South, which was the lowest division in Dublin at that time. There were four junior divisions in South Dublin and four additional junior divisions in Dublin North. There was also a separate Fingal League, which covered points north of Dublin Airport. In the summer of 1986 the status of adult football in the club was a little precarious.

We were up and running for a couple of years but did not seem to be going anywhere very fast. It was difficult to run adult teams as most players were from the country with all the associated difficulties of weekends away, college matches, work commitments etc. There seemed to be no particular club interest in adult football if the level of support was any indication. This was probably understandable at the time as many of the club members had children on the under-age teams and concentrated their energies on running or supporting the juvenile teams.

Players were getting a little disillusioned with the lack of progress and in addition some of the existing mentors at adult level wanted to step down after a few hard years. Jim Coghlan who was manager of the junior team also wanted to step down at the end of the 1985/86 season. Jim had given sterling service in keeping adult football afloat in difficult circumstances and was going to be a big loss. Don Lehane (Waterford) took over management of the St Judes Junior A side for the season 1986/1987 and also for the seasons 1987/88 and 1988/89. Don Lehane played his early junior football for Kinsalebeg in the parish of Clashmore, Co Waterford and underage football/hurling to minor level with the Ardmore club with whom he won a couple of minor championships.

He played minor football for Waterford in 1966 before heading off to London at seventeen and subsequently Holland. He returned to Dublin in the mid seventies and played Intermediate football with Aer Lingus in the Fingal league before joining St Judes in 1979.

Don Lehane was assisted in running the Junior A team by a number of people over the period including Gerry Quinn (Longford), Cyril Loughlin (Leitrim), John Boyce (Dublin) and Ernest Kenny (Meath). Gerry Quinn was one of a number of Longford people who were involved with St Judes in the eighties and nineties including Declan, Kevin and Frank Clabby, Bert Smith, Jimmy Hanniffy, Paddy O'Donnell and Peadar Carbery. Gerry Quinn played originally with Killoe Emmetts in Longford and lined out with the Post Office based St Colmans and Post Office Telephones teams, with players like Larry Gillen before the demise of that team when a number of Post Office players came across to St Judes. St Judes maintained good links with Killoe who were a senior Longford side and played them home and away on a few occasions in the eighties. Gerry Quinn was a good musician who featured in a number of medal presentation ceremonies in St Judes. He was once persuaded by Ernest Kenny and Joe Morrin to lead the parade of Summer Project GAA finalists around the Green while playing the accordeon before finishing off with a rendering of the National Anthem. If anyone has a video of this performance would they please hand it in to the clubhouse or the nearest police station. It inspired the Damien Carroll captained team to an unlikely win against the Gary Percy captained hot favourites in the final.

The Junior B team during this period was run by Ernest Kenny (Meath), with assistance from Donnchadh Lehane (Dublin), and Don Lehane (Waterford). Ernest Kenny played his early football with junior club Dunshaughlin and Meath minors before transferring to senior club Skryne where he won a senior football championship in 1954 having won a junior championship with Dunshaughlin a few years earlier. Ernest made a few appearances as an emergency goalkeeper with St Judes in the early days and was the first Judes player to set a fashion trend by playing in wellington boots. Ernest was the primary driving force behind early St Judes adult teams and had an amazing capacity to ferret players out of the most unlikely corners including we suspect the confession box in St Judes Church. He was the St Judes delegate to the Dublin Junior Football board for most of the first twenty five years of the clubs existence. He was a manager or mentor on a number of St Judes teams during this period and also served as a mentor on the Dublin Junior football team for a number of years.

Our resources at the start of the 1986/87 season were fairly limited. A number of our existing players were probably getting to the end of their careers at the "top level" including Charles Moran, Don Lehane, Joe McDonnell, Martin

McCabe, Danny Lynch, Jimmy Hanniffy, Hugo Devine, Mick O'Brien, Frank O'Grady, Moss Keane, Eddie Egan and Peadar McGlinchey. We had not yet reached the stage of having any throughput of players from underage level.

We drew up a rather ambitious ten-year plan to get from Junior Division 4 South to senior football. Promotion up through junior ranks would mean in effect to progress through the eight junior divisions plus two/three intermediate divisions. The North city junior teams and the South city junior teams played out their leagues separately in those days. At the end of the season north side winners of each league played south side runners-up at the same level and vice-versa.

The winners played in the All-County league final for that division. Stage One of the plan was to get to Junior Division 1 South in five years, which basically meant getting three promotions in a five year period. Stage Two was to get into Intermediate level within the following two years and finally Stage Three was to push on into Senior level over the next three years. This was the ten year plan, which I would have to say was never discussed with anyone but I felt we needed to have some target to aim at, to keep us focused and to give us some sense of achievement or failure as the years progressed.

The ten year plan was the easy part but now back to the reality. We had an ageing team with a number of the players approaching retirement age. Most of the players were "country" players residing temporarily or permanently in Dublin. We had a mixture of aging parents, students, teachers, Gardai, postmen, civil servants and other assorted "jackeens" and "culchies". We had one good thing going for us however – most of them could play a bit of football and with a number of reinforcements we had something to work on. Experienced mentors were also in short supply – in fact almost non-existent. The lower junior football divisions were competitive particularly at the top end of each division and we felt that it would be important to get out of the lower levels of junior football as quickly as possible in order to be able to offer emerging club players a good platform. Junior 4 was no environment for eighteen year olds back in the mid eighties.

Our first decision was to put out two adult teams in the 1986/87 season. Considering we were struggling to get out one team the season before, the decision did not find immediate favour with everyone. We felt that it would give us the twin benefits of getting us immediate promotion to Division 3 and at the same time providing some backup to the Junior A team. It would also give us a platform to introduce younger players to junior football in the B team without any pressure as we had decided that our A team really was going to attempt to push on up the promotion ladder.

Junior A matches were generally arranged to be played on Sunday mornings and Junior B games took place on Sunday afternoon. It normally meant that some mentors and players had to turn out for two matches each Sunday.

We started a recruitment campaign of which one of the elements was a parish seven-a-side football competition, which was highly successful both from a point of bringing in some new players, and also as a form of pre-season training. We also put in place a serious training program well before the start of the 1986/87 season.

In addition to our outdoor training we hired out a hall in Cheeverstown for winter physical training and Joe McDonnell persuaded Eugene Griffin to do the physical training as it would look good on his CV and we would not charge him for the privilege ! Eugene Griffin was a qualified PE instructor working in Cara and was the first external PE trainer to come into the club.

1986/87 SEASON

The Junior A team managed by Don Lehane and Gerry Quinn competed in Division 3 South and the Junior B team under Ernest Kenny and Donnchadh Lehane competed in Division 4 South. The 1986/87 season started with a number of competitive friendly games against good opposition including St Marks, Peregrines and Ballinteer St Johns. Our first Division 3 league match was against Postal Gaels on 12th October 1986 and hopefully a good omen for our target of Division 4 to Intermediate in seven years. St Judes ran out winners on a scoreline of 2-12 to 0-2. Judes defence played very well and our work in training on minimising close-in frees worked well. It should be said that moving Seamus McCartin into goals helped enormously in reducing the number of frees against us ! Our early season training, friendly matches and seven-a-sides has got us to a good level of fitness and there is a good spirit in the squad. Eamonn Curran, Seamus Clifford and Tom Maguire formed a very solid half-back line. Patsy Kenneally, Christy Kilcoyne and Ger Treacy were the pick of the midfield/forwards and Liam Reilly played very well when moved to full-forward. Our Junior B football team also fielded for their first Division 4 league game against St Annes and came away with a 2-11 to 0-4 win, even though we had to double up in a few positions.

This was a great start to 1986/87 league season and for the record these are the two teams that played on that October day in 1986.

Division 3/Division 4 Teams for 1st League Games of 1986/87 Season

Date: 12/10/1986 Competition: Division 3 Junior League 1986/87 (1st game). Result: St Judes A (2-12) V Postal Gaels (0-2). Team:

Tommy Walsh	Tommy Quinn	Dermot Clifford
Christy Kilcoyne	Ger Treacy	Ger Kenny
Liam Reilly		Patsy Kenneally
Tom Maguire	Eamonn Curran	Seamus Clifford
Luke Mooney	John Brown	Brendan Gill
	Seamus McCartin	

Subs: Frank Clabby for Tommy Quinn, Matt Farrelly for Brendan Gill, Don Lehane for Tom Maguire, Joe McDonnell

Date: 12/10/1986 Competition: Division 4 Junior League 1986/87 (1st game). Result: St Judes B (2-11) V St Annes (0-4). Team:

Ciaran O'Reilly	Tommy Quinn	Mick Ryan
Joe McDonnell	Eugene Loughlin	Don Lehane
Conor Lehane		Patsy Kenneally
Tom Clarke	Eamonn Curran	Seamus Clifford
Frank Jordan	Dessie Coyle	Charles Moran
	Mick O'Brien	

Subs: Billy Fogarty, Ronan Boylan, Seamus McCartin, Peadar O'Donnell, Brendan Gill, Ger Kenny

On 25th January 1987 we beat a good Bank of Ireland team in the league on a scoreline of 1.14 to 3.05. This was a good game of football with St Judes on top for most of the game but conceded three sloppy goals, which put unnecessary pressure on us towards the end. Patsy Kenneally and Kevin Clabby played well at midfield and up front Denis Murtagh, Ger Kenny and Ger Treacy played very well. Donal Brennan will be great asset at full-forward when he regains full fitness. The next league game against Liffey Gaels in the Phoenix Park ended in a 2.05 to 2.05 draw. It was a scrappy game played in the usual windy conditions of the Phoenix Park. Good performances from Michael Barrett and Donal Brennan but we missed the hard tackling Seamus Clifford in defence.

On the 24th May 1987 we beat Churchtown Dundrum by thirty four points in the league. Judes were leading 7.08 to 0.02 at half time with Christy Kilcoyne getting four goals, Liam Reilly contributing 3.02 and five well taken points from Danny Corbett. The second half was a non-event if we exclude Joe McDonnell's debut as a replacement keeper for Seamus McCartin – surely he was not going to get himself sent off from that position!

A feature of the game was the high fielding of Kevin Clabby who caught evertything around the middle including a couple of pigeons who had the temerity to come below cloud level.

On 14th June 1987 we had a convincing win in a league fixture against Ballyfermot on a scoreline of 3-11 to 2-8. The game had to be replayed at a later stage as it was deemed a friendly in the absence of the official referee. Fine performance from Derek McGuckian with good support from Ger Tannam, Eugene Loughlin and Eamonn Curran. This was the last official appearance of Eamonn Curran and Patsy Kenneally in a Judes jersey (in fact Patsy finished up refereeing the game as he was injured and the referee failed to show). They are both returning to Spiddal having completed their studies at UCD. They will be missed not only for their tremendous performances for St Judes at junior and U21 level over the last few years but also for their good humour and social input to the club. Their "As Gaeilge" discussions and arguments were a feature of their presence here and confused many a referee in the heat of battle. On 17th June we drew our next league game against St Mary's Saggart on a scorelinc of 1-9 (Judes) to 2-6. We should have won this game but conceded two poor goals due to goalkeeper and full-back line misunderstandings and mistakes. Fine games from Declan Clabby, Jimmy Hanniffy and Danny Corbett.

On 21st June we had a comprehensive league win against Thomas Davis in Kiltipper on a scoreline of 3-11 to 1-3. This continued our unbeaten league run in Division 3. Fine games from Seamus Clifford at centre-back and Ger Tannam at midfield with good support from wing-back Denis Evoy and centre-forward Michael Barrett. Don Lehane was a late second half substitute and scored three good points. On 12th July the re-fixed league fixture against Ballyfermot was due to take place in Tymon. Ballyfermot failed to show and the match was awarded to St Judes. Judes B team travelled to play Round Towers in Clondalkin but they did not turn up either so we finished up playing a friendly game beteeen Junior A& B teams. The joys of junior football in Dublin!

Our next league fixture did not take place until 6th December 1987 when we had a good win against a potentially dangerous Portobello side on a scoreline of 1-10 to 1-2. Very solid defensive display from Seamus Clifford, Cyril Loughlin, Denis Evoy and Declan Clabby. Up front Jimmy Hanniffy played best in a forward line which did not really click until the last twenty minutes. On 13th December Fr. Murphy's failed to turn up for our league fixture in Tymon and we were awarded the points. It is a crazy time of the year to be playing games and we understand that the league will resume in early January, which means we really have to keep in training over the Chistmas holidays. This team has really not had a break from football for a couple of years and it says a lot for the organisation at board level that we are still playing the 1986/87 league even though we are now moving in to 1988. We will drive on regardless.

On 17th January 1988 we played a crucial league game against St Patricks of Palmerstown. The Division 3 league is coming down to a battle between St Judes, St Patricks and Caislean so this game against St Patricks had a lot at stake. St Judes came out winners after a very committed performance in poor conditions on a scoreline of 1-4 to 5 points. This effectively means that we have won the Division 3 South league even though there is still an outstanding fixture against AIB to be played. We had tremendous defensive performances from Ger McSweeney, Declan Clabby, Seamus Clifford and Luke Mooney. Cathal Travers and Bert Smith were outstanding around the middle of the field and up front the forwards battled hard against both the poor conditions and a strong St Patricks defence. We were missing twelve of our first team panel for this game mainly due to injuries and it says a lot for our progress this year that we are still able to put out a strong side capable of getting a good result in a top of the table clash.

Conor Lehane, who did not start the game as he arrived after the throw in, came on as a midfield substitute in the second half and played very well. This is his last game for St. Judes as he is transferring to Intermediate side Caislean. It is a pity to lose one of the first good players to come up through St Judes underage teams. In any case we wish him the best and hopefully he will return to help the parish in the future.

Our final Division 3 league game against AIB was fixed for 24th Jan but was called off due to unplayable pitches in Tymon. We have won the league at this stage so the match did not really matter. As we are now into 1988 the board is anxious to start 1987/88 league fixtures. The All Dublin semi-finals and finals for Division 3 cannot be played as apparently the Division 3 North Junior League is even further behind than our league. It looks probable that we will be competing in Division 1 Junior League in the 1987/88 season after an unbeaten run in Junior 3 coupled with some very impressive cup performances against Division 1 junior sides throughout the past year. We had deliberately entered the higher cup competition to gain experience and in retrospect this has worked very well for us. After much behind the scenes discussions at both club and junior board level it was finally agreed that St Judes would progress to Division 1 South League for 1987/88 season. We are confident that we are capable of holding our own at this level and even though it will probably be very tough I hope we do not live to regret the decision. We will soon find out as our first Division 1 league fixture is due to be played in the next few weeks.

ST. JUDE'S . . . rounded off their season in fine style with a resounding victory over Round Towers

ANOTHER SCORE . . . Michael Barrett bursts through to score another point for St. Jude's in their runaway win over Round Towers on Sunday.

St. Jude's finish in fine style

ST. JUDES	1-13
ROUND TOWERS	0-1

St. Jude's picked up two Murphy Cup points and finished their season in fine style, after easily disposing of a ragged Round Towers' side at Tymon North on Sunday.

Round Towers, with only fourteen players, chose to face the wind and the slope in the first half. They soon found themselves in arrears, and with only twelve minutes gone, were three points adrift.

The home side stamped their authority as early as the fifth minute, when a pass from Michael Barrett found Don Lehane in the centre. The corner forward turned, and from twenty yards, lobbed over the bar. This was followed by points from play by Barrett and bustling full forward Martin Reynolds.

It was obvious, even at this early stage of the game, that Jude's were the superior side. A combination of poor kickouts by Towers and good fielding by midfielders Cathal Travers and Conor Lehane, ensured that play would remain in the visitors goal area.

Indeed, St. Jude's should have scored more, but rather than go for points they pursued a policy of planting hopeful balls into the arms of the opposing goalkeeper.

Byrne, Reynolds and Barrett all missed scoring opportunities, before Barrett — enjoying the freedom of the park — burst through and was taken down, leaving referee Tom Davis with no alternative but to award a penalty. Martin Reynolds stepped up and calmly stroked the ball low and left of the keeper to make the score 1-3 to 0-0, fifteen minutes into the game.

● Round Towers, although aware tht the game was slipping away form them made no attempt to tighten up their

The big match—
BY EAMONN GIBSON

marking or re-organise their side. There were plenty of idle forwards who could have been brought back into midfield in order to win the ball and attempt long range points. Unfortunately they failed to do so, and it was St. Jude's who kept up the pressure. A poor kick out was fielded by Conor Lehane, who swept by his marker before knocking the ball over for a point. Five minutes later a sweet move involving Tannam, Travers and Kenny ended with Barrett pointing, and putting his side into an eitht point lead at the interval.

Round Towers played with a new confidence for the opening minutes of the second period but, sadly for them, a solid home defence kept them at bay, and they failed to reap any reward for their brief spell of superiority.

St. Jude's , . playing now against a stiff breeze, adapted their game to suit, and began a display of fast, attractive football. Driving low into the

wind they linked well, moved the ball freely and set up speedy attacks.

● With the visitors reeling after scores from Barrett and Conor Lehane, Don Lehane, pointed off an upright to make the score 1-8 to 0-0, ten minutes into the second half. Then, man of the match, Martin Reynolds added two more points to increase his teams lead, and effectively end the game as a contest.

Just five minutes remained when Shane O'Neill pointed from a free to register Round Towers' solitary score.

ST. JUDE'S — C. Moran, S. O'Connell, B. Gill, C. Dolan, G. Tannam, D. Evoy, C. Redmond, C. Travers, C. Degane, G. Kenny, M. Barrett, H. Oakley, T. Byrne, M. Reynolds, K. Lehane.

ROUND TOWERS — D. HJogan, S. Mansfield, L. Croke, A. Cummins, L. Broderick, S. Lombard, E. McCabe. P. Doran, S. O'Neill, E. Tully, s. McDaid, C. Fitzsimons, K Naughton, D. McCabe.

. **SCORESR: St. Jude's** — M Reynolds (1-1), M. Barrett, D. Lehane, C. Lehane (0-3 each). G. Denny, H. Oakley, C Travers (0-1 each). Round Towers — S. O'Neill (0-1).

Junior Division 3 league results 1986/87:

1987/JFL3	86/10/12	V Postal Gaels	Win 2.12 to 0.02	Home
1987/JFL3	87/01/25	V Bank of Ireland	Win 1.14 to 3.05	Away
1987/JFL3	87/05/03	V Liffey Gaels	Draw 2.05 to 2.05	Away
1987/JFL3	87/05/24	V Churchtown	Win 9.13 to 1.03	Away
1987/JFL3	87/06/17	V St Marys	Draw 1.09 to 2.06	Home
1987/JFL3	87/06/21	V Thomas Davis	Win 3.11 to 1.03	Away
1987/JFL3	87/07/12	V Ballyfermot	Win W/O	Home
1987/JFL3	87/12/06	V Portobello	Win 1.10 to 1.02	Home
1987/JFL3	87/12/13	V Fr. Murphys	Win W/O	Home
1987/JFL3	88/01/17	V St Patricks	Win 1.04 to 0.05	Away
1987/JFL3	88/06/17	V Caislean	Win 2.08 to 1.03	Away
1987/JFL3	88/08/28	V AIB	Win W/O	Home

St Judes won the Junior Division 3 league (South) in the 1986/87 season and were promoted to Junior Division 1 league for the 87/88 season. St Judes also won the All-Dublin Division 3 league title when they defeated Whitehall CC in the semi-final which did not take place until the 16th October 1988 on a scoreline of 3.10 to 0.02. They went on to beat St Patricks in the final, on a scoreline of 2.07 to 0.03 (in replay) at O'Toole Park on 11th December 1988. At this stage St Judes had won the intervening Division 1 league (South) and were already competing at Intermediate level.

88/10/16	V Whitehall CC	Win 3.10 to 0.02	All-DublinJFL3Semi-Final/OTP
88/11/13	V St Patricks	Draw 1.04 to 0.07	All-Dublin Final /O'Toole Pk
88/12/11	V St Patricks	Win 2.07 to 0.03	All-Dublin Final /OTP/Replay

In the 1986/87 Junior Football Championship St Judes were knocked out in the first round by Caislean after a replay. The drawn game was played in very poor weather conditions and St Judes were missing a few key players including Declan/Frank Clabby, Ger Treacy, Christy Kilcoyne and Tommy Quinn but should have won the game with the amount of possession they obtained. St Judes were beaten in the replay after a disappointing performance even though they were still missing a number of key players.

87/03/01	V Caislean	Draw 1.03 to 1.03	JFC Round 1 /Tymon
87/03/15	V Caislean	Loss 0.08 to 1.07	JFC Replay /Tymon

The Junior B team was competing in Division 4 and finished well up the table having played 12 league games, won 7, drew 2 and lost 3. Our U21 team were beaten by a point in the first round of the championship.

AOB: The new St Judes clubhouse was officially opened on the 11th October 1987 and part of the celebrations included a friendly game between Dublin and Longford on pitch number two in Tymon. Three St Judes players made their appearance at various stages of the game, namely Ger Tannam, Ger Kenny and Mick Barrett and they all performed admirably in an entertaining game which Dublin won by a point.

The following Dublin team lined up on the day against Longford:

Conor Crowley	Anto McCaul	David DeLappe
Kieran Duff	Noel McCaffrey	Charlie Redmond
Declan Bolger		John Kearns
Eamon Heery	Paul Clarke	Ger O'Driscoll
Mick Kennedy	Kevin Fagan	David Carroll
	John O'Leary	

Substitutes: Ger Tannam, Mick Barrett, Ger Kenny (all St Judes), Gerry Hargan.

Longford sent up a strong team including Tommy Farrell, Seán O'Shea, Colm Bawle, Liam Tierney, Joe McCabe, Padraig Carbery, Brendan Lennon, Matt Duggan, Gerry Clarke, Kevin Smith, John "Spike" McCormack, Cosmos Gilmore, Noel Maguire, Frank McNamee, Michael O'Hara, Eugene McCormack, Kevin O'Rourke, Cathal Lee and John O'Brien. In November 1986 playing access to our main pitch was withdrawn, which was disappointing as the choice of location for our clubhouse was obviously influenced by the proximity of our main pitch.

1987/88 SEASON

St Judes started the 1987/88 season with Junior A team managed by Don Lehane, Gerry Quinn and Cyril Loughlin competing in Division 1 and the Junior B team under Ernest Kenny and Donnchadh Lehane in Division 4. This was a big step up in standard but St Judes had been competing against a lot of the Division 1 & 2 sides in the previous year's cup competitions and had competed very well. Whilst St Judes approached the challenge with confidence the last thing needed was to get demoted to Division 2 after one season at Division 1 level.

On 21st Feb 1988 we played our first Division 1 South league fixture against St Marks. St Judes put in a storming display against the Declan Bolger led Marks side in Tymon and came away with a tremendous 1-10 to 2-5 win against one of the sides favourites to win this division. We had a very poor start and were seven points down after fifteen minutes with John Boyce having a baptism of fire at right corner-back in his debut league match for St Judes before being substituted. The team never panicked however and we gradually worked our way back into the game.

Our defence confined St Marks to three points for the remaining 45 minutes of the game and this was the basis of our recovery. Kevin Clabby, Brendan Coughlan and Ger Tannam dominated in a three-man midfield where current Dublin senior Declan Bolger was playing for St Marks. In particular Kevin Clabby completely outplayed Bolger with some spectacular high catches.

Our forward line took a while to settle but gradually whittled back the scores with some well taken points from Ger Tannam, Kevin Clabby, Ger Kenny and Christy Kilcoyne. The decisive score was a well worked goal from Declan McSweeney following a good move involving Ger Kenny and Brian McSweeney. Sterling displays from Kevin Clabby, Declan Clabby, Tom Maguire, Ger Tannam, Ger McSweeney, Brendan Coughlan and Christy Kilcoyne but overall is was a great team performance with everyone contributing. We were missing six first team players including Luke Mooney, Bert Smith, Cathal Travers, Paul McDermott and Richard Jordan but the level of competition in this squad is very strong which augurs well for the year ahead.

It is hard to believe that we have made a winning start in Division 1 against a strong St Marks team when we were playing in Division 3 last season and Division 4 two years ago. Rock on! For the record the starting team for this game was as follows:

Date: 21/2/1988 Time: 11.30am Venue: Tymon Competition: League Div. 1
Match: St Judes A (1-10) V St Marks (2-5). Team:

Declan McSweeney (8)	Christy Kilcoyne (8)	Ger Tannam (9)
Dermot Clifford (8)	Brian McSweeney (7)	Ger Kenny (8)
Brendan Coughlan (9)	Kevin Clabby (9)	
Tom Maguire (8)	Seamus Clifford (8)	Ger McSweeney (9)
Cyril Loughlin (8)	Declan Clabby (9)	John Boyce (7)
Seamus McCartin (7)		

Subs: Dave McGlynn (7) for John Boyce

On 6th March 1988 we went out of the Junior football championship after a 0-4 to 0-7 defeat against Thomas Davis. The match was played on Faughs pitch due to the length of grass and condition of the Judes pitch. Thomas Davis played with a very strong wind in the first half and led by six points at half time. Judes came into the game strongly in the second half but failed to turn good possession into scores. None of the forwards really got going and we missed the presence of injured Ger Treacy, Donal Brennan, Brendan Coughlan and Cyril Loughlin. Declan Clabby also cried off with flu on the morning of the game. Defence and midfield played well but forwards let us down on the day against a resilient Thomas Davis defence.

On 10th April we had our first league loss in over two years since we left Division 4 when we went down by 0-6 to 2-4 against Guinness at the Iveagh Grounds. Our poor performance, rather than the defeat itself, was the most disappointing aspect of this game. We conceded two sloppy goals including an own goal by Ciaran Cribbs. Declan Clabby's experience was missed at the back even though minor Peter Ryan had a promising debut on the first team. We missed the free-taking and general play of Bert Smith and also Brendan Coughlan's defensive covering. Our next league match was a tough encounter against St Annes in Fettercairn. St Judes ran out winners by 2-7 to 1-8 on a poor pitch riddled with potholes, hoof marks and manure. Liam Reilly injured his troublesome knee early in the game. It is a shame that he cannot get an injury free run together as he is a very talented footballer. Cyril Loughlin was back after injury in a defence where Ger McSweeney, Luke Mooney and Declan Clabby excelled particularly in the first half when St Annes were playing with a strong wind. The match was level at half time. Judes found scores difficult to come by in the second half until a speculative long range shot from Brian McSweeney finished up in the back of the net – Brian of course insisting that this was precisely his intention. A couple of converted frees from Bert Smith put us ahead in the closing stages and we held out for a hard earned win.

On 24th March 1988 a spirited St Judes side had a good 2-5 to 0-9 league win against a typically mobile Synge Street team. As usual our defence played very well led by Luke Mooney at corner back, who turned in a marvellous performance, with good assistance from Ger McSweeney, Tom Maguire, Cyril Loughlin and goalkeeper Seamus McCartin. Luke Mooney shipped a lot of punishment particularly in the second half. Tremendous second half performance from Declan McSweeney as he repeatedly rounded his marker – he set up a couple of goals for Christy Kilcoyne. He had good support from Ray O'Connor and Ger Tannam.

On 8th May 1988 we had a disappointing league loss to Postal Gaels on a scoreline of 1-6 to 1-8. Postal Gaels had a very strong side out with a particularly strong Kerry player at left half-forward who gave both Ger McSweeney and John Boyce in turn a bit of a roasting. Judes had the edge at midfield with Kevin Clabby and Bert Smith but we laboured up front with the exception of the evergreen Jimmy Hanniffy who scored a tremendous goal and added on a couple of points from play. Judes were ahead entering the closing stages but conceded a very poor goal. Mick O'Brien and John Boyce failed to clear a ball when they had the opportunity and the resulting cross-kick from the Postal Gaels corner forward deceived Seamus McCartin and crept into the net to leave us two points down at the final whistle.

Paddy Russell blasts pass Johnny O'Gara in Dubs v Culchies 1988 classic.

Above: High speed action shot from Dubs v Culchies match in 1988.

Left: Dubs versus Culchies in Tymon (over-35s), Sean Conway and Davy Griffin.

We bounced back from our two point defeat to Postal Gaels with a resounding twelve point league win against Portobello on 29th May on a scoreline of 1-15 to 0-6. This was Judes back at their best with big displays all over the pitch against a formidable Portobello side who have had some good league wins in recent months. Judes were ahead by a couple of points at half time but really upped the tempo in the second half and stormed into a big lead with some well taken points particularly from Declan McSweeney, Ger Tannam and Jimmy Hanniffy. Seamus Clifford, John Boyce and Declan Clabby were extremely solid in defence backed up by Seamus McCartin who had an excellent game in goals particularly in the first half when we were under a bit of pressure. Bert Smith also had a tremendous game at midfield and gave valuable link support between our defence and attack. Declan McSweeney has developed into a top class corner forward with his determination in winning possession coupled with an ability to score himself or pick out a better placed forward.

On 17th June 1988 we were back to the future with a Division 3 league play-off fixture against Caislean to decide play off positions for the All-Dublin Division 3 league title. Judes had gone through this league unbeaten but there was a bit of pride to play for in getting to the Division 3 league semi-finals. The experience of playing in Division 1 showed up in the extra sharpness of St Judes around the pitch. Judes led by seven points at half time but really should have been fifteen points ahead. The pattern in the second half was similar with Judes dominating but missing scoring opportunities. St Judes eventually ran out eight point winners on a scoreline of 2-8 to 1-3 to ensure our place in the All-Dublin county semi-finals against the runners-up in the North Dublin Division 3 league. This was a good all round team performance where everyone from Seamus McCartin in goals to John Brown at corner-forward played their part.

On 6th July 1988 we had a good nine points win against Thomas Davis in the Division 1 league on a scoreline of 3-9 to 2-3. Weather conditions were poor with a crosswind and torrential rain in the second half. Judes did not play particularly well but stuck with the task and eventually ground down Thomas Davis. Declan McSweeney caused all sorts of problems for Thomas Davis defence with good support from Paul McDermott and Greg Hanlon. Judes led by five points at half time and built on this lead in the second half. Another class display from Ger McSweeney at wing back supported by the aggressive Seamus Clifford on the other wing. John Boyce in an unaccustomed centre-back role completed a very resolute St Judes half-back line.

On 17th July St Judes put in another convincing Division 1 league performance with a comprehensive 3-11 to 0-7 win against Ballyboden Wanderers.

We were missing a number of players including Seamus/Dermot Clifford, Bert Smith, Tom Maguire, Ciaran Cribbs, Ray O'Connor and Danny Corbett. A number of younger players were introduced and played very well including Ray Whelan, Peter Ryan and Leo Doyle. Judes led by 1-6 to no score at half time, following a lucky goal from Ger Tannam and an excellent defensive performance from St Judes. Cyril Loughlin and Kevin Clabby picked up a lot of possession around midfield with good assistance from Ger Tannam who is playing tremendous football at the moment – his work rate is very high and he is getting on the scoreboard much more frequently. Ger got good support at half-forward from Ray Whelan and Brian McSweeney.

In the full forward line Christy Kilcoyne and Declan McSweeney looked likely to score each time they got possession and a goal apiece from them during the second half finished off the game. Our defence as usual was rock solid as they have been all year. We have almost come to take their performances for granted at this point. Over the past number of months there has been a consistently high level of performance from players like Declan Clabby, Luke Mooney, Tom Maquire, Seamus Clifford, Ger McSweeney, John Boyce, Ciaran Cribbs, Cyril Loughlin, Mick O'Brien, Frank Clabby, Brendan Gill and Seamus McCartin. In this particular game Seamus McCartin did not start due to a slight strain in his kicking leg. He did however make a brief appearance as a corner-forward and in no time at all he had scored a point, annoyed the referee with back-chat and started a row with the corner back. St Judes ran out thirteen point winners and consolidated their position at the top of Division 1 league. On 28th August 1988 we were down to play AIB in a 1986/87 Division 3 league match. We are not sure why this match should be played as we have already won this division and have also won the play-off game with Caislean. In any case AIB failed to show and we were awarded the points.

On 16th October 1988 we had a big win against Whitehall Colmcille on a score of 3-10 to 0-2 in the semi-final of the All-Dublin Division 3 league. The midfield dominance of Bert Smith and Kevin Clabby gave our forwards an endless supply of good ball. Christy Kilcoyne, Declan McSweeney, Cyril Loughlin, Brian McSweeney and Ger Tannam in the forward line took full advantage of the possession to chalk up a big score. St Judes defence was never stretched, in particular the half-back line swept up any possession getting past midfield. Overall there was a good competitive edge to the St Judes performance which augurs well for the tough games coming up including the Division 3 league county final against St Patricks Palmerstown.

The 6th November 1988 was another historic day for adult football in St Judes with our first competitive match at Intermediate level against Kilmacud

Crokes in the Loving Cup 1988/89 at Silverpark. It was a tremendous achievement to go from Division 4 junior to Intermediate in two years and great credit is due to the squad of players who have achieved this landmark. The team has gone through this period with the loss of only two league matches and they are fully deserving of their promotion to this level. Our ten year plan was going better than expected as we had reached Division 1 junior in one year instead of the planned five years and we had now gone to Intermediate level the following year instead of the planned two years. Overall we had gone from Div 4 Junior to Intermediate in two years rather than the projected seven and hopefully set a sound basis for adult football in the years ahead.

These events seem to have bypassed the GAA heartland of Templeogue if one could judge from the St Judes support in Silverpark. The team ran out onto the pitch to the thunderous applause of Frank McSweeney, Ernest Kenny, Ger Tannam's father and his dog. The match itself ended in a draw with each team scoring 1-5. This was a very competitive game against a Crokes side, which was relegated last year from senior level. Both defences were on top throughout the game and scoring opportunities were rare. Bert Smith was having a big game at midfield and in defence Seamus Clifford, Brendan Coughlan, John Boyce and Declan Clabby were best. Up front Declan McSweeney tried hard as indeed did Brian McSweeney, Ger Tannam, Christy Kilcoyne and Ger Kenny.

We had a long discussion in the dressing rooms about the lack of St Judes support at the game. It was charitably concluded that the supporters were at this instant setting up bonfires on the way to Tymon and that we would be officially welcomed back to the club by the club executive before heading off for the celebration banquet. We headed off with a spring in our step to be greeted by a wall of silence in Templeogue even though Declan McSweeney swore he heard a cheer as we were passing the graveyard opposite the Spawell.

On 13th November 1988 we played the All-Dublin Division 3 league final against St Patricks of Palmerstown with a team captained by Kevin Clabby. The game ended in a dour draw with St Judes scoring 1-4 against 0-7 for St. Patricks. This was to be the conclusion of the Division 3 league competition, which commenced in 1986 and is still unfinished. In the meantime the team has been promoted up to Intermediate level. We have also reached the semi-final of the All-Dublin Division 1 league having recently won Division 1 (South). We must be the first club in history that has played Intermediate, Junior Division 1 and Division 3 league football with the same team in the same month. A match report plus team photo was covered in the Evening Herald on 16th Nov. 1988.

Our second team with Ernest Kenny and Donnchadh Lehane at the helm has also reached the O'Broin Cup final, which is due to be played next Sunday 20th

November in O'Toole Park. Overall it is quite a historic month for the club. Anyway back to the match against St Patricks which was played at O'Toole Park in excellent conditions. The match itself was rather a tame affair with defences dominating. St Judes were generally on top but poor shooting meant that we were only four points up at half time. In the meantime our defence was playing very well with Brendan Coughlan, Seamus Clifford and Ger McSweeney to the fore. An injury to Kevin Clabby restricted his progress at midfield but Bert Smith had a good game until tiring towards the end. Judes maintained their four point lead into the closing stages when St Patricks rallied to eventually draw level. Fine game up front again from Declan McSweeney who has been our most consistent forward all year. Ciaran McGovern came on as a late substitute to make his debut on the A team – he looked promising. This is a game we should have won but we were happy to get away with a draw in the end.

On 20th November 1988 we played Cuala in the O'Broin Cup final at O'Toole Park. St Judes had an excellent win on a scoreline of 2-12 to 0-5 and brought home the first adult football trophy to the clubhouse. This was our B team managed by Ernest Kenny and Donnchadh Lehane and backed up by a couple of eligible A team players. The team itself was selected the night before after extensive consultation in the clubhouse between Ernest Kenny, Donnchadh Lehane, Don Lehane, Tommy Bassett, Padre Pio and St Jude himself (or is it herself).

The 1988 St Judes Ó Broin Cup team lined out as follows:
Venue: O'Toole Park St Judes B (2-12) V Cuala (0-5)

Ray Whelan (8)	James Durkan (8)	Leonard Fitzpatrick (9)
Ciaran McGovern (9)	Brian McSweeney (8)	Ger Kenny (8)
Cyril Loughlin (8)		Peter Ryan (8)
Shane McGovern (8)	John Boyce (9)	Ciaran Cribbs (8)
Brendan Gill (8)	Mick O'Brien (8)	Patsy Tyrrell (7)
	John Brown (9)	

Subs: Ger Keaty (8) for Patsy Tyrrell, Denis Evoy (8) for Ciaran Cribbs (inj), Dara Murphy (8) for Leonard Fitzpatrick.

St Judes Scorers: Leonard Fitzpatrick (2.01), James Durkan (0.02), Ray Whelan (0.04/3f), Ciaran McGovern (0.02), Brian McSweeney (0.02), Ger Kenny (0.01), Denis Evoy (0.01).

St Judes got off to a good start in bitterly cold but dry conditions. An early point settled the nerves and this was rapidly followed by a couple of more points and a goal from Leonard Fitzpatrick. St Judes were twelve points up at half-time (2.08 to 0.02) against a demoralised Cuala side. Cuala were playing with the wind in the second half but only got into the game for a ten minute spell before St Judes reasserted themselves. They were going for goals when they got the opportunity but found John Brown unbeatable in the Judes goals. St Judes half-back line was led superbly by John Boyce with great assistance from Shane McGovern and Ciaran Cribbs. The full back line did not have a lot to do but coped well with the exception of Patsy Tyrrell in the corner who was playing like a sleeping tablet against a fast, elusive Cuala corner-forward. News of Patsy's high fielding abilities had apparently reached Cuala as every ball was rattling into the corner about a foot off the ground. In recent years Patsy has had to restrict his playing activities to mainly summer matches as his high fielding always carried the danger of developing frostbite which was not covered by the players insurance.

At midfield Cyril Loughlin and Peter Ryan held their own despite the presence of a very good fielder on the Cuala side. Up front Judes thrived on the possession and took some very good scores from a variety of angles and distances. Leonard Fitzpatrick and Ciaran McGovern used their pace to great effect against a sluggish Cuala backline. Both these players went on to play intercounty football with Lennie becoming one of the first St Judes adult county representatives when he played Under 21 championship with Dublin and Ciaran turning out for Leitrim at senior level. Brian McSweeney and James Durkan got a lot of possession down the middle. Ray Whelan converted some excellent frees and generally played well. Ger Kenny at wing forward gained a lot of possession around the midfield area. St Judes ran out thirteen point winners to spark wild celebrations. The Evening Herald report on the game stated "St Judes playing some very skilful football combined exceptionally well to totally outclass Cuala in the first half" and also mentioned "a magnificent display from John Boyce at centre back". John Boyce was more noted as a hurler and in earlier years had won a Leinster club hurling championship medal with Crumlin.

On 27th November 1988 we were beaten by two points by Trinity Gaels in the semi-final of the All-Dublin Division 1 league. St Judes had won the Division 1 (South) league and were playing the runners-up from North Dublin. The month of November 1988 will go down as a historic and an unusual month in the club's history. The same Judes team managed to play in competitions spanning four divisions over this one month period from 6th November 1988 to 27th November 1988 commencing with our first Intermediate game and culminating in the Division 3 All-Dublin final win against St Patricks. These were in the sequence Intermediate, Division 3, Division 1 and involved five visits to O'Toole Park to compete in two semi-finals and three finals. It is no wonder we are confused but it is tremendous to be involved in the shake up for so many competitions even though it is hard to understand why these competitions have not been completed before now. St Judes had already won the respective Division 3 South and Division 1 South leagues and gained promotion to the next level and the current fixtures were mainly to complete the All Dublin finals of these leagues. St Judes Junior B won the O'Broin Cup final in the middle of this sequence of games and the following list covers the fixtures in the extended period from mid October to early December 1988.

16/10/1988   Div. 3 League SF   St Judes(3-10) v Whitehall CC (0-2) O'Toole Pk.
06/11/1988   Intermediate Cup   St Judes (1-5) v Kilmacud Crokes (1-5) Silverpark
13/11/1988   Div. 3 League Final St Judes (1-4) v St Patricks (0-7) O'Toole Pk.
20/11/1988   O'Broin Cup Final St Judes (2-12) v Cuala (0-5) O'Toole Pk.
27/11/1988   Div. 1 League SF   St Judes (2-4) v Trinity Gaels (1-9) O'Toole Pk.
04/12/1988   Intermediate Cup St Judes (1-5) v Robert Emmets (1-3) 8 Acres
11/12/1988   Div 3 Dublin Final St Judes (2-7) v St Patricks (0-3) O'Toole Pk.

Anyway back to this fixture. As winners of Division 1 Junior (South) St Judes were playing the runners-up of the Division 1 Junior (North) which was Trinity Gaels. The game lived up to expectations as a hard, physical battle with little between the sides. St Judes were playing up the hill in the first half and started off very tentatively against the winners of the Dublin junior football championship which has ensured their promotion to Intermediate grade already accompanied by St Judes as Div. 1 league winners from Dublin South. Trinity Gaels got a few early points and then what seemed a perfectly good goal from Christy Kilcoyne was disallowed as a square ball by the referee. St Judes turned over at half time four points down.

In the second half St Judes stormed into the game and drew level with some well taken points. A good goal from Vinnie Murphy put Trinity Gaels back in front. St Judes came back with a goal from Ger Kenny, which was followed by a couple of points from Trinity Gaels. Brian McSweeney cracked the ball to the back of the net for another St Judes goal. Trinity Gaels were leading by one point as the game entered the closing stages. Continuous St Judes pressure failed to get an equalising point and eventually Trinity Gaels broke away for a late point to leave them winners by two points at the final whistle.

This was a good St Judes performance against strong opposition. Good performance from our full-back line of Tom Maguire, Declan Clabby and John Boyce. Our half-back line led by Ger McSweeney battled hard against a very strong Trinity Gaels half-forward line even though they were caught out for pace on a few occasions. Kevin Clabby had an outstanding second half against Vinnie Murphy around midfield. Bert Smith was not 100% fit but played very well in the circumstances. Up front an improved performance by St Judes but our half-forward line found it difficult to get scores from a tight marking Trinity half-back line. The following team lined out in the Division 1 all county league semi-final: Venue: O'Toole Park St Judes (2-4) V Trinity Gaels (1-9) on 27/11/88

Declan McSweeney (8)   Christy Kilcoyne (7)   Ger Kenny (8)
Brian McSweeney (7)   Ger Tannam (7)   Leonard Fitzpatrick (7)
                  Kevin Clabby (9)   Bert Smith (8)
Ger McSweeney (8)   Seamus Clifford (7)   Cyril Loughlin (7)
Tom Maguire (8)   Declan Clabby (9)   John Boyce (9)
                          Seamus McCartin (8)

Subs: Ray O'Connor for Leonard Fitzpatrick.

On 11th December 1988 we finally got around to playing the replay of the All-Dublin Division 3 1986/87 final against St Patricks of Palmerstown. This time we were determined not to make any mistake. This was an outstanding display from St Judes who were playing against the wind in the first half. They put in an exceptional defensive performance to hold St Patricks scoreless in the first half. The whole defence played well with Declan Clabby in particular having an outstanding game at full back. Luke Mooney had a solid return after a five-week lay-off and John Boyce was coolness personified in the other corner. St Judes half-back line, led by the tigerish Seamus Clifford, never gave the St Pats forwards an opportunity to settle. At midfield Judes were never stretched whereas up front our forwards picked off some great scores.

Ger Tannam had a fine game at centre forward in what was his last game for the club before his departure to join the Hong Kong police. He will be severely missed by the team, as he has played consistently well over the past couple of years and had a great attitude both on and off the pitch. St Judes turned over at half-time leading by 1 goal 4 points to no score. Playing with the wind in the second half they maintained their concentration and ran out easy winners by ten points in the end. Tom Maguire settled in well in an unfamiliar position at half forward. Jimmy Hannify had his usual steady game and picked off a few nice points. Ger Kenny, Declan McSweeney and Ger Tannam also chipped in with some good scores against a stretched St Patricks defence. Ciaran McGovern played at right half forward and is developing into a fine player. He is inclined to over carry the ball at times but is learning all the time and will be a quality player when he has more experience under his belt. St Pats played disappointingly but were never really allowed to settle by an eager St Judes side. Another trophy for the club and no doubt there will again be bonfires all over Templeogue when captain Kevin Clabby returns with the cup later this evening !

All-Dublin Division 3 Final Replay Team
  Venue: O'Toole Park St Judes (2-7) V St Patricks (0-3) 11/12/1988
  Declan McSweeney (8)   Jimmy Hannify (8)   Ger Kenny (8)
  Tom Maguire (8)   Ger Tannam (9)   Ciaran McGovern (8)
         Bert Smith (8)   Kevin Clabby (8) (Captain)
  Brendan Coughlan (9) Seamus Clifford (9)   Ger McSweeney (9)
  Luke Mooney (9)   Declan Clabby (9)   John Boyce (9)
                  Seamus McCartin (9)
Subs: James Durkan for Declan McSweeney, Barry Cribbs for Ger Kenny, Ray
O'Connor for Ciaran McGovern.
  The St Judes results in the Division 1 league were as follows in 1987/88:

1988/JFL1	88/02/21	V St Marks	Win 1.10 to 2.05	Home
1988/JFL1	88/04/10	V Guinness	Loss 1.11 to 3.07	Away
1988/JFL1	88/04/14	V St Annes	Win 2.07 to 1.08	Away
1988/JFL1	88/04/24	V Synge Street	Win 2.05 to 0.09	Away
1988/JFL1	88/05/08	V Postal Gaels	Loss 1.06 to 1.08	Away
1988/JFL1	88/05/29	V Portobello	Win 1.15 to 0.06	Home
1988/JFL1	88/06/11	V St Patricks	Win w/o	Home
1988/JFL1	88/07/06	V Thomas Davis	Win 3.09 to 2.03	Home
1988/JFL1	88/07/17	V Ballyboden Wndrs.	Win 3.11 to 0.07	Away

St Judes Played 9 Won 7 Drew 0 Lost 2 Total Points 14 Winners Division 1
(South). In the 1988 Junior Football Championship St Judes (0.04) were knocked
out by Thomas Davis (0.07) on the 6th March 1988 in Tymon after a less than
inspiring performance in poor conditions. The Junior B team competed in Division
4 South and finished in the top half of the table having played eight matches, won
five and lost three. They had a tremendous run in the 1987/88 O'Byrne Cup
which they went on to win in November 1988 after the following sequence of
results:

1988/O'B Cup	88/02/28	V Shankhill	Win 0.04 to 0.02	Home
1988/O'B Cup	88/04/17	V St Annes	Win W/O	Home
1988/O'B Cup	88/04/21	V Ballyboden SE	Draw 2.06 to 2.06	Away
1988/O'B Cup	88/05/05	V Guinness	Win 1.04 to 0.01	Home
1988/O'B Cup	88/06/09	V Cuala	Win 1.12 to 0.06	Home
1988/O'B Cup	88/06/19	V Synge St PP	Win 1.09 to 2.04	Away
1988/O'B Cup	88/06/26	V Robert Emmets	Win 1.07 to 1.05	Away
1988/O'B Cup	88/06/29	V Naomh Eanna	Loss 1.08 to 2.06	Away
1988/O'B Cup	88/07/10	V Round Towers	Win W/O	Home
1988/O'B Cup	88/10/02	V Naomh Eanna	Win 2.11 to 1.04	Semi-Final
1988/O'B Cup	88/11/20	V Cuala	Win 2.12 to 0.05	Final

46   Evening Herald, Wednesday, November 16, 1988

Late burst by St Pats earns draw

ST. PATRICKS (P)..............1-4
ST. JUDES.........................0-7

Big Match Report

By Niall Scully

A DRAMATIC late surge gained St. Patricks of Palmerstown a replay in the League Division 3 86/87 Football final, at O'Toole Park last Sunday morning.

For a long while in that second half such an outcome looked unlikely as Pats missed several good chances of getting back into the match.

Overall it was a pretty tame hour, only bursting to life in the last ten minutes. Yet it was sporting, with hardly a word out of place.

Despite the bright sunshine the surface was slippy and the play rarely flowed. Pats struggled to find rhythm in either half.

And they owe special thanks to the three Walsh brothers for achieving equality. It was their scores that earned a fortunate draw.

Trailing by five points to two at the break, Pats attacked the road end in the second period. In the 42nd minute, David Walsh reduced the deficit with a fine point from play.

By the 47th minute, Judes were ahead by seven points to three. Pats got a free on the right and Jimmy Walsh's kick was allowed to drift all the way to the net from around 35 yards. Judes will ask themselves some serious questions about that one.

Only two minutes remained and Pats still were behind by a point. It was left to Declan Walsh to direct over a splendid effort from play. Walsh Brothers Limited had performed a good day's business.

Things were looking bleak for Pats after Damien Flood struck the bar a minute after the re-start. Then they experienced another near-miss when Judes defender, John Boyce, cleared off the line from a punch by Colm O'Muiri.

O'Muiri is one of the fittest men around. He is a chaplain in Belfield where he takes a huge interest in sport.

Judes, from Templeogue, enjoyed a terrific first half when Declan McSweeney caused Pats all sorts of problems, but they should have scored more.

The accuracy of Bert Smith was also admirable, and even St. Patricks thought Judes had it won when Ray O'Connor put them four points in front on 47 minutes.

Judes were not as convincing against the breeze, and at the end they were the more disappointed with the result. They realised victory was within their grasp and they should have made sure of it.

ST. JUDE'S . . . drew with St. Patrick's at O'Toole Park on Sunday.

ST. PATRICKS — Eddie Farrelly, Pat O'Halloran, Finian Christie, Manus Daly, Damien Henley, Donnie O'Mahony, Andrew Diggins, Declan Walsh (0-1), David Walsh (0-3), Nigel Slater, Colm O'Muiri, Brian O'Brien, Damien Flood, John Keaney, Jimmy Walsh (1-0). Subs. — Sean O'Mahony for Daly (25 mins); Padraig Farrelly for Slater (36 mins). Managers — John Daly, Tom O'Brien.

ST. JUDES — Seamus McCartin, John Boyce, Declan Clabby, Tom Maguire, Brendan Coughlan, Seamus Clifford, Ger McSweeney, Bert Smith (0-4), Kevin Clabby, Ray O'Connor (0-1), Ger Tannam, Brian McSweeney, Declan McSweeney (0-2), Christy Kilcoyne, Ger Kenny. Subs. — Ciaran McGovern and Cyril Loughlin for Maguire and Brian McSweeney (42 mins.); Peter Ryan for Declan McSweeney (inj. 50 mins). Managers — Don Lehane, Gerry Quinn, Ernest Kenny.

Referee — Sean MacTurlough (St. Marks).

The Under 21 footballers won Division 3 South of the 1987/88 season with a very strong team which included Paul Bealin and Kenny Rowe from St Kevins, Seamus Clifford, Dermot Clifford, Ray Whelan, Leonard Fitzpatrick, Patsy Kenneally, Michael and Eamonn Curran to name a few. They put out a very strong team in the championship but were beaten by St Mary's of Saggart much to the amazement of the St Judes mentors who felt there was an All-Ireland title in the squad!

1988/89 SEASON

The 1988/89 season at Intermediate Football level was very much a year of consolidation, after a rather breathless run from Division 4 Junior to Intermediate level. The team was managed by Don Lehane and Gerry Quinn with Ernest Kenny and Donnchadh Lehane again managing the Junior B team. The A team had been playing non-stop for the last couple of years, but were nevertheless determined to keep the run going at this level. Five wins from the first nine matches ensured a good finishing position in the league by the season break in July 1989 and we had achieved our objective in retaining our Intermediate status in our first year at this level. Don Lehane stepped down as manager of the team due to work commitments at this point and Charles Moran and Tony Gilleran took over for the last few games and the major part of the following season 1989/90.

At the summer break in July 1989 St Judes still had two league games left to play and were well positioned in the top five of the Intermediate league. At this point in the league Good Counsel were down four points but had a number of games to play.

Lucan Sarsfields were six points down with one game to play against St Judes. Crumlin were six points down with three games to play. St Judes were eight points down with two games to play against Lucan and Crumlin. Cuala also had an outside chance of getting into the play-offs if they won all their remaining games. The outstanding league games were played at the start of the new season in Sept-Nov 1989 and results elsewhere brought St Judes right back into contention as all the leading teams dropped points. St Judes were beaten by Lucan Sarsfields in September 1989 which put Lucan Sarsfields through to the playoff final.

If St Judes won this game or the following game against Crumlin they would have been through to the playoff final.

In the event St Judes were well beaten by Crumlin but the team was very close to gaining a play-off final place to go senior in its first year at Intermediate level. Crumlin played Lucan Sarsfields in the IFL play-off final on 2nd December 1989 in O'Toole Park.

It would have been a fairytale ending to go from Junior 4 to senior football in three years but in the event it was a bridge too far and with hindsight it may have been a blessing in disguise.

Few people doubted that the present team would have held their own at senior level for a couple of years, even though a couple of players including Luke Mooney, Christy Kilcoyne, Declan McSweeney, John Boyce and Ray O'Connor were contemplating retiring or moving down a level after a couple of hard years under Don Lehane and company. It was not so clear however whether the up and coming underage players in the club would be ready to be thrown in at senior level immediately without first going through junior and/or intermediate level. Most of the St Judes underage teams with one or two exceptions were unfortunately competing at levels below Division 1 standard at this point and the gap in standard between minor/U21 Division 3 and senior football would have been quite large. Enormous credit was nevertheless due to this particular St Judes team who had established St Judes as a club who had arrived as a force to be reckoned with at adult level in Dublin and really set the standard for future teams. It would take St Judes another four years at Intermediate level before eventually making the break through to senior ranks but we were now here to stay and from here on progress was on an upward curve.

The following is an overview of the Intermediate league games played during the 1988/89 season. On 22nd January 1989 we went down by two points to Kilmacud Crokes in our first Intermediate league match of the 1988/89 season on a scoreline of 1-3 to 1-5. We were missing quite a few players mainly through injury but put up a good performance against a Crokes side which were relegated from senior football last season. St Judes went four points up but a defensive mistake let Crokes in for a goal, which brought them right back into the game. They went ahead by three points in the second half and we just could not break down their defence to draw level. Seamus Clifford, Ger McSweeney (until injured) and Declan Clabby played well in defence. Kevin Clabby and Brendan Coughlan played well at midfield and up front Ger Treacy and Ciaran McGovern never stopped trying. The following team lined out in our first Intermediate league match: January 1989 1st Intermediate League Team:

Paul McDermott (7)	Christy Kilcoyne (7)	Ray O'Connor (7)
Ciaran McGovern (8)	Ger Treacy (8)	Brian McSweeney (7)
Kevin Clabby (8)		Brendan Coughlan (7)
Denis Evoy (8)	Seamus Clifford (9)	Ger McSweeney (7)
Shane McGovern (7)	Declan Clabby (8)	John Boyce (8)
	Seamus McCartin (8)	

Subs: Ger Kenny (7) for Ger McSweeney, Patsy Nugent (7) for Shane McGovern

On 29th January 1989 we had an excellent win against local rivals Robert Emmets in an Intermediate league match in Tymon. St Judes won on a scoreline of 0-11 to 1-5. This was a highly competitive game with total commitment from both sides. The game was level at half time but Judes put in a storming display in the second half with Kevin Clabby and Pat Clifford getting on top in midfield. Up front our movement was good and we tacked on some great points from Ger Treacy, Joe Duffy, Ray O'Connor and Ciaran McGovern. Luke Mooney had a tremendous game at corner back. This was a good win for St Judes against an experienced Robert Emmets Intermediate side, who were certainly keen to put the local upstarts in their place. Three cheers for the parish !

On 5th February 1989 we were defeated in the league by Good Counsel on a scoreline of 0-5 to 2-3. Good Counsel were a solid side who came down from senior two years ago and who were involved in Intermediate play-offs earlier this year. They had a very good full-back line and centre-back who mopped up a lot of our attacks. Good Counsel led by a point at half-time. They went further ahead in the second half and when Judes conceded a penalty Good Counsel went five points up. Judes came back with some good points but another goal for Good Counsel wrapped up the game for them, which they probably deserved over the hour. Good Judes performances from Brendan Coughlan, Declan Clabby and Seamus McCartin in goals who could not be faulted for either goal.

On 2nd April 1989 we were knocked out of the Intermediate championship by a hotly fancied Ballymun Kickhams on a 0-9 to 1-10 scoreline. Whilst St Judes were never playing at the top of their form they nevertheless took the game to Ballymun and were two points ahead with ten minutes to go. A couple of Ballymun points followed by a goal put a rather undeserved look on the scoreline. Tom Maguire, Brendan Coughlan and Ger McSweeney played very well in the half-back line which was just as well as our full-back line for once looked a bit shaky against a free running Ballymun full-forward line. Bert Smith had the proverbial blinder at midfield accompanied by an unusually subdued Kevin Clabby. Christy Kilcoyne and Ray O'Connor were best in a forward line where our full forwards never really got into the game. We were missing a few key players including Ger Treacy (car crash), Cyril Loughlin, Joe Duffy and Seamus Clifford.

On 16th April 1989 we got back into winning ways with a six point win against Thomas Davis in the Intermediate football league. The score was 1-11 to 2-2. These were two important points for St Judes in what is turning out to be the toughest Intermediate league of them all. The Intermediate league consists of three equal divisions covering North, South and Fingal so in theory they should all be roughly at the same level but this division is shaping up to be the hardest. Our aim this year is to hold our Intermediate status after a rather breathless sprint through junior ranks. Bert Smith had another great game at midfield – he has been one of our most consistent players over the last few seasons. St Judes were two points up at the interval despite playing against the wind and the hill. In the second half Judes stepped up a gear playing with the wind and ran out six points winners. Good performances from John Boyce, Cyril Loughlin and the above mentioned Bert Smith.

On 16th May 1989 we were beaten in the league by a tough, physical Churchtown side on an 0-8 to 1-9 scoreline. Judes lacked their usual edge tonight and we are wondering if the continuous treadmill over the past few years is finally catching up with us. We certainly looked a bit stale with a rather lethargic performance from our usually lively defence. Kevin Clabby came back into a bit of form after a few performances, which were below his usual standard. Mick Tobin also won a bit of possession but the distribution of both midfielders was erratic to say the least. Up front Bert Smith had an off day even with his frees and the rest of the forward line struggled somewhat culminating with a late penalty miss by Brian McSweeney. The team could do with a break but we will have to drive on to secure our position at Intermediate level which hopefully we will do before the summer break.

On 28th May we were defeated by Cuala in the league on a scoreline of 0-8 to 1-8. Cuala went into a four point lead after fifteen minutes but Judes fought back to level the scores. We conceded a bad goal before half time, which left us two points adrift at the interval. The second half was fairly even until Judes had a goal disallowed which would have put them two points ahead. Cuala came back with a few scores and eventually ran out three points winners. Kevin Clabby gave another tremendous display of high-fielding with good support from Mick Tobin until he tired in the second half. Our midfielders did not help out much in defence however on a day when our half-back line was overworked. Frank Clabby, Declan Clabby and Luke Mooney formed a very solid full back line.

On 7th June 1989 we got back into winning ways with great one point win against St Marks (1-9 to 1-8) in Fortunestown. This should have been a home match for St Judes but the current difficulties with pitches in Tymon has left us temporarily homeless. We are in a sequence of five away matches in a row, which is very unfair on the team as the pitch situation is outside our control. We were also understrength due to injuries, holidays and a few of the younger players like Ciaran McGovern and Ger McSweeney gone abroad to work for the summer. St Judes got on top early on against a young fast Marks side but failed to convert the hard won possession into scores with Christy Kilcoyne the leading offender on this occasion. At midfield Kevin Clabby dominated proceedings as he has been doing for most of the season. Brendan Coughlan gave him excellent support in the absence of the injured Bert Smith. Our defence was reasonably solid despite being stretched on occasions by a fast Marks forward line. Seamus McCartin played well in goals and got some great distance into his kickouts. Up front all the forwards contributed but the half-forward line of Joe Duffy, Ray O'Connor and Christy Kilcoyne in particular worked back a lot to help out midfield/defence. Ray Whelan had a good game in the corner and his reliable free-taking was an extra bonus. The game was tight all the way through but St Judes determination saw them win out by a point.

On 7th July 1989 we played St Finnians of Newcastle in our next league game and eventually ran out four point winners (1-11 to 0-9) after the usual tough struggle at this venue. This was an outstanding all round display by a very committed St Judes side. St Finnians are due to play Kevins in the semi-final of the junior championship and had obviously been training hard. As per usual we were missing a few players but we have good strength in depth in this squad. Luke Mooney and Declan Clabby were on holidays and some of our student players were also still abroad on holiday work, Ger McSweeney (Germany), Ciaran McGovern (London) and Ciaran Cribbs (USA). The speedy Tony Gillen made an able full back in the absence of Declan Clabby even though his rugby style dive on the ball in the square was a temporary loss of concentration. It resulted in an undisputed penalty, which Finnians failed to convert.

St Judes took a while to get going but points from Shane Gallen in his first Intermediate league match, Christy Kilcoyne and Ray Whelan (frees) settled the team. St Judes were three points up at half time. In the second half Judes increased the pressure and Kevin Clabby gradually got on top in a tough midfield battle with O'Reilly from St Finnians. Bert Smith is still not fully fit and needed the help of Christy Kilcoyne in the midfield exchanges. Mick O'Brien, Denis Evoy and Brendan Coughlan were best in defence and up front Christy Kilcoyne got good support from the Brian and Declan McSweeney in the second half. Shane Gallen had a promising debut on the first team until he received an injury. Ray Whelan and James Durkan continue to improve match by match.

St Judes eventually ran out five point winners which is no mean feat in Newcastle. This win really ensures our position in Intermediate football for next season.

On 9th July 1989 we were down to play Ballyboden St Endas in the Intermediate league but Ballyboden were unable to field a full side and conceded the points. We now have ten points in the league with a couple of games left to play. We are in the top six in the league and with two games to go could make it into the top two or three. These games will not now be played until after the summer and depending on other results we could still be involved in the play-offs to go senior. In the interim I will be giving some thought to my own position as work pressure is making it increasingly difficult to keep going with training a couple of nights a week and two matches most weekends. I think it would be a good time to pass on the baton to someone else. We are well positioned in the Intermediate league and there is a very solid squad of players available. Most of the senior players still have a number of years football still in them and their experience over the next couple of years will be invaluable. The younger players such as Ciaran McGovern, Ger McSweeney, Shane Gallen, Ray Whelan, Denis Evoy, James Durkan, Ger Kenny, Mick Fallon, Ger Keaty, Ciaran Cribbs etc are continuing to improve and with additional coaching are capable of playing at a higher level.

The current squad is capable of winning the Intermediate league and pushing on to senior football within a year or two. They have lost only four league games during this campaign so far and all these by only a couple of points. In the process the team has gained a lot of winning experience and should have no problems surviving at senior level.

Note: It is now autumn 1989 and Don Lehane has moved on from managing the Intermediate team as planned. Charlie Moran and Tony Gilleran have taken over the Intermediate team for the last couple of games of the 1988/89 season, which were played in September and October and will bring the team forward into the 1989/90 season.

The first game was against Lucan Sarsfields, which was played on 24th September at 12th Lock and we lost by five points on a scoreline of 1-5 to 0-13. The last game of the 1988/89 league season was against Crumlin in late October 1989 which we lost on a scoreline of 0-6 to 4-12.

The result of the Crumlin game was particularly disappointing with an eighteen point defeat, which must be higher than the accumulated points losses for the six league games the team has lost since we left Division 4 junior back in 1986. If St Judes had won either the Lucan or Crumlin games they would have been involved in the play-offs against the other two Intermediate divisions to go senior.

St Judes Intermediate League results for 1988/89 season were as follows:

1989/IFL	89/01/22	V Kilmacud Crokes	Loss 1.03 to 1.05	Away
1989/IFL	89/01/29	V Robert Emmets	Win 0.11 to 1.05	Home
1989/IFL	89/02/05	V Good Counsel	Loss 0.05 to 2.03	Home
1989/IFL	89/04/16	V Thomas Davis	Win 1.11 to 2.02	Away
1989/IFL	89/05/16	V Churchtown	Loss 0.08 to 1.09	Home
1989/IFL	89/05/28	V Cuala	Loss 0.08 to 1.08	Away
1989/IFL	89/06/07	V St Marks	Win 1.09 to 1.08	Away

1989/IFL	89/07/05	V St Finnians N'cstle	Win 1.11 to 0.09	Away
1989/IFL	89/07/06	V Ballyboden SE	Win w/o	Away
1989/IFL	89/09/24	V Lucan Sarsfields	Loss 1.05 to 0.13	Away
1989/IFL	89/10/??	V Crumlin (*)	Loss 0.06 to 4.12	Home

The St Judes V Crumlin game doubled as a semi-final play-off to meet Lucan Sarsfields.

In the Intermediate Football Championship St Judes were beaten by Ballymun Kickhams in a good game at Albert College on a scoreline of 0.09 to 1.10.

On the 20th November 1988 the Junior B football team beat Cuala to win the 1987/88 O'Byrne Cup in O'Toole Park on a scoreline of 2.12 to 0.05 after a tremendous performance. This was the first adult football trophy won by the club and the performances of the team were a great credit to the manager Ernest Kenny and Donnchadh Lehane. The team also had a tremendous year in Division 4 Junior Football League with eight wins and a draw from ten games ensuring St Judes won Division 4 (South). The last game against Naomh Eanna was a rather controversial draw, which meant that Naomh Eanna and St Judes went through to JFL Division 4 All-County semi-finals against Beann Eadair and Clontarf respectively. The Evening Herald reported on the St Judes V Naomh Eanna game as follows - " The sharing of the two points was a fitting result to two excellent sides". St Judes lost in the semi-final on 15th October 1989 as did Naomh Eanna. Beann Eadair (3.08) beat Clontarf (0.08) in the Division 4 All-Dublin final on 12th November 1989.

The Junior B team were beaten in the B championship by St Annes on a scoreline of 1.05 to 2.06 on 16th April 1989.

AOB: On 4th November 1989 a "Championship Celebration Night" was held in the club to honour Junior hurlers and U16 footballers on their championship wins. The function was attended by Phil Markey (R.I.P) County Board Chairman, Danny Lynch PRO CLG and Crumlin/Dublin senior hurler Brian McMahon.

MEMORIES OF THE GROWING YEARS

The repeated shouts of "Ah Jaysus lads" from the tigerish Kerryman Seamus Clifford in several matches as he strove to bring a bit of cohesion to the defence. Seamus was a model defender with a ferocious will to win regardless of the significance of the game. Seamus was part of a tremendous St Judes half-back line with a variety of combinations involving Ger Tannam, Ger McSweeney, Brendan Coughlan, Tom Maguire, Denis Evoy, Brendan Gill, Patsy Kenneally, Cyril Loughlin, Paul McDermott, Ciaran Cribbs to name a few. The Judes half-back line was the backbone of the team and had a tremendous ability to break up opposition attacks with their no-nonsense hard tackling style and initiate quick counter attacks before the opposition regrouped.

The classic high-fielding of Kevin Clabby was a feature of many St Judes games over the above period. Kevin was a throwback to the catch and kick era and many players will particularly remember his performances against Declan Bolger of St Marks and Paul Bealin of St Kevins in important league games. Kevin played senior football with Longford. Seamus McCartin played an important part in Kevin's game where his long high kickouts dropping down into midfield were ideally suited to high fielders like Kevin. We will also remember Kevin Clabby's hand pass which came at you like an Exocet missile and was capable of causing severe internal injuries unless proper precautions were taken, namely to get out of the way. A multitude of training sessions failed to improve the hand pass to a level, which would bring it within VHI guidelines and we eventually gave up. Bert Smith was an ideal foil for Kevin at midfield with his good hands, intelligent passing and great linkup play between defence and attack. Bert was also our primary free-taker during most of this period and was capable of doubling up in any of the forward positions. Other midfield combinations included Michael Barrett, Ger Tannam, Cyril Loughlin, Patsy Kenneally, Liam Reilly, Donal Brennan, Cathal Travers, Conor Lehane, Mick Tobin to name a few.

Declan Clabby, in conjunction with Luke Mooney, was the foundation of the St Judes full-back line in the eighties and early nineties and rarely missed a game despite having to travel a big distance for most games. Declan had played U21 football with Longford in a Leinster final and would no doubt have played senior for Longford if he had remained in the county. Declan, Kevin and Frank were the three Clabby brothers from Forgney in Longford who gave tremendous service to St Judes over a long period. Declan Clabby, Kevin Clabby, Ciaran McGovern and Ger McSweeney were four of the long serving St Judes players who spanned the era from Junior thru Intermediate and into Senior football. Declan Clabby was an extremely dependable full-back with good hands, great strength in coming out with the ball and a long delivery out of defence.

Declan was usually partnered by Offallyman Luke Mooney in the left corner and either John Boyce or Eamonn Curran in the right corner to form a very solid full back line. Over the period a number of other fine players played in the full-back line including Frank Clabby, Mick O'Brien, Brendan Gill, Hugo Devine, John Brown, Cyril Loughlin, Patsy Nugent, Patsy Tyrrell, Tom Maguire etc.

Luke Mooney repeatedly appearing out of numerous melees in the square with the ball tucked safely under his arm was a feature of many St Judes matches in the eighties. Luke was an outstanding player who up to this time was the best corner back to play for the club in my experience. Some people will remember a particularly great game he had against Synge Street in a league game in March 1988, when he attracted a lot of close attention. After one robust challenge Luke finished up motionless on the deck. The only medical conditions recognised by our medical team, in those days, was "dead" or "alive" and indeed our prognosis in this area was often questioned by the injured party. We also had a little experience of nuclear attacks and radiation sickness from time spent in the Civil Defence in the sixties.

As a general rule if you were alive you played on and if you were dead then you were allowed some leeway provided you personally handed in a death certificate to the team manager before or during the game. We were fairly certain that Luke was not suffering from radiation sickness as we had not heard any loud explosions and whilst there was some evidence of hair loss, there was no sign of a mushroom shaped cloud so we eliminated this option fairly quickly. We were now down to two options, either dead or alive. A couple of groans from Luke seemed to indicate the latter, so more water was introduced. He eventually recovered and as he slowly arose he seemed to have difficulty in remembering his name or what he was doing in Dolphins Park – the absence of a lake not to mention the dolphins did not help us in trying to explain the circumstances to him. Having informed him that he was Jack O'Shea and he was really playing in Croke Park, Luke roared back into the action to play the veritable "stormer" for the remainder of the game. In retrospect we should probably have told him he was Robbie O'Malley as he might not have deserted his corner-back so often in his eagerness to join the attack.

We were tremendously lucky to have a number of outstanding forwards during this period. Declan McSweeney and Christy Kilcoyne formed a great partnership in the full-forward line and engineered some great goals not to mention a plethora of points. Bert Smith was the primary free taker during the above period and his scoring contribution from frees and play was usually significant. Michael Barrett and Ger Tannam were very similar players with their hard running, end-to-end football being one of the strong points of earlier St Judes teams before their emigration to Australia and Hong Kong respectively.

Though initially a bit wild on the shooting side they settled down to become very effective scorers. Jimmy Hanniffy of course was a brilliant scoregetter and leader in attack even though at the latter stages of his career when he played for St Judes. Ger Treacy was a great long distance point scorer and also a valuable free-taker. Liam Reilly was a particularly good goal scorer with a great ability to take on players but his career was unfortunately blighted with a knee injury, which eventually forced his early retirement from football.

1988 Captain Mick O'Brien accepts the Ó Broin Cup – (l-r): Tony Gilleran (Junior Board), Mrs Ó Broin, Mick O'Brien (captain).

Above: 1980 early Judes mentors – Back row (l-r): Jimmy O'Dwyer, Eamon Reilly, Noel Curran, Seamus Durkan, Donnchadh Lehane. Front: Des Brannigan, Frank McSweeney, Ernest Kenny, Joe Morrin, Mick Kavanagh.

Left: 1993 Kevin Clabby raises Intermediate Cup – (l-r): Phil Markey (RIP) Junior Board Chairman and Kevin Clabby (captain).

Other good forwards during this period were Danny Corbett, Don Lehane, Derek McGuckian, Ray Whelan, Joe Duffy, Cyril Loughlin, Ger Kenny and Brian McSweeney who contributed hugely to the many big scores run up by Judes teams in this period.

A feature of Dublin GAA from the seventies on was the great rivalry built up amongst a lot of the newer clubs who were formed in Dublin after the sixties and seventies. These included clubs like St Judes, St Olafs, St Marks, Ballyboden St Endas, St Kevins, Trinity Gaels, Ballyboden Wanderers, Naomh Mearnog, St Finnians (Swords), Lucan Sarsfields, St Sylvesters, St Peregrines, St Patricks, etc. These teams were mainly established in suburban areas with fast population growth. Games between these sides were particularly competitive as quite often they had come up together through junior ranks and all were very ambitious to progress up to senior football. These teams would eventually transform the landscape of Dublin football by moving up to senior level and putting it up to the more established clubs. It was reflected in quite a high standard of football during this period which meant of course that you really had to work hard to make progress up through the leagues.

The sight of Seamus McCartin cycling around the pitch in the middle of winter as part of his training programme was another rare sight. Seamus was a diligent trainer who rarely missed training sessions or matches. Having picked up a hamstring injury, which ruled out sprints, Seamus introduced a bicycle to the training pitch and proceeded to complete the requisite laps on the bike until an "accidental" shoulder deposited him on the ground as he was winding up for a sprint finish. The goalkeeper position in St Judes was generally manned by the long kicking Leitrim man with occasional appearances from John Brown and at a later stage Tony McGinley. The shouts of "Seamus's ball" for anything passing the half-way has kept many a Judes full-back line awake over the past few years. He was prone to the odd eccentric move including a propensity to solo across the goal or to come out for a ball that was thirty yards outside his jurisdiction. He startled many a corner back by suddenly appearing out of nowhere and taking both ball and corner forward into the the next parish and maybe giving the corner back a clip on the ear on his way back to goal to keep him on his toes. It was no surprise to see him appearing suddenly up in the forward line with mentors and defenders screaming at him to return to the goals. He once appeared in goals for the second half of a championship game against Caislean without his football boots due to a foot injury. The missing boots did not seem to affect his play and his bare-footed kickouts were landing effortlessly around the middle of the field. He was playing extremely well until late in the game when he rushed out for an incoming ball, lost his footing in the greasy conditions and the ball bounced over his head into the unguarded net. He was however another stalwart player for St Judes over a number of years with a fierce committment both to training and playing and an uncanny knack of stopping penalties mostly by psyching out the penalty taker.

Picking up two Cork lads at Newlands Cross on our way to playing a game at St Finians of Newcastle was another recollection from the period. We were short a few players and the hurleys on the bags of the two hitch hikers was a dead give away. We picked them up and after some polite conversation gently enquired would they be interested in a game of football before travelling on to "The Real Capital". They seemed keen enough which brought our team up to full strength and we gratefully dropped them back on the main road at the Poitin Still a couple of hours later to continue their journey. St Finians knew they were in for a battle when they saw the hurleys appearing on the sideline for a football game.

The tremendous roar of the St Judes supporters when we played our first Intermediate football game against Kilmacud Crokes in November 1988. For the record the three supporters were Ernest Kenny, Frank McSweeney, Ger Tannam's father and his dog and with all due respect to the dog he departed from the sideline very soon after the throw-in.

A number of "schmozzles" often involving either Christy Kilcoyne, Joe McDonnell or Seamus McCartin also come to mind. In one highly competitive game against local rivals Declan McSweeney was coming in for a lot of aggravation from the corner back. Christy Kilcoyne decided to take on the role of minder with severe repercussions for the corner-back who eventually had to be taken off with, in the words of Declan McSweeney, "His jersey looking like a butcher's apron".

The climax of the 1988 Millenium celebrations in St Judes were the ladies and gents over 35's Dublin V The Rest football games. The games were promoted locally as the Jackeens versus the Culchies to give a bit of edge to the proceedings – as if an edge was needed with the players lining up on either side. Training for both teams was confined to a slightly quicker sprint to the bar on the call of "Last Orders" over the last few weeks. A couple of players thought it was an ideal situation to settle a few old scores and set about the task with abandon. My own immediate starting opponent was Garrett Edge and I knew I had "the legs" of him when he attempted to remove my jersey after the first ball to come in our direction. Declan Feore's St Judes club notes reported the games as follows " Former Kerry minor Jim Coghlan made a big comeback for the Rest against Dublin last Sunday evening in Tymon. Frank Carty failed to stop John Gallen on his way through for a great Dublin goal, which was helped by a hip swivel from Bob Carty, causing Coghlan to buckle at the knee. This was the finale, which was preceded by the ladies football challenge starring Essie O'Gara and Sylvia O'Reilly, of the St Judes contribution to Templeogue's version of the Millenium". It was a miracle that Stephen Willoughby was the only participant who required hospital treatment after he was kneed in the back by Seán Conway. We should be grateful that no one was killed or seriously injured in either encounter as some of the exchanges were vigorous to say the least. It is no surprise that the event has not been repeated – not at least for another Millenium.

A variety of games up in Glencullen against Stars of Erin would have to go into the hall of fame as games to be remembered. The Glencullen pitch backed onto Johnny Fox's pub, which is reputed to be the highest pub in Ireland. The games in Glencullen were usually associated with terrible weather and ferocious matches or ferocious weather and terrible matches. Most games seemed to involve a combination of rain, gale force winds, freezing cold, injuries, sheep, fights, broken limbs, hot whiskies, and a rake of players being sent off. However we always seemed to come away with a win which bore testimony to the team's refusal to be intimidated. In one particularly tough encounter a row broke out in the square involving over a dozen players. In the bedlam and red mist that ensued, Christy Kilcoyne had the misfortune to mistime a right hook and hit the notorious Stars full-back who was a veritable man mountain in boots. The punch had little or no effect on the full-back other than to put him into a violent rage and he spent the remainder of the game seeking retribution. Christy in the meantime had voluntarily retired to the safer confines of the outfield to "shore up the midfield", as he explained afterwards to a rather sceptical dressing room, leaving the Stars full back patrolling the edge of the square like the demented polar bear in Dublin Zoo.

Cathal Dolan, Patsy Kenneally and a number of other players had to depart the battlefield in Glencullen with a variety of injuries from the popular broken nose to severe bruising of the ribs. On one of these occasions we had travelled to Glencullen with only fifteen players plus a genuinely injured Joe McDonnell. (As distinct from the sudden Sunday morning ailments developed by a number of the younger players when the appalling prospect of a Trip to the Stars confronted them on awaking). Joe McDonnell was umpiring at the lower end of the pitch when Cathal Dolan went off with a broken nose and other facial injuries received in an off the ball incident. We had no substitutes but Joe seemed very eager to get on the pitch and discarding his coat he came on for the departed injured player and promptly confronted the protagonist. The referee, sensing danger, quickly intervened and if our recollection is correct gave Joe three directives: (1) Calm down (2) Stop shouting and (3) Keep his hands to himself. Joe thought briefly about the options on offer and did not seem to find any of them attractive. He promptly decided to go for an option of his own, which was to give the "*@#$ing gurrier" a haymaker and promptly started another major "schmozzle" in which we all got involved. Joe of course got sent off thus shaving forty seconds off his existing club record of the shortest time on the pitch from one minute to about twenty seconds – a record I am sure is unlikely to be broken before the next Wicklow junior championship.

Other memories were the "As gaeilge" discussions, arguments, comments both on and off the field between Spiddal Gaeltacht players Patsy Kenneally, Eamonn and Michael Curran who played U21 and Junior football for St Judes during their student years in Dublin. Patsy Kenneally, Eamonn Curran, Michael Curran, Ger Tannam etc were part of a good tradition of UCD U21 players togging out for St Judes during this period.

My first Junior Board meeting in Belvedere place with Ernest Kenny showing me the ropes was another occasion not quickly forgotten. Ernest was the first St Judes delegate to the Junior Board and maintained this position for most of the first twenty five years of the club's history. It did not take long to establish that we were in the presence of the greatest bunch of wheeler-dealers this side of Tammany Hall. There is little doubt that as many games were won and lost in Belvedere Place as in O'Toole Park. It established in my mind once and for all the importance of clubs appointing progressive board delegates with a willingness to see the bigger picture. In any case I resolved never to appear in the venue again without a solicitor and a bodyguard. Chairing the Junior Board meetings was a virtually impossible task with the wisdom of Solomon, the escape tricks of Houdini and the cunning of Charlie Haughey being absolutely minimum requirements for the incumbent of that position. The pressure must have been intense, with all sorts of wheeler-dealing going on behind the scenes and phone calls rolling in at all times of the day and night. One of the tricks of the trade was a game called "winner takes all". The Junior Board like all other board relied primarily on referee's reports to give them the results of matches. Of course not all referees would submit reports – indeed not all referees would turn up for matches in the first place. In addition not all clubs sent delegates to the Junior Board every week particularly if their team was not in contention for honours or in danger of relegation. This scenario had all the ingredients of an "occasion of sin" or "daylight robbery". If the referee's report for a particular match was not available at the board meeting the Chairman/Secretary would put the question to the delegates: "Anyone know the result of the Saints v Sinners game?"

A short delay in responding from the Saints delegate enabled him to have a quick scan of the hall to establish the presence or otherwise of the Sinners delegate. If the delegate was not present and the Saints had lost the match by fifteen points then a tentative hand would be raised and a fairly non committal response would be given: "Saints won by three points, I think Mister Chairman"

The "I think" at the end of the response was crucial in case the Sinners delegate happened to be tying his shoe laces at the time the room was scanned and you failed to see him. A short delay, no further interruptions and you had two more hard earned points in the bag. The above is an example only and is not intended to represent actual clubs who would partake in such activities.

A variety of games during this period stand out for particular reasons. These could be grouped into categories which would include crucial games and unusual games.

CRUCIAL LEAGUE AND CUP GAMES

The games which earned promotion from Division 4 to Intermediate obviously stand out when you look back over this period as this was after all the whole purpose of the exercise. These would include the All County Division 3 Semi-Final game against Whitehall Colmcilles in October 1988 which we won by seventeen points followed by the All Dublin Division 3 Final against St Patricks in November 1988 which we won by ten points.

The All County Division 1 Semi-Final against Trinity Gaels, which we lost by two points was also a game which most players and mentors will recall. The two league games, which we narrowly lost in Division 1 to Postal Gaels and Guinness will also be recalled, if only that they were the only league losses from Division 4 to Intermediate.

Our first Intermediate league game against Kilmacud Crokes in Silverpark was a big game for the team but not apparently a big game for the club as we had no support. The games against local big rivals Ballyboden and Thomas Davis were also important particularly in setting down markers as we invariably beat them in the important games. Our June 1989 away win against St Marks in the Intermediate league was a benchmark game for us as we considered the Declan Bolger led Marks side to be one of the top Intermediate teams.

This should have been a home game for St Judes but we had no home pitches available as Tymon North is basically closed until issues over pitches have been resolved.

The O'Byrne Cup final victory over Cuala by thirteen points in O'Toole Park was also a big occasion for the club and particularly for manager Ernest Kenny and Donncadh Lehane. Some friendly matches particularly against outside Dublin teams like Emmetts Killoe Longford, St Marys Ardee, Two Mile House can also be recalled.

GAMES WHICH TOOK PLACE IN UNUSUAL CIRCUMSTANCES
Joxer arrives in Tymon
Date: 11/06/1988 Time: 7.30pm Venue: Tymon Competition: League Div. 4
Match: St Judes B (1-08) V Round Towers (0-03)

The Division 4 Junior league game between St Judes B and Round Towers was scheduled to take place at 7.30 pm on the June 1988 day that Ireland beat England 1-0 in the first round of the European Championship in Stuttgart. This was not in itself unusual, in fact the only surprise was that the County Board did not set the fixture to coincide with the Ireland-England game. A massive crowd watched the game (the soccer one) in the bar in St Judes clubhouse and of course celebrations on beating the old enemy continued well after the game. The celebrations were halted by the arrival of the Round Towers team in the car-park at 7.20 pm and only a couple of Judes players in the dressing room. Panic stations all round as whereas everyone knew about the fixture most of the players seemed to believe that Round Towers would not turn up – the day that was in it and all that.

A number of desperate phone calls from the mentors enquiring about the whereabouts of players yielded little or no response which was not surprising as most of them were up in the bar having a whale of a time. Finally a quick reconnaissance of the Judes bar established the severity of the situation with a big sing-song taking place and evidence of copious amounts of alcohol having been consumed. At least half of the players present were immediately eliminated from possible involvement in the game even as spectators as their legs were incapable of getting them to the pitch without the use of some additional assistance such as a stretcher, wheelchair or a motorised vehicle. A motley crew was eventually pulled together in the dressing room with some insisting on bringing their unfinished refreshments with them. A number of these were eliminated at the second cull having failed a fitness test which involved bouncing a ball on the floor of the dressing room and catching it either with or without a pint glass in the other hand.

If truth be told then a couple of them would have had difficulty in achieving this task even when stone cold sober as they proved on many subsequent occasions.

A final head count established that fourteen players would be in a position at least to walk unaided to the pitch even if a couple of them looked unlikely to be able to complete the task in the designated time which was five minutes max. A frantic search for the final piece of the jigsaw eventually uncovered the presence of John McGoldrick in the vicinity. John was an up and coming sports journalist in the Evening Herald at the time and even though he sometimes trained with St

Judes as a colleague of Brendan Gill, he apparently had only ever played once for the club in a cup match. He immediately agreed to take up the troublesome right-half forward position in front of Ciaran Nolan who was picked to play in the corner.

The game eventually started at 8 o'clock and it was immediately obvious that a number of the Round Towers players were not in any better shape than our own.

They had obviously also been on the sauce themselves earlier in the day. This gave Judes a tremendous fillip and they proceeded to give Towers a football lesson. The Judes defence was solid as a rock shandy with sterling performances from Patsy Tyrrell, Mick O'Brien, Denis Evoy (teetotaller) and John Brown. John Boyce and Ger Kenny ruled the skies at midfield and up front Brendan Gill and Ray Whelan gave a display of point scoring to which Towers had no answer. St Judes led by five points at the half-time whistle, which heralded the fastest sprint of the day to the ditch on Pitch #2 as the contestants proceeded to offload excess fuel. Judes went on to win the game by eight points on a scoreline of 1-8 to 0-3, with Denis Evoy the star performer, which proves the adage that alcohol and football are poor bedfellows.

John McGoldrick may also have established that sports journalism and football are unlikely soul mates as his right wing partnership with Ciaran Nolan failed to ignite the game.

St Judes defeated in thriller at Tymon North

Another game which springs to mind was the September 1989 clash between St Judes B and St Patricks B in a Murphy Cup game in Tymon. This was the oldest St Judes team to take the field in the club's history to that point. The following is the match report of this game:

Date: 13/09/1987 Time: 11.30am Venue: Tymon Competition: Murphy Cup

Match: St Judes B (0-1) V St Patricks B (1-8)

This was definitely the oldest team ever fielded by the club. A disastrous turnout with a number of regular players failing to show. It seems difficult to get commitment from some of the local younger players particularly in cup games. The B team is performing well in the league but the Murphy Cup turnouts have been disappointing despite some good cup wins. In any case we refused to give a walkover and went immediately for plan B.

We scoured the local highways and bye-ways and seduced a number of "senior citizens" to Tymon on the promise of sweets before the game and a pint afterwards. A few of the less trusting individuals refused credit and insisted on reversing the order of the inducements.

Great credit to Seán Conway, Denis Reid, Tommy Hartnett, Tommy Mulready, Don Lehane, Joe McDonnell amongst others for turning out in an assortment of gear from wellington boots to three piece suits.

We failed to locate Jim Coghlan, Donnacha Lehane, Paddy Russell or Tommy Bassett, which considerably weakened our hand. Jack Lernihan had a prior engagement with a dog and Ernest Kenny felt that the responsibilities of management were too onerous to allow him to tog out.

We dispensed with the warm up on the basis that it might have a detrimental effect on team performance and resorted instead to growling and menacing signals in the direction of the opposition, to no great effect as events transpired. At half time St Pats led by 1gl 4 points to no score and in the immortal words of Moss Keane we were lucky to have nil. Nevertheless a good spirited performance from St Judes despite woeful lack of punch up front – indeed if the performance of the forwards had been repeated outside the environs of Tymon the whole sextet would have been arrested for "loitering without intent". Tommy Hartnett, Joe McDonnell, Seán McBride and Denis Reid wreaked considerable damage down the centre but unfortunately the bulk of this damage was to the pitch itself and did not manifest itself on the scoreboard.

Seán Conway had a very solid game in goals and marshalled the full back line very well. Only a shortage of taxis prevented Ernest Kenny from moving Seán to midfield. Mick O'Brien played very well at full back but in fairness had youth on his side.

Tommy Mulready won some good ruck ball in the corner and left the pitch with his ears ringing from a string of instructions from Seán Conway who had taken an instant dislike to the cocky St Pats corner forward. Seán was only prevented from an assault and battery charge by a hamstring twinge and an uncooperative pair of wellington boots. The relatively youthful half-back line of Paul McDermott, Brian Kiely and Don Lehane played well and got good support from Brian McSweeney and Ger Kenny at midfield. Up front, well we have seen more movement in the local graveyard and an early injury to Ger McSweeney brought total gridlock to the area. Joe McDonnell broke yet another club record by starting and finishing the same match. Jim Coghlan and Donnchadh Lehane we believe opted for 11 o'clock Mass over a Junior B cup game in Tymon and no doubt will eventually reap their deserved reward but no prayers were said for them in Tymon. A rousing finish by St Judes yielded a deserved point but we were eventually unhinged by a lack of pace particularly on our left flank.

The following team took the field that day – the numbers in brackets were my crude performance marks out of ten for participants and on reflection were a tad on the generous side but we had to reward courage in the face of adversity:

Joe McDonnell (7)   Denis Reid (7)   Seán McBride (7)
Tommy Hartnett (7)   Eugene Loughlin (7)   Ger McSweeney (8) inj
          Brian McSweeney (8)   Ger Kenny (8)
Paul McDermott (8)   Brian Kiely (8)   Don Lehane (8)
Tommy Mulready (8)   Mick O'Brien (9)   Martin McCabe (7)
                     Seán Conway (8)
Subs: Who needs subs with that line up !

Shenanigans in Bushy Park

Another unusual game took place in October 1989 between St Judes B and
Naomh Eanna in a league play-off encounter. St Judes had scorched through this
league with eight wins and only one loss but still found themselves in a three way
tie with Geraldine Morans and Naomh Eanna to establish the two teams to go
through to the All Dublin County semi-finals.

Date: 01/10/1989 Time: 11.30am Venue: Bushy Park Competition: Div. 4
League. Match: St Judes B (2-6) V Naomh Eanna (2-6)

This was a crucial league match for both teams. A defeat for either team
would have resulted in a play-off for the losing team against Geraldine Morans
to clinch the final place in North/South All-Dublin county semi-finals/finals. The
winning team would go straight through to the county semi-finals. In the unlikely
event of a draw both St Judes and Naomh Eanna would go through to the semi-
finals at the expense of Geraldine Morans and of course this scenario proved very
attractive to certain individuals from both camps who shall have to remain
nameless in case of litigation.

The match was originally fixed for Tymon North at 3pm but in a late change
of plan the fixture was switched to Bushy Park at the earlier time of 11am. The
junior board were duly informed of the fixture change, which was apparently due
to a severe bout of bad weather in the Tymon area. The weather rendered all the
pitches in Tymon unplayable but fortunately this did not seem to effect the Bushy
Park pitches half a mile down the road. It proved impossible to contact the
designated match referee in time for the 11 o'clock start despite strenuous efforts
all round. A neutral referee was conveniently present at the game in a spectator
role and kindly agreed to referee the game in the absence of the nominated
official. The original match referee was finally contacted at a later stage to inform
him it was not necessary to travel for the evening fixture.

Needless to report the match ended in a draw after a less than pulsating
affair.

Both teams put up a brave struggle before finally settling for a draw. A few
representatives from Geraldine Morans arrived in Tymon for the 3 o'clock game

to run the rule over their expected play off opponents and were extremely disappointed to find the fixture had already been played and they were out of the competition. It will be an interesting Junior Board meeting next week. The following team took the pitch against Naomh Eanna:

Ger Kenny (2)	Don Lehane (1)	John Malone (1)
Shane Gallen (2)	Paddy Denver (1)	Ciaran McGovern (2)
Mick Tobin (2)		Barry McGovern (2)
Declan O'Reilly (0)	Pat Corcoran (2)	Stephen O'Connell (1)
Colm O'Brien (1)	Mick O'Brien (0)	Frank Clabby (0)
	John Brown (2)	

Man of the Match: Frank Clabby (0), Mick O'Brien (0) and Declan O'Reilly (0)

Battle of Glencullen

Date:19/10/1986 Time:3.30pm Venue:Glencullen Competition: Parsons Cup
Match: St Judes A (2-6) V Stars of Erin (0-5)

This may have been the Parson Cup but there was very little sign of any form of Christianity in most inhospitable conditions in Glencullen. I have no recollection of ever playing Stars of Erin other than in Glencullen. It seems very difficult to coax them out of their eyrie in the mountains. In fairness to St Judes we tried to be gracious visitors and went so far as to clear the sheep from the pitch before engaging in pleasantries. Our gesture was not reciprocated, as you will deduce from the following report. Excellent performance from an understrength St Judes team (Short 9 first choice players including Declan/Kevin Clabby, Cyril/Eugene Loughlin, Luke Mooney, John Brown, Ger Treacy and Eamonn Curran). This was a very physical game played in very cold, windy weather conditions.

St Judes played with the very strong wind in the first half and led by just seven points at half time, which on the face of it did not look sufficient considering the elements. The match in the interim had deteriorated from the normal tough encounter in Glencullen to what could only be described as a war zone. Patsy Kenneally had already departed the scene with a broken nose. The referee was about to send off a Judes player for the incident but grudgingly accepted that he may have made a mistake. Lets face it, we may not be saints but we do draw the line somewhere and hitting one of the last seminarians to enter Milltown was definitely out of bounds. The real culprit got away unpunished until he unfortunately ran into an unusually mistimed Seamus Clifford tackle which left him gingerly massaging his backside. Patsy Kenneally follows a noble tradition of broken limbs in Glencullen. Cathal Dolan was similarly hospitalised in our last game up here with another broken nose.

Patsy Kenneally was replaced by Don Lehane, who delayed proceedings by having to change from wellington boots into more suitable footwear – steel capped, hob nailed boots would have been most suitable in the circumstances but we had to do with a pair of aging football boots. He was promptly booked by the referee for time-wasting – the whole game had descended into farce !. A further three Stars of Erin players were sent off and Tom Walsh from St Judes was sent off for retaliation. The referee had completely lost control of the proceedings at this stage. He was reduced to a blubbering wreck and it was difficult to deduce whether it was the severe cold or the tough exchanges was having the most serious effect on him. In any case the combination of the two seemed to introduce a feeling of complete inadequacy to his being. His earlier piercing blasts on the whistle had now been reduced to a polite whimper and at any moment one expected him to merge seamlessly into the grazing sheep behind the lower goals whom he had already joined in spirit if not in body.

Meanwhile in between the disturbances there were periodic outbreaks of football. St Judes restricted Stars of Erin to a couple of points in the second half. Liam Reilly had an outstanding performance in attack in the first half (two goals) and in defence in the second half. The defence played generally well all through with good performances from Tom Maguire, Seamus Clifford and Dermot Clifford. Seamus McCartin played well in goals but had severe difficulty with the kickout in the second half due to the very strong winds. St Judes ran out winners by seven points. We will have to get these boys down to Tymon some day to see if they travel well. The win and a couple of pints in Johnny Fox's restored our spirits and we headed down the mountain to Tempelogue with Brendan Gill and Frank Clabby riding shotgun in case of any guerilla attacks. The team lined out as follows:

Tom Walsh (7)	Tommy Quinn (7)	Tony O'Donnell (7)
Christy Kilcoyne (8)	Liam Reilly (9)	Ger Kenny (8)
Patsy Kenneally (7)		Frank Clabby (8)
Seamus Clifford (8)	Brendan Gill (7)	Tom Maguire (8)
Dermot Clifford (8)	Dessie Coyle (8)	Patsy Tyrrell (8)
	Seamus McCartin (8)	

Subs: Don Lehane (7) for Patsy Kenneally (inj)

The Green

Jimmy O'Dwyer

ORWELL GREEN can at times be a bleak place. As the wind howls down from the mountain and the next fleeting shower comes, the lack of shelter and warmth becomes even more evident. However this dreary picture changes totally on Saturday mornings when the green is invaded by a drove of small indigenous natives who scurry to the centre of the park to listen to the elders issue instructions.

The younger of this tribe can be identified by the wearing of oversized socks which usually reach above the knee, where they meet long shorts. This combination makes one wonder if the tribe have any knees at all for they are rarely seen. The experienced elders are bedecked in an array of outfits that can hardly give credit to their tailors. However, they have one essential item – a whistle around their neck which helps keep the little tearaways in tow and also helps prevent a lemming-like exodus to the shops when the tasks of punt kicking or ground striking become all too demanding for their little bodies to execute.

Anthropologists and historians connected to the tribe's big nest on Wellington Lane – The Clubhouse, Cumann Luthchleas Gael Naomh Jude - attribute the word "nursery" to the activities on the Green on Saturday mornings. Colloquially it will be forever referred to as simply "The Green". This term conjures up many images. It does not just refer to location but to the many voluntary hours of coaching that have been enjoyed by all connected with the Green since its inception towards the last quarter of the last century.

It is a matter of no importance as to who instigated the Green. Credit in some quarters has been given to this writer and I am happy to take the some of the plaudits, but it was by no means a solo run. I have seen almost every present day mentor as a coach on the Green at some stage. When school holidays came, the late Joe Morrin kept the flame burning through involvement in the Summer project. Jim Coghlan was of magnificent help to him in those days.

But to my mind the Grand Panjandrum of the Green is Joe McDonnell. Many miserable mornings when I would leave the hills of Rushbrook and cycle down to the Green hoping that Joe would decide to call it off, I would be faced with a scene of military activity that ignored the weather and we just got on with it. By the end of the session even the grumpiest mentor would be in good spirits because of Joe's infectious humour. Big Mac became mentor, nurse, psychologist and even babysitter to many. His house became HQ for the Green and Joe became the Quartermaster. Through winter and summer he has soldiered on enthusing and caring for the young boys and girls of the parish and beyond, aided and supported by enthusiastic mentors, Padraig McManus, Seán Ward, Pat Brady, the redoubtable and cheerful Bobby Carty, Seán Breheny, Peter Ryan, John Halpin, Niall Graham and hordes of willing parents.

The Green has served the club well. Its purpose is to build a sense of community among the very young – children of five, sometimes even younger, often begin their life-long association with the GAA on the Green. Social skills, team spirit, sharing, acceptance of talents and shortcomings as well as mutual effort are deemed essential first steps in a growing community and these are consciously cultivated. These necessary skill abilities are carefully rehearsed through play and fun. And while many of our charges may never be crowned champions, the Green cultivates a life-long love of Gaelic games and a grounding in community spirit.

Last year a returned yank came in to my place of work to renew old acquaintances. He had been in the States for almost twenty years. He spoke at length about the fun he and his friends had on the Green on Saturday mornings and he was delighted to hear that it was still vibrant.

In recent times the Green has moved to the more posh setting of the All Weather pitch and this is no bad thing. However, Orwell Green won't be abandoned

The Green kept many a parent content, boasted many a child a star and challenged many a volunteer. Long may it flourish.

Cork coaching session – Brian Corcoran and Mark Landers with Jimmy O'Dwyer (Tipperary) in the background, with young players.

It's History Now: notes on Dublin's GAA story

Willie Nolan

S T JUDES Club was born on a rising tide as the glamour and romance of the golden days of the 'Dubs' in the 1970s rejuvenated the GAA in Dublin. Now a settled though still young club in the context of the long history of the Association, it is appropriate that it should mark a notable benchmark by casting an eye on the past twenty-five years. Memories and histories revolve around anniversaries of life and death but a GAA club should have an ongoing commitment towards preserving the paper record of its existence. As one of the people now endeavouring to research and write the history of the GAA in Dublin it is precisely the absence of publications, such as that now in preparation by St Judes, which has left so many unfilled gaps in the story. Not all Dublin GAA clubs responded to the call by the Association to produce a history for the centenary year in 1984. Thankfully many did and these, and other fine accounts of the origins, development, failures and successes of clubs, constitute an important record, not only of the role of sport but of the life of the people. Some examples of published histories may give a flavour of what has been done.

SOURCES

Neighbours Faughs published *One Hundred Years of Faughs Hurling* by Marcus de Búrca to celebrate its centenary in 1985. Faughs also maintains a club archive, something which every club should aspire to. In 1981 St Vincents, Marino celebrated its jubilee with *Cumann Iomáine agus Peile Naomh Uinsionn 1931-1981 Na Blianta Órga* compiled by Paddy Donnelly. In 1987 the *History of Civil Service Gaelic Football Club*, with many contributions by the indefatigable Tom Wolfe, was published. *Crumlin GAA: A History* written by hurler John Murphy came out in 1985; *An Cumann Parnell 1893-1993* marked the centenary of the famous northside club in 1993; *The St Maur's Gaelic Football Story*, which documents the engaging history of a north county club, was published in the 1960s; Brother DJ Vaughan did a marvellous job in recording the many clubs based through the years in the Inchicore district in *Liffey Gaels: A Century of Gaelic Games*, published in 1984.

In more recent times two books - *Scéal Oileán na hÉireann: A history of Erin's Isle GAA Club Finglas (2000)* by John Campbell and Liam Casey and *St Laurence O'Toole GAC 1901-2001* a centenary history by Jimmy Wren - have contributed enormously to our understanding of two very distinctive parts of north Dublin and the linkages between the GAA and economic, cultural and political themes. There are many other shorter accounts such as Carmel O'Brien's The Golden Jubilee of the Rolestown football team now Fingal Ravens 1920-1976 and we must not forget the publication by St Judes to mark the official opening of the clubhouse by Mick Loftus, president of the GAA.

Many clubs, as does the County Board, publish yearly handbooks and nearly all contribute club notes to newspapers and church information leaflets. A neighbour in the southwest county, St Annes, has managed to maintain a consistently high standard in its regular newsletter which is on file in the Public Library in Tallaght. Minute books constitute the most important single source for the history of any club and they should be retained safely in a central location. Dublin County Board Minutes have survived from 1908 and those for one other year (1897) are in the GAA Museum in Croke Park. Unfortunately, because so many clubs in Dublin had no permanent homes, minute books and other club records were kept by the secretary. When he/she passed on the records were either dispersed or destroyed and we are left with no information on clubs which have disappeared over the years. Newspapers are key sources and in many instances it is the journalists, who were eyewitnesses and not the players who were participants, whose words we must take that such and such happened during a particular game. Since the 1880s newspapers have taken sport and the GAA seriously, although many complaints were voiced by delegates at County Conventions concerning the lack of coverage. The most important early source is the weekly newspaper Sport, a subsidiary of the Freeman's Journal, which runs from 1885 to 1931 with a break in the 1920s. The Evening Herald and later its rival the Evening Press, until its demise, are particularly important for Dublin club competitions and team lists. On 5 September 1931 the Irish Press was launched and it is widely perceived to have marked the beginning of a new era in sports journalism with extended coverage of GAA games. Yet it would be unwise to ignore The Irish Times, which many GAA historians tend to do. From the 1920s on, probably the greatest GAA commentator of all time, PD Mehigan, wrote a GAA column for the Times under the pseudonym Pat'O. Because the Times was more widely sold in Dublin than, for example, Tipperary at the time there is good coverage of Dublin GAA affairs. Mehigan, who played hurling with London and Cork, his native county, had a keen appreciation of the nuances of hurling and football apart from a writing style which still conveys the heat of battles long forgotten. The GAA made a number of attempts to produce a regular journal devoted to gaelic games but never managed to maintain continuity. An Caman published in the 1930s faltered as did the excellent Gaelic Weekly/Gaelic

Sportsman brought out in the 1950s. The Association usually subsidised these newspapers rather than being responsible for their production. The Gaelic Weekly had a column, from Dublin and Vincents footballer Jim Crowley, which gave good insights on a decade from which many date the rise of support for Dublin football teams.

POPULATION, PARISH AND SCHOOL

In 1881 the last census taken before the foundation of the GAA at Thurles in November 1884 recorded the population of County Dublin as 419,000. One hundred and fifteen years later (1999) the numbers living in the county reached 1,058,300 people. When we note that there were 636,200 in the county in 1946 and 852,200 living in the same space in 1971 it is obvious that there has been major changes in both population numbers and the landscape of the county in the period between 1961 and 2001. Such change can be highlighted by the response of the Catholic Church in creating new parishes to cater for what was, nominally at any rate, a Catholic population. In 1935, Dublin had divided into 35 parishes. Today (2003) that number is 168. Fifty-three new parishes were created in the 1970-'80 decade including the parish of Willington dedicated to St Jude. Many of our neighbouring parishes, such as Greenhills, Firhouse, Castleview, Ballyboden, Kilnamanagh and Knocklyon were constituted in the same period. It would be misleading to think that every new Catholic parish fostered a GAA club. Indeed the total number of affiliated clubs in the county in 2000 was 82 whereas there are 168 parishes.

Associated with the parish structure since the beginning of the National School system in the 1830s has been the school. Sometimes, as in the parish of St Jude, the school and church are located side by side. The early Dublin clubs were largely based on adult teams but from the 1900s onwards the connection between the school and the club became important. In 1901, for example, the St Laurence O'Toole club was founded in the Christian Brothers School in Seville Place. Based on the school and the inspiration of teachers such as Frank Cahill the club prospered and provided the material for the successful Dublin teams of the 1920s. The foundation of the Primary Schools League in 1928 formalised juvenile competitions and again linked schools to adult clubs. St Vincents founded in 1931 was drawn from the boys of Scoil Mhuire, Marino and then linked into St Josephs CBS, O'Connell Schools(until this school founded its own club in 1950) and Árd Scoil Rís at second level. Crumlin CBS, closer to home, brought the players to St Columbas and Dublin championship victory in 1956. Common denominators in all of these cases are the Christian Brothers and the lay primary teachers. Dublin's Christian Brothers were drawn from the hurling counties of the south-indeed in its early days St Vincents was mainly a hurling club. The Christian Brothers have almost disappeared and it is the work of lay primary teachers which provides the bedrock for gaelic games in Dublin. St Judes has benefited from its association with Bishop Galvin NS. Players have graduated through the primary leagues and teachers, such as principal Jimmy O'Dwyer, Seán Breheny and Peter Lucey, have rendered great service to school, club and county. The loss of the Christian Brothers has fragmented the chain which linked primary and secondary schools and is perhaps the single most important reason for the decline of hurling standards in the county.

BEGINNINGS

When the Dublin County Board met for the first time on 12 December 1886 delegates from 26 clubs attended and the first county championship in 1887 had fifteen clubs in football and four in hurling. Football has always been the more popular game in Dublin, indicating that it may have stronger roots than hurling in the county. The evidence for either game in the Templeogue district is scant. A club known as Harps of Erin, Templeogue was one of 120 clubs affiliated in 1888 but we have no idea where it was located in the district. In his reminiscences published in 1943 under the title *Malachi Horan Remembers* the Killinarden man has no reference to Gaelic games even though he does refer to other athletic pursuits. Templeogue and adjoining Tymon was villa and big farm country, not always nurturing environments for Gaelic games.

Two major controversies almost destroyed the GAA in County Dublin in the 1890s. The revelation that Charles Stewart Parnell, one of the three patrons of the GAA, leader of the Irish Party at Westminster, was having an affair with Kitty O'Shea, whom he subsequently married, caused mayhem in Irish politics. Archbishop Croke and his fellow bishops published their public disapproval of Parnell but the GAA held firm in its support for the beleaguered leader. After Parnell's premature death, in October 1891, his subsequent funeral was attended by thousands of Dublin GAA members marching in the cortege to Glasnevin. Perhaps because of the Parnell controversy, it was not until the twentieth century that the Catholic Church, through the Christian Brothers and some parochial clergy, became actively involved in promoting the GAA. Indeed in contrast to other counties, clergy of the Dublin archdiocese have never held key positions such as chairpersons of the Dublin County Board. Neither did many clubs in Dublin in the early years carry parish names: most of them commemorated people or events in nationalist history. The second controversy related to the election of Michael Cusack as secretary of the County Board in 1893. Cusack, by now sidelined by the Association he founded, had, according to his opponents, rigged the election. It took outside intervention to restore an uneasy peace. Both controversies impacted upon the young organisation as the number of affiliated clubs plunged to a mere 35 in 1896.

THE 1920S

Dublin GAA has always overcome adversity and a number of positive occurrences brought new members and vitality. The Gaelic League founded in 1893 to promote the Irish language and Irish culture brought many young and articulate people to the forefront of Irish cultural organisations including the GAA. The games, hurling in particular, became badges of nationality and were regarded as central in the de-Anglicisation of Ireland. Sinn Féin established in 1908 by Arthur Griffith set about establishing a parallel administration to that of Dublin Castle and the GAA clubs gave it a basis on which to operate. Dublin County Board was fortunate in attracting administrators of high calibre such as Dan McCarthy , a youthful Harry Boland and Tipperary man, Andy Harty. Harty stood in for Boland when political business called him from the chair and the Faughs clubman as County Board chairman brought the GAA safely through the stormy years of the 1920s. McCarthy a native of Dolphin's Barn, was a journalist with the United Irishman. He was chairman of the Leinster Council and in 1923 became the first, and since then the only, Dublin born President of the GAA. McCarthy was director of elections for Sinn Féin in 1918 and a Cumann na Gaedheal TD in the Dáil. He retired from politics in 1924.

The games survived the cataclysmic events of the Easter Rising, the War of Independence and the Civil War. Perhaps the most dramatic occurrence in the long history of the GAA in Dublin was the shooting dead of thirteen people at a football match between Tipperary and Dublin on 20 November 1920 in Croke Park. The identity of those killed included a cross-section of the GAA supporters in Dublin at the time. Although the bitterness engendered by the Civil War persisted to recent times the GAA survived relatively unscathed. Its greatest loss was the deaths of Harry Boland (I August 1922) and Michael Collins (21 August 1922). Boland was chairman and then president of the Dublin County Board; Collins believed in all the ideals of the GAA. There are poignant photographs of the two friends attending games in Croke Park in the summer of 1921. The All Ireland final of 1923 played in September 1924 between the great O'Toole's Dublin selection and Kerry is seen by many as part of a healing process to which the GAA contributed a major part. Kerry had suffered greatly during the Civil War and many of its key players were interned.

The records tell us that a team known as Gavan Duffy's played at Riversdale, Templeogue in the late 1880s. Terenure Sarsfields, subsequently St Josephs, were associated with the tram depot in the village. Todd Andrews in his autobiography *Dublin made me* (1979), recalls playing for them but he soon abandoned Gaelic games for soccer in 1918. Andrews had a poor opinion of the art of Gaelic football. 'In my view' he wrote, 'three skills only were required for playing Gaelic football: a capacity to field a ball, ability to kick it high and hard in the direction of goal and at least elementary boxing skills' (p.113). The 1900 'home' All Irelands were played in Terenure. Tipperary and Galway featured in the hurling and football matches played on the same day. It is presumed that they took place in what is now the VEC grounds on Templeogue Road but some maintain that the pitch was on Fortfield Road close to the KCR. A club named Seán Doyles, in honour of Seán Doyle from Inchicore who was shot dead at Kilmashogue Mountain in September 1920 in an engagement with the Auxiliaries, was founded in Templeogue in the 1920s. It survived until the early 1940s but we only have scattered accounts of games it played at minor and junior grades. In the 1930s a club known as the Wolfe Tones was based in Firhouse with its headquarters at Delaney's pub. The team won the Junior Football Championship in 1938 and had a couple of seasons in senior ranks before fading from the scene.

GAMES

Two accounts, one referring to a junior Leinster Championship football game in 1912 and the other to the All Ireland final of 1917, may help to highlight the hardships faced by players in the early years of the GAA. In late January 1912 Dublin's junior footballers had to travel to Wexford to play the local team. Thomas Davis FC. Tallaght, as junior champions, had the selection of the team and their spokesman told a newspaper reporter of the difficulties their players had. 'Eight [players] will have to rise at 3.30am, do some two hours work, and then travel nine miles to get to town in time for the train'. The train journey to Wexford took five hours and when the Dublin team arrived on a miserable January day they found the pitch unplayable. Yet they went ahead having decided to 'play with the tide' if they won the toss.

Tommy Moore, Faughs, who played on the Collegians(afterwards UCD) selected team who beat Tipperary in the 1917 All Ireland hurling final gave the following account of his All- Ireland final day:

'The match was played in the middle of the day at twelve-o-clock and don't forget that I was working in the bar business and had to be back at work at half-past-one. I was staying in digs at the time and after I had my breakfast about 8.30 I went to Mass and then walked to Jones' Road where the match was being played. We took the field at 12 o'clock and came off winners after as tough and hard a game as ever you looked at. When you played against those Tipperary fellows you knew all about it. Seasoned campaigners every one, and as hard as the anvils they hooped their hurleys on. I played on Jack Power at right-half-forward. That was always my position. One of the vital scores of the match, a sizzling goal came from Brendan Considine who came on for us instead of Hugh Burke. Well, the final whistle saw us All Ireland champions and saw me and a lot of the lads with the marks of battle fresh on us. Then we made a dash for the dressing room tore into our clothes and away helter skelter to our jobs. I had eaten my breakfast at 8.30 that morning and all I had between that and seven o'clock was a drink of water. These were tough times, tough games and tough men that played them.

Dublin were successful in both hurling and football in the 1920s. The hurling team captured the All-Ireland crown in 1920, 1924 and 1927. Dublin footballers won All-Irelands in 1921, 1922 and 1923, It was not until the 1970s that the winning of three titles in one decade was again accomplished. Indeed by 1923 Dublin had 14 of its 2003 total of 22 titles in football and 3 of its 6 titles in hurling. Critics regard the 1920s O'Toole selection, featuring the McDonnell brothers, the Synotts, Norris, O'Reilly and Carey, as capable of matching Dublin teams of the 1950s and 1970s. PD Mehigan believed that 'the fifteen representing Dublin are the best I have ever seen'. He was referring to the Garda hurling team of 1927 who beat Cork in the All Ireland of that year. It was in effect an Ireland team with Tommy Daly and Fowler McInerney (both Clare), Mick Gill (Galway), Garrett Howard (Limerick), Matty Power (Kilkenny) and Dinny O'Neill (Laois) the stars. Yet Dublin were to win only one more senior hurling All Ireland - in 1938 - for the remainder of the century. Apart from Rule 27 (the Ban), the rule which caused most problems in Dublin was the so called 'declaration rule' introduced in 1925. This allowed players residing in Dublin to play club competitions there, but to play inter-county for their native county. The declaration on an official form had to be lodged with the general secretary before the last day of February. Players could play for Dublin in the League and then play for their home county in the Championship. This rule and other factors lead to the break-up of the Garda team and caused much debate at many Dublin Conventions.

St Judes GAA Club inherits a long tradition.

Siopa Naomh Jude

Mary Joyce

IT WAS during Summer 1995 at the invitation of Joan Molamphy that Rita Gallagher and I became involved in setting up SIOPA NAOMH JUDE. We went in search of appropriate premises and, low and behold, the lease on container No.1 was available. After some deliberation we realised this was the best we were going to get so we signed up. We hastily drafted in shop fitters "Gallagher and O'Dowd" (Jamsie has since migrated to Tralee).

Within two weeks shelves were fitted, electricity was laid on and we were ready for business. "O'Neills Sports" promptly dispatched tracksuits, shorts and socks. Tom Fitz supplied hurleys and helmets. We advertised through the local primary schools and in our club notes. On the 7th October 1995 the shiny blue ribbon (supplied by Rita) was cut by Jimmy O Dwyer and Paddy Russell.

Our takings on the first day were £208 and by Christmas everyone knew where the shop was. We struggled in the container for three years, freezing in the winter and sweltering in the summer. Thankfully we were re-accommodated in the main club building in 1998 on completion of the club extension. Rita had to retire due to her dedication to the Community Games and Áine Ní Shuibhne stepped into the breach. Siopa is now very much a focal point for club members on Saturday and Sunday mornings. We have greatly expanded our stock and our takings often exceed €1,000 over a weekend.

Míle Buíochas d'ár gcuistiméirí go léir - ar aghaidh linn

Official opening of shop in portacabin, 1995 – (l-r): Bernie Gallagher, Jimmy O'Dwyer, Mary Joyce and Paddy Russell.

25 caʀð game

Neil Doyle

THE FIRST fund-raising and longest running social activity in St Judes is the weekly 25 card game. This is held every Thursday night all year round in the back lounge. The game started in the early 1980s in Bishop Galvin School and after some time moved to St MacDaras. After a short sojourn in the Spawell it settled in its present home when the new clubhouse was built in 1987, first in the Members' Lounge and since 1998 in the Back Lounge.

For the dedicated band of 25 players the week would not be complete without the Thursday night game. It is a very enjoyable social occasion and at very modest cost. The game has been the avenue for a number of social members into the Club. The card players provide a link to other 25 games in the area such as Cheeverstown, Ballyboden St Endas and Harolds Cross. From time to time special games with expanded attendance take place in aid of various charitable causes. A number of successful Poker Classics have also been held. A highlight of the year is the annual pre-Christmas game which always draws a bumper attendance. What other show in town can boast a prize (bottle of wine) for everyone in the audience!

In recent years the card players have spread their wings and a very active Bridge Club is now based in St Judes.

Because of its earliest origins the 25 card game enjoys a certain sentimental niche in the history of the Club, particularly among the older founding members. Long may it continue, together with the Bridge Club, as an essential and enjoyable dimension of the social scene in St Judes.

Card players – (l-r): Finbarr Murphy, Ann Mullan, Eileen Lyons and Maura O'Keeffe.

Cumann Bridge Naomh Jude
1998-2003

Eoin Heraty

WHEN the new lounge was opened a call went out to all members to consider ideas that would best utilise the magnificent facilities available. Finbarr Murphy, an ardent bridge player, came up with the wonderful idea of forming a Bridge Club. He felt that Monday nights were quiet in the club and would be ideal to play cards and the fresh activity would generate much needed funds to boost the turnover of the club. He sourced a number of interested parties to recruit new people with an interest in learning to play bridge. He offered his knowledge and experience of the game to tutor all those who were interested. He exchanged his idea with that great octogenarian Jack O'Donoghue who agreed to assist him and offered his services as Treasurer, a position he held for two years. Finbarr was elected the first President of the Club and Ann Marie Tierney was elected Secretary. The committee consisted of Eoin Heraty, Eileen Lyons, Gerry Hurley, Marian Mahon, Alicia Sweeney.

Finbarr started the first class in March 1998. There was a tremendous interest and Finbarr really enjoyed bringing his pupils through their paces. A small number found the going difficult but the vast majority stayed with it resulting in the formation of the backbone of a very vibrant, thriving, enthusiastic and innovative new club. The membership has now grown to around 40 members and about 10 visitors who call from time to time. Unfortunately we have lost Eileen Levins, Peggy Smythe and Eamonn Martin to the ravages of time. Go nDéana Dia trócaire ar a n-anamacha go léir.

In 1999 the club successfully obtained sponsorship from Hibernian Insurance and very successfully launched an annual tournament for beginners. All other grades of players were catered for and the event is now very firmly fixed into the calendar of the Bridge Association. A charity event is also run along the same lines and the spread of food provided after these events is legendary. A special "Thank you" to all the ladies for the exceptional effort in providing the food and the men in assisting with the tables and chairs. A special thanks, also, to Michael Hartnett who is always available to move and return the furniture from the Bridge Centre. We must also give special mention to the Competition monitor, Seán Treanor.

We host a number of club nights such as the Presidents Prize, Christmas party, Jack O'Donoghues party and the Table quiz. My thanks to our Quizmaster

Gerry Hurley. After these events the parties are legendary and have unearthed brilliantly talented people. One would go a long way to find a better group- talent, enthusiasm and effort abound. Beannacht Dé orthu go léir.

The Bridge Club Members are very proactive and have a powerful history of fundraising for the Club and local charities. To date the bridge club have raised in excess of €12,000 for the direct benefit of the GAA Club and in excess of €7,000 for charities such as the St Vincent de Paul, Cheeverstown, The Hospice Harolds Cross and the Special Olympics. This is a superb achievement, achieved through the generosity and good will of our members who constantly supply spot prizes for the raffles held on the Gala and charity fundraising nights.

The club continues to grow and prosper. We owe a debt of gratitude to our tutors over the years namely Finbarr Murphy, Maura O'Keeffe and Seamus Dowling and our hard working tournament Director Jennifer Cullen who keeps a watchful eye on proceedings every Monday night. Kathleen Feehily ensures all the members get a nice cup of tea and coffee and an ample supply of chocolate biscuits for the hard working Secretary!! We welcome visitors and guarantee them a game if they are in attendance by 8pm. The confidence and experience of our players are progressing extremely well and we visit other clubs from time to time. We have entered teams in the Fanagan League over the past three years and have improved on our overall rating each year. Who knows- we may well win it very soon. Special thanks to all those participating.

Our biggest success to date is a carefree and happy bridge club and long may it continue to grow.

Year	President	Secretary	Treasurer
1998	Finbarr Murphy	Ann Marie Tierney	Jack O'Donoghue
1999	Eoin Heraty	Marian Mahon	Jack O'Donoghue
2000	Marian Mahon	Eoin Heraty	Eileen Lyons
2001	Declan Feore	Eoin Heraty	Eileen Lyons
2002	Declan Feore	Eoin Heraty	Eileen Lyons
2003	Eoin Heraty	Martin Molamphy	Alicia Sweeney

To Jack O'Donoghue

TO JACK O'DONOGHUE – On the occasion of his 80th birthday celebration at Cumann Bridge Naomh Jude (CLG). Monday 14th January 2002.

With deep affection and recollection
His dreams in fancy go back to times,
When a child played gaily and wandered daily,
And o'er his city rang Shandon's chimes.

Oh! He played and sported at games assorted
Beneath the elms of the Mardyke grand,
And on Grand Parade where the gentry strayed,
He marched behind the buttery band.

At the butter market when gold was carted
From western roads and from far flung farms,
He saw the wheeling and loved the dealing,
And learned the ways of the traders' charms.

No middling scholar when taught by collar,
His learning earned him a little fame,
So civil servant, quick and observant,
Be-collared and tied he soon became.

Now stones were thrown in waters flowin'
And if they sank 'neath the river Lee,
That was an omen to go to Dublin,
And a wider view of life to see.

In Baile Atha Cliath where fliúrseach bia
And grander living became his norm,
He worked in sleeved shirt with future Taoiseach
And learned to listen and study form.

A task to ponder caused him to wander
Down Shannon side to vintner's joint,
When affairs concealing became revealing
He lowered the price of the Limerick pint.

Now agonistic and patronistic,
He became what once he could not guess,
As liquidator and legislator,
He cleaned up many a monied mess.

Though oft conceited when sometimes feted
By close connections in church and state,
'Though they be grander he will not pander
To mitre, minister or to mate.

He's now reached eighty and maybe weighty,
Still memory won't forget those hours,
With the friends of youth, though a few uncouth,
On mossy banks and in happy bowers.

When young love's dream had ways to scheme,
And girls met boys in the lanes to sing,
Then brown haired Bridget on her third left digit
Was wearing a golden wedding ring.

Oft they pressed wild daisy and life was aisy,
As gold sun sank 'er the river Lee,
And they raised a brood of which Jack is proud,
And pride's in his eye for all to see.

So let's drink a toast, for it is our boast
To know a man who enriched our lives,
It is our anthem that fate will grant him,
The mildest winter and soft demise.

Seamus Dowling (wordsmith).

With due acknowledgement to certain songs and ballads, the influence of which you will recognise.

St Judes GAA Golfing Society

A BRIEF HISTORY by Michael Fortune

IT WAS in the area now known as the 'Confession Box' that the Golfing Society was born. After weeks of chatting and planning, the 'founding eight' consumed gallons of Arthur's Brew as they drew up the articles for the new body. While golf was the number one priority, right from the start the new committee placed the emphasis on fun. And what fun has been had by all in the ten years of its existence!

The first Committee was selected that night late in 1993 and Tony Gilleran was nominated to be the inaugural Captain with Tommy Hickey as his right hand man, the Secretary. Not surprising, the banker Eoin Heraty became Treasurer and JP Leahy the Handicap Secretary. Liam Larkin was named Vice Captain while the three-strong committee comprised of Mick Hartnett, Colum Grogan and Michael Fortune.

After a few months of intense planning, the calendar for 1994 was announced on February 16th and the honour of staging the first outing fell to Castlewarden. Liam Larkin came up with the sponsorship from Gouldings and has remained the sponsor for the first outing of the year ever since. My garden spade is a lasting testament to the sponsorship!

For the record, Oliver O'Connor won that inaugural outing from Tom Fitzpatrick and Noel Lyons while the class winners were John Boyce, Tony Gilleran and Tommy Hickey.

Captain Gilleran brought us to Stackstown for the first Captain's Day, sponsored as ever by Mick Hartnett. And it was JP Leahy who landed the prize from Mick O'Boyle and Noel Lyons.

The first Away Trip was to the West Park Hotel, known now as the Shannon Oakes Hotel, where the all-in rate for Golf, Evening Meal and B&B was a massive £35. By now the Society was on a very sound footing and the first AGM was staged following the Bodenstown outing on 21st October, 1994. Tommy Hickey reported that a balance of £675 was being carried into 1995. Liam Larkin introduced Colum Grogan as his Vice Captain.

Since then the society has prospered. The first Classic was staged at St Margarets on 27th August, 1997. It was a splendid success and raised a huge sum for the club. The Classic has now become part and parcel of the club year and has generated substantial and much needed finance for the club.

In recent years the Society has grown significantly with the limit on the number of members lifted. Nowadays it is a case of getting your name on the timesheet early - or else you could be too late. For the first time this year there was a President's Day and it has now joined the Captain's Day, the Classic and the Away Trip to Portumna as the great social happenings of the year.

Of particular pleasure to the 'founding fathers' is the number of young members who have joined the Society and derive great pleasure from their involvement. It has proved to those original doubters that the Golfing Society is very much a benefit to the Club. Not alone does it contribute handsomely in a financial manner but it also plays a very vital social role in the life of St Judes GAA Club.

The 2003 Captain is Martin McCabe who took over from Peter Coates at the 2002 AGM. Stepping forward in November to captain the good ship will be Michael O'Boyle.

Golf Society Captains – Back row (l-r): Michael Fortune (1999), Eoin Heraty (2001), Mick hartnett (2000), Tommy Hickey (1998), Peter Coates (2002). Front: Tony Gilleran (1994), Liam Larkin (1995), Martin McCabe (2003), Colum Grogan (1996), J.P. Leahy (1997).

Irish music classes

Tommy Hartnett

IN 1992 after making enquiries regarding interest we set up Irish music classes for all age groups. The venue for these classes was the committee room and dressing rooms of the clubhouse. We asked an excellent teacher Mary O'Halloran to take the classes and she agreed to do so. The classes ran for 18 months until the summer of 1993. The classes were once a week and the instruments taught were Tin Whistle, Fiddle, Accordion and Banjo. At the height of the classes we had approximately 25 pupils. In December of 1992 we held a concert for parents at which all the pupils played and this was a great success. After 18 months the music classes stopped. At the time the classes finished there were several players accomplished at playing instruments. These included: Tin Whistle – Michael Hartnett, Gerard Hartnett, Bart Lehane, Greg Lehane, Donal Ward, Maeve Ward, Joseph Bermingham, Conor Delaney, Liam Lyons, Aoife Hurley, Fergal Hurley, Kevin Coughlan, Michael Hanahoe, Donagh O'Dwyer, Andrea Hartnett, Jennifer Hartnett. Fiddle – Ross Mac Mathuna, Andrea Hartnett. Accordion – Micheál Lyons

Music session with Scoil Naithi at St Judes during Sevens tournament.

CLUB NEWS LETTER

The first news letter was produced by Tommy Hartnett, Betty Collard, Killian McCaffrey and Joe Mc Donnell in December 1987. This newsletter was delivered to the whole parish to introduce the club and to give details of some of the teams and times for training, meetings, and bar opening. Two further issues gave details and update on the teams and match reports and again were delivered to all houses in the parish the last issue being in March 1988.

The newsletter was revived again in 1990 with club PRO Jimmy O'Dwyer as editor and with the help from Joe Mc Donnell and again lasted for three issues. This newsletter gave reports on teams and activities. It gave details of upcoming events and had a quiz corner and tips on football and hurling. The newsletter came equipped with photographs and was called the "CROSS BAR".

THE NIGHT WE WENT TO THE DOGS!

Saturday, June 8 ... It's getting on towards 9.45pm and Paddy Nolan strides up the hallowed turf at Shelbourne Park. Is he going to do a sprint up the track, we wonder? No, realisation dawns, he is simply there to hand over the trophy for the Nolan Kitchens 525. The name of the winner, Ardfert Mick, is firmly etched in Paddy's mind.

But then there were other strange sightings on the Shelbourne track that night. Donnachadh Ó Liatháin strode out impressively along with Tommy Hartnett and Tipperary's own Jimmy O'Dwyer. an eyecatching workout, the spies suggest they could do a nifty run for the 525 yards.

Eileen Hartnett handed over the Tolmac Trophy and husband Mick was even seen to be holding a dog's lead. Upstairs in Room 4, Eoin Heraty was proving evasive in his role as "Mine Hoste".

Yes, it was a great night and St Judes "Night at the Dogs" proved to be a roaring success. But word has it that Conway and Carty still haven't mastered the art of backing winners! As for the Karaoke, Tobin was surely the star performer.

St Judes held a race night at Shelbourne Park on June 8th, 1991 and it was a marvellous success. Feature race of the night was the Friends Of St Judes Open 525 and it was won by a dog called Ardfert Mick who a few months later went on to win the Irish Derby.

Our picture shows club chairman Donnchadh O'Liathain presenting the trophy to Noel Clifford while Joe O'Reilly is holding the winner. Also included are PRO Jimmy O'Dwyer and Secretary Tommy Hartnett.

Incidentally, the club ran a Buster competition on the race and the £1,500 prize was won by Eddie Brassil.

Hillwalking and Rambling in the Wicklows

Declan Doyle

W HEN I climbed my first hill almost 25 years ago little did I know the profound influence it would have on me in the years ahead. Since that first ascent of Kippure and surrounding hills I have become almost addicted to this most rewarding pastime. My treks have taken me to almost all peaks and hills in Ireland and to the Rockies in Colorado. Although I have trekked a number of those hills many times, each walk has thrown up new experiences and challenges. In this short article I will attempt to give a brief walkthrough of some of the trails, which I have traversed most often with my good neighbour and friend Willie Nolan.

Less than 30 minutes drive from St Judes clubhouse lies one of our great natural treasures – the Wicklow Hills. They are the largest area of uplands in Ireland and shaped like a great spine they divide the Garden County in half. It is a vast reservoir of mountains, glens and lakes, a place of stunning beauty. The gateway to this walkers' paradise is located at the Ballinscorney gap, just a short distance 0.4km beyond the golf club. Taking a left turn at the monument we head for Kilbride military camp, which nestles in a great amphitheatre at the slopes of SeeFingan. This is a great walking trail for the beginner. Once you have ascended the gently sloping track to the left of the camp you are on a ridge, which will take you to the summit of Seahan mountain where you will find the first of three megalithic tombs on this walk. From there we head South along the ridge on an eroded path along the county boundary to the summit of SeeFingan and the second buriel chamber. Dropping to a nearby shallow col to the west we soon reach the heathery slopes of Seefin (the seat of Finn) which boasts by far the most impressive cairn.

It was to this very trail yours truly led the U21 hurlers and mentors for a post Christmas constitutional in early January 2002. Mentor Declan Feore had approached me some weeks before Christmas to organise a trek – "not a training session" said Declan "but more a bonding exercise". Along with other mentors Garrett Edge and Donnie Cummins we were joined by club President Jack Lernihan. Jack assured me he would have no difficulty in staying the pace. He was well used to walking. Didn't he bring "Bouncer" for walks almost every day around Tymon. He said, he had also got new runners (plimsolls, in fact). I said nothing. We told all the lads to bring suitable refreshments.

Needless to say they did, but not quite the kind we had in mind! We travelled by coach to the foot of Seefin to begin our ascent. It was a vigorous and challenging climb. The tea and sandwiches were scoffed, when we took a break at the summit. "Do we go down now?" asked one of the players. I pointed towards SeaFingan, our next peak. Feigned shock. Manfully the lads made the ascent. Jack was seen taking little breaks. Was he wilting? Garrett was encouraging him. I saw someone giving him a little sustenance.

Dusk was upon us as we crossed Seahan on our descent. The lads and mentors defied the winds, which were now rising, with tribal war cries of "Up the Rebels"!. "Come on Tipp"! "Up de Dubs"!

When we made our descent – all without exception dirty, wet and tired – we rested by the roadside, awaiting our coach. One of the elder lemons produced a brandy flask and we elders drank from it with relish. The young lads had a can. I think the day turned out to be a memorable and enjoyable one and was certainly a great "bonding experience" for everyone involved.

As you stand on the summit of Seefin spread out in front we can see Kippure, the Coronation plantation and the source of the river Liffey, Sally Gap and the well defined trail along the peaks of Gravale and Duff Hill leading to Mullaghcleevaun.I have vivid memories of crisp winter mornings on this trail years ago... The glistening waters of Blessington lakes completed this awe inspiring vista.

At the Sally Gap you can see the peaks of Djouce and Maulin on our left and Luggala or Fancy mountain which rises like a colossus from Lough Tay on whose northern shore sits the Guinness ancestral home where Garech De Bruin now resides. This is great walking country with paths and trails to suit all walking abilities and breathtaking scenery to match. A lovely walk for all the family begins at the Pier Gates and leads down to the valley below.A well defined trail through the valley eventually leads to the shores of Lough Dan.

Back at the Sally Gap the road takes us in the direction of Glendalough. We pass vast plains of blanket bog and see Lough Dan in the distance before arriving some 11 miles on at our destination. Much has been written about Glendalough but one cannot describe the breathtaking scenery that awaits you once you have ascended the summit of Lugduff and the Spink overlooking the Upper Lake. A three hour trek will take you around the Glen along the summit where you can see the upper ramparts of the reservoir at Turlough Hill in the distance.

Some of my favourite walking routes are located in Glenmalure and Glen of Imaal both of which lie south of Glendalough.It was here we made our first attempt many years ago to climb Lugnaquilla (925m), the highest mountain in Ireland outside Kerry.

President Jack Lernihan on the inaugural mountain trek to the Dublin mountains in January 2001.

Once you have forded the river at Baravore you enter the Fraughan Rock Glen one of the most desolate but scenic regions in the Wicklows where a map and compass are compulsory items to bring. One can take an easier trek from Glenmalure across the gap into Glen of Imaal, which houses the largest military firing range in Ireland. By far the most popular and easiest approach to Lugnaquilla is via Camarahill which is accessed from the village of Donard. Parking our car at Fentons Pub (which we have done on many occasion!) we head for Camarahill along a fairly rutted military access road. The ascent of Camarahill is steep but not difficult. It will knock the wind out of you though! Once on the summit of Camarahill (480m) the path is well defined. This is a lovely stretch with the cliffs of the north Prison ahead, Ballineddan mountain on your right and the vast expanse of the Artillery Range on your left. You will know when you have arrived at the base of Lug. The ground rises steeply and is strewn with boulders. Once you have navigated this short but steep stretch you arrive on a grassy plateau where a well defined path will take you to the summit itself.The scenery is breathtaking and affords a 360 degree view of the Wicklows. We must have climbed Lug at least 100 times over the past twenty years including 2 night walks to the summit. Every trek is special during which you discover something new about the mountain.

Hill walking has given me great fitness and stamina, has taught me much about patience, perseverance and commitment, about nature and given me great insight on how we fit into the greater scheme of things. There are times during the working week when I crave for the hills, to feel the wind in my face as I reach the summit of a desolate mountain top.The great thing about trekking in the Wicklows is that you have total isolation and freedom but you never feel isolated.

Whether it is a daily trek around our magnificent Tymon Park, a ramble through Pine Forest or a more arduous trek up Lugnaquilla there is something there to suit all tastes and walking abilities. I hope that this short article has given the reader a flavour of what is literally on our doorstep. Perhaps like the U21 hurlers, more of our teams will want to experience the "pleasures" of a day on the hills. Maybe the time is right to establish Naomh Jude Hill Walking club in this our 25th year. Equip yourself with a sturdy pair of walking boots, some good quality rain gear, a rucksack with flask and food and you are on your way. As they say "Carpe Diem" and enjoy what nature has provided. Once you start you will never look back...

Down from the hills! U21 hurlers after their hill walking trek, tired but happy!

Adult hurling (1988-2003)

Peter Lucey and Seán Breheny

A CCORDING to his post-match notes 5th September 1988, trainer Joe Clavin commented that "the lads need a lot of training and hard match practice. Fitness levels are very low." For all of us involved, we can indeed confirm that under Joe's training schedule fitness levels did improve and subsequent "hard" matches were followed by even tougher training sessions on the green swards of Tymon Park. This first ever adult hurling game was a friendly against our near neighbour Faughs and for the records the team was : Jerry Maguire, Colum Grogan, Christy Reidy, Dave O'Connell, Seán Boyce, Martin Hayes, Davy Mahon, John Dwane, Liam Larkin, Seán Doherty, Eamonn Moloney, Peter Ryan, Michael Ryan, Frank Carty, and John Kearns. Man of the match award went to Seán Boyce!!

Credit must go to Frank Gallagher who was instrumental in attracting Joe Clavin to St Judes in 1988. Frank, a true gentleman and long-serving member of the club, regularly asserted that while his knowledge of the finer aspects of the game of hurling were " limited", he saw the need for the development of an adult hurling team in the club to provide continuity for the ever – increasing juvenile section. Frank has been a selector to many Junior and Intermediate club hurling sides since, as well as long-serving Junior Hurling Board delegate. They were joined by Martin Molamphy, the Tipperary guru, in the first management team set – up. Our next outing in 1988 was against St Marks in McGee Park and a much improved performance saw us win on a score line of 5 – 10 to 1 – 1. Recorded scorers that day were: John Dwane 2-2, Peter Lucey 2 – 1, Colum Grogan 1 –0, Frank Carty, Eamon Treacy, Ray O'Connor 0-2 each, Liam Quinlan 0-1.

This Junior hurling team started off originally in the Junior C league. However, following our first competitive outing, we were quickly promoted to Junior A. The team was back- boned by former Robert Emmets players, by then disbanded, along with a group of Garda players who were clubless on the Dublin scene. Michael Ryan was instrumental in bringing these hurlers to Tymon and it started a long and fruitful relationship with the "law"!!! A number of players who were living locally were also recruited along with local school teachers Eamonn Treacy and Peter Lucey.

The post-match sing-songs those days lasted well into the night with regular tenors Frank Carty and Colum Grogan entertaining the squad.

Renditions of The Old Bicycle and Twice Daily were close to perfection and it was oft suggested that both Frank and Colum might have a greater talent for the singing! The spirit and comraderie in that squad was remarkable and bore fruit when St Judes, the minnows of Junior hurlers, defeated a fancied St Vincents team in the Junior A Championship final in Parnell Park on Wednesday 26th July 1989.

The management skills of Joe, Martin and Frank were stretched to the limit in the week leading up to the final. Regular keeper Shay O'Connor announced he would be unavailable – he was getting married that day!! Along with that, captain Davy Mahon was cutting short his Spanish holiday to return for the final. However, these problems were handled with "diplomacy" by the wily Clavin, who had himself won a Junior championship medal with Ballyboden St Endas in 1973, before a long involvement with the Robert Emmets club. The one and only Christy Reidy took over between the posts, ably protected by his brother Mick on the edge of the square. Commitment was the most admirable trait of that evening's final. The stage held no place for those without courage.

A final score-line of 1-8 to 1-4 brought great joy to this magical night for all in St Judes, in our very first year in Junior hurling ranks.

Well held … John Boyce (St Judes) clutches the sliothar as he is challenged by St Vincents forwards Tony O'Boyle and John Lambe during the Dublin Junior 'a' hurling final at Parnell Park.

1989 PANEL

Christy Reidy, John Boyce, Mick Reidy, Noel Egan, Martin Hayes, Eamonn Moloney, Davy Mahon (C), Ray O'Connor, Liam Quinlan, John Kearns, Liam Larkin, John Costello, Peter Lucey, Donal O'Connor, Seán Doherty, Peter Ryan, Mick Fallon, Colum Grogan, Denis Ryan, Eamonn Treacy, John English, Michael Ryan, JP Leahy, John Gordon.

CUMANN LUTHCHLEAS GAEL
COISTE SOISEARACH
IOMANA
BAILE ATHA CLIATH

1989
Junior *A* Hurling Championship
Final

St. Judes V St. Vincents
at Parnell Park on
Wednesday 26th July - 8 p.m.
Réiteoir: P. Power (Kilmore)

St. Judes *Championship Finalists*
(Naomh Jude)

1. A. N. Other
2. John Boyce   3. Mick Reidy   4. Noel Egan
5. Martin Hayes   6. Eamonn Maloney   7. Dave Mahon **(Capt.)**
8. Ray O' Connor   9. Liam Quinlan
10. Eamon Tracy   11. Liam Larkin   12. John Costello
13. Peter Lucy   14. Christy Reidy   15. Mick Minnogue

Fir Ionad:
16. Mick Fallon, 17. Frank Carthy, 18. Colm Grogan, 19. Michael Ryan, 20 Sean Doherty, 21. John English, 22. Peter Ryan, 23. Sean Gordan, 24. Denis Ryan.
Manager: Joe Clavin
Selector: Martin Molamthy
Board Delegate: Frank Gallagher.

Judes Joy!

THIS was a magical night for St. Judes, the progressive young club from Temple-ogue.

In their very first year in adult hurling, they captured one of the most sought after prizes of them all, the Junior Hurling Championship.

Magical moments for a young club

ST. JUDE'S................. 1-8; ST. VINCENT'S................. 1-4

Big Match Report

By
**NIALL
SCULLY**

Vincent's won the event four times, and to defeat such a proud name added to the merits of Jude's victory.

Captain, Dave Mahon, said so when he was presented with the trophy. "It's a great honour to beat Vincents", he said.

Mahon summed up the enthusiasm of Judes. He cut short his holiday in Spain to return for the final, which was the final chapter in the club's solid bid for glory.

And nobody doubted the influence of Joe Clavin in the win. "I put our victory down to hard work", he said. "We have been training twice a week since May".

TOUGH

Joe has done a huge amount for hurling at Judes. Back in '73, he won a junior championship hurling medal with Ballyboden and he also served Robert Emmets.

A difficult breeze, mainly blowing from the pavilion end, but also across the pitch, made life uncomfortable. The surface was hard and the light faded quite fast.

Commitment was the most admirable trait of the evening. The stage held no place for those without courage. The wholehearted pulling saw plenty of hurleys crumble with the impact.

Judes were behind just once after five minutes. In the last twenty minutes, Vincents as expected, put up a mighty surge. The response from the Judes defence was firm.

And in those last five hectic minutes, Judes turned their level all over the pitch. Their control and distribution of the sliothar was really excellent when it mattered most.

ST. JUDE'S . . . beat St. Vincent's 1-8 to 1-4 in the Junior Hurling "A" Championship final at Parnell Park.

This was Vincent's third team, but some of their numbers have tasted life at the top table. Full-forward Dave Billings, is among them.

His craft would worry any defence, and he did show some worthy touches. Yet Mick Reidy produced a marvellous display to curb his threat.

At half-time and defending the pavilion end, Judes led by 1-3 to 0-2. Their goal came on 22 minutes and it was a reward for all the fine spirit they showed.

CRISP

John Costello turned crisply and fired sweetly to the net.

Billings, with a neat point on the left after five minutes, warned what he was capable of, and goalkeeper, Christy Reidy, normally a forward, had to be alert to save a snap shot from Senan Moylan on the right, but, in general, the Judes defence

was in commanding mood.

Judes were encouraged when Liam Larkin scored a lovely point after a solo run early in the second half, and John Kearns of Judes like his colleagues, was sparing no energy as Vincents began to move with added purpose.

Judes had an ace in their pack, substitute, Peter Ryan, on the Dublin minor hurling team last season at centre half-back. On 45 minutes he scored a neat point which left Judes 1-6 to 0-4 in the clear.

Vincents, true to their renowned name and beliefs, never give up, and their hearts rose when former minor footballer, Moylan, drove the ball to the Judes net on 48 minutes, 1-6 to 1-4.

The tension was mighty on the Judes bench. Were they, after their supreme effort, going to be deprived? Mahon, playing the skipper's role, knocked over a crucial

point from play before coming off with an injured left leg.

That point helped to settle anxious nerves, and when Larkin struck over a majestic point from play on 58 minutes, the dream was slowly turning into hard wonderful reality.

ST. JUDES — Christy Reidy, John Boyce, Mick Reidy, Noel Egan, Martin Hayes, Eamonn Maloney, Dave Mahon (0-1), Ray O'Connor, Liam Quinlan, John Kerins (0-2), Liam Larkin (0-2), John Costello (1-1), Peter Lucy, Donal O'Connor, Sean Docherty (0-1). Subs — Peter Ryan (0-1) for Lucy (37 mins.); Mick Fallon for Mahon (inj. 52 mins.) Managers — Joe Clavin, Martin Molamthy, Frank Carthy.

ST. VINCENTS — Eamonn Burke, Brendan Pocock, David O'Leary, Fergal Curley, Pat McGrane, Dara Litle, Liam Foley (0-1), Peter Lucy, Donal O'Connor, Sean Cronin (0-1), Tony O'Boyle, Anthony McGinley, Barry Halpin, Niall Lambe (0-1), David Billings (0-1), John Lambe. Subs — Hugh O'Neill for John Lambe (half-time); Gerry Regan for Niall Lambe (¾ mins.) Managers — Dick Brennan, Kevin Drumgoole, Paddy Lillis.

Referee — Paddy Power (Kilmore).

Evening Herald, Wednesday, August 2, 1989

While this great achievement had put Naomh Jude on the hurling map, the tremendous work at juvenile level would soon reap even greater rewards. Success at Minor 3 level in 1990 would soon provide a number of players for the 1991-92 season and beyond. Such names as Fallon, Feore, Orr, Ryan, Nolan, Duggan, McLoughlin, Reen, Colgan, McGovern, Molloy, Crennan and Sheehy would soon be entering the fray.

In the Autumn of 1990 Joe and Martin left the management of the team to be replaced by "rebel" Peter Lucey, Martin Hayes and Mick Reidy. Lucey took over training duties also and all three continued as players for some time. By now also the noteworthy "Mines" man, Gerry Ryan had joined the panel. Gerry would go on to captain many club teams and become the only Judes hurler to hold championship winning medals at Junior A, B, C and D level – a remarkable achievement indeed. Having one Ryan (Denis, aka Mr. Borrisoleigh 1987) on the panel was difficult enough, but now two from Tipp. (Have you ever been to Borrisoleigh?)

And of course the Ryan name was prominent on the team sheets for many years. That great Rossmore (via Limerick) family of Michael, Eoghan, Niall and Colm are still involved with the club; and then there was the truly great Peter "Hippo" Ryan, our first Dublin Minor star who performed such heroics, both on and off the field!!

With many of the players from the 1989 side moving on, the onus fell on the younger players to step up a grade. Lucey's first two seasons were diligently spent consolidating the team's position and bringing players through from the minor and subsequent grades. League status was maintained and by 1993 the future of adult hurling was on solid foundations. Whilst defeated by St Vincents in the Junior A championship, the team had a successful league run and had added such players as Quigley, Kennedy, Carty, Molloy and dual star Peter Keohane to its ever increasing numbers. Our statistician extraordinaire, Gerry Ryan confirms that in the 1992-93 season we played a total of 16 matches, winning 8, drawing 2 and losing 6. Total scores for 26 – 116, scores against 30 – 121. (How Gerry found the time to record these facts we will never know. Had it anything to do with the fact that he was our top scorer with 3 – 40 and he also had a 100% training attendance record!!)

The 1994 season saw this Junior team make a serious impact, going through the entire league campaign undefeated but losing narrowly to St Vincents in the play-offs. However, promotion to the Intermediate grade was achieved through victory over St Vincents in the Top Four final. A noteworthy addition to the panel by now was Eugene Murray, that talented hurler who had until then played with Kevin's, along with Martin Hayes, in Dolphin's Barn. Eugene was to play a pivotal role both on and off the field over the following years, as he still does today in his role as Senior Hurling manager. Another stalwart to take this same route was Padraig Kennedy. Our talented footballer John O'Riordan decided to pick up the camán once again and Seán Hegarty found the Dublin lads to be very welcoming and threw in his lot with us. Competition for places was indeed intense – the training ground was no place now for the faint hearted (memories of 1989 come flooding back and the great duels between Frank Carty and one Colum Grogan on the edge of the square as Joe pucked in sliotar after sliotar in our "backs and forwards" sessions. The hurley bill was some sight in those years!!).

Judes Blast On Inter Scene

Intermediate Hurling League
Division Two

ST. JUDE'S 2-11
ST. VINCENT'S 0-9

By Stephen Leonard

ST. JUDE'S blasted on to the Intermediate hurling league scene with a stunning eight point victory over the mighty St. Vincents last Sunday in Tymon North Park.

Having only recently handed Vincents a disturbing Doyle Cup defeat, their northside opponents were looking to avenge this loss last weekend, but fell far short for a second time.

Full forward, Jerry Ryan launched Judes' match campaign with a goal after only nine minutes which midfielder, John O'Riordan and former Dublin Minor hurler, Declan Molloy followed up with a flurry of points.

Yet Sean Fox, it Boland and Mick Roberts all struck between the posts to leave both sides deadlocked at halftime by 1-4 to 0-7.

Some effective deep defending was a quality of both teams, yet Judes slowly overpowered at midfield, which eventually led to an unstoppable surge on the scoreboard.

Led by John O'Riordan, who proved to be the engine at centrefield, the home side added a further six points to their tally within a ten minute period compliments of Sean Fallon, Alan Kennedy, O'Riordan and substitute, Niall Ryan.

Vincents' only response came from Mick Roberts and Niall Boland, who each hit for a point. And when Peter Duggan, L. Quinlan, Ryan connected with Jerry Ryan's long free for a 52nd minute goal and the latter struck over the bar five minutes later the nails were firmly fixed in Vincents' coffin.

ST. JUDES : B. McGovern at M. Reidy, P. Kennedy, E. Murray, F. Feore,

K. Quigley, P. Keohane, J. O'Riordan, S. Fallon, P. Ryan, D. Molloy, P. McGovern, A. Kennedy, G. Ryan.

SUBS. : N. Ryan for A. Kennedy in 52nd minute.

ST. VINCENT'S : B. Kelly, S. Sheen, J. Roberts, M. Hogan, B. Moore, J. King, G. McCary, S. Fox, P. Considine, J. Lambe, N. Boland, P. Gray, P. Boland, M. Roberts, S. Greene.

St. Judes star Eugene Murray (right) attempts to block down St. Vincent's Niall Boland in their intermediate clash last Sunday in Tymon Park.

The Echo, Thursday, October 20, 1994

The 1994-95 season will long be remembered in the hurling history of the club. With the under 21s having a great league run and reaching the quarter final of the championship, a remarkable treble was on the cards. Victory in the Intermediate Division 2 league and promotion to Division 1 was achieved at the expense of Lucan Sarsfields in a league play-off. The Doyle Cup found its way to the club following a great win over St Vincents in a replayed final.

The treble dream was however shattered by a narrow defeat to Naomh Mearnóg in the final of the Junior A Championship. The All-Ireland Junior Sevens Shield also found a home with us. This wonderful season came about as a result of a number of factors. The club policy of developing committed, skilful players at juvenile and minor level was bearing fruit. The work of such people as Declan Feore, Michael Glover, Noel Lyons, Seán Breheny, Seán Ward, Tommy Hartnett, Jimmy O' Dwyer, Don Lehane, Pat Quigley, Jack Crennan, Gus Barry, Garrett Edge, Joe Clavin, John Fitzpatrick, Mick Hartnett, Michael Ryan and Oliver O'Connor amongst others ensured that the number of lads swinging the caman in Tymon Park was at an all-time high. Records show that the Minor Team of this year had a panel of 24 players and finished in the top three of their league. The under 21 squad of 22 under the watchful eye of Denis and Gerry Ryan, Seán Ward and Pat

St. Judes who were narrowly defeated by Naomh Mearnog last weekend.

St. Judes regret
missed chances

Junior A Hurling Championship Final

Naomh Mearnóg 1-5
St. Judes 1-3

By Cian Murphy

THE low score accurately sums up the close-ness of the contest, but it was a bitterly disap-pointing result for a Jude's side who never played as they can and missed several crucial chances as Nh. Mearnóg claimed the title at O'Toole Park last Sunday.

A scrappy game, low in skill content, was always a close affair with the opening half ending 0-2 each and only one point from each coming from play.

The fortunes of the two sides altered dra-matically on the back of two half-time switches. St. Judes inspira-tional Eugene Murray moved out from full for-ward, where the poor supply going in meant he was wasted, while Mearnóg's switched their big Dublin player Dermot Harrington from mid-field into full for-ward where in a 14-minute spell he was in-volved in the northsiders hitting 1-3 to win them the cup.

Prior to this, veteran defender Padraig Kennedy was a class act in the Jude's full-back line, constantly thwarting Mearnóg's threats.

Jude's problems, however, lay in an attack that failed to fire and hit 14 wides. St. Judes had made the better start to the second half with Eugene Murray very ef-

fective upon moving out, and along with Kieran Quigley, Peter Ryan and Sean Fallon were work-ing hard.

When Gerry Ryan finished Murray's high ball into the net in the 38th minute, it seemed like the flood gates would open for the Tem-pleogue men. However, from the puck out, Kevin Quinn pointed for Mearnóg's and for the remaining 22 minutes, Judes would have an abundance of chances agonisingly fail to go in.

No doubt inspired by the performance of their defence, Mearnóg's raised their game and Paul De Loughrey's long shot was scrambled in by Jack Ryan to put them back in the game, before Harrington snatched what would prove to be the winning points.

At the other end St. Judes could do every-thing except score. With six minutes left, a terrific shot from Murray was superbly stopped by Pat Monaghan; the ball fell to Gerry Ryan who faced an empty net, but pushed

St. Jude's Alan Kelly goes to launch an attack during his side's Junior A cham-pionship final with Naomh Mearnog last Sunday.

it inches wide of the post.

That miss seemed to deflate the predomi-nantly youthful St. Judes side and in the closing couple of minutes they failed to get scores from two 65's that could have earned them a deserved draw. Alas it was not to be and in the end, they were thankful that they weren't relying on the game for promotion to

Intermediate, where they arrived this season and have performed a lot bet-ter than they showed on Sunday.

Scorers: St. Judes: G. Ryan 1-0, S. Fallon 0-2, P. Ryan 0-1.
Naomh Mearnóg: J. Ryan 1-1, D. Harrington 0-2, K. Quinn, A. Toft 0-1. **Teams: St. Judes:** B. Duggan, L. Quinlan, M. Reidy, P. Kennedy, D.

Roche, F. Feore, K. Quigley, S. Fallon, P. Keohane, S. Hegarty, P. Ryan, N. Ryan, D. Molloy, E. Murray, G. Ryan. A. Kennedy for Hegarty 20 mins, P. McGovern for A Kennedy 35 mins. **Nh. Mearnóg:** Monaghan, Fallon, Larkin, Walsh, Woods, Staunton, Quinn, Doherty, Harrington, Madden, Aston, Toft, De Loughrey, Reilly, Ryan. **Referee: Stephen Fahy** (Kilmore).

The Echo, Thursday, June 15, 1995

☐ **WINNERS: St Jude's who beat Civil Service in the Junior Hurling A semi-final. Back row (L to R): S Fallon, D Molloy, F Feore, C McLoughlin, M Fallon, C Quigley, M McGuigan, J Reen. Front: D Roche, M Reidy, K Fitzsimons, B Duggan, E Murray, M Keenan, P Kennedy.**

Saints' last gasp winner

St. Jude's 1-9
Civil Service 1-8

Niall Scully

THE four umpires at O'Toole Park on Friday night could have been taking part in a Daz advertisement.

Their bright and clean white coats, freshly ironed, had them looking like doctors in the Blackrock Clinic. Instead, they had a Junior Hurling A semi-final to examine, and it turned into a cracking contest that only found a winner in additional time.

"We are making a habit of winning like that," said Jude's mentor, Peter Lucey. "It was a good, tight, hard game, and the lads have shown plenty of spirit during the campaign."

A stiff breeze, blowing towards the road-end goal, played a leading part. With it, Civil Service led at the break, 0-4 to 0-1, a slender enough advantage.

But Service stuck to their task on the resumption, even though the brilliant half-back line of St. Jude's didn't give them much leeway. Padraig Kennedy, in particular, was outstanding in his positioning, movement, control and distribution.

Dave Fleming was the Service ace, scoring all his points from frees. Service led

from the start until the 37th minute when the game welcomed its first goal, a thundering drive from Declan Molloy that escaped the clutches of Liam Myles to make it 1-4 to 0-5 for the Saints.

Fleming's frees kept Service in and, in 54 minutes, they constructed a fine goal that, unexpectedly, brought them level. Paul Swaine, on the left, passed inside to Martin Mullen, who struck a rasping drive just inside the left-hand post for the equaliser, 1-7 each.

A minute later Swaine, a valuable substitute for Service, sent them into the lead with a point from play, but two minutes from time Eugene Murray equalised for the Templeogue Saints.

The game had popped into injury time when a foul on Fiachra Feore presented Ciaran Quigley with the opportunity to win the game. Alas for Ciaran, his free, from the left, drifted to the right and wide.

Yet, two minutes into additional time, Jude's won another free, and this time, Quigley, with the hopes of the village on his shoulders, propelled Jude's into the final.

Evening Herald, Wednesday, June 5th, 1996

Quigley were also having a successful season. Another factor in this successful season was the professional approach of the team management. Training sessions were well planned, outside coaches invited to take sessions, goals were set, training intensified and team morale developed. A second adult team was now fielded under the management of Michael and Denis Ryan and Jim Kelly. They had a very successful first season, being runners up in both the Fletcher Shield and the Murphy Cup. The roll-call of honour in Con Ryan's Junior Hurling Board records for 1996 makes interesting reading for all Judes supporters as it proudly shows not one, but two, championship trophies returning to the club. Our Junior D side had a sweet win over Naomh Mearnog in their final in Parnell Park. They also reached the Fletcher Shield play-offs.

However, this hurling season truly belonged to the Intermediates who brought the Junior A championship trophy to the club once again, for the second time in the club's short history. A determined side saw off Na Fianna and Liffey Gaels before meeting Civil Service in the semis. A pointed free, two minutes into injury time by Kieran Quigley saw us through on the narrowest of margins to the final against Setanta. Playing superb roles on that fine victory were Padraig Kennedy, Eugene Murray, Bryan Duggan, David Roche and two "former" footballers Mick Fallon and pal Martin Mc Givergan, that super Kerry dual star, (a rare breed, Jim). Lucey ensured that all was in order for the encounter with Setanta in a packed O' Toole Park. A pre-match puck-around in Tymon settled the last minute nerves of the younger players, and the team was under no illusions as to the enormity of the task in hand as they travelled the short journey to the Crumlin venue. Leading at the interval by just 2 points having played with the wind, the half-time mood in the Judes dressing room was anything but "cosy". The magical Spawell water and, more-so in reality, the free-taking of centre back Kieran Quigley, were the crucial ingredients in this famous victory.

As reported by Niall Scully in the Evening Herald : "On a night of big match nerves, he was the coolest saint of all. Simon Templar and Steve Silvermint rolled into one!" As captain Eugene Murray collected the silverware on that balmy June evening, every Templeogue parishoner was there to applaud the success of this fine team.

Path to the final: St Judes 2-16   Na Fianna 4-8.
                  St Judes 1-13   Liffey Gaels 3-6.
                  St Judes 1-9   Civil Service 1-8.

Final: St Judes 1-14   Setanta 1-11.

VICTORS: The St Judes team. Back row (from left) — Sean Fallon, Declan Molloy, Fiachra Fiore, Mick Reidy, David Roche, Ciaran Quigley, Mick Fallon, Ciaran McLoughlin, Niall Ryan. Front — John Reen, Paul McGovern, Martin McGivern, Eugene Murray, Brian Duggan, P adraic Kennedy.

Quigley has sights tuned

ST. JUDE'S	1-14
SETANTA	1-11

Niall Scully

ST. JUDE'S chief, Peter Lucey, quipped that the magical water from the Spawell was the crucial ingredient in the famous Junior A Hurling Championship victory at O'Toole Park.

But reality says that the free-taking of Peter's centre half-back, Ciaran Quigley, might have had a bigger say. From all angles, distances and positions, Quigley was the master, sending over nine points from placed ball.

If you required double top for the jackpot, then Quigley's your man. On a night of big match nerves, he was the coolest Saint of all. Simon Templer and Steve Silvermint rolled into one!

"We weren't under any illusions coming here," noted Peter Lucey. "Setanta gave us a tough match, and I'll predict they'll be back next year. We lost this final last year, but this makes up for everything. We are all absolutely delighted."

Setanta, the pride of Ballymun, are held fondly in the folklore of Dublin hurling. "We are disappointed," said mentor, Padraig O'Maoilsteighe. "I felt we stood a good chance going in at half-time just two points down, with the wind behind us in the second half."

The interval mood in the Templeogue camp didn't resemble that of a cosy tea-party. They had 13 wides to ponder, and it was only a goal on the half-hour from Paul McGovern that allowed them that 1-6 to 1-4 advantage at the break.

A swift turn and strike from Anton Keating, at the pitch and putt end, swept stylish Setanta into a 1-1 to 0-2 lead on twelve minutes.

A delivery by centre half-forward Fiachra Feore McGovern strike to the far corner from a tight enough angle for Jude's welcome goal.

Two points from Sean Fallon and another from Quigley saw Jude's lead by 1-9 to 1-4 inside the opening eight minutes of the resumption. Four minutes later, Setanta had reduced the deficit to one point, with scores from Matt Kearney, Alan Breathnach, Keith MacAdhaimh and Pat Berigan.

Nobody dared to put their mortgage on the outcome at this tense, compelling stage. Quigley and Berigan swopped points, before two more points from Quigley, and one from McGovern, pushed Jude's ahead by four points, 1-13 to 1-9, on 51 minutes.

Yet Setanta remained extremely dangerous, and the closing sequence, just like the game itself, was never a comfortable journey for the now renowned Templeogue Tigers, who just had enough Holy water in their cultured tank!

MATCHFILE

● **Scorers: St. Jude's:** C Quigley 0-9 (8f 1 65). P McGovern 1-1, S Fallon F Feore 0-2 each. **Setanta:** A Keating 1-0, M Kearney (2f), A Breathnach, P Berigan (2f, 1 65), 0-3 each. K McAdhaimh 0-2.

St. Jude's: Brian Duggan 7; Ciaran McLoughlin 7; Mick Reidy 7, Padraig Kennedy 7; Eugene Murray 7, Ciaran Quigley 8, David Roche 7; Sean Fallon 7, Martin McGivern 7; Mick Fallon 7, Fiachra Feore 8, John Reen 7; Paul McGovern 8, Niall Ryan 7, Declan Molloy 7. **Subs:** Ken Fitzsimons 7 for Molloy.

● **Setanta:** John White 8; Colm Breathnach 7, Pat Berigan 8, Brendan Gregan 7; Brian Murphy 7, Niall de Craig 7, Gary Fitzpatrick 7; Paul Conlon 7, Jason Buckley 7; Rodney Hussain 7, Alan Breathnach 8, Keith McAdhaimh 7; Matthew Keating 8, Anton Keating 7, Thomas O'Mongain 7. **Subs:** Warren Carroll 7 for O'Mongain; Eoin Murray 7 for Hussain.

● **Referee:** Tony Clarke (Lucan Sarsfield).

● **Ratings:** Match: Very close duel – 8. St. Jude's: Always able to pull out that bit extra – 8. Setanta: Kept knocking on the door - 8.

● **Conditions:** Bright evening.

● **Wides:** St. Jude's: 16 (13). Setanta: 5 (3).

● **Mentors:** St. Jude's: Peter Lucey, Frank Gallagher. Setanta: Padraig O'Maoilsteighe, Matt Berigan, Michael Holian.

● **Man-of-the-Match:** Ciaran Quigley (St. Jude's).

Sponsored by

SPAWELL

VICTORIOUS PANEL

Bryan Duggan, Ciaran Mc Loughlin, Mick Reidy, Padraig Kennedy, Eugene Murray, Kieran Quigley, David Roche, Seán Fallon, Martin Mc Givergan, Michael Fallon, Fiachra Feore, John Reen, Paul Mc Govern, Niall Ryan, Declan Molloy, Ken Fitzsimmons, Liam Quinlan, Gerry Ryan, Barry Heraty, Peter Ryan, Seán Hegarty, Kevin O'Dwyer, John Nolan, Neil Guinan, Ronan Colgan, Colm Ryan, Barry McGann.

Follow that do I hear you say! Well, follow it we did and in 1997 the Corn Ceitinn found its way to the trophy cabinet. A Ken Molloy goal proved the decisive score in the replayed final with Naomh Mearnog. By now the Judes squad had been further strengthened by the arrival of Killanena stars Joe Moloney and Shay Collins. Also featuring strongly was Neil Guinan and Gareth Roche had decided that "hurling was your only man".

Further team building continued throughout this season to help us achieve our long-term goal – Senior Status. How long more would it take? Participation in tournaments i.e. Muintir Uibh Fhaili and our own Colum Grogan instigated Corn an Earraigh were further developments, as were the weekend trips to Galway, Kilkenny, Portumna etc.

The 1997 trip to the home of the Cats was noteworthy indeed, from a morale development point of view, of course. A large contingent of hurlers, would-be hurlers and hurlers on the ditch enjoyed this trip. When the going got tough, those of mature years – like Feore, Grogan, Lucey, Gallagher, Ryan, Quigley and company kept the ship afloat. Partaking of the Happy Hour in Judes may not have been such a good idea after all, Denis, but it sure set the tone for the weekend. Some managed to re-design a local golf course on the Saturday, with Mick Fallon literally losing the head, and with young Ryan (Borrisoleigh) and Declan Feore tearing up their cards, Neil Guinan slipped in to snatch a late victory.

Templemore recruit Bugsy Fallon gave everyone his annual ear-bashing on the theories of iomaint. (When both he and "Glocko" McLoughlin hit the streets in uniform, we could all rest easy in our homes, safe in the knowledge that any poor gurrier they came across got the proverbial earful!). The swimming gala took place at a very unreasonable hour of the morning. Ryan took the 400M freestyle, Quigley (junior) took the breast - stroke with ease but there was a tie in the 200M back-stroke between O'Dwyer (junior) and Coghlan. "Longest in the Tub" went once more to Mick Reidy and Dessie Keating retained his Sauna title. Dancing trophies had earlier in the evening been awarded in Langtons to those who tried – but ultimately failed!!

While 1989, 1995 and 1996 holds many fond memories for all hurling fans, 1998 was the year when senior status was attained.

☐ **WINNERS: The St Judes team with the Corn Ceitinn trophy in O'Toole Park after they beat Naomh Mearnog in the final on Sunday last.**

Molloy's golden goal captures Corn Ceitinn

ST. JUDE'S.............1-6
N. MEARNOG........ 0-6

KEN MOLLOY'S golden goal proved decisive in St. Jude's Junior Hurling Corn Ceitinn final replay victory at O'Toole Park last Sunday lunchtime.

Molloy struck five minutes into the second half in a close,intriguing tie that overcame the dark, greasy conditions.

Jude's were never behind in the contest, which was level twice, both in the opening half.

The Templeogue attack had several aces, and in a compelling finish, their defence defied Mearnog with some brave defending.

Mearnog poured on high

By NIALL SCULLY

pressure in their last-ditch effortat salvation, and a Portmarnock goal looked quite possible in the growing excitement.

"It was a good game from two teams, who provided two good games," said Jude's mentor, Peter Lucey.

"There was only a puck of the ball in it. It was very sporting. Mearnog are a fine side, and we'd like to follow them into senior ranks."

FATHER AND SON

On the Mearnog half-back line were Jack and Shane Ryan, father-and-son. Jack, at centre-half back, was majestic, always in the right place at the right time, and never wasting a pass, or a clearance.

Shane is obviously learning well from the master, for he worried Jude's with his strong,

menacing runs in the latter part of the second half.

At the interval, it was 0-3 to 0-2 for Jude's, and the critical goal came at the pitch and putt end.

Following a little bout of Jude's pressure, the ball ran to Molloy, lurking to the left of the posts, and he fired in a crisp drive that found the net, despite a gallant bid by 'keeper, Cormac Doherty.

A brilliant point from Neil Guinan extended the Saints' lead before Mearnog responded with a free from their captain, David Aston, and a fine point from Shane Ryan, leaving a goal in it, 1-4 to 0-4.

Joe Moloney's 47th minute free was answered by Mearnog's diligent, dangerous substitute, Andrew Rittweger.

Guinan sent over another point for Jude's with four minutes left, but, two minutes

from the end, Rittweger was on target for Mearnog once more, insuring that hectic conclusion.

MATCHFILE

● **Scorers: St. Jude's:** K Molloy 1-0, N Guinan 0-3, F Feore 0-2, J Moloney 0-1 (f). **Naomh Mearnog:** D Aston 0-3 (2f), A Rittweger 0-2, S Ryan 0-1.

● **St. Jude's:** Brian Duggan 7; Ciaran McLoughlin 7, Ciaran Quigley 7, Padraig Kennedy 7; Eugene Murray 8, Joe Moloney 8, David Roche 7; Sean Fallon 7, John Nolan 8; Shay Collins 7, Martin McKiverghan 7, Fiodhra Feore 7; Neil Guinan 6, Alan Kennedy 7, Ken Molloy 7. **Sub:** Kevin Rodhe 7 for P Kennedy.

● **Naomh Mearnog:** Cormac Doherty 7; Colm Larkin 7, Sean Walsh 7, Rory Breen 7; Simon Woods 7, Jack Ryan 8, Shane Ryan 8; David Aston 8, Alan Toft 7; Ciaran Reale 7, Declan O'Reilly 7, Kevin Quinn 7; Damien Reale 7, David Breen 7, John Madden 7. **Subs:** Andrew Rittweger 8 for Woods; Peter McDonnell 7 for Breen; Colm O'Driscoll 7 for C Reale.

● **Referee:** Donny Ryan (Kilmacud Crokes).

● **Ratings: Match:** Tight and interesting — 7. **St. Jude's:** Lively, well-balanced crew — 8. **Naomh Mearnog:** Didn't have the finishing power — 7.

● **Conditions:** Moist.

● **Wides: St. Jude's:** 8 (7). **Naomh Mearnog:** 8 (6).

● **Masters: St. Jude's:** Colm Grogan, Michael Fay, Jack Ryan. **Naomh Mearnog:** Tony Larkin, Mick Fay, Jack Ryan.

● **Player-of-the-Match:** Joe Moloney (St. Jude's).

Judes in top flight

THE scent of celebration still lingers across the Templeogue's Tymon North.

The St. Jude's hurlers are in the big time for the first time, having emerged from the Intermediate Premier division at the third attempt.

Following the disappointment of being overwhelmed in the Intermediate Championship Final by St. Vincent's, Jude's had four games left in the League.

By NIALL SCULLY

"That was the big worry," admits captain, Eugene Murray. "But the lads reacted very well by getting stuck back into training, and we won the four matches to clinch the title."

The critical tie was their last game to St. Olaf's. Jude's had won seven games and drawn one; Olaf's had also won seven but had lost one.

A win or a draw was the Jude's requirement, and they managed to win by three points.

"It was a winner take all situation, and our big fear was that we would have nothing to show for our season's work," explains Eugene, who, by all accounts, has proved a real captain Fantastic.

Yet the skipper deflects all praise on manager, Peter Lucey, and his fellow mentors, Declan Feore, Colm Grogan and Michael Ryan.

HURLING KING

Peter the Great has long been regarded as a Hurling King within the corridors of Tymon. Lucey's seasoned eye, and thorough approach, inspired this success.

And the prospects for the Senior grade are appealing, as Eugene outlines:

"Ten of the team all went to school together and the oldest of that group is 25. And since 1994 we have managed to win some competition or other."

Now that the main mission has been accomplished, Jude's can focus on the semi-finals in the Corn Fogarty and Corn Ceitinn tournaments, plus their own prestigious All-Ireland Junior Seven's, where they reached the semi-final last year.

"It's been a very long season," muses Eugene. "It's been the same every year. You hardly get a break at all."

Evening Herald, Tuesday, September 1, 1998

Lucey's dream of seniority was finally realised following the capture of the Intermediate Premier Division title. The league title that year came down to the wire. The final game of the season saw the visit of Naomh Olaf to Tymon Park on 23rd August. Victory for Olafs would see them gain promotion while a draw would be enough to see Judes join the senior ranks. The non-appearance of the appointed referee saw the match delayed before both clubs agreed to inter-county ref Aodhán Mac Suibhne doing the honours. A thrilling game saw Judes victorious on a score-line of 2-7 to 1-7 and an emotional and proud team and the large crowd saw Eugene Murray lift the trophy and lead St Judes to the senior ranks. Both the squad and team management of Peter Lucey, Declan Feore, Colum Grogan and Michael Ryan deserve great credit for this fabulous achievement.

Earlier in the season they tasted defeat in the Intermediate championship final against an awesome St Vincents side. Following this defeat Judes still had four league games to play but as captain Murray commented, "The lads reacted very well by immediately getting straight back into training and winning all four matches to clinch the title". The semi-final of the Corn Ceitinn and the final of the Corn Fogarty were also contested in 1998 by the now senior side.

INTERMEDIATE PANEL 1998

Bryan Duggan, Kevin Roche, Kieran Quigley, Eamonn Coghlan, Ken Molloy, Niall Ryan, Gareth Roche, Seán Fallon, John Reen, Enda Sheehy, Alan Kennedy, Fiachra Feore, Sé Collins, Neil Guinan, Eugene Murray, Fergal Hourihan, Martin McGivergan, Joe Moloney, Gerry Ryan, Padraig Kennedy, David Roche, Kevin O'Dwyer, Ronan Colgan, Barry Heraty, Barry Mc Gann.

Not to be outdone however, the Junior hurlers, now guided by Denis Ryan, Gerry Ryan and Joe Kane did the glorious double with victory in the Junior C league and Championship. Both Martin Hayes and Mick Reidy from this squad had been on the Junior A winning side in 1989.

JUNIOR C PANEL

Seán Hegarty, Gerry Ryan, Kevin O' Dwyer, Mick Reidy, Fergal Hourihan, Tadgh O' Connor, Barry McGann, Enda Crennan, Ciaran Mc Loughlin, Dara Kane, Greg Lehane, Barry Heraty, Cathal "Roundy" Nolan, Donagh O' Dywer, Bart Lehane, Robbie Mc Cabe, Padraig Finnerty, Kevin Roche, Eamonn Coghlan, Ken Molloy, Martin Gaughran.

Templeogue men hold out for victory despite late onslaught

ST JUDES............ 1-13
CRAOBH CHIARAIN. 3-4

ST JUDE, the patron Saint of hopeless cases.

And a hopeless case was precisely the predicament Craobh Chiarain found themselves in O'Toole Park last Friday night in the Junior Hurling "C" Championship quarter-final.

All bets were off as the highly impressive Templeogue team were coasting to a predictable victory.

At half time it was 1-12 to 0-2 to Jude's, and although they had enjoyed the breeze, it looked like their superior sharpness and craft was just too much for the Donnycarney side.

With nine minutes remaining, that still was the picture, as Jude's were ahead by 1-13 to 0-4.

NIALL SCULLY

Then, the climate suddenly changed as Chiarain's grabbed three goals in six minutes. Cruise control had become emergency exit drill for Jude's as Chiarains strove to bridge a three-point gap.

"We surely are relieved," quipped Jude's mentor, Denis Ryan, at the close.

MATCHFILE

● SCORERS: St Jude's: G Ryan 0-8 (7f), T O'Connor 1-1, M Murnane 0-2, F Hourihan, B McGann 0-1 each. Craobh Chiarain: C Kope 1-1, G Fagan, D Kane 1-0 each, G Maher, A Abernethy, G McCormack 0-1 each.
● St Jude's: Kevin O'Dwyer 7; Barry Herrity 7, Mick Reidy 7, Ciaran McLoughlin 8; Sean Reen 7, Martin Hayes 7, Sean Hegarty 8; Fergal Hourihan 7, Michael Murnane 8; Daragh Keane 7, Gerry Ryan 8, Barry McGann 8; Donough O'Dwyer 7, Cathal Nolan 7, Tadgh O'Connor 8. Sub: Robbie McCabe 7 for D O'Dwyer.
● Craobh Chiarain: Mark McGucklan 7; Paul Browne 8, Joey Maher 7, Derek Ryan 7; Fergus O'Riordan 8, John Satall 8, Stephen Heery 7; Gerry Maher 8, Sean Shanley 7; Ciaran Kope 8, Darren Abernethy 7, Kevin Clune 7; Stephen Norton 7, Joe Sullivan 7, Graham McCormack 7. Subs: Gary Fagan 8 for Norton; David Kane 7 for McCormack; Christian Leonard 7 for Heery.
● Referee: Gene Hernon (O'Toole's).
● Ratings: Match: Saved the best for last — 7. St Jude's: Got a fright — 8.
● Conditions: Pleasant with a stiff enough breeze.
● Wides: St Jude's: 3 (3). Craobh Chiarain: 5 (2).
● Mentors: St Jude's: Denis Ryan, Jim Kelly, Joe Keane. Craobh Chiarain: Mick Maher, Michael Barry, Derek Connolly.
● Player-of-the-Match: Gerry Ryan (St Jude's).

And more high drama is promised between the clubs again as Jude's, in their final match, need to beat Chiarains, to clinch the League title.

Jude's, attacking the road end, were majestic in that opening half when the Ryan line was most definitley open.

Gerry Ryan, their ace marksman and hard-working centre half-forward, was in inspiring form, scoring seven first half points, six of them frees.

The Jude's goal arrived on 24 minutes. Cathal Nolan placed Tadgh O'Connor, who finished to the net with a tidy strike.

The fixture was easing towards an unexciting end when the Donnycarney three injected the welcome sting to the plot.

They had restricted Jude's to just one point following the break, but despite a increased share of the sliotar, Chiarains were not making much impres-

sion on the scoreboard.

Then, on 51 minutes, Ciaran Kope drilled in a cracking goal, and three minutes later, Gary Fagan sent another crisp drive to the Jude's net.

On 57 minutes, a long delivery from David Kane brought Craobh's third goal, forcing the men of St Jude's to begin saying prayers for themselves.

Jude's just couldn't comprehend how their position of authority had been wiped away so quickly.

Yet they held on by their fingernails, and in the tension of the hectic conclusion, a skirmish ended with the Chiarains full-forward, Joe Sullivan, being sent off.

Evening Herald, June, 1998

1999 saw St Judes compete in Senior hurling, both league and championship, for the first time in the club's history. This indeed showed great progress for a club whose first adult hurling team had been fielded only 10 years previously. Team mentors were Peter Lucey, Michael Ryan and Colum Grogan.

Our first league match against Oliver Plunketts/Eoghan Ruadh saw us win on a score-line of 2-13 to 2-7. Damian Garrihy, that great "Banner" man (Wolfe Tones) was a welcome new addition to the scene as was "Rebel" John Mc Carthy, who immediately found favour with Lucey!! (Only Feore and Lucey would ever

The St Jude's team which marched into the final of the Junior C Hurling Championship after beating Faughs last weekend.

JUDE'S CUT THROUGH FAUGHS

A LATE flurry of points proved invaluable to St Jude's Junior C Hurling Championship cause and propelled them into the final of the competition at the expense of their neighbouring rivals.

Deadlocked at 3-5 each heading into the closing five minutes of play, both sides began to separate as Enda Sheehy, Fergal Hourihan and Enda Crenin combined for four late points that effectively killed off the Faughs' challenge.

Indeed the former proved crucial in his side's bid to reach the title match, proving a hindrance to the Faughs' rearguard from the moment he was introduced

ST JUDE'S	3-9
FAUGHS	3-5

to the action just after the break.

The Saints enjoyed a commendable start and were two points up before Gerard Ryan delivered the first of their big scores when his early free found the net just before Liam McCabe answered

in similar fashion for Faughs.

It was tit-for-tat throughout the opening half and for much of the second period with Jude's managing to establish only a two-point cushion by the interval, thanks largely to the efforts of Ryan who delivered in another couple of points. Darragh Kane was in fine form for Jude's also and wrote his name on the goal-sheet but Faughs stayed well in touch through the likes of McCabe who added another goal just prior to the half.

With the elements Faughs in the second period, the gap began to be closed when McCabe, Martin McKenna and Martin Sheridan all struck over the bar while Tony Spellman let fly from the edge of the square past goalkeeper Kevin O'Dwyer. It helped Faughs pull level, and for a moment the possibility of a semi-final upset looked set to materialise.

Yet St Jude's dug deep and produced the gritty performance that has helped them climb to the peak of the Junior C Division One ladder.

The Echo, June 16, 1988

really understand Mac's mutterings). Noel Nash had also joined the fray, along with Shane O'Connor, Eamonn Ryan and George Frisby and retaining senior status was achieved comfortably.

Our first championship game at senior level saw us take on Eugene Murray's former club, Kevins, who had too much experience on the night.

SENIOR PANEL

Bryan Duggan, David Roche, Ciaran McLoughlin, Eamonn Coghlan, Gareth Roche, Kieran Quigley, Ken Molloy, Seán Fallon, John McCarthy, Fiachra Feore, Alan Kennedy, Damien Garrihy, Eugene Murray, Joe Moloney, Tadgh O'Connor, Kevin O'Dwyer, Ronan Colgan, Eamonn Ryan, Gerry Ryan, Barry McGann, Kevin Roche, Michael Lyons, Niall Ryan, Ciaran O'Brien, Aidan O'Gorman.

The Junior hurlers won the B league with a 2-12 to 2-6 win over neighbours Ballyboden St Endas.

ST KEVINS... 1-8
ST. JUDE'S.. 0-7

A STORMING display by 18-year-old Sean O'Shea saw Kevins become the first club to book their place in round two of the *Evening Herald* Dublin Senior Hurling Championship at O'Toole Park yesterday.

The big midfielder dominated the early exchanges in a well-contested clash to assure his side a 0-5 to 0-1 lead after the first quarter, in a match spoiled by the inclement weather.

If O'Shea tired somewhat for a period of the second half his fellow midfielder, Darragh O'Mahony, from Cork, took control of the area to complete another fine personal display.

And whatever got by this midfield pairing had to contend with a very effective half-back line in which Donal Tutty's experience and judgement sealed off the middle.

On Tutty's wings some whole-hearted play by wing-backs Paul Crompton and John Murray was in evidence.

EXPERIENCED

St. Jude's will be disappointed by their display in their very first Senior Hurling championship outing but they can take heart in that the experienced players for the winners were the difference between the sides.

For, although O'Shea and O'Mahony were outstanding for Kevins, it was the presence of older stagers like Tutty, Colm Murphy, Sean Gleeson, Joey Dalton, and goalkeeper Cian Murphy that actually saw them through.

One has to pay tribute to St. Jude's for the way in which they tried right to the finishing post. In fact they forced a penalty, taken by Damien Garrihy, and saved by substitute Aidan Flynn in the 64th minute.

It was all St. Jude's pressure in those closing minutes but the almost impenetrable full-back line

of Kevins held out as Cian Murphy in goals also covered anything that came his way.

St. Jude's had good performances from their two big men at full-back Kieran Quigley, and at No. 6, Sean Fallon. These two switched in the last quarter but the lack of real penetration in their full-forward line failed them.

In attack Fiachra Feore showed great pace but his control let him down on a few times when he had shaken off the cover. Apart from Feore, Tadhg O'Connor and veteran former Kevins' player, Eugene Murray, worked hardest for the losers.

The Templeogue side missed their injured trio, Alan Kennedy, Padraig Finnerty and Joe Moloney. A win over St. Oliver Plunkett's/Eoghan Ruadh in the league on Wednesday night proved expensive with injuries to these key men.

SCORERS: Kevins: E O'Mahony 1-0, S O'Shea 0-3 frees, D Tutty 0-2 65s, D O'Mahony, C Murphy, B Scott 0-1 each. **St. Jude's:** D Garrihy 0-3 frees, T O'Connor 0-2, F Feore, E Murray 0-1 each.

Kevins: C Murphy; T McDaid, S Gleeson, S Curran; P Crompton, D Tutty, J Murray; S O'Shea, D O'Mahony; B Scott, C Murphy, J Dalton; P Daly, J Browne, P Synnott. **Subs:** E O'Mahony for P Synnott, A Flynn for B Scott.

St. Jude's: M Lyons; K Roche, K Quigley, E Coughlan; G Roche, S Fallon, K Molloy; N Ryan, T McCarthy; F O'Connor, D Garrihy, F Feore; E Murray, T Colgan, C Lehane. **Referee:** D Grogan.

 IN FRONT: Brian Scott of Kevins takes the ball past St Judes' Kevin Roche in yesterday's clash

Evening Herald, April 26, 1999

The Juniors also added the Miller Shield to their fine collection in 1999. After ten glorious years, our top team was in the Senior grade and our Juniors were back at Junior A level. Some achievement in a short period of time. Yes indeed, Denis, two leagues, two championships and a Miller Shield was a handsome return for the King of Borrisoleigh and your fellow-mentors!! At the end of the 1999 season, Peter Lucey decided it was time to take a well-earned rest.

Jude's clinch Junior B title

ST. JUDE'S.....................2-12
BALLYBODEN ST. ENDA'S 2-6

ST. JUDE'S wrapped up the Junior "B Hurling League in Tymon North with a victory over neighbours Ballyboden St. Enda's in their final match.

Having already won eight out of eight matches in the league, Jude's needed the two points to make sure of the title and

they achieved their goal with a six-point winning margin.

One point down at half time, Jude's turned in a very impressive second-half performance with centre forward Gerry Ryan and full forward Mick Fallon very much to the fore. Fallon finished the game with a personal tally of 1-4 with Ryan contributing six points.

St. Jude's were the winners of the Junior "C League and Championship in 1998 and they can now carry their winning form into Junior "A next season, where they will be striving to capture their

third league title in-a-row.

A very interesting aside to the match was the fact that Ken Ryan was playing his final game for Ballyboden, having played with distinction for the club for many years.

Ken's son David, a prominent member of St. Jude's minor team, was a sub on the night and it was nice to see him involved in a junior game at the start of his adult hurling career as the carrer of his father drew to a close.

July 13, 1999

ST. JUDE'S

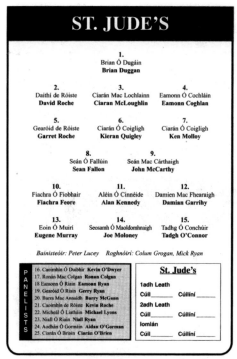

1.
Brian Ó Dugáin
Brian Duggan

2.
Daithí de Róiste
David Roche

3.
Ciarán Mac Lochlainn
Ciaran McLoughlin

4.
Eamonn Ó Cochláin
Eamonn Coghlan

5.
Gearóid de Róiste
Garret Roche

6.
Ciarán Ó Coigligh
Kieran Quigley

7.
Ciarán Ó Coigligh
Ken Molloy

8.
Seán Ó Fallúin
Sean Fallon

9.
Seán Mac Cárthaigh
John McCarthy

10.
Fiachra Ó Fiobhair
Fiachra Feore

11.
Aléin Ó Cinnéide
Alan Kennedy

12.
Damien Mac Fhearaigh
Damian Garrihy

13.
Eoin Ó Muirí
Eugene Murray

14.
Seosamh Ó Maoldomhnaigh
Joe Moloney

15.
Tadhg Ó Conchúir
Tadgh O'Connor

Bainisteóir: Peter Lucey   Roghnóirí: Colum Grogan, Mick Ryan

PANELISTS
16. Caoimhín Ó Duibhir **Kevin O'Dwyer**
17. Ronán Mac Colgan **Ronan Colgan**
18. Eamonn Ó Riain **Eamonn Ryan**
19. Gearóid Ó Riain **Gerry Ryan**
20. Barra Mac Annaidh **Barry McGann**
21. Caoimhín de Róiste **Kevin Roche**
22. Mícheál Ó Liatháin **Michael Lyons**
23. Niall Ó Riain **Niall Ryan**
24. Aodhán Ó Gormáin **Aidan O'Gorman**
25. Ciarán Ó Briain **Ciarán O'Brien**

St. Jude's

1adh Leath

Cúil_____   Cúilíní _____

2adh Leath

Cúil_____   Cúilíní _____

Iomlán

Cúil_____   Cúilíní _____

His contribution to hurling in the club will long be remembered and appreciated. His dedication and commitment over the years as player, manager, coach and trainer played a significant part in the progress hurling had made in the club. His retirement was celebrated in style in the clubhouse when among the many guests were Rebels Brian Corcoran, Ger Cunningham and, along with the captain Mark Landers and his prize possession, the Liam Mc Carthy cup.

Management of the Seniors was taken over by a young and enthusiastic Ken Ryan, (not another Ryan from the Premier county!) along with Eugene Murray and Denis Ryan. In 2000, Senior status was once again maintained with some very impressive performances.

The Junior side, now under the watchful eyes of Gerry Ryan and Corkman Donie Cummins, contested the Junior B championship final, losing narrowly to a strong Naomh Mearnog side.

The 2001 season saw the Seniors promoted to Division 1 following a hard fought league campaign. Many skilful young players had come up through the ranks and this blend of youth and experience paid off handsomely.

By the start of the 2002 season David Ryan and Bart Lehane were regular starters on the senior team and Vincent Kelly, Seán McLoughlin, Gerard Hartnett, Timmy McCarthy, Colm Manning and Seán O'Connor were seriously challenging for senior positions. Liam O'Reilly and Aidan Hassett were also wearing the Judes jersey at this stage.

Our Juniors once again excelled and under Ryan (Gerry) Cummins and Grogan, brought the only remaining Junior championship title, the Junior B, to the trophy room with a deserved win against neighbours Boden. This victory completed the full complement of Junior Hurling Championship titles for the club and that great sportsman, Gerry Ryan, proudly holds winning medals in all four championships – surely a remarkable achievement !

As we enter the new season, Eugene Murray has taken over the reins at

Jude's fightback to earn a share of the honours

ST JUDE'S senior hurlers produced a superb fightback in the 'B' Championship last Sunday morning as they held Cuala to a 0-12 to 1-9 draw in O'Toole Park.

Trailing by seven points early in the second half, Jude's looked to be cruising to a heavy defeat but they turned the game around with a string of superb scores.

Ciaran Quigley kick-started Jude's revival with a fine goal and this was followed up with scores from Fiachra Feore and Damien Garrihy.

Jude's grew in confidence as the game went on and with defenders Gerry Hartnett

| ST JUDE'S ......0-12 |
| CUALA ....1-9 |

and Eamon Ryan not giving an inch, Cuala found it hard to clock up some scores.

Garrihy added another two points for Jude's to round off a

St Jude's senior hurlers drew with Cuala in the championship.

superb revival by the Templeogue men.

Jude's face

Setanta in the next round and they will have to improve if they are to

qualify for the play-off stages of the competition.

Echo, May 31, 2001

senior level, ably assisted by Aodhán Mac Suibhne and Padraig Kennedy. Failte mhor ar ais, a Phadraig. The Junior team are being guided once again by Donie and Colum and are intent on bringing another championship title to the club. But the best news of all is the fielding of a third adult hurling team in the club, under the experienced eyes of Oliver O'Connor and Michael Ryan. Both Ollie and Michael have given years of dedication to the club and it is a credit to them to have the vision and enthusiasm to manage this team. Best of luck lads.

The successes and progression of our current adult teams are solidly founded on the excellent work done down through the years at juvenile, minor and Under 21 level by a dedicated squad of coaches, with the assistance of the club executive and, in particular, the Adult Games Committees.

In recent years, the expertise of our Director of Coaching, Niamh Leahy, has been of immense assistance to many of our teams. While there has always been a warm welcome extended to all our "country cousins" in Judes, our teams are largely made up of home-grown players.

The 2001 season saw our Under 21 hurlers reach the B County championship semi-final, losing narrowly to eventual winners St Mark's. An epic campaign against Na Fianna at the quarter-final stage was the highlight of this season. The non-appearance of a referee for the original fixture, a draw the following Saturday in Mobhi Road (remember the free Declan?!!) and a sweet victory in the replay in Tymon on the following Bank Holiday Monday had the management

Jude's cruise past Setanta

ST JUDE'S cruised to a comfortable 3-11 to 0-10 victory over Setanta in Senior Hurling Championship action last weekend.

Damien Garrihy was the indisputable hero of the Templeogue side's victory, accounting for two goals and five points.

Indeed his double strike to the net in the second period effectively killed off the Setanta challenge.

Looking for a dramatic improvement on their disappointing draw with Cuala in their opening championship fixture, the saints made no mistake against their Ballymun rivals.

Loran Luby's first-half goal was just what they needed to get the momentum going, and, together with points from Vinny Kelly, Pauric Ryan, John McCarthy and Fiacra Fiore, they led by four points heading into the second period.

Their good run in the championship coincides with a fine league display that has seen them go top of Division Two, having taken seven points from a possible 10.

The introduction of a number of young stars – the likes of Kelly, Ger Hartnett and Sean O'Connor – has served to bolster the team this season.

The Echo, Thursday, June 21, 2001

team of Mick Hartnett, Garrett Edge, Jack Crennan and Declan Feore gasping for breath. This was followed in 2002 with victory in the league (Southside) before encountering a more determined Craobh Chiaran in the semis.

Those who wore the Dublin jersey at Under 21, Junior and Intermediate grade include Bart Lehane, Bryan Duggan, Niall Ryan, Fiachra Feore, Seán Fallon, Martin McGivergan, Joe Moloney, Mick Fallon, Noel Nash and Garreth Roche. Damien Garrihy was the first hurler in St Judes to receive a Blue Star nomination, in 2001.

And so, while we celebrate 25 years of sporting activity in Cumann Luthchleas Gael Naomh Jude, we celebrate all that hurling has given us in a much shorter time-scale. We have been fortunate to have collected much silverware in that time and we look forward to a senior county title in the near future. May the minors of today be the stars of the future. Whatever the next 25 years will bring, the good Lord only knows, but let there be absolutely no doubt that the greatest field-game in the world will be alive and well on " De Banks" – of the Dodder!!!

Presentation of jerseys to Intermediate hurlers 1991 – Back row (l-r): Martin Molamphy, Seán Doherty, Mick Fallon, Denis Ryan, Patsy Tyrrell, John Boyce. Middle: Frank Carty, Frank Gallagher, Tosh Murray (Terenure House), Davy Mahon, Joe Clavin. Front: John Gorey, Peter Hanrahan, JP Leahy, Seán Gordon.

Presentation of jerseys… sponsor Paul Mangan with Bryan Duggan. The Glenside and Doheny & Nesbitts are one of our club's major sponsors.

Press launch of 1997 Bank of Ireland/St Judes All Ireland Junior Sevens.

The huRLeRs

Gerry Ryan

As we celebrate our club's first glorious 25 years
We recall moments of victory and joy, moments of defeat and tears
I'm sure there will be many with great football stories to tell
But don't forget that we play Adult Hurling and Camogie here as well

We begin as the young club was just about finding its feet
Back in the late eighties a group of hurling men did meet
They had seen all the fun, that the footballers were havin'
So they got a team together, to be managed by Joe Clavin

As the great team of '89 they'll forever be known
Though in some of the photos their faces weren't shown
Famous men whose names trip right off the tongue
But the big problem was there was none of them too young

Men like Larkin, the Reidys, Grogan, Boyce and Hayes
The truth of it was that they had all seen better days
It was clear new blood was needed if hurling was to survive
And a plan was put in place to keep the dream alive

The club knew it was time to put their faith in youth
And throw in a few lads a bit long in the tooth
And just to make certain that their clever plan would work
They gave the manager's job to Peter Lucey from Cork

Peter knew he'd need help his job for to do
He called on men who were hurling through and through
Pat Quigley, Frank Gallagher and Jimmy O'Dwyer
And Declan Feore, the world's best umpire

They knew for the team to be any good
They should play all the hurling they possibly could
So they played in everything, even the Sevens
And brought a couple of young fellas up from Kevins

And now with Padraig Kennedy and Eugene Murray signed up
The team they started to win many a cup
But with players like Duggan, Quigs, Bugsy and Feore
The only surprise is that they didn't win more

After ten years in charge Peter decided to stop
But by that stage he had brought them all the way to the top
And everyone involved had fulfilled their dream
And the Club now had what it wanted - a Senior Hurling team

The goal now was to take it to the next level
They needed a manager who in the challenge would revel
The choice was Ken Ryan - a man with no hidden agendas
Although he had links with Ballyboden St Endas

For his selectors he chose Eugene Murray and Denis Ryan
Eugene knew it was over, it was time to move to the line
And Denis had won two leagues, two championships and a Miller Shield
Although not even one of them was won on the field

To build up their team they wouldn't spend the club's cash
The found cheap recruits in the Gardai, like Reilly and Nash
And Duggan and Feore, Quigs and the Roches were still there
Along with Johnny Mac from Cork and Damien Garrihy from Clare

So the panel was there and the work had to be done
But the goal has been reached, we are now Senior One
And from Ken on to Eugene, the baton has been passed
And Senior One status, long may it last

But just Senior Hurling is not what it's all about
And there are plenty of hurlers who like a drink of stout
But they wouldn't be too fond of all the laps and the training
And they don't even bother to turn up if it's raining

But Judes have been lucky from the very beginning
To have had Junior Hurlers who had a habit of winning
And mentors like Grogan, Cummins, Mick Ryan and Jim Kelly
And quite a few players with a bit of a belly

A football championship in the Club, we have yet to see
While the Hurlers have won Junior A, B, C and D
Which shows the teams have always been strong
And there's quite a few players who've been there all along

The McLoughlins and the two Barrys, Heraty and McGann
Ronnie, Coughlan and Finnerty always ready to take out a man
Martin Hayes and Mick Reidy who hung around for ages
And Hegarty and Kenno played at various stages

The Ryan brothers of Rossmore, Colm and Niall
Both of them hurlers with plenty of style
And Gerry from the 'Mines, a Ryan but no relation
He has been the cause of many a celebration

For a lot of our success we must be thankful to the West
Because the Fallons and the Roches were some of our best
But we'll take them from anywhere as long as they can play
And anyone who joins us always wants to stay

Shane O'Connor and Eamonn Ryan have been around a while
And George Frisby and Hassett bring their own hurling style
So here's to the next quarter century of hurling success
Let's hope we can keep our place up with the best

Summer Project 1983/84 – Included: Deirdre Feore, Sylvia O'Reilly, Mary Farrell, May Hughes, Rita Moran, Jimmy O'Dwyer, John Malone, Fiachra Feore, Callaghan McCarthy, Paul Farrell, David O'Reilly.

Club hurling team, official opening of clubhouse, 1987 – Back (l-r): Brendan Byrne, Ciarán McLoughlin, John Nolan, Declan O'Boyle, Barry Jeffries, John Reen, Darren Orr, Eoghan Ryan, Kieran Durkan, Dara Murphy, Joe Denver, John O'Riordan. Front: Martin Carty, Fiachra Feore, Colin Farrell, Ger Farrell, Paul Farrell, Enda Sheehy, Terence Orr, Bryan Duggan, Seán Fallon, Ted Russell.

U10 hurling 1991 with mentors Bobby Carty and Noel Lyons.

St Judes U11 team who played Faythe Harriers in Wexford in 1990.

1992 U11 Camogie Championship winners – Back row: Marie O'Brien, Lorna Cowzer, Sarah Hughes, Lisa Sheehan, Jacinta Bradshaw, Aoife Farrell, Anne Marie O'Brien, Deirdre Ryan, Ruth Maguire, Seamus Massey, Front: Elaine Sherry, Niamh Cunningham, Caroline Scanlon, Michelle Carey, Elaine Clarke, Imelda Molloy, Sarah Massey (captain), Aoife Kelly, Ailish Reid, Fiona O'Frighil.

1992/93 Dual Division 1 Hurling and Football Champions U12 – Back row (l-r): Ronan Potts, Brian O'Brien, Ross McDermott, Kevin Hayes, Andrew Glover, Mark O'Brien, Paul Molamphy, Donagh O'Dwyer, Conaire Fitzpatrick, Anthony Reilly, Bart Lehane, Sean McLoughlin. Front: Aidan Russell, David Ryan, Ger Hartnett, Fergal Daly, Caoimhin Joyce, Eoghan Mangan, Stephen Murray, Alex Meade-Wilson, Colm McGovern, Eoghan O'Neill.

1996 U11 Hurling panel – Back row (l-r): Eoin Conway, Simon McCann, Darren Kennedy, Stephen O'Reilly, Rory Bannigan, Dermot Hanaphy, Kevin O'Malley, Ronán Joyce, Brian Meade-Wilson, Peter Daly, Sam Lehane, Ciaran McNamara. Front: Michael Byrne, Ciarán Dowd, Feargal O'Rourke, Ross O'Brien, Brian Roche, Éadhmonn Mac Suibhne, James Kilcoyne, Vincent Walsh, Karl O'Gorman, Brian Monaghan.

1995 U14 'A' Feile Hurling team – Back row (l-r): Conaire Fitzpatrick, Seán McLoughlin, Alex Wilson, Anthony Reilly, Ross McDermott, Paul Molamphy, Donagh O'Dwyer, Bart Lehane, Kevin Hayes, Andrew Glover. Front: Sean Breheny, Donal Ward, David Ryan, Vincent Wallace, Caoimhin Joyce, Ger Hartnett, Eoghan Ward, David Edge.

U10 Footballers 1979/80 – included at back are: James Durkan, Niall Murphy, Pat Brien, Sean Feehan, Seán Feeney, Gavin Kavanagh, Gary Irvine, Gerard Keaty, J. Brady. Front: Barry McGlynn, Alan Mulgrew, Pat (Lefty) Byrne, Michael Denver, Jim Dolan.

Centenary Cup winning team for 1984.

1988 winners Corrigan Cup U10 – Back row: Jim Mulready, Enda Crennan, Alan Bowe, Karl O'Boyle, Ken Molloy, Dermot O'Reilly, Trevor McDonald, Thomas Quinn, Padraig O'Shaughnessy, Ian Fortune, Patrick McLoughlin. Front: Antoin Doyle, Trevor Percy, Owen McBride, Shane Lynch, Paul Carroll, David McGovern, David Barry, Philip Kearns, Aidan Lawlor, Niall Tierney.

U10 Football 1988 – Back row (l-r): Hugh McBride, Robert O'Grady, Greg Lehane, Kevin Faley, Dave Reynolds, Colm Murphy, Stephen Culhane, Brian Moran. Front: Tadgh O'Brien, Keith Kelleher, Ian O'Shea, Padraig Joyce, Brendan Leahy, Gerry Quinn, Barry O'Connor, Carl Butler, David Coates. At back: mentors Mick O'Brien and Kevin Clabby.

U10 'B' Football team 1992/93 – Standing (l-r): Andrew McFeigh, Brian Geraghty, David Dunk, Donail Ó Nuallain, John Conlon, Pat Tyrrel, Dara Carty, Fintan O'Brien, John Ryan, Ronan O'Riordan. Kneeling: Vincent Kelly, Paudie Rooney, Dave McGuire, Niall Cullen, Kevin Coghlan, Cathal Feehily, Cillian O'Neill, Paul McCabe, Fergal O'Connor.

1992 Corrigan Cup winners (U10) – Back row (l-r): Terence Meade-Wilson, Ciaran O'Brien, Seán Breheny, Kevin Edge, Ciarán O'Brien, Neil Roche, Barry Faulkner, Kevin Shanley, Shane O'Brien, Richard Collins, Graham Crawford, Cormac McNamara. Front: Eoin McGowan, John Ryan, Shane Guckian, Mick Lyons, Colm Daly, Mark Carthy, Dara Carthy, Conor McBride, Fergus Grimes.

U14 Division 1, U15 Division 1 and McCarthy Cup winners – Back row: Pat Quigley, Gerald Coburn, Brian Farrell, Alan Kennedy, Jeff Kane, Colm Ryan, Derek McGrath, Robert Hyland, Anthony Gilleran, Philip Shaughnessy, John McKeon, Paul McSherry, Tommy Hartnett. Front: David Campbell, Brendan Culhane, Kieran Quigley, Alan Lenane, Ross Mac Mathúna, Michael Mahon, Ian Healy, Michael Hartnett, Declan Molloy, Colm Farrell.

Feile na nGael winners 2002 and U15 Championship finalists 2003 – Front row: Sean Walsh, David McGann, Shaun Ó Cuiv, Conor Finnerty, Gerard Fehily, Kevin McLaughlin, Neal Mangan, Ciaran Conroy, Kris Green, Donal Grimes. Middle: Colm Murphy, Seán Walsh, Peter Morgan, Brian Malee, Niall Dervin, Chris Guckian, P. Mac Fhlannchadha, Gearoid Gilmore, Stephen Larkin. Back: Chris Hilliard, Seán McMahon, Mark Colgan, Andrew McCann, Colm Kilcoyne, Martin Hartnett, Gerard Hanahoe, David Browne.

You can't beat class! DJ Carey meets Jack and Mary Crennan in Judes.

Cumann Bridge Naomh Jude 2000.

Martin and Seán at Sevens, 1998.

Our first chairman Fr John Greene cc, with Seán Conway and Ernest Kenny.

Bishop Galvin NS, the first team to represent the school in a Cumann na mBunscoil final in Croke Park in 1980 – Back row: Derek Doherty (Rushbrook), Sean Feeney (Orwell), Stephen O'Connell (Rossmore), Gerard Keaty (Templeogue Wood), David McGlynn (Orwell), Diarmuid Healy (Butterfield), Niall Robinson (Rossmore), Brendan Finn (Glendown), Stuart Cahill (Willington), Mark Dempsey (Rushbrook), Peter Kernan (Rossmore), Michael Lalor (Glendown). Front: Gregory Irvine (Glendown), Declan O'Reilly (Orwell), Niall Murphy (Orwell), Kevin Hogan (Glendown), Eoin Darcy (Kennington), Eamonn O'Reilly (Glendown), Jim Dolan (Glendown), Gerard McSweeney (Orwell), Patrick Byrne (Willington), Alan Healy (Rossmore), Michael Kavanagh (Orwell), Barry McGlynn (Orwell).

Bishop Galvin NS, winners Cumann na mBunscoil Corn Oideachais Junior Hurling Division 1 final and winners Corn Oideachais 'B' 2003 – Back row (l-r): Alan O'Beirne, Paul Kiernan, Danny Riordan, Keith Duane, Niall Conroy, Niall Murray, Ciaran Mangan, Gerard McManus, Paul Maguire, Stephen Elliott, Eoin Larkin, Conor McMahon, Evan Griffin. Front: Mark Hannon, Carl Dunne, Emmet McKenna, Killian Ó hÓra, Danny Devine, Michael Scanlon, Killian Morgan, Robert Hardy, Robert Martina, Darragh O'Connor, Oisín O'Donnell, Ross Murphy.

1989 U16 All Dublin League and Championship – Back row: Brendan Byrne, Raymond Walsh, Jim Fields, Kieran Durkan, Dara Murphy, Seán Dunne, Declan O'Boyle, Niall Bowe, Ray Waterhouse, Joe Denver, Joe Moran, John Farrell, John O'Riordan. Front: Louis Dockery, Brian Howlin, Christy Cullen, James Weldon, Craig Fitzpatrick, Gary Percy, Carl Coleman, Alan O'Connor, Peter Keohane. Managers: Seamus Durkan and Michael O'Boyle.

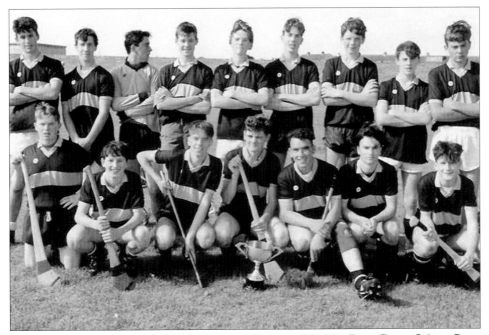

1990/91 winners Division 3 Dublin Minor League – Back row (l-r): John Reen, Ronan Colgan, Bryan Duggan, Eoghan Ryan, Marcus Mallon, Fiachra Feore, Barry Heraty, Mark O'Reilly, Ciaran McLaughlin. Front: Paul Farrell, Paul McGovern, Niall Ryan, Sean Fallon, Darren Orr, Jonathan Duffy, Brian Ward.

1994 winners Division 1 South City League U16 – Back row (l-r): Neil Doyle (Asst Manager), Thomas Quinn, Stephen Joyce, Antoin Doyle, Ian Fortune, David Dickens, Eoin McBride, John O'Loughlin, Michael Glover, Enda Crennan, John Barr, Philip McGlynn, Seán McBride (Manager). Front: Ciaran Fitzpatrick, Kevin O'Dwyer, Ross Kinsella, Ken Molloy, Gareth Roche, David Edge, Gary Downes, Patrick Brien, James Kelly, Dave McGovern.

1997 U16 'B' Hurling Champions – Back row (l-r): Joe Clavin (mentor), Donnacha Ryan, Anthony Reilly, Ger Hartnett, Paul Molamphy, Donagh O'Dwyer, Bart Lehane, Michael Lyons, Shane Hartney, Eoghan O'Neill, Brian Eighan, Seán McLoughlin, Don Lehane (manager), Tommy Hartnett (mentor). Front: Ross McDermott, Paul Goodall, Ciaran Coates, James Dennehy, Eoghan Mangan, Donal Ward, Tomas Mangan, Seán Breheny, Alex Meade-Wilson, Ciaran O'Brien, Vincent Wallace, Gavin Duffy.

1999 U16 Football promoted to Division 1 – Back row (l-r): Damien Devins, Mark Molloy, Dave O'Hara, John Conlon, Dara Carty, Padraig Griffin, Pat Waldron, Liam Coffey, Barry Lyons, Fergal O'Connor, Kevin Coghlan, Fintan O'Brien. Front: Ben Savage, Ciaran Lalor, Joey Donnelly, Dara Lowe, Vincent Kelly, Conor Foley, Alan Lowe, Shane Lynch, Niall O'Shea. Mentors: John Foley, Mick O'Brien, Eamonn Treacy, Danny Lynch.

2000 winners Division 1 Dublin Minor League – Standing (l-r): Declan Feore (manager), Garrett Edge (selector), Timmy McCarthy, Seán Breheny, Dave O'Hara, Neil Roche, Shane Guckian, Michael Lyons, John Waldron, Kevin Coghlan, Mick Hartnett (selector), Seán Breheny (selector). Middle: Ciaran O'Brien, Kevin Edge, Mark Molby, Barry Lyons, Fintan O'Brien, Seán O'Connor, Trevor Dickens. Kneeling: Eamon Treacy (coach), Vinny Kelly, John Conlon, Seamus Ryan (captain), John Ryan, Fergus Grimes, Aidan Smylie. Absent: Niall Guckian.

2001 U16 Division 1 Hurling League winners – Back row: Ross O'Brien, Stephen O'Reilly, Raymond McLoughlin, Brian Meade-Wilson, Sam Lehane, Vincent Walsh, Conor Ward, Ciaran Dowd. Middle: Philip Ryan, Michael Teehan, Kevin O'Malley, Ronán Joyce, Redmond O'Hanlon, James Kilcoyne, Brian Monaghan, James Hurley. Front: Peter Daley, Ciaran McNamara, Eadhmon Mac Suibhne, Conor Kelly, Fergal O'Rourke, Gavin Coyne, Paul Teehan. Mentors: A. Mac Suibhne, Paul Dowd, Fonsie McNamara.

2002 Minor Hurling Championship finalists v St Vincents – Back row (l-r): Ciaran McNamara, Niall Guckian, Seamus Dwyer, Patrick Crean, Colm Manning, Ronan Joyce, Seán O'Connor, Andy McLoughlin, Conor Kelly, Vinny Walsh, Sam Lehane, Niall O'Shea, Ian Murray, Timmy McCarthy. Front: Kevin O'Malley, Eamonn Mac Suibhne, Paul Teehan, Ross O'Brien, Mark Whitmore, Redmond O'Hanlon, Adam Smiley, Stephen Hyland, Michael Teehan, Howard Walsh, Martin McCabe.

2003 Minor Hurling Championship finalists v St Brigids – Back row (l-r): Brian Meade-Wilson, Seamus O'Dwyer, Ray McLoughlin, Ciaran Dowd, Kevin O'Malley, James Hurley, Ronan Joyce, James Kilcoyne, Vincent Walsh, Philip Ryan, Conor Ward, Kevin McManamon. Front: Paul Teehan, Conor Kelly, Paddy O'Shea, Brian Monaghan, Ross O'Brien, Redmond O'Hanlon, Michael Teehan, Ciaran McNamara, Sam Lehane, Paul Mangan, Eamonn Mac Suibhne.

The Captains from 1999 – Seán Hegarty, Eugene Murray, Jade McGurn, Niall Lawlor, Fiona Guckian, Odhran O'Brien.

Under 11 Championship winners, 1994 - Back row (l-r): Ann Kelly (mentor), Sheena McDonnell, Helena O'Brien, Roisin Eighan, Blaithin Keane, Jennifer Hartnett, Maeve Ward, Sinead O'Friel, Siobhan Reid, Ann Dennehy (mentor). Front: Toni Cowzer, Niamh McGann, Karen Byrne, Claire Dennehy, Claire Mangan, Bhróna Maher, Suzanne Waine, Niamh Skelly.

Tommy Hickey (Bar Manager) and Patrick Tyrrell (Assistant Manager).

UnδeR 16 anδ MinoRs

Neil Doyle and Seán McBride

G IVEN the structure of competitions within the GAA, Under 16 and minor levels are an extremely important element in the overall organisation. These levels represent the transition from juvenile and youth to adult level. It is vital for any Club with ambitions for success at adult level to give special attention to Under 16 and minor football and hurling teams.

However, it is not just as a feeder for future adult teams that these teams should be seen. First and foremost, the Under 16 and minor competitions are significant in their own right.

With the progression of juvenile and youth teams from the foundation of the Club, St Judes readily rose to the challenge of entering teams in the highly competitive environment of Under 16 and minor leagues and championships engaging with such well established powers as St Vincents, Thomas Davis, Ballyboden St Endas and Erin's Isle.

Football teams at Under 16 and minor level took the field in the period 1982/1984. The former performed creditably but the minors had to rely to some extent on Under 15 and Under 16 players, understandably for a such a young Club. However, success was not that long coming. In 1985 an Under 16 team managed by Donnchadh O Liathain, and ably captained by Séan O'Conaill, won Division 3 of the South Dublin League but were beaten in the All-Dublin final by Rosmini Gaels after a hard fought encounter in Ringsend Park. Stalwarts on that team included Seán O'Conaill (Captain), Philip Doyle, Alan Carr, Stephen O'Brien, Seán O'Driscoll, Philip Stokes, Ian Kelly, Jim Dolan, Eamonn O'Reilly, Seán Coffey, Mark Dempsey, Fergus O'Hanlon, Shay Howlin, Denis Evoy, Ger McSweeney, James Durkan and Conor Lehane. The last three are still giving sterling sevice to the Club.

In 1987 an Under 16 football team managed by John Gallen, Charles Moran, and Frank McSweeney won Division 2 of the South Dublin League. In the same year the Club fielded an Under 16 hurling team, under John Gallen, Charles Moran and Finbarr Murphy, for the first time. They achieved instant success winning Division 2 of the League beating Raheny in the final in O'Toole Park. Peter "Hippo" Ryan represented Dublin at Minor level in 1988. Minor mentors in those early years included Mick Hartnett, Garrett Edge, Ray O'Connor and Martin Molamphy.

In 1988/89 a minor football team managed by Tommy Bassett and Donnchadh O Liathain won Division 1A (South) of the Minor League and were beaten in the Dublin Final. They reached the quarter-final of their championship. The records show the Minor B team in 1987/88 under Seán Conway and John Gallen as "enjoying their football"! In 1988/89 and 1989/90 the Minor B team finished midway in their Leagues. The mentors were Tommy Hartnett, Bernie Gallagher, Martin McCabe, Charles Moran, Máire McSherry and Bobby Carty.

However, it was in 1989 that St Judes made a real impact on under age football in Dublin for the first time. In that year the Under 16 team, flushed with success from juvenile years, under the astute guidance of Seamus Durkan and Michael O'Boyle won the Dublin Championship and Division 1 of the League. This was the Club's first championship win and a tremendous achievement for such a relatively young Club. The team was: Brendan Byrne, Raymond Walshe, Jim Fields, Kieran Durkan, Dara Murphy, Liam Dunne, Declan O'Boyle, Niall Bowe, Ray Waterhouse, Joe Denvir, Joe Moran, John Farrell, John O'Riordan, Louis Dockery, Brian Howlin, Christy Cullen, James Weldon, Craig Fitzpatrick, Gary Percy, Carl Coleman, Alan O'Connor and Peter Keohane. Of these, Kieran Durkan, Dara Murphy, John O'Riordan and Declan O'Boyle (Senior Manager) are still active with the Club.

In football in the period 1990 to 1994 the Club continued to compete at the highest levels at Under 16 and minor. Normally, there were two teams at each level thus ensuring a steady supply of players for the adult teams in subsequent years. Players from the 1991 Under 16 teams still involved in the Club include Barry Heraty, Stephen Willoughby, Ronan Colgan, Niall Lawlor, Peter Gilsenan, Garrett Evans and Ciaran Cash. In 1991 the Minor A team under Seamus Durkan and Michael O'Boyle reached the quarter final of the Championship. Kieran Durkan was selected for the Dublin Minor team. In 1991/92 the Under 16 A team finished in the top half of Division 1 of the League going out in the first round of the Championship. Tommy Hartnett, Pat Quigley and Gary Kane were the mentors. Jeff Kane was selected on the Dublin Under 16 team. In both 1992/93 and 1993/94 the Minor A team under Tommy Hartnett and Tony Gilleran finished in the top half of the Premier Division of the League going out in the second round of the Championship in 1992/93. In 1992 and 1993 Enda Sheehy played for the Dublin Minors. Mentors who kept the flag flying at Under 16 and minor level in this era, in addition to those mentioned, included Leslie Percy, Pat Brien, Tommy Bassett, Martin McCabe, Paddy Russell, Jack Lernihan, Stephen Willoughby, Johnny O'Gara, Charles Moran, Jack Crennan and Frank McCarthy.

In hurling in 1991 the minors under Joe Clavin, Michael Ryan and Seán Ward brought the first piece of silverware at that grade to the Club. They won Division

3 of the League defeating Northside team Naomh Fionnbarra in the final having won all their matches in the Southside League. They lost the second round of the Championship to Thomas Davis. The following year they beat the all powerful O'Tooles in the Championship before losing to St Sylvesters. Bryan Duggan played in goal for the Dublin minor team and Enda Sheehy and Niall Ryan were also Dublin minors. The team was invited to Portumna for the O'Meara minor hurling tournament losing in the final to Portumna. Players from that era who are still active in the Club include Seán Fallon, Fiachra Feore, Bryan Duggan, Ciaran McLoughlin, Niall Ryan, Barry Heraty, Ronan Colgan, Declan Molloy, Alan Kennedy, Ciaran Quigley, David Roche, Barry McGann, Paul McGovern and Colm Ryan.

In 1991 we had an Under 16 hurling team under Pat Quigley and Tommy Hartnett in Division 1 of the League for the first time finishing in 4th position. Declan Molloy, Ciaran Quigley, Alan Kennedy and Colm Ryan made the Dublin South team in the Leinster League. In 1993 the minor hurlers under Michael Ryan and Pat Quigley finished 3rd in Division 2 of the League and lost the quarter final of the championship by a point. Enda Sheehy played centre field for the Dublin minors and Ronan Colgan, Declan Molloy and Ciaran Quigley made the Dublin B League team. In 1994 the team finished in the top half of the League. Declan Molloy was selected for the Dublin Minor Championship team and Ciaran Quigley, Declan Molloy and Alan Kennedy were on the Dublin League team. In 1994 the Under 16 hurling mentors were Peter Ryan and Jack Crennan and the minors were managed by Jimmy O'Dwyer and John Fitzpatrick. Players from the Club played a significant role in back to back VEC All-Ireland B Championship wins for Dublin in 1993 and 1994 - Enda Sheehy, Ronan Colgan, Alan Kennedy, Ciaran Quigley and Declan Molloy starring throughout with the last mentioned three all scoring in a thrilling encounter with Laois in 1994.

The year 1994 brought some further football successes. The Under 16A team under Seán McBride and Neil Doyle won Division 1 of the South City League and reached the quarter final of the Championship. They were also runners-up in a Clontarf Under 16 Blitz tournament. Enda Crennan was selected for the Dublin Under 16 team. Members of the team who are still playing with the Club include Tom Quinn, Stevie Joyce, Antoin Doyle, Ian Fortune, Enda Crennan, Philip McGlynn, Ken Molloy, Gareth Roche and David Edge. The Minor B team under Charles Moran, Pat Russell and Jack Crennan were beaten in the semi-final of the Shield by St Bridgids. Players on that team included Damien Carroll, Gavin Russell, Paul Crennan, Michael Murphy and Jimmy McGurn.

In 1995 and 1996 the Under 16 and two minor football teams performed creditably, generally finishing midway in their leagues. New mentors in addition to those already mentioned included Eamon Brady, Mick O'Brien, Noel Lyons, Donal O Loingsigh, B Kennedy and Gus Barry. Enda Crennan and Ken Molloy made the Dublin Minor panels, in football and hurling respectively, in 1996. The year 1997 again saw success at under age level. The Under 16 hurlers under Don Lehane, Joe Clavin, Tommy Hartnett and Seán Ward won the B Championship after a one point win over St Peregrines in a thrilling final in Parnell Park. This was the first underage hurling championship won by the Club. The Under 16 football team, managed by Don Lehane and Tommy Hartnett, were unlucky to be beaten by only one point by St Brigids in the Championship (A) final. The achievements of these teams is dealt with in more detail in the section entitled "Juvenalia" as they essentially had been together from under 10 days. A highlight of the year was the visit of Nicky English to the Club to present medals to the Under 16 football and hurling teams. A well deserved accolade from such a prominent figure.

Representative honours included -

Dublin U16 Football: Ger Hartnett, Paul Goodall, Kevin Hayes, Andrew Glover

Dublin U16 Hurling: Bart Lehane, Anthony Reilly, Donncha Ryan, Ger Hartnett

Dublin Minor Hurling: Ger Hartnett (1998)

Leinster U17 Football: Paul Goodall

Dublin Minor Football: Kevin Hayes, Aidan Lawlor (1997)

Dublin Vocational Schools Football: Declan McCabe, Kevin Hayes (1997), Andrew Glover, Ger Hartnett, Ross McDermott (1998), Seán Breheny, Micheál Lyons, David O'Hara and Brendan McManamon (1999). In 1999 Dublin won the All-Ireland, beating Tyrone in Croke Park.

Dublin Vocational Schools Hurling: Seán McLoughlin, Donagh O'Dwyer, Colm McGovern, Bart Lehane.

Dublin U15 Football: Seán Breheny, Micheál Lyons, Brendan McManamon, John Waldron

The year 1998 saw Seán Breheny (Senior), Bartle Faulkner and Tom Ryan in charge of the Under 16 football team. Seán Breheny, Micheál Lyons and John Waldron made the Dublin Under 16 panel. With the addition of a few second year minors, the 1997 Under 16 team progressed to Minor A in 1998. Noel Lyons joined the management team. They were beaten in the first round of the Championship, after a replay, by the eventual winners, Ballyboden. They finished third in Division 1 of the League. Andrew Glover made the Dublin Minor panel.

The same team essentially again represented the Club at Minor A level in 1999. They were defeated in the quarter final of the Championship again by the eventual winners, Kilmacud Crokes, and finished mid-table in the League. Paul Goodall was selected for the Dublin Minors. John Waldron and Seán Breheny were subsequently selected on the Dublin Minor panel which went on to win the Leinster Championship. In 1998/99 St Judes fielded three minor football teams, the only Club in Dublin to do so.

A feature of the activities of the 1997/99 Under 16 and minor teams was the number of games played, with quite good success rate, against top class opposition outside Dublin - Louth Under 16 footballers, The Heath (Levins) Celbridge, Dunboyne, Sarsfields, Ballymore Eustace, Kilcock and Summerhill and runners up in their group in the Carlow town Under 16 All-Ireland Club Hurling Tournament. Finally, a point in relation to the 1997/99 teams that deserves mention. Taking football and hurling together about 50 players are still playing with the Club in 2003 - surely a worthy legacy. It is to the credit of players and management that they are still making such a significant contribution to the playing strength of St Judes.

Mick O'Brien, John Foley and Eamon Treacy managed the 1999 Under 16 football team. They finished well up in Division 2 of the League and reached the quarter final of the Championship following a great second round win over Ballyboden St Endas. Fintan O'Brien was selected for the Dublin Under 16 footballers. This team went Minor A in 2001 with Paddy Kehoe replacing Eamon Treacy in the mentors. They reached the top level of Division 1 eventually finishing in fourth place and lost in the second round of the Championship. The team made a memorable trip to Ballinskelligs during which certain parties were reported as having got "lost"! Of that team Stephen Earley, Damien Kehoe, and Joey Donnelly are now with the Senior Panel. Paul Copeland kept goal for the Dublin Minor team beaten in a replay by Tyrone in the 2001 All-Ireland final. Paul was also goalkeeper for Dublin at Under 21 level in 2003 when, together with Michaél Lyons and Brendan McManamon, they secured the ultimate honour of All-Ireland winners.

In 1999 the Under 16 hurlers under Eamon Treacy, John Foley and Pat Griffin finished fourth in Division 1 of the League and were beaten by five points in the semi final of the Championship by hot favourites and eventual winners, Ballyboden St Endas, in a closely contested encounter. In what perhaps was the team's best performance they led at half time and the game was in doubt until Ballyboden got a lucky goal late in the second half.

The panel, which had been together under the same management since Under 11, was Barry Lyons, Fergal O'Connor, Dara Lowe, Alan Lowe, David O'Hara,

Mark Molloy (Captain), Dara Carty, Conor Foley, Lorcan Farrell, Vinny Kelly, Kevin Coghlan, Fintan O'Brien, Damien Devine, John Conlon, Pat Waldron, John Ryan, Shane Lynch, Padraic Griffin, Alan Barry and Stephen Early. Mark Molloy and Vinnie Kelly were members of the Dublin Hurling Development Squad.

The year 2000 was a good year for our Under 16 footballers. The A team under Oliver O'Connor, Luke Mooney and Paul Manning won Division 2 with the B team under Oliver O'Connor and Noel O'Rourke taking Division 4. Both league final play-offs took place on the same morning, the A team beating St Olafs and the B team accounting for Ballymun Kickhams.

The Under 16A panel was: John Behan, Michael Boyce, Mark Brennan-Whitmore, Patrick Crean, Brian Doran, Dermot Groarke, Niall Guckian, Stephen Hyland, Jim Lawless, Ciaran Lawlor, Colm Manning, Martin McCabe, Tim McCarthy, Alan Mooney, Ian Murray, Anthony O'Connor, Seán O'Connor, Niall O'Shea, Paddy Reynolds, Conor Sanfey, Ben Savage, Patrick Tyrrell and Howard Walshe.

The Under 16B panel was: Mark Fleming, Paddy Fleming, Karl Johnston, David Lonergan, Paul McCabe, Brian McCurtain, Seán McLoughlin, John Paul O'Reilly, Paul O'Reilly, Kevin O'Shea, Paudie Rooney, Hugh Smith, Adrian Tallon, Aidan Walshe, Andrew Farrell, Seán Dwyer, Conor O'Byrne, Aidan Smylie, Ian Daly, Joseph Meehan, Mark McGovern and Cathal Fehily.

In 2001 the Under 16 hurlers won Division 1 of the league for the first time in the history of the Club. This panel had been together and won a number of trophies from under 11 under mentors Phonsie McNamara, Aodhán MacSuibhne, Paul Dowd, Padraic Monaghan and Martin O'Rourke. The members of the panel were Conor Kelly (Captain), Gavin Coyne, Peter Daly, Ciaran Dowd, Dermot Hanaphy, James Hurley, Gerry Hughes, Ronan Joyce, James Kilcoyne, Sam Lehane, Eadhmonn MacSuibhne, Paul Mangan, Raymond McLoughlin, Ciaran McNamara, Brian Meade-Wilson, Brian Monaghan, Ross O'Brien, Redmond O'Hanlon, Kevin O'Malley, Fergal O'Rourke, Stephen O'Reilly, Bryan Roche, Philip Ryan, Michael Teehan, Paul Teehan, Vincent Walshe, Conor Ward.

In the year 2000 the Minor hurlers did us proud bringing home the Lorcan Uí Tuathail Cup by winning Division 1 of the League for the first time. They scored an impressive victory, 5-8 to 1-11, over favourites Naomh Mearnóg in the decider. A strong backline which included Seamus Ryan, Seán Breheny and Mark Molloy kept the Mearnog's lethal attack at bay. Vinnie Kelly, Ciaran O'Brien and John Ryan starred in a brilliant and hardworking attack. St Judes were undefeated in the League overcoming tough opposition such as St Sylvesters, Cuala, Ballyboden St Endas, St Brigids and St Oliver Plunketts. Ciaran O'Brien and Vinnie Kelly were selected for the Dublin County Minor team.

By 2001 we were fielding two minor hurling teams and for the last two years our Minor A hurlers have reached the county championship final.

In 2002 the minors, coached by Oliver O'Connor, Christy O'Shea and Con O'Brien won their way to our first ever Minor A Championship final. Victories along the way over Crumlin, Ballyboden St Endas and St Brigids gave us great encouragement as we faced St Vincents in the final. And what a cracker that turned out to be. In a pulsating finish the Judes lads went down by 4 points. However, the display of hurling skills that evening brought delight to the many supporters and, of course, minor mentors of previous years who saw all their hard work coming to fruition. The 2002 Minor hurling panel was: Aidan Smylie, Niall Guckian (C), Martin McCabe, Stephen Hyland, Niall O'Shea, Timmy McCarthy, Seán O'Connor, Colm Manning, Seán McLoughlin, Howard Walshe, Mark Brennan – Whitmore, Patrick Crean, Paudie Rooney, Andrew McLoughlin, Conor Sanfey, Ian Murray, Paul Teehan, Ray McLoughlin, James Hurley, Kevin O'Malley, Vinny Walsh, Ross O'Brien, Conor Kelly, Sam Lehane, Ronan Joyce, Ciaran McNamara, Raymond O'Hanlon, Eadhmonn Mac Suibhne.

To play in a county final is every hurlers dream and in 2003 this dream was fulfilled by another fine squad of hurlers. Fonsie McNamara led the management team on this occasion and was assisted by Con O'Brien, Padraic Monaghan and Paul Dowd. This final was reached by victories over Craobh Chiaran and Round Towers but the trophy eluded us once again. It was won by a superb St Brigids outfit, whose display on the day was indeed worthy of county champions. A very successful table quiz to fund the return of Aidan Smylie from Crete for the final exemplified the spirit of this squad.

The 2003 Minor hurling panel was: Paul Teehan, Ray McLoughlin, Ciaran Dowd, James Kilcoyne, James Hurley, Kevin O'Malley, Brian Monaghan, Vinny Walsh, Ross O'Brien, Conor Ward, Ciaran McNamara, Redmond O'Hanlon, Ronan Joyce, Conor Kelly, Sam Lehane, Michael Teehan, Kevin Mc Manamon, Eadhmonn MacSuibhne, Patrick O'Shea, Brian Meade-Wilson, Philip Ryan, Paul Mangan, Gerard Hughes and Aidan Smylie.

The 2003 Minor hurlers also reached the League Division 1 final only to be beaten again by St Brigids after a hard fought encounter in O'Toole Park. While there is naturally disappointment at failing twice at the last hurdle, players and mentors alike can hold their heads high. Their team was up there at the top with the best in Dublin minor hurling. Players from the 2002 and 2003 teams to represent Dublin at Minor county level were Seán O'Connor, Timmy McCarthy and Ronan Joyce.

Footballers at Under 16 (2001) and minor (2002 and 2003) were managed by Padraic Monaghan, Martin O'Rourke, Paul Dowd and Luke Mooney. After two mid-table finishes the minors finished third in Division 1 of the League in 2003. This team won the Minor Cup, Division 1 on 2nd November 2003.

In each year the teams competed in Division 1 of the League and the A Championship. Nearly all the players involved are still with the Club carrying with them to adult football the experience of playing in a highly competitive environment against top class opposition. In 2001 the team made a trip to Glasgow taking in a Celtic match and playing a friendly with the local GAA Club.

All in all the Club can take satisfaction from its involvement at Under 16 and minor level in both football and hurling. The teams have consistently performed very well at the highest level in League and Championship. There will, understandably, be some disappointment at the lack of Championship success, particularly at Minor level. However, if the dedication and commitment shown over the years by players and mentors alike is maintained it will surely only be a matter of time, hopefully a short time, before this position is rectified. Certainly, the Club can look forward with confidence to its future in both football and hurling given the quality of teams and players, and the stage of development which they have attained, coming through from the Under 16 and Minor ranks.

1990 U16 Hurling Squad – Back row (l-r): Charles Moran (Manager), Barry McGovern, Mick Davis, Damien Fallon, Aidan Malone, John O'Riordan, Peter Ryan, Shane Gallen, Tarla Kelly, Dara Murphy, Mick Quinn. Front: Brendan Byrne, Mick Fallon, Alan Gallagher, Fiachra Feore, Kieran Durkan, Raymond Moore.

"Mister, gissa lift over the stile"

A CHILDHOOD MEMORY – Brady Bunch

A PLEA that reverberated around Croke Park in a bygone era! A time when, as far as we youngsters were concerned, hurling and football were played by giants. I had the privilege of being born and reared under the shadow of the Cusack Stand and Hill 16, separated only by the Belvedere ground which now no longer exists. The location of my house in Foster Terrace stood at the confluence of access roads to the Hill and the Cusack Stand for spectators travelling from the city and points beyond. It provided a crucial stand for the "hawkers" as we termed them, those most entrepreneurial of spirits who flogged everything from caps and badges to fruit and lemonade. It amazed me that the same old lady with rusty grey hair always occupied our stand, a most desirable spot. Maybe it was the fact that on days after the game our fires crackled with the splinters of old apple and orange boxes and fruit bowls brimmed over with bruised apples, pears or bananas. The scent, which still assails my nostrils to this day, is that of tobacco smoke, body odour and oranges, that wafted around the periphery of Croke Park on the big match days.

The privilege of living beside this cacophonous cauldron was not limited to big match days. Any given Sunday, Croker was the target no matter who was playing. Indeed, we were encouraged to go. However a request for the admission price or for refreshments was seldom, if ever entertained. Once out of the front door, in two minutes flat we would be standing at the entrance stiles, eyeing the burliest and strongest of patrons. Experience had taught us to slip in front of our chosen benefactor and with all the innocence of a timid deer cast our eyes heavenward and intone "Mister, Gissa lift over the stile". I can't remember the tactic ever failing. Once over, we scrambled up the hill and no matter how often we made the climb the sight of the vast green sward struck us and the desire to walk one day behind the Artane Boys' Band welled up.

On such days we could pick our spot, one of our favourites was to climb on to the toilets on the Hill and watch the proceedings. During those informative years we watched in awe the hurling skills of Ring, Rackards, Doyles and Walsh and the football wizardry of Heffernan, Stockwell, O'Connell and Doherty to name a few.

Perhaps it was a different world, but it gave us grounding in all that was exciting and enthralling in our national games.

The inner sanctum

Declan Feore

L AST WEEK I was fortunate enough to be a privileged guest in the Premium Section of the New Cusack Stand for the National Football League semi-finals between Cork and Donegal and Mayo and Derry. I met as arranged, with a very good friend, Eoin Heraty, in the Bankers in Trinity Street. We got a taxi across. The driver, a Dub, was slagging us, being from Cork and Mayo, about our prospects and warning us not to forget that whatever about the league the DUBS and KERRY would be there for the Championship. He was old enough to remember.

Alighting at the barricades on a side street leading directly to the new Cusack Stand we were courteously ushered through by the Gardai. Stewards at entrances to and in Croke Park proved equally courteous. The mere sight of a Premium Ticket appears to command great attention. "Over to the right gentlemen. In to your right there. Straight through the door on your left Sir". And my God! There it was - an escalator! Did I ever think I'd see the day when I'd be going to a match on an escalator? Slowly, silently up she went. Passing action - packed banners, representing all codes and counties along the way. Up and up until finally we reached the palatial reception area, sumptuously but tastefully laid out. We stood there in awe. A glass partition between us, the seats and the pitch below.

Two nice pints. At £2.20 a head, a little above the odds - but what the hell! we've come a long way.

A quick call to the Gents. The craic and the banter there and in the reception area was as good as in any country town for any important game.

In to our section through a glass door and out to our seats, strategically positioned right on the halfway line. Cork jerseys out on the pitch. Wow! This is the life. We're in the Inner Sanctum. The view is magnificent. The luxury of the New Cusack Stand contrasts beautifully with the panoramic view from here of the surrounding seedy elegance of Dublin, with its skyline dotted with spires, domes and chimney-stacks.

My mind goes back some forty years to when Tom Feore, my father, would bring us from Ballyhea to matches in Buttevant or Kilmallock and the like. He'd give us a tanner a piece with the stern admonition – "don't spend it foolishly". The sideline was the Inner Sanctum then. Getting in there was achieved by contriving a disinterested shuffle and holding out a tentative hand to the coat-tail of some gentleman, actively engaged in healthy banter with the opposition while paying his sideline entry fee.

Come next September, if I'm lucky enough, I'll probably end up on the Hill or the Canal. Looking up at those fortunate enough with Premium Level tickets I'll be regretting that adults cannot emulate the contrived innocence of ten year olds.

Declan Feore
28th April 1996

I sent this article to Croke Park. Liam Mulvihill, Director General, asked that it should be filed in the archives for the New Stand. Danny Lynch PRO promised me two good tickets for the All-Ireland, if I got it published. It was published in the Irish Independent on 1st May 1996. Danny got me the tickets. They cost me 60 pounds.

St Judes trip to the new stand, 15th June 1995, spnsored by "The Spawell". Driver Charlie Dolan.

A peRsonal view

Ernest Kenny

T HE PARISH of St Judes was founded in the seventies, which was the golden age of Gaelic Football. The glamorous Dubs exploded onto the scene awakening a new generation of football supporters and young players anxious to emulate their heroes on the field of play. The existing clubs struggled to cater for the new wave of enthusiasm.

Meanwhile the boundaries of Dublin were also exploding as new suburban developments sprawled further and further in the direction of the Dublin Mountains. At that time you could buy a 3 bedroom semi-detached house for less than £14,000. Estates built by Gallaghers, Crampton and McInerney developed in the fledgling parish of St Judes. In January 1973, Fr. Paul Boland was the lone resident of the new area which would grow to 1,600 households by August 1976, and ultimately 2,300 households by the end of the decade. Progress was marked by the arrival of things which today's residents take for granted. A single phone box by the roundabout was the only phone in the area apart from the doctor's or the priest's phone. A sparse bus service was provided by the 15C, which travelled as far as the Orwell roundabout. The area was really taking shape when the shopping centre was built and the various units opened for business. Although some have since changed hands, the Paintpot, Maxwell's Pharmacy, Brady Butchers, Danny Horkans and West End Dry Cleaners were always with us and were to become great supporters of the Club.

The new residents traipsed through the enormous building site to hear Father Boland (himself an ardent supporter of the Dubs) celebrate mass in the little hut on the site of the present church. This little hut quickly became a community focal point, where jumble sales were first held to raise much needed money to fund school and church buildings. Soon a second priest was appointed directly from the seminary and indeed it was Fr. John Greene who decided to initiate a summer project for the children in 1978. He approached me to organise the Gaelic competition. As part of the project we ran two competitions at U10 and U14 levels and all matches were played off on the Orwell Green. The Gaelic side of the Summer Project proved to be a great social occasion and on its final day we organised some novelty matches including father and son game, over forties game and a Dubs versus culchies game. Notably among the stars of the culchies were Jim Coghlan, Mick O'Brien, Seamus Durkan, Charlie Moran and Don Lehane.

The awesome Dubs included Donnchadh Lehane, Joe McDonnell, John Gallen, Bobby Carty, Tom Mulready, Frank O'Grady and the demure Tommy Bassett.

From these summer evenings the GAA club was formed and first competed in the season 1978/79. The Club was fortunate that so many great people committed themselves wholeheartedly to its development over the years. Its growth was due in no short measures to the energy and the enthusiasm of my neighbours Cyril Bates, RIP and Joe Morrin Snr. RIP. The new school was staffed by fellow enthusiasts such as Seán Healy, Jimmy O'Dwyer and Dónal O'Loingsigh. Links between the school and the club forged in those early years continue to this day with the additional work of Bláthnaid Clancy, Peter Lucey, Seán Breheny, Eamonn Treacy, Alan Dodd, Kathryn O'Connell, Elaine Dromey, Sinéad Curley and Lisa Farragher. Teams grew rapidly and their meeting point was the Orwell Shopping centre. Young lads hanging about were "encouraged" to fill any vacancies which arose on the morning of a match.

In our early years we had difficulty holding onto good players as neighbouring Clubs were busy poaching our players, but gradually the problems were resolved as successes increased at both juvenile and adult level. In particular by winning the Ó Broin Cup St Judes announced its arrival on the Club scene as a force to be reckoned with. Many funny incidents occurred in the twenty-five years of the Club. A lot of them I wouldn't like to commit to paper but I enjoy recounting and reliving those memories with all my friends in the Club. The Club's strength lies in the calibre of its members. Many lifelong friendships have been formed in St Judes and I am proud to count many of its members as my friends. I am also proud to be a founder member of a club with such a great Gaelic tradition. As founders we were extremely ambitious for the Club and are delighted to have seen so many of those ambitions realised in a relatively short space of time. We set goals high in St Judes and no doubt the coming years will bring further achievements.

I would like to wish the Club every success in the future.

Danny Lynch – The St Judes eagle who landed in Croke Park
by Martin Breheny

F OR reasons which we can only surmise upon, history has displayed an unwavering determination not to leak any details of the response to questioning of the famous American bald eagle which strayed across the Atlantic before flopping exhaustedly on Irish shores in 1987.

It might reasonably be assumed that having completed such a spectacular voyage, the bird would be granted asylum in Ireland but no, the authorities decided to send him back home. Accompanying the feisty explorer on the return journey was a job which called for... well... what exactly?

The neck to walk through Dublin Airport clutching a squawking bunch of feathers while telling curious on-lookers: "I'm taking him home to America – honestly"? Yes, definitely a priority requirement.

And what else? A specialist knowledge of how bald eagles react in a pressurised cabin at 40,000 feet? The courage to face stony-faced US immigration officials on the other side, announcing chirpily: "Lads, I just thought ye would want this boyo back, so here we are."

Then again, the most important criteria for this major diplomatic assignment could have been an up-to-date American visa. Whatever the combination, the obvious man for the job was Mr Daniel Lynch, diplomat, spin doctor and adventurer. Plus, of course, a fully paid up member of St Judes GAA club.

Younger club members may be unaware that prior to taking over as Public Relations Officer for the GAA in 1988, Danny filled a similar role at the Department of Public Works, a job which involved making the relevant Minister and various others look so creative and caring that people went to bed at night praying for an election so that they could express their thanks at the ballot box.

Promises weren't delivered on (not much change there then) but it didn't prevent them being made. So then Danny, let it be firmly recorded that the entire population of the West of Ireland holds you personally responsible for not having the Shannon drained. It was repeatedly promised by various politicians but it never happened. Never mind, Danny put a good spin on the excuse, sugar-coating it with a layer of Dingle 'Blarney'. Still, there's a limit to how long any sane citizen could keep doing that. And when Danny's job gave him a chance to contemplate life from high over the Atlantic in the company of an extradited eagle, he decided it was time for a change.

Those of us in the media business were extremely interested in who would become GAA PRO in succession to the late and revered Pat Quigley.

We speculated among each other and even took bets but nobody predicted the winner. I still recall how Michael Fortune, a colleague of mine in the Irish Press back then, arrived in the office one morning to announce that the word from St Judes was that Danny Lynch was to be the next GAA PRO.

Who? What's he like? Do we know anything about him? "He's the guy who brought the bald eagle back to America last year," declared Fortune conspiratorially as if that was in some way relevant to publicly relating for the GAA. In hindsight, maybe it was, since it gave Danny a good grounding in dealing with 'fliers', although he would later turn his attention towards attempting to curb the activity of the species he hates most of all – the dreaded 'mole'.

I have had many jousts with Danny over the years, especially in his early years at Croke Park when he took regular umbrage over articles I wrote in 'The Sunday Press'. The nib of his pen was usually very sharp when it came to writing 'A Chara' letters to the paper's editor, castigating Mr Breheny (you knew things were serious when he got formal) for some comment on GAA affairs.

Still, neither of us ever took it personally. We both had a job to do and while that brought us into conflict from time to time, it didn't mean we couldn't park our respective views and have a pint together. In the midst of one particularly protracted bout of critical 'A Chara' letters winging their way from Danny's office to 'The Sunday Press', we travelled together to a match in Ballinasloe.

We were having lunch in Hayden's Hotel when Cyril Farrell walked in, marched over to our table and declared: "What a pair of bloody rogues. Look at today's Sunday Press. Breheny is having a go at the GAA, Lynch is having a go at Breheny and ye're sitting here having lunch together. I'll never believe anything I read again."

We have travelled to some far flung spots around the world since then where the arguments have continued to rage but the crack has been good too. Danny knows that if the occasion demands I'll call it as I see in the Independent, just as I know that he'll fire off an 'A Chara' letter if he feels it's justified. No hard feelings either way.

However, what I still don't know is how that bald eagle viewed his travelling companion as they shared a glass of red wine on the flight to America all those years ago. I must make a few enquiries under the Freedom of Information Act. Better still, I might ring a 'mole'.

The Lotto early years

Peter Hanrahan

I REMEMBER when Mick O'Brien (who else?) approached me in 1992 and asked if I would be interested in getting involved in establishing and running the Club Lotto. This seemed to be a reasonable request at the time but little did I realise that it would have far-reaching consequences for myself and for the Club. I agreed to "give it a go" and see how it might work out.

The Club Lotto was at the time becoming a common fund raising tool for many clubs in Dublin and throughout the country. It was seen as a decent regular money-spinner for any club that was prepared to put in the effort. A lot of the groundwork had already been done when I got involved. Visits to other clubs where the Lotto was already up and running had taken place in order to learn from their experiences.

Initial decisions on issues such as price of tickets and prize money had been taken and a basic plan on how to go about "encouraging" people into selling and buying lotto tickets had already been hatched. I attended a number of meetings with Mick and the late Dick Fox (RIP) and we set out our stall. The initial plan was to get every club member to take at least five lotto tickets to sell each week. This would have given us a very good income from the venture but like many a good club plan, in this club and in all others, it didn't quite work out. A number of "likely candidates" who might be willing to make an ongoing regular effort were identified and approached (too many in number to name them all here) in order to get the ball rolling. We also recruited a Sunday night team that would help with the checking etc. every Sunday night. In order to win, one would have to select the three numbers that would be drawn on the Sunday night in the Clubhouse. Tickets were printed and distributed and there was no going back at this stage.

Mick went out and bought the first club "lotto machine". I am sure many of you remember it well. It was a circular red wire basket that you placed your numbered balls in and rotated it using the handle. You twisted one way to ensure that all the balls got a good mix and then you slowly twisted it in the opposite direction and "hey presto"! one ball would emerge into the pocket! You repeated this procedure to get your three numbers on the night. It was a far cry from the futuristic machine that is now used to draw the numbers for the Club Lotto. Times were simpler then!

The response was quite good and the Club Lotto was born. The first Club Lotto draw was held in St Judes GAA Club on Sunday 22nd March 1992. (The winner of this first draw was Deirdre Feore who was working as a lounge girl in the Clubhouse at the time. The grand prize of £220 seemed like a fortune to the poor student.) Week in, week out we went through the same procedures. Tickets were distributed to sellers for sale outside the Club. Various club members took turns to sell tickets in the Clubhouse on different nights and on Sunday night the Lotto Team was present to carry out the draw and to check for winning tickets and publish the results. It was quite successful, even if I do say so myself and the club now had another regular source of income to compliment the bar takings. If my memory serves me correctly, one of the first winners of a large jackpot was Susan Collard, the daughter of Betty and Tommy. It should be pointed out here that as well as full members, many social members made an invaluable contribution to the running of the Lotto.

I lasted for about three years or so and I don't remember whether I decided myself that it was time to remove myself from the Lotto Committee, or whether I was prompted to do so by someone who shall remain anonymous. So that was it. The Lotto Team moved on to be replaced by a new group of people headed by Martin McCabe and Bernie Gallagher with new ideas and suggestions. The Club Lotto has gone from strength to strength and thanks to the hard work of Betty Collard, Tommy Collard and their crew over the past number of years, the Lotto has become a major ongoing fundraiser for the Club and plays a vital role in the success of the Club in these expensive days.

From little acorns mighty oaks do grow.

The website

Joan Molamphy

http://homepage.eircom.net/~stjudesgaa

This is the website address for St Judes GAA Club but an alternative way of logging on is to open the search engine Google and type in St Judes GAA. A lot of people find this is a quicker method and saves typing time.

St Judes although a young club was not slow to establish itself on the playing front at local, County and All Ireland level and from there to have a presence on the World Wide Web.

The St Judes Web Page contains an enormous amount of information and is organised into easy to access pages by a simple click of the mouse. Our Home Page which is the first Page you see when you log on to the site is set out so that you can access your area of interest as quickly as possible but also allows you the freedom to browse other areas.

Each part of the club has a page assigned to its activities and by clicking on the appropriate button you have the information at your fingertips.

Football, Hurling, Camogie, Ladies Football, Football Sevens, Hurling Sevens, Lotto, Picture Page, Coaching news, Our Story, Summer Camp, Current news, Twenty Five Years, Guest Book , The Dream Team and The Executive are all there for you to click on and explore. Of particular interest is the "Our Story" Page, which outlines the history of the club from its earliest days.

The two pages dealing with the "Sevens" give a comprehensive outline of how that particular competition has grown over the years. Indeed, the first webpage for the "Sevens" was launched for the 1998 All Ireland. It was designed with the technical expertise of Ronan Murphy and the secular advice of Declan Feore and Jimmy O'Dwyer, together with the wizardry of Ronan's father, Finbarr, who showed how to upload photographs using a hand- held scanner. We were the first GAA club to provide real-time results on line. It is at "Sevens" time of year that the webpage comes into its own when clubs often email the club for information. After the Sevens the traffic on the web increases with pictures of competitors and winning teams being sent to the clubs who have email addresses. The list of clubs grows every day who are now contactable by email.

We have a special "Links" page where we list all GAA Clubs with whom we are in contact or who have asked to be linked to our website.

To facilitate people travelling to us for competitions there is a map showing our location as well as our address, phone/fax number, on the Home Page.

Pictures abound on our site and we have a special section for dignitaries who have visited the club on occasions e.g the Taoiseach was here to open the All Weather Pitch in November 2002. We have consistently tried to put pictures of our young players up as we are aware that they are probably more internet aware than the adult population of St Judes and consequently more likely to see the webpage.

It is hoped eventually to have all aspects of club life featured and we hope to see the website becoming an integral part of St Judes life with an interactive section or even a discussion board for members. Mentors should be able to send messages about training or matches to their teams via email very easily and eliminate the endless phone calls which plague every manager's life.

One of the more lighthearted web pages features "The Dream Team", a group of young men in the club who take their football seriously but also put a lot of emphasis on the enjoyment side of club life. They are very consistent in their input to the site and contribute match results and features regularly to the webmaster.

It is also our dream that in the very near future membership can be taken out on line and that a few people will become involved in the updating of the site as this is quite an onerous task as the site grows year by year.

The current site was designed by Joan Molamphy in 1996 and is updated as regularly as possible by her, but new blood is always welcome.

Adult Football history (1979-2003)

Don Lehane

PART 3 – THE PUSH TO SENIOR 1 (1989–1996)

1989/90 SEASON

Management of the Intermediate Football Team was taken over by Charles Moran for the season 1989/90. Charles was assisted by Tony Gilleran (Longford), with Cyril Loughlin (Leitrim) and Ger Treacy (Waterford) providing training backup. Charles Moran played his early football with St Michaels in Roscommon before he moved to Dublin. He was one of the founder members of the St Judes club and had played a key role in the development of the clubhouse facilities in St Judes particularly in his period as chairman. The Intermediate league included St Judes, Thomas Davis, Good Counsel, Lucan Sarsfields, Wanderers, Naomh Eanna, St Finnian's, Cuala, St Mark's, Churchtown, St Kevin's, Kilmacud Croke's, St Olafs, Round Towers, Robert Emmets and Civil Service.

St Judes entered the year with great confidence after their exploits in the preceding year when they narrowly missed out on a playoff position to go senior. Unfortunately as it transpired the team had a disappointing year and lost most of their early matches. There was considerable danger that the team would be on its way back down to junior. They had only four points in the bag as the league entered its final stages in the summer of 1990. A crucial win against St Finnian's of Newcastle halted the decline and put St Judes on six points. St Judes finished up with 8 points and avoided the drop and thus retained their Intermediate status for the 1990/1991 season. Ger McSweeney made an impassioned speech in the dressing room before the St Finnian's game to fire up the troops. Though still not involved with the team Tommy Bassett made a half time intervention to talk to the team and in the process stripped the remainder of the paint off the walls of the steel container that served as a dressing room in Newcastle. In any case the team came away with a great win and went on to pick up two additional league points to ensure safety. Intermediate team management was taken over by Tommy Bassett towards the end of the 1989/90 season with Luke Mooney and Bert Smith as mentors. Luke and Bert had just retired from active service on the football field. St Judes were beaten in the first round of the Intermediate Football Championship by Naomh Barrog on 18th March 1990 at Parc Barrog on a scoreline of 1.04 to 0.09.

St Judes should have won this game but a disappointing last ten minutes meant they were out of the championship for another year.

The Junior A team were beaten by Craobh Chiarain in the first round of the junior championship at Tymon. They played in Junior Division 3 (JFL3) in a league which included St Judes, St Annes, Kilmacud Crokes, Synge Street, Churchtown, Geraldine Morans, St Marys, Cuala, AIB and Ballinteer St Johns.

At U21 level St Judes were competing in Division 1 (South) with Thomas Davis, St Brigids, Kilmacud Crokes, St Olafs, St Patricks and St Annes in a double round league. They had a disappointing season with four defeats in their first four games followed by the concession of a walkover to St Patricks on 19th May 1990.

AOB: St Judes All-Ireland Junior 7s hurling started in 1990 with football in 1991.

On the 25th October 1990 Phil Conway the ex Irish international hammer thrower and trainer of Tipperary senior hurling team visited the club to give a talk on coaching techniques. We should be grateful that none of our forwards showed any interest in hammer throwing as I'm afraid with their accuracy over the last season every semi-detached in the vicinity of Tymon would have been reduced to rubble.

Luke Mooney played his last game for St Judes in the game against Lucan Sarsfields and it would have to be said that the young leggy blond corner forward (male) was giving him a hard time of it. For one of the few times in his distinguished career Luke resorted to underhand tactics to slow down the "blond bomber" and he departed the scene with some attractive red highlights running through the blond hair.

Match Report on Intermediate Football championship game between St Judes and Naomh Barrog: Date: 1990/03/18. Venue: Pairc Barrog. Competition: 1st Rnd Intermediate C'ship. Teams: St Judes (1.04) V Naomh Barrog (0.09)

This match was spoiled as a spectacle by the persistent wind, which caused havoc to attempts at accurate shooting. St Judes travelled northside with great hopes of gaining success but unfortunately it wasn't to be. They will regret missing many scoring opportunities. In fact all their scores came from free kicks.

Within fifteen minutes of the start Bert Smith had converted three frees from all angles. Two points from Barrog's Brennan and one from Carolan kept the scores level. The Kilbarrack side then raised their game and two further points came after good bouts of play by their forwards. Almost on the stroke of half time, St Judes were awarded a penalty, which Leonard Fitzpatrick converted expertly to leave St Judes ahead by a point at half time.

After five minutes of the second half, Naomh Barrog had equalised with a fine free from Aidan Brennan, despite the fact that St Judes had restarted well, putting some good moves together. David Lyons added another fine point for the northsiders and the game swung in their favour at this stage. A further two points were added by Naomh Barrog, with Bert Smith getting a point from a free for St Judes.

St Judes Team: Seamus McCartin, John Boyce, Declan Clabby, Patsy Nugent, Gerard McSweeney, Peter Ryan, Brendan Coughlan, Kevin Clabby, Michael Tobin, Leonard Fitzpatrick, Bert Smith, Ciaran McGovern, Ray O'Connor, Justin Delaney, Ger Treacy.

Subs: Shane Gallen for Ger Treacy (24 mins), James Durkan for Mick Tobin (41 mins), Declan Mcsweeney for Peter Ryan (45 mins)

1990/1991 SEASON:

St Judes consolidated their position at Intermediate Level in the 1990/91 season. While not exactly setting the world on fire they were never in danger of relegation and finished up around mid table. Tommy Bassett (Dublin) with Luke Mooney (Offally) and Bert Smith (Longford) had taken over management of the Intermediate team from Charlie Moran (Roscommon) for this season. Tommy Bassett was the first Dublin born manager of the St Judes top adult football team and had played his earlier football in Dublin with Intermediate/Junior side O'Connell Boys. In the late sixties that team reached three finals in the same year all against Thomas Davis - the Loving Cup, the Junior A Championship and the Junior Division 1 final of which they lost the first two and won the last. Tommy Bassett played U21 championship with Dublin around 1968. In an U21 championship fixture against Louth the game was delayed for repairs to the crossbar and the Louth goalkeeper as both had finished up on the ground after a "spirited challenge" from a combination of Tommy Bassett and Leslie Deegan. Tommy also played over half a dozen league games with the Dublin senior football team. Luke Mooney had played his earlier football with St Carthage's in Offaly before moving to Dublin and Bert Smith was an ex Longford Slashers player who had played underage football for Longford as a goalkeeper. They had both been key members of the St Judes team on its journey to Intermediate football. The Intermediate league in 1990/91 included St Judes, St Marks, Wanderers, Clan Na Gael, Civil Service, St Kevins, Robert Emmets, Thomas Davis, St Finnians, Portobello, St Olafs, Round Towers.

The Loving Cup competition included St Judes, St Marks, Civil Service, St Kevins, Robert Emmets, Thomas Davis, St Finnians, Portobello, St Olafs, Round Towers, Kilmacud Crokes and Lucan Sarsfields.

St Judes were runners-up in the inaugural All-Ireland Junior Football 7-a-side competition, which was won by St Olafs (Dublin). St Judes went on to win the competition in the following two years with players coming mainly from the Intermediate team. Of course all teams competing in the sevens were technically first year Intermediate level teams as winners of their respective county junior championships.

When St Judes went senior in 1993/94 then the sevens team was composed of players from junior level only. St Judes involvement in the sevens in the early nineties was of great benefit in the push on to senior football. It meant that a large group of the Intermediate football panel were getting in some hard training in August/September before the Dublin leagues started and this level of fitness was carried into the league. The Junior All-Ireland Seven's run by St Judes has been a very popular and successful competition, which enabled junior clubs from around the country to test themselves against similar junior clubs in other counties. The event has been of great educational value for the young Dubs in the parish who can be seen eagerly looking up their notebooks and maps to establish the exact location of Sixmilebridge, Fivefootgrogan, Fourmilewater and Twomileborris. A pastime amongs the older supporters is attempting to establish the county of origin of each team based on the style of hurling or football which they are playing. Some teams are easy to identify - Kilkenny teams all flicks and wrist work, the power and direct style of the Wexford or Cork lads, the Waterford lads clearing all before them in the first half but over indulging in the large bottles at half time and failing to appear after the break, the distinctive accents of the northern teams, Mayo for their ability to avoid hitting or kicking the ball between two widely spaced poles.

Championship: St Judes were beaten in the 1st round of the intermediate championship by Kilmacud Crokes in a game which they should have won with a late burst. Peter Carney missed an open goal, which would probably have won the game, and I am sure he still has nightmares about the miss. St Judes (1.08) were also knocked out of the junior championship by Ballyboughal (2.11) in the first round in Parnell Park on 20th July 1991. The Evening Herald reported "While the final scoreline reads a difference of a goal and three points, in reality this was a cliff-hanger with the Southsiders only lacking experience in taking their scoring opportunities early in the game. St Judes attacked and attacked but the mighty Ballyboughal defence held firm under pressure". Ballyboughal were later beaten by St Vincents in the quarter finals.

AOB: Mick Fallon and Mick Tobin had their first holiday abroad with a trip to Greece and came back looking like a pair of ripe tomatoes.

In the early to mid 'nineties St Judes went on a number of trips to various parts of the country including Milford (Donegal), Killarney (Kerry) and the Slieve Russell Hotel (Cavan). Details of these trips are largely clouded under a veil of secrecy to protect the guilty we suspect!. On the Kerry trip Mick and Seán Fallon were credited with introducing the first fully automatic car to the south-west county and it is rumoured that the vehicle can be seen to this day in the museum in Killarney. The presence of rain apparently interfered with the finely tuned auto pilot system necessitating a return to manual controls. Some external functions, like the operation of the belt & pulley driven windscreen wiper system apparently required the intermittent presence of Seán on the bonnet of the vehicle while Mick steered a "steady as she goes" course. There were no reported arrests.

Night at the Dogs took place in Shelbourne Park on 8th June 1991 followed by social in St Judes – great night all round and even the dogs seemed to enjoy it. The senior football league was made up of two divisions in 1990. The following teams played in Senior Division 1 : Parnell's, Ballymun Kickham's, St Vincents, Na Fianna, Thomas Davis, Whitehall CC, Erin's Isle, Fingallians, Scoil Ui Chonaill, St Annes, St Patricks, Garda, Kilmacud Crokes, Round Towers (Clondalkin). Senior Division 2 comprised Civil Service, St Margaret's, Synge Street, St Mary's (Saggart), Caislean, Clontarf, Crumlin, Kilmore, O'Dwyers, O'Toole's, St Sylvester's, Clann Colaiste Mhuire, Cuala, Inisfails and St Oliver Plunkett's.

Update from the Brother-in-Law:

The Brother-in-Law (BIL for short) joined the club in the early nineties as a freelance "troubleshooter" with a roving brief from the club trustees to tackle problems and issues which were outside the scope of existing committees within the club. His first major task was to tackle the lack of recent championship success. The BIL has decided that the club needs to shed its "friendly" image and "harden up" before meaningful championship success will be achieved. He has initiated a long term program designed to turn around the club image and to turn Tymon into a venue to be feared throughout the land. Of course our founding fathers left us in a difficult position by naming the club St Judes in the first place – the patron saint of hopeless cases was a rather unfortunate choice for the fledgling club. It was unlikely that the name would strike the fear of God into visiting teams in the manner that a visit to Man O'War, Killavilla, Crossmaglen or Kill might do. The first step will be to turn Tymon into an impregnable fortress and ensure that visiting teams and supporters will quake with fear at the first sign of the new St Judes flag complete with skull and crossbones logo flying high over the clubhouse.

The sign over Hell's gate in Dante's Inferno "Abandon every hope, ye that enter" is to be placed at all roads leading to Tymon and over the door of the visitor's dressing rooms. The temperature in the visitor's dressing room is to be reduced to minus 30 degrees Centigrade and tapes of Dana to be broadcast continuously. All St Judes players to be issued with a new standard set of equipment including hob nailed boots, knuckle dusters, compass and a couple of sticks of garlic per game.

St Judes supporters are to be given instructions regarding the recommended dress code for attendance at matches, which would include a flat cap, blue overalls, wellingtons or hobnailed boots, blackthorn stick and a minimum of a week of stubble (two weeks for the ladies).

The away strip must be the full Hell's Angels outfit (black glasses optional). Effeminate items such as umbrellas, suede shoes, gloves, scarves, ties, boxer shorts, books of poetry and light coloured suits will be completely banned from the sidelines and club environs.

The brother-in-law has also grown increasingly concerned with the tendency of some St Judes supporters in bringing small dogs to matches in Tymon. It would be difficult to get a decent Chinese meal from the entire population of these dogs and the BIL has decided that they have to be replaced by dogs with "attitude" such as Doberman Pincers, Rotweilers or cross-bred Alsations. He has already called in the Crennans, Joyces and Lernihans and warned them regarding their future conduct in this area. Some of our resident genial hosts in the club including Jack Lernihan, Frank McSweeney, Seán Conway, Jim Coghlan and Jack Tierney have also been warned to cut out the bonhomie and largesse to visiting players and supporters and replace it with an attitude and demeanour more appropriate for the occasion.

1991/1992 SEASON

In 1991/1992 the Intermediate Football team was managed by Tommy Bassett with mentors Luke Mooney and Seamus Durkan. Seamus Durkan (Mayo) had replaced Bert Smith (Longford) as mentor for the 1991/92 season. Seamus Durkan was one of the founder members of the club and had played his earlier football with Swinford in Mayo before emigrating to England. He was manager of a very successful St Judes underage football team who won the first underage A football championship for St Judes in 1988/89 when they won the U16A football with Michael O'Boyle as co-mentor.

A number of players from that side went on to play senior football for the club in later years including Kieran Durkan, Declan O'Boyle, John O'Riordan, Peter Keohane and Dara Murphy.

It was unfortunate that Bert Smith did not take any further part in team management in St Judes after this period. He was a very good coach who got on very well with the players and would have made a big contribution to St Judes in the period ahead.

On 15th July 1992 Intermediate Football league Section B league positions were as follows in a sixteen team competition (15 matches).

15th July 1992 Intermediate League Section B

Teams	Played	Won	Drew	Lost	Points
St Mark's	14	13	1	0	27
Lucan Sarsfield's	14	10	1	3	21
Parnell's	15	10	1	4	21
Trinity Gaels	10	9	0	1	18
St Judes	13	7	4	2	18
Kevin's	15	7	3	5	17
Na Fianna	15	7	3	5	17
Good Counsel	15	7	1	7	15
Thomas Davis	13	7	0	6	14
Kilmacud Crokes	14	6	2	6	14
Robert Emmets	15	5	1	9	11
Civil Service	15	4	3	8	11
Portobello	14	3	2	9	8
Scoil Ui Chonaill	15	3	0	12	6
Wanderers	14	0	0	14	0

St Judes drew with St Marks in their last match and finished up third in the league. A win for St Judes in this game would have put them into joint second position but a draw left them one point behind in third place.

St Judes had a great run in the Intermediate championship in 1992 before finally bowing out at the semi-final stage to a very strong St Brigids senior side who went on to win the Intermediate championship final with a three point win over St Olafs on 5th July. In the second round St Judes had a four point win over Raheny.

At the quarter-final stage St Judes had a great two point win against Kilmacud Crokes who brought on experienced senior players Pat Burke and Mick Leahy during the game in an attempt to pull the game out of the fire. In the semi-final against St Brigids St Judes were leading until just before half-time when a Brigids goal gave them a morale-boosting half time lead. The second half was dominated by St Brigids who went on to win easily.

St Judes won the 1992 All-Ireland Junior Football Sevens title run by St Judes at Tymon North in September 1992. This was the second year of the football sevens and St Judes won the trophy by beating An Spideal in the final with the following squad of players: Enda Sheehy, Ciaran Gallagher, John O'Riordan, Kieran Durkan, Colm O'Brien, Declan O'Boyle, Ciaran McGovern, Dara Murphy, Mick Fallon and Ger McSweeney.

1992/1993 SEASON:
The Intermediate Football team was again managed by Tommy Bassett with mentors Luke Mooney and Seamus Durkan. This was a tremendous year for the club with the Intermediate team gaining promotion to senior football for the first time. Promotion to Senior Football League Division 2 (SFL2) was achieved after a great win against Raheny in a play-off game in Parnell Park.

On 30th June 1993 the Intermediate league positions were as follows. This was a fifteen team league so all teams had to play fourteen games.

30th June 1993 – Intermediate Football Lge.

Team	Played	Won	Drew	Lost	+Points	-Points
St Judes	11	10	0	1	20	-2
Raheny	7	6	0	1	12	-2
Parnell's	9	6	1	2	13	-5
Kevin's	8	6	0	2	12	-4
Lucan Sarsfields	9	5	0	4	10	-8
Clann Colaiste Mhuire	12	4	1	7	9	-15
Trinity Gaels	10	3	2	5	8	-12
St Mark's	10	4	0	6	8	-12
Thomas Davis	7	3	1	3	7`	-7
St Olafs	7	3	1	3	7	-7
St Monicas	8	3	1	4	7	-9
Naomh Fionbarra	11	3	1	7	7	-15
Craobh Chiarain	9	3	0	6	6	-12
Crumlin	8	2	1	5	5	-11
St Patricks	10	2	0	8	4	-16

This set up an exciting finish to the league with the top four teams of St Judes, Raheny, Parnell's and Kevin's still very much in contention for promotion to senior. Thomas Davis, St Mark's and Lucan Sarsfields were still not out of contention. The top two teams in this group would play-off in semi-finals against the top two teams of the Fingal Intermediate league.

On Thursday 8th July 1993 St Judes played Kevin's in the first of a crucial series of league matches in Tymon and lost. On 11th July St Judes beat St Olafs in the league on a scoreline of 2-05 to 0-06 bringing St Judes total points to 22. On the 15th July 1993 St Judes played their last league game against Raheny in St Annes No. 9 (Referee B Nugent) and were beaten on a scoreline of 0-07 to 0-09 leaving St Judes on 22 points and Raheny now on 21 points with two games to play. Parnells had lost to St Mark's in their last game when on 19 points and so were now out of contention for the top two positions. On 22nd July Raheny beat Thomas Davis (0-13 to 0-06) and drew with Craobh Chiarain in their last game on 25th July 1993 to bring their points total to 24 points, with St Judes runners-up on 22 points and Parnells third on 19 points. Kevins were unlucky not to be involved in the shake up. They refused to field for a league match against one of the bottom teams on the basis that some of their players were involved in a Dublin match. They lost the points and also the subsequent appeal and these two points dropped would have put them right in contention.

1992/93 Final Intermediate League (City) placings:

Raheny: Played 14 Won 11 Drew 2 Lost 1 Total 24 points
St Judes: Played 14 Won 11 Drew 0 Lost 3 Total 22 points
Parnell's: Played 14 Won 9 Drew 1 Lost 4 Total 19 points

Fingal Ravens and Garristown finished up level on points in the Fingal Intermediate League and tossed for their position in the semi-finals where runners-up in City Intermediate League (St Judes) played the winners of the Fingal Intermediate League and vice versa. St Judes beat Fingal Ravens by a big score in one semi-final at O'Toole Park. Ger McSweeney put out his shoulder during this game and had to put it back into place himself due to the slow arrival of the medical corps. Raheny beat Garristown easily in the other semi-final thus setting up an exciting play-off final between St Judes and Raheny with the winning team going senior. Raheny had already beaten St Judes in the league itself and were favourites to take the title. The following match report was written at the time by Jimmy O'Dwyer and we include it here in its entirety:

Senior status for Super Judes

St Judes (1-16) V Raheny (0-11)

A superbly taken goal after seven minutes of play by Enda Sheehy, similar to the one scored by John O'Driscoll in this year's All Ireland Final, made all the difference in this absorbing Intermediate League Final at Parnell Park. Played before a huge crowd of mainly St Judes supporters, the standard of football was quite excellent and the stylish play by the St Judes side was much admired by all.

St Judes began the game in great style and went into a three point lead early on with points from John O'Riordan and Declan O'Boyle and that magic goal from Enda Sheehy (scored incidentally while Mick Fallon was off the field for running repairs on his boot!). Raheny were certainly no pushover and with Maurice Curran's accuracy from frees keeping them in touch, the pressure was always on St Judes to maintain the lead. John O'Riordan, whose brilliant free-taking was also a feature of the game, was terribly unlucky not to score a goal, when in the 24th minute he latched onto the end of a high kick from Kieran Durkan, but his fisted effort went inches over the bar. He quickly made amends for the goal miss with a point from a well taken free two minutes later. By half time Judes had a well earned lead of four points. Raheny came out after the interval in a far more determined mood, and with Dublin star, Niall Guiden, sprung from the bench, the stage was set for a tremendous second half. Within two minutes they had scored two points from play, through Ian O'Connor and Jim Woods. A John O'Riordan free and a Kieran Durkan point from play after a fine movement that started with a save from Tony McGinley, settled Judes again. For the next ten minutes points were exchanged and after Niall Guiden pointed in the nineteenth minute, Raheny did not score again and Judes finished with two points each from Declan O'Boyle and Shane Gallen and then another from Declan O'Boyle.

The team is a great credit to St Judes. Their dedication to training and to their games is an example to the younger teams in the club. Well done to mentors Tommy Bassett, Luke Mooney and Seamus Durkan. This victory raises the spirits of all of us involved in developing the club. We have come a long way in fifteen years. The sky is the limit now – what chance a senior title this century.!

Raheny Team: Colin McMahon, Brendan Keane, Brendan Fitzpatrick, Barry Roche, Jim Woods (0-1), Stephen Molloy, Aidan Hurley, Neil Curley, Ian O'Connor (0-1), Damien Reville (0-1), Brian Madden, Marcus Herbert, Greg Hogan (0-1), Dermot Morris, Maurice Curran (0-6, 5f).

Subs: Seán Keating, Dave Cahill, Jimmy Malone, Brian Somers, Niall Guiden (0-1), Mick O'Sullivan, Eamon Clarke.

St Judes 1992/93 Intermediate League Winners

John O'Riordan (0-7,6f)	Dara Murphy	Shane Gallen (0-2)
Kieran Durkan (0-2)	Declan O'Boyle (0-3)	Enda Sheehy (1-1)
James O'Dowd (0-1)	Kieran Gallagher	
Ciaran McGovern	Peter Keohane	Ger McSweeney
Mick Fallon	Declan Clabby	Colm O'Brien
	Tony McGinley	

Subs: Kevin Clabby (capt), Peter Gilsenan (inj), Peter Ryan, Declan O'Reilly, Dermot McCarthy, Brendan Coughlan, Alan Gallagher, Mick Tobin, Denis Evoy.

St Judes Intermediate footballers also won the Loving Cup in 1992/93 season. The following were the final Loving Cup positions in a fourteen team competition (13 games each).

7th July 1993 – Loving Cup Final Table

Team	Played	Won	Drew	Lost	Points
St Judes	13	10	2	1	22
Thomas Davis	13	8	4	1	20
Ballymun Kickhams	13	9	1	3	19
St Olafs	13	8	1	4	17
Erin's Isle	13	7	2	4	16
Parnell's	13	6	4	3	16
Trinity Gaels	13	7	0	6	14
Lucan Sarsfields	13	6	1	6	13
Kevins	13	6	1	6	13
Raheny	13	5	0	8	10
Naomh Fionbarra	13	2	4	7	8
Kilmacud Crokes	13	3	1	9	7
Beann Eadair	13	2	1	10	5
Portobello	13	1	1	11	3

The Intermediate footballers won the first round of the championship on 21st Feb 1993 with a big win against Inisfails on a scoreline of St Judes 4-12 V Inisfails 2-05 but were beaten by two points in the second round by St Olafs. St Olafs went on to win the Intermediate Football championship and gained promotion to senior level. The match followed the St Judes V Raheny play off match in Parnell Park and so St Judes preceded St Olafs into senior ranks by just over an hour. St Judes won the 1993 All-Ireland Junior Football Sevens title run by St Judes at Tymon North in September 1993. This was the third year of the football sevens and St Judes won the trophy by beating Kilcummin in the final with the following squad of players: Enda Sheehy, Ciaran Gallagher, John O'Riordan, Kieran Durkan, Colm O'Brien, Declan O'Boyle, Ciaran McGovern, Seamus Lynch, Jamsie O'Dowd and Shane Gallen.

St Judes Junior A team finished bottom of Division 3 Junior League with one win and two draws from their fourteen matches.

AOB: Ciaran Gallagher was called up to the Mayo senior football panel after the Raheny V Judes game. He was almost denied the opportunity by Tommy Bassett who was Intermediate manager at the time. Tommy took a call in the clubhouse from the Mayo manager Jack O'Shea but refused to accept that he was talking to the great "Jacko".

He assumed that it was another of Jamsie O'Dowd's windups and told him to "$#ck off Dowdie and stop annoying me" much to the surprise of the speechless Jacko. The penny eventually dropped and Gags duly got his place on the Mayo panel where his accurate point scoring ability will not be out of place on a Mayo team abounding with sharp shooters! In the Loving Cup game against Parnells Brian Talty was sent off the Parnells team by referee Jim Turner for pulling Ciaran McGovern's immaculately groomed ponytail in a vain attempt to slow him down.

Update from the Brother-in-Law:

The Brother-in-Law has been called in again by the club trustees who are concerned that the club is being taken over by the Tipp crowd who are apparently breeding like rabbits around Orwell and have taken over a number of key executive portfolios in recent months. The first sign of danger was the transportation of the self-appointed "Welcome to Tipperary – Home of Hurling" sign from its previous location on the Tipperary border to the Red Cow roundabout. To cap it all Hell's Kitchen appear to have been given the franchise for the bar and hospitality functions within the club. This is causing severe discomfort and an element of physical danger to residents of the Nook who are now having their pints delivered to them topped with a dash of venom instead of the more traditional creamy head. This is frequently followed up by a third man tackle or full frontal assault as a barperson appears with blades lowered from the Nook exit of the bar wielding an ice bucket and scattering bewildered tipplers to the left and right.

1993/1994 SEASON

This was the first year that St Judes competed at senior football level. It was a tremendous achievement to go from Junior Division 4 in 1986 to senior football in 1993. It took seven years to complete that journey which was a remarkably short time considering the team had to transgress in effect through 11 divisions of football with eight junior divisions (North/South) and three Intermediate divisions. We had started with a very ambitious plan in 1986 to progress from junior 4 to senior in ten years and now we have achieved this objective in seven years which was beyond our wildest expectations back in the mid eighties. Don Lehane and his team of players and mentors including Gerry Quinn, Cyril Loughlin and Ernest Kenny achieved the first step in the plan by moving from Division 4 Junior to Intermediate football in two seasons. Tommy Bassett and his team of players plus mentors Luke Mooney, Seamus Durkan and Bert Smith achieved the second step in the plan by going from Intermediate to Senior 2 in the period between 1989/1990 and 1992/1993 seasons.

Kevin Clabby, Declan Clabby, Ger McSweeney and Ciaran McGovern are four players who will go down in club history as having played right through this period as St Judes journeyed from Junior, through Intermediate and on to Senior football level.

Our first year senior was a year of consolidation mainly to ensure we retained our Senior 2 (SFL2) status. The team was again managed by Tommy Bassett with mentors Luke Mooney and Seamus Durkan. Our first game at senior level was away against the Mick Galvin led St Oliver Plunketts on the 31st October 1993. It was a baptism of fire for St Judes with Oliver Plunketts running out winners on a scoreline of 4-14 to 0-13. This Plunketts side was quite strong and eventually finished up fourth in this league behind Round Towers, St Sylvesters and Clontarf. Nevertheless it was a wake-up call for St Judes and showed the gap in standard between Intermediate and Senior football.

St Judes made a great recovery from the heavy defeat in the first game and proceeded to win the next four games against Synge Street PP, Caislean, Naomh Barrog and St Maurs respectively. These results were crucial at the end of the season as St Judes lost eight of their final ten games to finish up in twelfth position in the league with twelve points and ahead of Synge Street PP (16), St Maurs (15), Skerries Harps (14), St Vincents B (13). The league was won by Round Towers (29 points) followed by St Sylvesters (24 points) and Clontarf (23 points). The following are the results of the SFL2 matches in the 1993/1994 season with the number in brackets indicating the position of each team at the end of the season:

93/10/31	V Oliver Plunketts (4)	Loss	0.13 to 4.14	Away
93/11/14	V Synge Street PP (16)	Win	1.10 to 2.05	Home
93/11/28	V Caislean (10)	Win	1.08 to 0.08	Home
93/12/05	V Naomh Barrog (9)	Win	1.06 to 1.05	Away
93/12/12	V St Maurs (15)	Win	2.12 to 0.02	Home
94/02/13	V Clontarf (3)	Loss	0.09 to 2.06	Home
94/03/06	V Scoil Ui Chonaill (8)	Loss	0.06 to 0.10	Away
94/03/17	V St Patricks (5)	Loss	0.13 to 2.09	Away
94/04/06	V St Vincents B (13)	Win	1.11 to 1.07	Away
94/05/06	V St Olafs (11)	Loss	0.06 to 3.11	Away
94/05/08	V Skerries Harps (14)	Win	4.05 to 0.05	Home
94/05/25	V St Sylvesters (2)	Loss	0.08 to 1.09	Home
94/06/22	V Round Towers (1)	Loss	1.06 to 1.07	Home
94/06/26	V O'Tooles (6)	Loss	0.07 to 1.10	Away
94/08/14	V O'Dwyers (7)	Loss	0.07 to 0.09	Away

St Judes (12) Played 15 Won 6 Drew 0 Lost 9 Pts 12. Finished 12th in league

On 24th April 1994 St Judes were beaten in the first round of the Senior Championship by Clontarf at O'Toole Park on a scoreline of 0.07 to 1.09. This was a game that should not have been played as the O'Toole Park pitch was virtually unplayable after very heavy rain. It was decided that the game should go ahead despite the reservations of the referee and both teams. The turning point of the game was the Clontarf goal, which came about as a result of a high ball being dropped by the Judes goalkeeper who wishes to remain anonymous. Brian Barrett (Galway) played for St Judes in this game. Declan O'Boyle received a cruciate injury in this game which was not helped by the condition of the pitch. After a long layoff he returned to play for St Judes and Dublin in 1995 but a re-occurrence of the injury effectively ended his footballing career at the top level, which was very disappointing for a very talented footballer.

St Judes competed in Section A of the 1993/94 St Vincent De Paul Cup competition and had wins against An Caislean and St Marys Saggart but were defeated by Fingallians, Synge Street PP and St Patricks. Fngallians won the section and eventually made it to the final where they were beaten by Ballyboden St Endas. In the AIB Cup competition (Section C) St Judes beat Synge Street PP and had losses against Civil Service, St Sylvesters, Clontarf, St Brigids and Na Fianna. St Sylvesters came out of the group and went on to the final where they were beaten by Parnells.

The Junior A team had a poor year in the league but had a good run in the championship before eventually being beaten in the quarter finals. They had beaten Intermediate team St Finnians in an earlier round. Our Junior B team entered competition for the first time in Division 8 and finished runners up to St Marks thus gaining promotion to Division 7 for 1994/95. The U21 team was beaten by St Sylvesters in the second round of the championship having beaten Trinity Gaels in the first round.

In the 1994 All-Ireland Football Sevens in September 1994 St Judes were runners up with a panel comprising: Brendan Coughlan, Declan O'Reilly, Enda Crennan, Kieran McSherry, Peter Ryan, Gavin Russell, Damien Carroll, Colm Gough, Peter Harlow and Jeff Kane. The team was managed by Christy Kilcoyne.

AOB: Declan O'Boyle played for Dublin in the 1993/94 National League before picking up a cruciate injury with St Judes which sidelined him for a long period. He did not return to training with the Dublin team until around 1994 before eventually having to retire from senior football due to another cruciate injury. Enda Sheehy played U21 football and hurling with Dublin and at this stage was figuring in the Dublin senior football panel.

Update from the Brother-in-Law:

In an attempt to liven up the social aspect of the club the brother-in-law is planning is to introduce a "Conversation Menu" to the bar whereby patrons can order a selection of moderately priced conversations to go with their selected tipple. "Conversation Appetizers" or "A small one" come in at 1 Euro and would cover basic topics of conversation like the weather, family matters, gardening tips and the price of the pint.

A pint and a small one has now become the standard request when a member enters the bar for the first time and the bartender is encouraged to throw in a welcoming smile free of charge. "Conversation Starters" come in at 2 Euro and you have a selection here covering items like local politics, budgets, soaps and progress of the U14 hurling team. The "Main Course" at 5 Euro per fifteen minute conversation offers topics under a number of heading such as religion, philosophy, literature, national and international politics, sport and sex. Issues such as management of the senior hurling team, the state of Fine Gael, the life of Rembrandt and the rise of Fascism would be covered here. "Conversation Desserts" finish off the menu options and are only allowed if you have completed the full set of menu options and have consumed a minimum of ten pints or the alcoholic equivalent in spirits. Options here are left to the discretion of the bartender and the management as it largely depends on the level of alertness in the client – a number having difficulty in remembering their name at this point in the proceedings. The brother-in-law was considering replacing this option with an argument but felt it might be a non-runner as this particular genre was already well established. Patrons or bar staff might consider they were losing a perk if they could not start an argument with whoever they liked and whenever they liked, without the added complication of bringing a stop watch and calculator into the proceedings.

The menu options are changed on a weekly basis and each club member is confined to a maximum of five conversations per night and no more than twenty conversations a week. Group conversations are offered at 10% discount. The new system has been a roaring success with old members flocking back to the club in droves from Faughs. Of course mistakes were made in the early days and one unfortunate member having initiated a conversation on the influence of Vincents found himself embroiled in a night long discussion on Van Gogh. He left the club 100 Euro lighter in the pocket and missed the last bus home. The club management committee has had to issue notices to the effect that they cannot be held responsible for any conversations going on in the bar and will not be held responsible for conversations or arguments lost on the premises.

1994/1995 SEASON

The 1994/95 season was a very successful year for the senior football team who finished up third in the Senior Football League Division 2 (SFL2) behind Fingallians and St Marks with a team managed by Tommy Bassett, Luke Mooney and Seamus Durkan. The team had a great run in the senior championship with wins against O'Tooles and St Sylvesters before going down to Kilmacud Crokes in the quarter finals by two points in O'Toole Park before a massive crowd.

The league campaign started with a game against Scoil Ui Chonaill in Tymon on 9th September 1994 which St Judes won by six points on a scoreline of 2.09 to 1.06. It finished with a loss against our old bogey team St Olafs on 16th July 1995 in Tymon on a scoreline of 0.08 to 0.09. St Judes had found it very difficult to beat St Olafs during the nineties and invariably Olafs seemed to raise their game against St Judes. St Judes played fifteen league games in the 1994/95 season with nine wins, three draws and only three losses. St Judes needed two points from their last two games against St Marks and St Olafs to get the runners-up slot. A draw against St Marks and a loss to St Olafs left St Judes just out of the promotion positions. St Judes finished the season in third place with 21 points behind Fingallians (24 points) and St Marks (23 points).

The following are league results for the season with finishing league positions of each team in brackets:

94/09/09	V Scoil Ui Chonaill (8)	Win	2.09 to 1.06	Home
94/10/23	V St Patricks (7)	Win	1.09 to 1.07	Home
94/11/06	V Naomh Barrog (12)	Win	1.06 to 0.06	Away
94/12/04	V StO. Plunketts(15)	Win	0.10 to 0.06	Home
95/01/15	V Fingallians (1)	Loss	1.10 to 2.11	Away
95/03/12	V O'Dwyers (13)	Win	3.07 to 0.04	Home
95/03/26	V Skerries Harps (11)	Win	0.09 to 1.05	Home
95/05/03	V St Marys (5)	Draw	1.10 to 2.07	Away
95/05/07	V Trinity Gaels (14)	Win	1.15 to 1.12	Away
95/05/31	V O'Tooles (9)	Draw	1.08 to 0.11	Home
95/06/21	V St James Gaels (10)	Loss	1.07 to 3.07	Home
95/06/25	V Clontarf (6)	Win	0.15 to 0.07	Home
95/06/28	V St Vincents B (16)	Win	0.12 to 0.06	Home
95/07/12	V St Marks (2)	Draw	1.13 to 2.10	Away
95/07/16	V St Olafs (4)	Loss	0.08 to 0.09	Home

St Judes (3) Played 15 Won 9 Drew 3 Lost 3 Pts 21. Finished Third in league

The following were the leading scorers on the St Judes senior team in the 1994/95 league campaign: John O'Riordan (1-55), Enda Sheehy (1-15), Peter Gilsenan (4-6), Liam Keogh (3-8), Kieran Durkan (0-16), Conor Lehane (0-16), Shane Gallen (0-12), Declan O'Boyle (1-4), Jamsie O'Dowd (0-6), Ger McSweeney (1-1), Kieran Gallagher (0-4), Peter Harlow (0-2), Peter Ryan (0-2), Brendan Coughlan (0-1), Colm Gough (0-1) and Peter Keohane (0-1).

St Judes had a great run in the senior championship starting with a ten points win against O'Tooles in O'Toole Park on 8th April 1995. They followed this up with a tremendous four point win against one of the championship favourites St Sylvesters at the Iveagh Grounds on 19th April 1995. This was a tremendous contest between two good footballing sides even though the recent death of corner back Colm O'Brien's father cast a shadow over the proceedings. Enda Sheehy had probably his best game ever in a St Judes jersey and of course went on to bring home an All-Ireland winners medal with Dublin later in the year. Judes led at half time by four points (0-8 to 0-4) but a good goal from Niall Guiden early in the second half really set up this for a nail-biting contest. A Shay Keogh point brought Sylvesters level but Judes stepped up a gear in the last quarter and outscored Sylvesters by five points to one. Enda Sheehy roamed all over the attack and finished with four points. Jamesie O'Dowd worked very hard around the middle of the field and with Kieran Gallagher ensured that Judes were on top for most of the hour in the vital midfield battle. Up front the Judes forward line of Liam Keogh, Declan O'Boyle, Enda Sheehy, Peter Gilsenan, Conor Lehane, Ciaran Durcan and substitute Shane Gallen gave the Sylvesters defence a torrid time. The Judes defence of Terence Orr, Ger McSweeney, Mick Fallon, Peter Keohane, John O'Riordan, Dara Murphy and Ciaran McGovern kept a tight rein on the Sylvesters forwards for most of the game with the exception of a fifteen minute period early in the second half. The game threatened to overheat on a number of occasions and at one point Tommy Bassett shipped a heavy punch from a Sylvester's player in an altercation on the sideline but it was not sufficient to prevent a large grin from Tommy after the match.

St Judes were eventually beaten by two points by Kilmacud Crokes in a great game at O'Toole Park on 21st April 1995 in the championship quarter-finals. Kilmacud Crokes had recently been crowned All-Ireland Club football champions and so St Judes were overwhelming underdogs for this game. One of the biggest crowds ever seen at O'Toole Park turned up for the game with supporters right round the pitch. A large contingent came to see the All-Ireland champions in action, an even bigger crowd it seemed were supporting St Judes team and no doubt quite a few expected St Judes to get a hammering. St Judes put in a tremendous performance in the circumstances and were winning the game into the second half after a couple of early goals from Peter Gilsenan. A late revival inspired by substitutes Mick Dillon, Pat Burke and Maurice Leahy put Kilmacud Crokes ahead going into the final stages and their experience enabled them to hold out for a two point victory.

The championship was eventually won by Ballyboden St Endas, who defeated Erins Isle by a point in the county final with Paul Bealin making his championship debut for Ballyboden as a substitute. This was Ballyboden's first senior football championship success. St Judes competed in Section B of the St Vincent De Paul and had wins against Naomh Barrog and St James Gaels, a draw against Round Towers (Clon) and losses against St Sylvesters, Clontarf, St Marys and St Patricks. The section was won by St Sylvesters who went on to beat Thomas Davis in the final. In the AIB Cup competition St Judes competed in Section A and had one win against St Margarets and five losses against Parnells, St Sylvesters, St Marks, Naomh Barrog and Trinity Gaels. The group was won by Parnells who were beaten by eventual winners Ballyboden St Endas in the semi-final. St Judes Junior A team were runners up in Division 4 and gained promotion to Division 3. They were beaten by eventual winners St Vincents (Intermediate) in the quarter final of the championship. They also reached the Sheridan Cup final. The Junior B team won Division 7 and gained promotion to Division 6. They lost to St Brigids in the quarter final of the Junior B championship. The U21 team was beaten by a good St Sylvesters team in the 3rd round of the championship.

AOB: Another club milestone was achieved when Enda Sheehy brought the Sam Maguire Cup back to St Judes in 1995 after the great win by Dublin in All-Ireland final. Enda was the first St Judes player to win an All-Ireland senior football medal. The official welcome of Sam to the club took place at a function on the 3rd November 1995 and was a great success. Ciaran McGovern played senior football with Leitrim and on his debut scored a point with his normally redundant left foot. Peter Gilsenan and Enda Sheehy were on the Dublin U21 football panel. The club dinner dance was held outside the clubhouse for the first time since it was built with a very enjoyable function in Stackstown in February 1995. Conor Lehane and Jeff Kane transferred back to St Judes from St James Gaels and Ballyboden respectively.

1995/1996 SEASON

The 1995/96 season was St Judes third season in Division 2 of the Senior Football League (SFL2). There was a quiet confidence around Tymon that the 1995/96 season was the season to push onto Senior 1. St Judes had finished the previous season in third place after a great campaign.

The loss against St James Gaels and the draw with O'Tooles were two games which Judes were expected to win and the results in these games were to prove crucial at the end of the season. The season ahead was not going to be easy however as three strong additional teams were now residing in SFL2 namely Lucan Sarsfields, Ballymun Kickhams and St Margarets. As events transpired these three teams finished third, fourth and sixth respectively. The team was again managed by Tommy Bassett, Seamus Durkan and Luke Mooney.

St Judes started their league campaign with a one point loss against St Margarets (Away) on 24th September 1995 and followed this up with a draw against Ballymun Kickhams (Home) on 8th October 1995. This was not the start St Judes wanted in this league with three points dropped in the first two games. However, extraordinarily, they went on to win all bar one of their remaining games in the league culminating in an eight point home win against St Marys on the 3rd July 1996. It was not however sufficient to topple the Noel O'Mahony led Clontarf who won the league on 26 points with only two defeats in the whole campaign. St Judes finished second on 25 points and Lucan Sarsfields finished third on 20 points. St Judes were promoted for the first time to Senior Division 1 level (SFL1) which sparked wild celebrations in the parish. Tremendous credit due to Tommy Bassett, Luke Mooney, Seamus Durkan and a great bunch of players who had a brief two year stay in Division 2 before pushing on to Senior 1 level for the 1996/97 season. The climax to the 1995/96 league season was disappointing when St Patricks were only able to put out thirteen players in the final league match against a fired-up St Judes side and had to concede the points. A friendly match was played with a couple of Judes players togging out for the opposition.

In the championship St Judes (0.16) had a good three points first round replay win against St Brigids (1.10) in Parnell Park on the 31st March 1996. The second round pitched us against St Olafs in Parnell Park and Olafs nicked a draw in the first game with a goal scored with the last touch of the game. St Judes eventually went out of the championship in the replay on 10th April 1995 against St Olafs on a scoreline of 1.04 to 2.03. This was a tough, dour game with little good football due partly to the tight marking and poor shooting. St Judes conceded a crucial goal when the normally immaculate John O'Keeffe dropped a ball on the line but in fairness to "Johno" he was one of the St Judes better performers on the night. Corkman John O'Keeffe was one of a group of talented Munster footballers who played for St Judes around this period including Kerrymen Martin McKivergan, Jamsie O'Dowd and Martin Dennehy.

The 1995/96 league campaign went as follows with final league placings in brackets:

95/09/24	V St Margarets (7)	Loss	1.09 to 1.10	Away
95/10/08	V Ballymun Kickhams (4)	Draw	2.11 to 2.11	Home
95/10/22	V St Oliver Plunketts (15)	Win	1.08 to 0.06	Away
95/11/05	V James Gaels (11)	Win	1.14 to 1.05	Home
95/11/19	V O'Dwyers (5)	Win	1.08 to 1.07	Home
95/12/03	V O'Tooles (8)	Win	1.09 to 1.07	Away
95/12/10	V Skerries (6)	Win	2.13 to 1.08	Away
96/03/03	V Trinity Gaels (9)	Loss	1.06 to 0.14	Away
96/05/24	V Naomh Barrog (13)	Win	0.14 to 1.04	Home
96/05/26	V St Olafs (10)	Win	1.09 to 1.04	Away
96/06/12	V Lucan Sarsfields (3)	Win	4.10 to 2.15	Away
96/06/16	V Scoil Ui Chonaill (16)	Win	1.12 to 1.03	Away
96/07/03	V St Marys (14)	Win	2.12 to 1.07	Home
96/07/07	V St Patricks (12)	Win	0.12 to 0.02	Home
95/96	V Clontarf (1)	Win		

St Judes (2) Played 15 Won 12   Drew 1 Lost 2 Total 25 Points

The leading St Judes scorers in the 1995/96 league campaign were as follows: John O'Riordan (1-47), Peter Gilsenan (6-16), CiaranDurkan (2-17), Martin Dennehy (3-14), Enda Sheehy (2-15), Conor Lehane (2-11), Shane Gallen (2-6), Declan O'Boyle (0-10), Ken Lenihan (1-6), Jamsie O'Dowd, Kieran Gallagher (0-3), Martin McKivergan (0-3), Ciaran McGovern (0-2), Liam Keogh (0-2), Peter Harlow (0-2), Dara Murphy (0-1), John O'Keeffe (0-1) and Peter Ryan (0-1).

St Judes competed in Section B of the St Vincent De Paul and lost to Lucan Sarsfields, Clontarf, St Margarets, Naomh Barrog, St James Gaels, St Sylvesters and Round Towers. The section was won by St James Gaels. In the AIB Cup competition St Judes competed in Section A and had wins against St Sylvesters and Trinity Gaels and losses against Kilmacud Crokes, Parnells, St Margarets, Naomh Barrog and St Marks.

St Judes had three junior football teams in the 1995/96 season and all three teams gained promotion, which was a tremendous achievement. Therefore all four St Judes adult football teams gained promotion in the same season which must be some kind of a record in Dublin football.

For the record the teams and mentors were as follows: St Judes Junior A won JFL 3 league and gained promotion to JFL 1 under the guidance of Mick O'Brien, Gary Kane, Ernest Kenny and Maura McSherry. They were beaten by Whitehall CC in the third round of the championship. The Junior B team won JFL 6 and gained promotion to JFL 5 led by Christy Kilcoyne, Donnchadh Lehane, John Brown and Joe Fallon.

They also had a good run in the B championship before being beaten in the semi-final by AIB on a scoreline of 0.05 to 1.12 in O'Toole Park. AIB went on to beat St Vincents in the final on a scoreline of 2.14 to 0.11 after extra time on 21st July 1996. The junior C team entered competition for the first time and were runners-up in JFL 8 gaining promotion to JFL 6 with Charles Moran, Eamonn Brady and Paddy Russell on the bridge. The following were the league tables on 24th July 1996 with all teams having completed their league programs with the exception of the St Judes Junior A team (Junior 3) who had two matches to complete which they duly won to top the table by season end.

Division: Junior 3 (16 teams)

Team	Played	Won	Drew	Lost	Points	
St Finnians	15	13	0	2	26	
St Judes A	13	12	0	1	24	(2 games left)
Paveh	15	10	1	4	21	
AIB	14	10	0	4	20	
Kilmacud Crokes	14	10	0	4	20	

St Judes A finished with 28 points to top table

Junior 6 (16 teams)

Team	Played	Won	Drew	Lost	Points
St Judes B	15	14	0	1	28
Naomh Fionbarra	15	13	1	1	27
Cabinteely	14	10	0	4	20
Garristown	13	9	1	3	19

Junior 8 (13 teams)

Team	Played	Won	Drew	Lost	Points
Stars of Erin	12	11	0	1	22
St Judes C	12	10	1	1	21
Ballinteer St Johns	12	10	0	2	20
Raheny	11	8	0	3	16

AOB: St Judes were fined 50 pounds as a result of the abandoned St Judes v St Marks Under 21 football match in Tymon.

The match was played on a dreadful day and from the throw in it was clear that there was trouble ahead as minor skirmishes broke out almost immediately in various parts of the pitch. The referee unfortunately failed to stamp his authority on the match and it eventually developed into an all out brawl involving players and mentors from both sides. Tommy Bassett and Don Lehane entered the fray in non user friendly mode.

Jack Crennan was slowed down severely by a pair of over sized wellington boots and entered the arena just as hostilities were coming to a conclusion. The match was later rearranged for a neutral venue.

St Judes were also fined 50 pounds by the County Board due to substitutes kicking a ball around at half time during the senior football championship match against St Olaf's in Parnell Park. The club should have recouped the money by fining the remainder of the team for not kicking the ball around during the actual 60 minutes when the game itself was in progress – it was a very poor game. At an Adult Games meeting in September 1995 it was reported that the senior footballers had a full set of jerseys except the number 12 jersey which was reported as "damaged". There was no report on the condition of the unfortunate wearer of the jersey on the occasion of the "damage" or no get well soon messages so we have to assume he made a complete recovery.

The rapid promotion of St Judes up through the ranks was of course an exciting time for both players and supporters with new teams, new venues and of course new hostelries being the order of the day. Our first visit at senior level to St Margarets in North County Dublin ended in a one point defeat but did not deter a number of supporters from participating in the delights of the local Brock Inn. Seán Conway, Joe McDonnell, Jim Coghlan, Jack Lernihan and Patsy Tyrrell were the team selected by the club to represent them in competition with the local St Margarets supporters in an attempt to salvage something from the day. The event started with the usual sombre post match analysis with player performances being dissected at length. It rapidly developed into an all out session complete with sing-song and Jews harp and culminated in an energetic waltz involving Seán Conway and one of the locals (male we understand). St Judes left St Margarets with no points from our on pitch endeavours but with a whole new set of North County Dublin pen pals.

The club presentation night was held in the Springfield Hotel on 22nd November 1996.

The suppoRteR

Donnchadh Ó Liatháin

Let's go St Judes – right from the start
(The ball's just been thrown in)
Grant us Dear Lord an early score
This time we have to win.
A mighty catch, a brilliant pass
A goal is surely on!
Six bloody steps – can he not count? –
A golden chance is gone.

Come on St Judes – we cannot lose
These points we badly need
Our backs are driving forward
Inter-passing at great speed
Their Number six has won the ball
His long punt is no threat
Oh no! the Bloody keeper's slipped
It's in our bloody net!

Cop on St Judes – we're three points down
(It's thirteen points to ten)
Why is it when we win the ball
We give it back again?
Our forwards couldn't skin a spud
Despite their weave and bob
My sister's kids (both under ten)
Would do a better job.

St Judes – a chance to close the gap
We've won a close-in free
The hopeless case miscued the ball
Its hit the referee!
A ricochet from off his knee
I can't believe my eyes

It's crossed the line a goal's a goal –
I knew we'd equalize.

Now see St Judes break from defence
And solo down the field
(I never for a second thought)
that we'd lie down and yield)
A lofted point from out the field
We've pipped them at the post
O brave fifteen – o gallant team
You really are the most.

Forever Judes – Forever Judes
My faith has never faltered
When fortune smiles or fate's unkind
My passion burns unaltered
At home, away, in rain or shine
You have my rapt attention
I don't complain or bad mouth you
Unlike some I could mention!

The supporters – St Judes v Raheny 1993 final.

The Role of Umpire

Don Lehane

T HE important role of umpires is very often underestimated in the scheme of things in a club. The ideal umpire will have a number of important characteristics, which do not include honesty and a sense of fair play. The most important feature of an umpire is a calm and commanding nature when all hell is breaking out around him. The ability to decisively wave a wide for any opposition ball that goes over the bar but within two feet of the upright requires courage. The first task of an umpire is to undermine the confidence of the opposition goalkeeper. If he wears gloves or is of a nervous disposition, subject to hopping around the goals and talking incessantly you know you are on the pig's back. A reminder that our full-forward is just back from a six month suspension for GBH and that in your opinion he should have been banned for life for "destroying that poor lads career" often has the desired unsettling effect. Most goalkeepers are paranoid about their kick-outs so this is another area worth focusing on initially. If he shows any weakness in getting distance into his kicks then regular shouts to the full-forward to "Watch the poor kick Peter" will often undermine his confidence even more. If he is the type that insists on digging a large divot to place the ball on then it should be pointed out to him that this is not within the rules and you will have to inform the referee and/or the local park ranger if he persists. Umpires should watch out like a hawk

"Yerra, sure 'twas a mile wide!"

for any perceived weakness in opposition goalkeepers when coming out for the high ball and make sure that outfield players are aware of it. Regular shouts at one of your midfielders to "Kick it in long Tom – he doesn't like the high ones" will often rattle the best of goalkeepers. It will often reduce him to a nervous wreck before the end of the game, particularly if each high kick is accompanied by the early arrival of a sixteen stone full-forward in a threatening and abusive manner. Disrupting the goalkeeper's concentration is not to be confused with intimidation which is generally frowned on except in ultra serious confrontations such as games against local opposition or maybe an important play-off match.

Tommy Bassett and Charles Moran on umpiring duty at 1988 Division 3 Football final.

The All-Ireland Sevens

Colum Grogan

IN 1989 St Judes won the Dublin County Junior A Hurling Championship – the club's first ever adult hurling trophy. Later that year the possibility of creating a competition of All-Ireland proportions for Junior clubs was being formed within the club. An application to host a sixteen team seven-a-side Junior Hurling Competition in September 1990 was submitted to Croke Park. The criteria for participating teams from each county to compete in this competition in 1990 would be they being the previous year's Junior A County Champions.

INAUGURAL 1990 EVENT - A MAJOR SUCCESS

In 1990 permission was granted by Croke Park to host the competition and the Dublin County Board allocated the date to be the eve of the All-Ireland Senior Football Final. This was changed in 1993 to eve of Senior Hurling Final, with the footballers being given eve of Football All Ireland.

Credit for the concept of a Junior All Ireland Sevens Competition is given to Limerickman Martin Hayes of Doon. The inaugural competition was organized by Colum Grogan, Chairman of the Hurling/Camogie Committee and its Secretary and Club PRO Jimmy O'Dwyer, with the assistance of other committee members Martin Hayes, Peter Lucey, Declan Feore, Denis Ryan, Mick Hartnett and Joe Clavin. Hayes, Grogan, Ryan and Lucey were, of course, members of the victorious Junior A Championship team, managed by Joe Clavin.

Finance was a major concern when St Judes first embarked on a venture of this scale but they were fortunate and forever grateful to the ESB for committing £1,000 each year for the first three years of the competitions.

Club stalwart Mick Hartnett of Tolmac Construction, as generous as ever and an ardent supporter of both Limerick and St Judes, purchased the magnificent Corn Naomh Jude Hurling Cup. Club member and another of the Junior A hurling team, Liam Larkin now CEO of Goulding Chemicals, purchased the Player of the Tournament (now Laoch an Lae) Trophy. The Club is most grateful to both Mick and Liam who have continued their support ever since.

Because of the detailed preparation and organisation and the local club commitment the competition was a great success. Mullinahone of Tipperary defeated Faythe Harriers of Wexford in the final. Player of the Tournament was won by John Leahy of Mullinahone and Tipperary fame.

Since then many other famous clubs and inter-county players have graced the fields of Tymon North in these championships -Seán Treacy of Galway, Nicky English of Tipperary, Damien Quigley of Limerick, Joe Deane of Cork in hurling, Darragh O'Shea and Darragh Ó Cinnéide of Kerry and our own clubmen Declan O'Boyle, Enda Sheehy and Enda Crennan of Dublin and Ciaran McGovern of Leitrim to name but a few, in football.

Following the 1990 success of the Hurling Sevens, the following year the Football Committee decided to run a Football Sevens It's organization was coordinated by Donegalman Tony McGinley with the assistance of fellow Football Committee members. A Perpetual Trophy for this competition was presented to the Club by Don Lehane from Waterford and we are greatly indebted to him for his generosity. Dublin club St Olafs were the inaugural winners with the host club St Judes as runners up. St Judes learned from this and were successful for the next two years, 1992 and 1993.

In 1992 the Club arranged that one committee should be responsible for the two competitions. Declan Feore was elected Chairman with Club PRO, Garrett Edge as Secretary and Martin Hayes as Treasurer. The committee members were Mick Hartnett, Billy O'Frighil, Paddy Russell, Tommy Hartnett, Peter Lucey, Tony McGinley and Seán Breheny.

Having spent three years as Chairman, Declan retired. He was succeeded in 1995 by Colum Grogan, who has retained the position to date. Participation in each competition had extended to 20 teams in Hurling and 24 in Football which is the present competitions format. However in 1998 thirty two teams participated in the Football competition and also that year the Sevens organised a Ladies Football Sevens consisting of 20 teams nationwide which was won by Kenmare of Kerry who defeated Carrigtwohill of Cork in the Final. Also during that Ladies Competition the Dublin Ladies Football team played an exhibition game against the Meath Ladies Footballers which the Royal County Ladies won by two points.

STEPPING STONE

It must be said that winners and finalists of the St Judes Junior Hurling and Football sevens have gone on to greater things in competitions in their own counties. Our first seven's winners Mullinahone have since won the Tipperary county senior hurling championship as indeed have Na Piarsaigh of Limerick. In football, St Judes, winners of the sevens in 1992 went on to become senior football league champions in 2000. An Ghaeltacht of Kerry, winners of the St Judes sevens on two occasions, have had plenty of success in the Kingdom.

Many other winners of the Seven's have moved up the ranks and have since established themselves as potential senior contenders for major success in their own counties and we in St Judes are delighted that the standard of our Sevens competitions in organization and play is a major contributor to these developments.

The Sevens are undoubtedly a Junior Club's stepping stone to success.

SPONSORS

Following the success of the hurling competition in 1990, our application to host a Junior Football Sevens in 1991 was approved. This, too, was a great success. From 1993 to 1994 ACC Bank became main sponsors and the Club was also fortunate to receive sponsorship of sliotars and footballs from Kevin Reynolds of Nuri Sports. This sponsorship was then taken up by Gouldings Chemicals and this year Azzurri took over the mantle as sponsors of sliotars and footballs. During the period 1993 and 1994 the dates of the competitions were altered to coincide with the respective All-Ireland weekends.

In 1995 the Bank of Ireland became our major sponsors and since then the competition has increased from 16 teams competing in 1991 to 32 teams in 2000 in the Football Sevens. The involvement of a major financial institution such as Bank of Ireland in sponsoring these competitions was a contributing factor in its increasing popularity and its establishment as a permanent fixture in the GAA calendar. Since then we have had EBS as sponsors from 1999 to 2001 and last year and to date our sponsors are McCloskey Engineering (Ireland) Ltd.

VISITORS TO THE SEVENS

Apart from participating famous players and visits by GAA presidents, over the years many famous GAA personnel have visited St Judes through their involvement with teams and friends taking part in the Sevens. GAA giants such as Paddy Doherty of Ballykinlar and Down, Donie Nealon of Burgess and Tipperary, Willie John Daly of Carrigtwohill and Cork to name but a few.

LIFE MEMBER

Along with all our welcomes to all visitors to the Sevens there is too a big welcome for the Presidents of the GAA, both past and present. Various Presidents have visited us during these competitions and we were delighted to have conferred Honorary Life Membership of St Judes on former GAA President Jack Boothman.

2003 SEVENS COMMITTEE

Chairman: Colum Grogan, Martin Hayes, Donie Cummins, Jack Lernihan, Jack Crennan, Declan Doyle, Nick Finnerty, Marie O'Brien and Seán Breheny.

THANK YOU

It must be stated that without the cooperation and assistance of a number of other groups it would have been very difficult, if not impossible to host and organise these competitions. The Club will be forever grateful to our friends and neighbours Faughs GAA Club, to the Dublin Hurling and Football Boards, Coiste Reiteori Atha Cliath, South Dublin County Council Parks Dept., Bishop Galvin NS, St MacDara's Community College, and of course, the media, particularly the written press.

Finally the Sevens Committee is most grateful to the members of St Judes, who by their ceaseless and dedicated work have most of all made the Sevens the success that they are today.

Left: Mick Hartnett presents his All-Ireland Hurling Trophy, 1991.

Bottom: Don Lehane with his All-Ireland Football Trophy, 1995.

The All-Ireland Sevens' plaque

Declan Feore

FRIDAY 22nd April 1994 was a memorable date in the history of St Judes and the All Ireland Junior Sevens. It was on this date that the plaque commemorating the Laoch an Lae and Buaiteori of the "Sevens" was unveiled by Seán O Síocháin, former General Secretary and first Director General of the GAA. Seán came out of retirement for this occasion. We were greatly honoured, as it was his last official function on behalf of the Association.

Following an introduction by the then "Sevens" Chairman, Declan Feore, the Plaque was unveiled by Seán. "Tá áthas orm an phlac seo a nochtú" and then at the request of our Club President, Frank McSweeney, Seán gave what many regard as his finest rendition of Sigerson Clifford's ballad "The Boys of Barr na Sráide"

At the unveiling of a Roll of Honour for the All-Ireland Sevens at St Judes GAA Club, Templeogue, last night (from left): Nicky English (Captain of last year's winners, Lattin Cullen), former Director General of the GAA, Seán Ó Siochain, Seán Breheny, Chairman of St Judes GAA Club and Seán Treacy (Captain 1991 winners, Portumna). (Irish Press, Saturday 23rd April, 1994)

242

John Mangan, a woodcarver in Marley Park Craft Centre, was contracted to bring to fruition the concept of Declan Feore, Jimmy O'Dwyer and Seán Breheny. The carving of the two players at the top of the plaque is of Tomás Mulcahy, Cork and Johnny McGurk of Derry.

In the 1986 All Ireland Final against Galway, Mulcahy scored a goal, after being seen, but not by the referee, John Bailey, to have fouled the ball. Afterwards, Tomás explained that following a solo run he gave a handpass, but as there was nobody there to receive it, he took it himself before scoring.

In the 1993 semi final against Dublin, Johnny McGurk came from wing back to score the winning point, knocking the Dubs out of the All Ireland.

Many notable names have been engraved on the plaque. In hurling, the first Laoch an Lae was John Leahy of Tipperary fame, who was selected when his club Mullinahone won the inaugural "Sevens".

Nicky English, who captained Lattin-Cullen to victory in 1993, was pipped by his club mate, Gerry Maguire for the title. That night Micheál Ó Muircheartaigh presented Maguire, who scored 24 goals throughout the day, with his trophy on "CEILI HOUSE", which was broadcast live from St Judes Clubhouse. On the same programme Donnchadh Ó Dúlaing interviewed the famous NICKY. Another player interviewed that night by Ó Muircheartaigh was Joe Hennessy of James Stephens, Kilkenny, who was there as a guest.

In 1992 Damien Quigley (he of the 2 goals 3pts against Offaly in 1994) of Na Piarsaig, Limerick had his name engraved and the famous goal snatcher from Killeagh and Cork, Joe Deane was honoured in 1996.

No hurling club has, to date, won the double in Sevens. That honour belongs to the footballers. Our own St Judes had back to back victories in 1992 and 1993. Kerry is represented, twice with Sneem in 1999 and 2000 and An Ghaeltacht, whose Ian Larmer was Laoch an Lae in 1996, when they won the Sevens. 1994 was the other year of their double.

It will be interesting to see what illustrious names will be added in the future.

Footnote : The day before the unveiling the legendary John Kerry O'Donnell died in New York, aged 94. Our own clubman Danny Lynch GAA, PRO, who was at the unveiling flew to New York the following day with former President Paddy Buggy to represent the GAA at the funeral.

The Biter Bit – Bobby Carty and trainee.

Billy O'Frighil with Peter and Ciara Lucey. In the background are Martin Hayes and Bernie Gallagher.

Liam Larkin presents the Laoch an Lae Trophy to Joe Deane (Killeagh) 1996.

Irene Feore, Marie O'Dwyer (RIP) and Eileen Breheny at the unveiling of the Sevens Plaque 1994.

"Have you got one for me?", asks Gerry Wright of Garrett Edge as Pat Brady looks away in disbelief.

St Mac Daras Community College

Seán Breheny

THE CONNECTION between St MacDaras and St Judes goes back to the foundation of the College. There has always been a spirit of co-operation between the College and the Club in many areas, as we are next door neighbours. One of the most practical applications of this co-operation is the coaching help provided by St Judes Director of Coaching Niamh Leahy to the College. Another is the wholehearted assistance the Club receives each year from the College when the pitch, the carpark and changing facilities are provided for the Hurling and Football Sevens. Indeed the experience of the Club in dealing with the College has been very rewarding and the Club is only too eager to respond in a like manner wherever necessary. St MacDaras has a proud sporting tradition over a wide spectrum of sports.

The Sports Awards Night celebrated each year in the College is a fitting tribute to the excellence of sport in the College. Gaelic Games are very well catered for in College life. Beginning with Seán Ryan and continuing all the way up to the present with Derek Ward and Liam Cormack, there is a good spread of Gaelic sporting achievement.

The very first Gaelic football team that represented St MacDaras played Firhouse Community College in a challenge on Wednesday 17th November 1982. The team was (1) Brian McFeeney, (2) Michael Denvir (3) Mark Dempsey (4) Alan Healy (5) Ronan Moore (6) Stephen O'Connell (7) Eoin McDonagh (8) David McGlynn (9) Patrick Byrne (10) Barry McGlynn (11) Alan Egan (12) David Heather (13) Conor Molloy (14) Michael Tobin (15) Derek Landy (16) Bernard Colgan (17) Brian Downes (18) Kenneth Morrin (19) Mark Kearns (20) John Cullen (21) Paul Fitzpatrick.

The first Gaelic Football title won by the College was the Donegan Cup (Under 14 1984-85), which was won in Croke Park when St MacDaras beat St Finians, Swords after a replay. The Captain was Declan O'Reilly and one of the outstanding players was Shane Gallen. During the 1985-86 season the Donegan Cup was won again by the College who beat Skerries. The Captain of the College team was Dara Murphy. The first Under 18 Football win was in 1986-87 when the College won the Dublin Under 18 Vocational Schools Murphy Cup with star players Alan Healy, Shane Gallen, Declan O'Reilly and Barry McGlynn. They beat Balbriggan in Terenure VEC grounds.

The College's first Football title was won in 1992-93 when St MacDaras became the Dublin Under 18 Colleges champions having beaten Coolmine CC by nine points to eight in O'Toole Park. The current captain of St Judes Senior Football team, Peter Gilsenan, was captain of that victorious College team. The team went on to contest the Leinster Final which they lost in extra time to Bagenalstown, Carlow. Outstanding in the Leinster Final were Peter Gilsenan and Terence Orr.

St MacDaras became Dublin and Leinster Champions in the 1993-94 season at Under 16C under captain Michael Glover. Enda Crennan and David McGovern were outstanding. The College defeated Beneavin College in the Dublin Final and they beat Bagenalstown in the Leinster Final.

During the 1996-97 season the College were again victorious winning both Dublin and Leinster Under 14C. In the Dublin Final they beat Beneavin College and Presentation College Carlow fell to them in the Leinster Final. During that series of wins it is worthy of note that they were struggling in the Leinster semi-final against Ardscoil Chiarain from Clara, being 10 points down at half time, and going on to win by 2 points! The team was captained by Shane Lynch, son of Danny and included Stephen Early, Shane O'Brien, Barry Faulkner, David O'Hara, Liam Coffey, Stephen Lynch, Fintan O'Brien, Gerard Bambrick, Kevin Edge and Conor McBride.

Being promoted to Under 16B in 1997-98 did not prevent St MacDaras from winning their fourth Colleges title. They beat St Marks 1 – 11 to 1 – 10. Shane Guckian was the Captain and outstanding players were Micheál Lyons, Seán Breheny, Stephen Lynch and Fintan O'Brien.

Successes prompted promotion yet again in the 1998-99 season when St MacDaras found itself in the Under 16A for the first time. A notable feature of the season was the first A game in which the College beat St Davids Artane 2-10 to 2-6. St Davids was managed by St Judes senior manager Brian Talty! Subsequently the College lost the Dublin semi-final by four points to Coláiste Cholm, Swords.

During 1999-2000 St MacDaras contested the Dublin B semi-final and lost by two points to eventual Leinster Champions St Marks. Seán Breheny was unable to play due to injury.

St MacDara's was proudly represented by Micheál Lyons, Brendan McManamon, David O'Hara and Seán Breheny when they were part of the Dublin team that won the Leinster title and the All-Ireland title for the first time since 1963. Seán Breheny scored a goal in the final in Croke Park against Tyrone. The Dublin team was captained by Seán Breheny the following year, but they were unlucky to be beaten in the first round.

The year 2000 saw the College select its team of the Millennium. This is the team, among whom are many stars of St Judes:

MILLENNIUM GAELIC FOOTBALL – *1982-2000*

(1)
Terence Orr
1987 – 1993

(2)	(3)	(4)
Fintan O'Brien	Shane O'Brien	John O'Toole
1996-2001	1995-2000	1987-1993
(5)	(6)	(7)
Seán Breheny	Gary Colleran	Michael Kelly
1995-2001	1988-1993	1993-1999

(8)
Fergal O'Donoghue
1985-1990

(9)
Paul Keogh
1989-1994

(10)	(11)	(12)
Barry McGlynn	Enda Crennan	Micheál Lyons
1982-1987	1991-1996	1994-2000
(13)	(14)	(15)
Peter Gilsenan	Pat Burke	Shane Gallen
1988-1993	1996-2001	1984-1989

During the 2001-02 season St MacDara's won the Dublin and Leinster Under 14B Championships.

In the Dublin Trial they beat Colaiste Eoin 0-8 to 0-7 and they beat Carlow CBS 2-10 to 1-8 to win the Leinster Final. Notable players in these victories were Paul Teahan, Chris Guckian and Ger Fehilly. During the 2002-03 Season the College reached the Under 18B semi-final losing by 2 points to Malahide CS. Stars for the College in the semi-final included Ross O'Brien and Ronán Joyce.

Hurling and camogie have always been fully supported in St MacDaras. Both codes are in the healthy state, and with the help of Coaching Director, Niamh Leahy, major success is not too far away. Over the years, notable hurlers have included Eoghan Ryan, John Reen and Seán Fallon (1988 Under 14C winners). In 1990 the first year shield was held aloft by Ciaran Quigley, and he was supported by Star players Damien Keating, Alan Kennedy and Colm Ryan. In 1999 Under 14C hurling was won by St MacDaras who had players of the calibre of Brian Monaghan, Conor Kelly and Aidan Smylie. Under 16B hurling was won by the College with Dublin Under 21 Seán O'Connor as Captain, and included star players Ronán Joyce and Kevin O'Malley.

Camogie has proved itself in the College over the years. In the 1992-93 season the college minor team won the Dublin Colleges Championship and went on to contest the Leinster Final in Carlow losing to Ballyfin College by one point. In 1995-96 the junior team won the Dublin Colleges Junior Championship, which was followed in 1998-99 by a Dublin Colleges Senior Trophy. Success has been elusive since, but signs are good for success in the near future. The College owes a great debt of gratutide to Seamus Massey, Marie O'Brien and Joan Molamphy for their dedication and hard work in the great achievements of College Camogie teams.

The present Junior and Senior camogie panels in St Judes is made up largely of past pupils of the College. The College is proud of its association with St Judes and is equally proud of the fact that its past pupils are members of a club that fields teams in the top division in football, hurling and camogie in the county!

Ar agaidh le chéile.

1996-97 Dublin and Leinster U14 Champions – St Mac Daras
Back row (l-r): Derek Ward (Manager), Pat Burke, Stephen Earley, Stephen Devlin, Shane O'Brien, Barry Faulkner, Dave O'Hara, Mark Kelly, Liam Coffey. Front: Stephen Lynch, Shane Lynch, Fintan O'Brien, Gerry Bambrick, Kevin Edge, Conor McBride, Mark Molloy.

Ladies Football in St Judes

Máire McSherry

ST JUDES entered their first team in Juvenile Football in 1997 at Under 12 Division 2. The formation of this team was in response to representations by local teacher Peter Lucey who had gathered a starry panel of players at Bishop Galvin School and was anxious that they continue at Club level.

In 1999 the section grew when teams were entered at Under10, 12 and 14 levels. The following season saw the introduction of a team at Under 16 level. From small beginnings in 1997 the Juvenile Ladies section of the Club now caters for over 100 players. During this period St Judes has enjoyed considerable success on the field of play.

ROLL OF HONOUR

Under 10	Shield winners	1999
Under 12	A Championship Runners-up	1998
	C Championship Runners-up	1999
	League Runners-up	2000
	Shield Winners	2001
Under 14	C Championship winners	1999
	B Championship Runners-up	2000
	League Runners-up	2001
Under 16	B Championship Runners-up	2000

The following Players have been selected at Intercounty level to play for Dublin:

Under 12   Leah Barry, Olivia Ryan, Emer Lowe, Aoife Rafferty, Ann Holland, Sarah Curran, Ciara Tyrell, Roisin Murray, Katie Grehan, Sarah Walsh, Niamh Grogan, Amy Seery.

Under 14   Leah Barry, Susan Hughes, Katie Grehan, Roisin Murray, Helen Cosgrave, Niamh Grogan, Helena Ryan, Emma Blake.

Under 16   Susan Hughes and Leah Barry.

ADULT SECTION

The first Adult Ladies' team competed in 1996. The team was made up of young girls from the Parish and surrounding area, many of whom had no previous football experience. They fielded for five years despite having a very tight panel and surviving the loss of players to exams, work and Australia at various times. In 2002 the girls of the previous year and some current Under 16 players joined the Senior panel. They competed in the Senior Division 4 League and finished in second place, earning promotion to Division 3 for the current year.

Our hopes for the future are high with a steady supply of well trained players coming through from under age from now on. We hope for many more successes in this fastest growing of sports.

Celebrations — (l-r): Anne Marie O'Brien, Ciara Brien, Sarah Massey, Aoife Farrell, Cathy Dickens, Deirdre Ryan, Imelda Molloy.

2000 Bishop Galvin NS winners of the Cumann na mBunscol Corn Royal Breffni Division 1 Girls' Football League.

Feile na nGael 1988

Seán Ward and John Browne

THE CLUB'S under 14 teams had been very successful in 1988, winning the all Dublin Division 2 titles in both hurling and football. Most of the Feile team in 1988 was drawn from this under 14 team: Alan Byrne, Marcus Mallon, Terence Orr, John Reen, Enda Sheehy, Niall Ryan, Ronan Colgan, Andrew Moore, Mark O'Reilly, Brian Ward, Conor Lyons and Paul McGovern. In those years, the reckonable date of birth for most competitions was mid-year, whereas for the Feile competitions the relevant date was 1 January. For the Hurling Feile in 1988, the hurling panel was strengthened by the addition of several older players, including Bryan Duggan, John Nolan, Seán Fallon, Colin Farrell and Gerard Farrell: these players had been ably coached by Willie Nolan from Tipperary and Young Irelands. There were also some U13 players on the panel, Alan Kennedy, Kieran Quigley and Brendan Culhane, from the team managed by Pat Quigley and Tommy Hartnett.

The semi final match was against Good Counsel on Saturday 10th June in Fairview Park. This was a very exciting match as Good Counsel had some good players, most notably Stephen Perkins, who now plays senior hurling with Dublin. However, he was ably marked by Terence Orr, wherever he went, and this greatly reduced the effectiveness of the Good Counsel team. Other Judes players to play well were John Reen, Enda Sheehy, John Nolan, Ronan Colgan and Colin Farrell (not the actor). The final score was Judes 4-4, Good Counsel 2-3.

The final was played on the following day, also in Fairview Park against Setanta. This team was very energetic whereas the Judes team was very tired, having played the previous day. As all the Setanta instructions were given 'as gaeilge', the Judes players felt they were missing something! Bryan Duggan made some very fine saves to keep us in the match. Other players to catch the eye were Colin Farrell, John Nolan and Mark O'Reilly. The final score was Judes 2-1, Setanta 1-2.

The team went on to the Leinster Feile in Aughrim, and won the shield, beating Coill Dubh (Kildare) in the final.

Two of the players went on to play minor hurling for Dublin - Bryan Duggan and Enda Sheehy.

Under 14 Hurling Féile na nGael winners, 1988
Front row: Colin Farrell, Ronan Colgan, Andrew Moore, Alan Kennedy, Brendan Culhane, Gerard Farrell, Mark O'Reilly, Brian Ward, Conor Lyons, Paul McGovern. Back row: Seán Ward (mentor), Bryan Duggan, Alan Byrne, Marcus Mallon, Terence Orr, John Reen, Enda Sheehy, John Nolan, Seán Fallon, Niall Ryan, Kieran Quigley, Gus Barry (mentor).

Junior B Division 10 Runners-up – Back (l-r): Joe McDonnell (mentor), John Foley (mentor), Niall Guckian, Pat Crean, Dave O'Kelly, Conor Ryan, Ciaran O'Brien, Conor Foley, Tadgh O'Brien, Dara Lowe, Ciaran Wynne, Alan Lowe, Rory O'Connell, Mark Carty, Mick O'Brien (mentor), Neil Doyle (manager). Front: Mark Worrell, Eadhmonn MacSuibhne, Alan Mooney, Darragh McGivern, Fintan O'Brien, Vinny Kelly, Alan Tierney, Donal Evoy, Colm Manning, John Conlon, Fergal O'Connor, Shane Lynch, Ger McSweeney, Brian Sommers.

All weather pitch

Seán McBride

AN TAOISEACH, Bertie Ahern TD on Sunday, 3rd. November 2002, officially opened the All Weather Pitch in Tymon Park in the presence of the Mayor of South Dublin County Council, Councillor Jim Daly. The opening was attended by hundreds of adults and children from inside and outside the parish, by our local and national representatives, by officials from SDCC and by officers of both the GAA & FAI.

The opening marked the completion of a project that was a number of years in gestation and it was brought to a successful conclusion as the result of a lot of hard work carried out by our members in St Judes and our neighbours in Templeogue United FC.

The history of the project went back five or six years when officials from SDCC approached a number of clubs and organisations in the area to seek expressions of interest in developing the disused site where the pitch now stands. Various ideas were mooted before the idea of an AWP took hold and, while a number of parties considered the idea, only St Judes and our neighbours were prepared to make the necessary commitment to proceed with the project.

At an EGM of the club on the 28th January 2001, the members of St Judes gave their approval to proceed with the development and to undertake borrowings if this were necessary to complete the scheme.

Because of the considerable costs involved, we decided to build the development in two stages. The first phase, involving the clearance of the site, extensive drainage works, the installation of ducting for the lights and the laying of sand based surface, was completed in the summer of 2001 at a cost of €300,000.

This was a good start but we recognised that if we were to get maximum advantage for our players, particularly for our hurlers and camogie players, we would have to improve the playing surface. But this next step would come at a considerable cost, as it would involve the installation of a state-of-the-art plastic carpet with sand and rubber inlay.

This was in addition to the installation of the lighting, which had not yet been put in place. When we did our sums we realised that we were talking about additional expenditure of €450, 000, bringing the total cost of the project to €750,000.

Finance was critical to the success of the project and we assiduously used all our know how and contacts in the Club in the applications we submitted for National Lottery funding. We received three grants totalling €300,000 in 2001/02 but even still there was a considerable gap to fill if we were to finish phase two.

This was where our members showed their real mettle in their total endorsement of the proposal to run a limited draw to raise the balance needed.

To achieve our goal, we had to raise about €300,000 after prize money had been allocated. This in turn meant having to sell 4000 tickets at €127 each, a daunting task by any standards.

We had brilliant supporters and committee members who just got stuck in, displaying courage and commitment in the best traditions of St Judes. People who had sworn never again to sell tickets door to door found new energy. Members, who had never sold anything in their lives, found they had a real talent for parting their friends from their money. Particularly heartening was the input from new members who saw this development as their way of making a contribution to the development of St Judes. In a joint fund raising scheme with Templeogue United, we got huge support in the parish for a project that was seen as a cross community exercise.

We launched the draw in October 2001 and by the following March we had achieved our goal and we netted about €300,000 from the fundraising exercise. With the necessary finances secured, we were in the position to choose a supplier and product at a competitive price.

Before deciding on a supplier the committee had travelled the country looking at other installations and talking to people. This was an important decision for the Club after all the hard work our members had put into the development and we wanted to get it right. After considerable consultations and deliberations, we chose Tarkett, a French manufacturer whose pitch was then installed by Peter O Brien Ltd., a prominent landscape company based in Dublin. Since its installation in Autumn 2002, the response from our players and visitors has been overwhelmingly positive and the pitch has met and exceeded our expectations.

While pressure on the facility is tremendous because of the number of teams who are using it, all our players are guaranteed training even in the harshest weather conditions. Utilised properly, it gives our members an advantage in terms of meeting their training needs and it ensures that more and more players attend for training. The local schools also use it during daylight hours.

Because the two clubs own it, a unique ownership and management structure is in place and representatives from the two associations meet on a regular basis to deal with all issues relating to the management of the pitch.

Apart from our own members and friends, over the years leading to the completion of the AWP we received huge support and encouragement from Dr Christy Boylan and his colleagues in SDCC. We are also indebted to our political representatives, including Conor Lenihan TD, Charlie O Connor TD, Pat Rabbitte TD, Seán Ardagh TD, Senator Brian Hayes, Councillors Marie Ardagh, Stanley Laing, Cait Keane and Eamonn Walsh.

This development stands alongside the building of the clubhouse in 1987 and the extension to it in 1998 as one of the three major investments undertaken by St Judes in its first 25 years history. It is a credit to all those who have worked so hard for the Club since its foundation in 1978 and it is a facility of which we can all be proud.

Bertie Ahern (Taoiseach) with kids at opening of All-Weather Pitch in 2002.

Intermediate hurling panel 1995 – Back row (l-r): Peter Lucey, Sean Fallon, Padraig Kennedy, Declan Molloy, Ciaran McLoughlin, Fiachra Feore, John Nolan, Kieran Quigley, Mick Reidy, Mick Fallon, Peter Ryan, Frank Gallagher. Front: Bryan Duggan, David Roche, Gerry Ryan, Paul McGovern, Eugene Murray, Liam Quinlan, Ronan Colgan, John Reen.

All Ireland Junior Hurling Sevens Panel 1992 – Back Row (l-r): Peter Lucey (Manager), Niall Ryan, Peter Ryan, Mick Reidy, Fiachra Feore, John Nolan. Front: Noel Egan, Davy Mahon, Bryan Duggan, Sean Fallon, Enda Sheehy.

Presentation of Junior 'A' Championship Cup, 1996 – John Leonard, Chairman Dublin Junior Hurling Board, presenting the Elvery Cup (Junior 'A' Championship) to captain Eugene Murray.

The Dublin hurling team who played Dicksboro (Kilkenny) at the official opening of club extension, May 1998 – Standing (l-r): Michael O'Grady (manager), Kieran Quigley, Fiachra Feore, Conor McCann, Seán Power, Derek Maher, Derek McMullan, Seán Fallon, Seán McDermott, Alan Kennedy, Stephen Perkins, Denis Ryan, Eugene Murray. Kneeling: Bryan Duggan, Ronan Colgan,s Neville Kelly, Lee Keogh, John Finnegan, Connie Ring, Seán Duignan, Joe Moloney.

Junior C League and Championship winners, 1998 – Standing: Denis Ryan, Jim Kelly, Bart Lehane, Kevin O'Dwyer, Mick Reidy, Kevin Roche, Cathal Nolan, Lorcan Looby Barry Heraty, Barry McGann, Gerry Ryan, Greg Lehane, Donagh O'Dwyer, Fergal Hourihan. Front: Martin Gaughan, Eamonn Coghlan, Tadgh O'Connor, Ken Molloy, Sean Hegarty, Daire Kane, Robbie McCabe, Martin Hayes.

1999 Junior 'B' League and Miller Shield winners – Back row (l-r): Denis Ryan, Shane O'Connor, Eoin O'Connor, Bart Lehane, Kevin O'Dwyer, Barry Heraty, Cathal 'Roundy' Nolan, Paul Molamphy, Donagh O'Dwyer, Mick Fallon, Mick Reidy, Barry McGann, Donncha Ryan, Joe Keane. Front: David Ryan, Colm McGovern, Eamon Ryan, Ger Hartnett, Gerry Ryan, Ciaran McLoughlin, Robbie McCabe, Donal Molloy, Fergus Hourihan, Seán Hegarty.

2002 Junior 'B' Hurling Championship Trophy, Gerry Ryan (captain) with Cup and Seán Fallon.

Happy Corkmen – Peter Lucey with Brian Corcoran, Ger Cunningham and Mark Landers, captain of Cork All Ireland Champions 1999.

On the waterfront – St Judes participants preparing for their Millennium March in 1988.

1998 first U10 Ladies Football team – Back row (l-r): Ailbhea O'Conner, Aishling Holland, Vanessa Daly, Sarah Walsh, Ann-Marie Hoare, Niamh Murphy, Aisling Ryan, Laura Clarke. Front: Ruth Hannon, Niamh Naughton, Amy Seery, Aoife Rafferty, Niamh Grogan, Róisín Murray, Leanne Brennan, Oonagh McCormack, Katie Grehan.

2001 Senior Hurling Panel promoted to Senior 1 – Back row (l-r): Ken Ryan (manager), Seamus Ryan, Seán Breheny, Ciaran O'Brien, Bart Lehane, Alan Kennedy, Seán McLoughlin, Damien Garrihy, Noel Nash, John McCarthy, Denis Ryan (mentor), Niamh Leahy (Physio). Middle: Eugene Murray (mentor), David Ryan, Eamonn Ryan, Kieran Quigley, Gareth Roche (captain), Bryan Duggan, Ken Molloy, Tim McCarthy, David Roche. Front: Barry McGann, Gerard Hartnett, Vinny Kelly, Michael Lyons, Shane O'Connor, John Ryan, Fiachra Feore.

2000 Senior Football Division 1 winners – Back row (l-r): P. Tyrrell, C. Kilcoyne (mentor), M. Fallon, A. Connell, G. O'Reilly, C. Lehane, P. Kenny, L. Belton, T. Morley, J. O'Riordan, C. Moran (mentor), B. Talty (Manager). Middle: J. McGovern, S. Cunningham, L. Kehoe, D. Carroll, T. Orr, T. Prendergast, P. Harlow, W. Linney, A. Glover, M. Lyons, C. Conneely. Front: D. Reynolds, E. Crennan, C. Voyles, E. Sheehy, C. Durkan, C. McGovern, A. Doyle, E. O'Neill, G. Quinn, S. Breheny, P. Cunney. Inserts: J. O'Gara, G. Russell, P. Gilsenan.

2002 Senior B Championship presentation.

2002 U21 County finalists – Back row (l-r): Paddy Keogh (mentor), Stephen Lynch, Liam Coffey, Robert Hyland, Ciaran Coates, Dara Lowe, Donnacha Ryan, Stephen Earley, Ger Hartnett, John Waldron, Andrew Glover, Seamus Ryan, Brendan McManamon, Shane O'Brien, Paul Cunningham, Bart Lehane, Tommy Hartnett (manager), Bartle Faulkner (mentor), Aileen Keogh (Physio). Front: Conor McBride, Eoghan Mangan, Joey Donnelly, Paul Sweeney, Seán Breheny, Paul Copeland, Niall O'Shea, Damien Keogh, Kevin Hayes, Ross McDermott, Barry Faulkner, Shane Guckian, Michael Lyons.

1986/87 Junior 'B' Football team – Back row (l-r): Conor Lehane, Ernest Kenny (mentor), Kevin Clabby, Ger Kenny, Joe McDonnell, John Browne, Don Lehane, Tommy Quinn, Brendan Gill, Frank McSweeney. Front: Stuart Cahill, Dermot Clifford, Mick O'Brien, Seamus Clifford, Seamus McCartin, Brian McSweeney, –, –.

1988 Junior Football Division 3 winners (full squad) – Back row (l-r): Patsy Tyrrell, Frank McSweeney, Don Lehane (manager), John Boyce, Ciaran McGovern (partly hidden), Cyril Loughlin, Brian McSweeney, Bert Smith, Tom Maguire, Peter Ryan, Declan Clabby, Gerry Quinn (mentor), Ernest Kenny (mentor). Front: Christy Kilcoyne, Ger Kenny, Brendan Coughlan, Ger McSweeney, Seamus McCartin, Kevin Clabby, Seamus Clifford, Ray O'Connor, Ger McSweeney, Ciaran Cribbs.

1988 Ó Brion Cup winners – Back row (l-r): Donnchadh Lehane (mentor), Tommy Bassett, John McGoldrick, Brian McSweeney, Mark Ingham, John Brown, Brendan Gill, Mick Tobin, Ger Kenny, James Durkan, Leonard Fitzpatrick, John Boyce, Shane McGovern, Ger Keaty, Ernest Kenny (mentor), Gerry Quinn. Front: Cyril Loughlin, Ciaran Nolan, Mick Kavanagh, David Nolan, Mick O'Brien (captain), Denis Evoy, Ray Whelan, Dara Murphy, Patsy Tyrrell.

1993 St Judes Intermediate team promoted to Senior – Back row (l-r): Seamus Durkan (mentor), Luke Mooney (mentor), Mick Tobin, Tony McGinley, Peter Gilsenan, Mick Fallon, Peter Ryan, Dara Murphy, Delcan O'Reilly, Declan O'Boyle, Denis Evoy, Edna Sheehy, John O'Riordan, Tommy Bassett (manager). Front: Kieran Gallagher, Declan Clabby, Ger McSweeney, Jamesy O'Dowd, Kevin Clabby, Brendan Coughlan, Kieran Durkan, Peter Keohane, Ciaran McGovern, Shane Gallen, Dermot McCarthy.

2000 Joy Cup winning team – Back row (l-r): Tommy Bassett (manager), Tony Gilleran (mentor), Gareth Roche, Antoin Doyle, Conor Lehane, Ciaran Cash, Ian Bassett, Andrew Glover, Declan Molloy, Ken Molloy, John Doherty, John O'Riordan, Donnchadh Ó Liathain (mentor). Front: Liam Keogh, Ger McSweeney, David Reynolds, Jeff Kane, Paul Goodall, Eoghan O'Neill, Ger Hartnett, Gerry Quinn, Declan Clabby, David Coates.

1994/95 Junior Division 7 winners – Back row (l-r): G. Russell, G. McSweeney, D. McCarthy, Greg Kane, T. McGinley, Glen Kane, P. McSherry, F. Nolan. Middle: M. O'Brien (mentor), P. Ryan, K. Clabby, F. Garivan, I. Bassett, F. Feore, D. Cambell, S. Fallon, Gary Kane (mentor). Front: E. Kenny (mentor), D. Clabby, S. Willoughby, M. Tobin (captain), D. O'Reilly, J. Kane, K. McSherry.

1995/96 Junior 'A' Division 3 winners – Back row: Christy Kilcoyne (manager), Joe Fallon, Seán Fallon, John McKeown, Michael Mahon, James Durkan, John Brown, Anthony Gilleran, Barry Heraty, Niall Lawlor, Enda Crennan, Barry Lawlor, Donnacha Ó Liathain (manager). Front: Colm Kilcoyne, Jeff Kane, Gavin Russell, Paul Byrne, Gerry Ryan, Daire Keane, Declan McSweeney, Damien Carroll, James Kilcoyne.

2001 Floodlit Cup winning team of Iveagh Grounds.

1998 Intermediate Championship winners – Back row (l-r): Peter Ryan (mentor), Alva Colgan, Deirdre O'Connor, Deirdre Massey, Sarah Massey, Tracy Culhane, Martina McGrath, Ruth Breheny, Caroline Scanlon, Sarah Breheny, Marie O'Brien (mentor), Seamus Massey (mentor). Front: Sarah Hughes, Emma Reynolds, Elaine Sherry, Aoife Kelly, Fiona Guckian (captain), Emma Reynolds, Suzanne Moore, Imelda Molloy, Lisa Rohan.

1998 Junior 'B' Championship winners – Back row (l-r): Marie O'Brien. Lisa Rohan, Sarah Hughes, Mary Howlett, Deirdre Massey, Lisa Kavanagh, Martina McGrath, Jennifer Hartnett, Helena O'Brien, Seamus Massey. Front: Suzanne Waine, Ailish Reid, Fiona O'Frighil, Jade McGurn, Jacinta Bradshaw, Imelda Molloy, Karen Walsh.

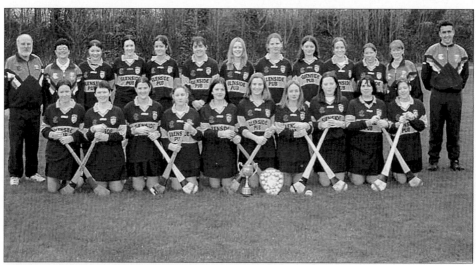

2000 Camogie Senior B Championship winners – Back row (l-r): Seamus Massey, Marie O'Brien, Ailbhe Colgan, Ruth Breheny, Bronagh Maher, Caroline Scanlon, Suzanne Waine, Tracy Culhane, Siobhán Reid, Fiona O'Frighil, Claire Sherry, Geraldine Mangan, Bryan Duggan. Front: Sarah Breheny, Andrea Hartnett, Roisín Fitzpatrick, Emma Reynolds, Sarah Massey, Fiona Guckian, Niamh Skelly, Aoife Kelly, Anne O'Gara, Claire Mangan.

1998 Ladies Football team 1998.

Official opening 1987 – Joe McDonnell, Seán Conway, Monsignor Seamus and Fr. Connolly PP.

St Judes Minor Football team 2003 – Division 1 Cup Winners

Ladies Football 2003.

Youth perspective

Kevin Coghlan

I AM a full member of St Judes GAA club who was born and grew up during the club's twenty-five year lifespan. Being the son of Jim Coghlan, a trustee, the club has always played an important part in my life. As Youth Representative for 2003, I thought I might give my views on the effect the club has had on my life.

I suppose my family background dictated that I would be involved with the club as soon as I was old enough. A grandfather who played for Cork and a father who played for Kerry had some influence of course! I presume it is genetically proven that GAA talent skips a generation...

My father's background was certainly steeped in GAA tradition. His home club, Beaufort GAA Club in Co Kerry, play in Pete Coghlan Park, named after my grandfather, who donated the land for the pitch.

I vaguely remember the building of the initial St Judes clubhouse in 1987. The growth and development of the club has mirrored the development in our whole community. It has been fascinating to see how our club has developed so quickly in such a short space of time.

We are situated in a very competitive catchment area surrounded by other sports clubs, both GAA and otherwise. However, we are consistently fielding more and more teams. I have never gone to a Judes match as a player or supporter when we have failed to field a team.

My playing career has not been as successful or distinguished as many of my contemporaries but it began at the same place as so many others did and continue to do so – on Orwell Green. Countless numbers of children have passed through Joe McDonnell's care and training regime there – some to greatness and others merely to U-10! The whole focus of my weekends was that Saturday morning on the Green. Some of Coghlan Jnr's finest moments on the playing field were seen on said Green when I won All-Ireland after All-Ireland. (I'm allowed to dream!)

The club is a meeting place for young people in our area. It is with great pride that I can say I know somebody on all the adult teams, from the Senior's to the Dream's. It is a place to go and watch one of our teams or to watch something on the big screen in the bar.

The Irish football matches in the World Cup are occasions that stick in my memory - fantastic occasions in the club.

I ran for the position of Public Relations Officer (PRO) at the 2001 Annual General Meeting (AGM). Although I was defeated, it was only by a narrow margin. It just shows that if young people are interested in getting involved in any of the club's committees, there is more than enough opportunity to do so. Perhaps the AGM would gain from a greater attendance from younger members though.

In the past, we have won trophies with adult teams containing players from outside the parish. Nowadays it is particularly satisfying to see homegrown teams winning competitions and developing players from the local area.

The facilities that our club has developed are fantastic. We have a clubhouse that is the envy of any in Dublin. I have been to matches all over the county and it is safe to say that our facilities are up there with the best. The new all-weather pitch is also a wonderful development. It will make the nights of winter training a little easier now that our players will at least be able to work on skills as well as fitness.

I suppose we've all seen the image of D'Unbelievable's crazed manager of the Juvenile Hurling team. My mentors at Juvenile level would not have been quite so blood thirsty, although we were encouraged on more than one occasion to "use the timber" because "they're no relation..." I have also got my fair share of bumps and bruises from the game. Amazing how the magic water always works though!

And of course there was always the struggle of getting to away games. I think the record of juveniles squeezed into a single car must have been at least seven or eight.

One particular memory was coming home from Malahide one Saturday after playing St Sylvester's. We had for some reason travelled through town to get to the match. However, on the way home we took the M50. When we reached the roundabout at the Spawell, our driver – let's call him AN Other (hint: his surname ends like a southern river) – asked us how to get back to the club. In disbelief, we informed him that it was just down the road. Hilarious stuff...

I was lucky enough to be involved in a few trips away with the club as well. Although some of the memories are more than a little hazy, they are experiences I will always cherish.

Now, in semi-retirement at the age of 20, I still enjoy club activities to the full and will continue to do so for many years to come.

Mary, Mary, Philip and The Dreamers

YOU'VE ALL heard about the Dream Team, ours was The Dreamers… well Daydreamers to be exact! We mentored them from Under 11 up to Under 16 and they were the loveliest, liveliest and chattiest bunch of girls in the club.

Talent they had in abundance but somehow they never managed to peak as a team, when it really mattered. However, as this article goes to print, we are still there with a chance of winning the Under 16 Camogie League. And we did get to the semi-final of the Championship, but we won't talk about that.

Of course they broke our hearts – many many times – but we still wouldn't trade those six years we spent with that group of young ladies for anything. Oh and those away matches and them fighting as to who would travel in which car. And the things you would hear on those journeys! Not to mention the singing along to the radio at full volume and the windows down. They loved the traffic jams – waving at this guy or that hunk – and conversing with strangers who would ask "Did yees win?" and the puzzled expression from the stranger if they replied in the negative. Oh they were such a happy bunch.

And the amount of jewellery we would be entrusted to mind before a match, and you could be left with it for the next week because they'd forget to get it back! Not to mention the mobile phones – "Answer it, if it rings, I'm expecting an important call".

Over the years some girls gave up the game. Remember Ciara, Siobhan, Aisling, Susie and Deirdre – maybe they'll take up the game again. Hope so. Then there's Julie and Jean. I think they'll be back. Don't know about the two Gillians or Emer or Amy. As for Helen, Vanessa, Orla, Fiona, the two Aislings, Aislinn, the two Niamhs, the two Aoifes, Sarah, Laura, Shona, Lindsey, Susan and Derval, we hope they will continue to play and enjoy the game.

The dReam Team

I
N EARLY 2002, a group of football enthusiasts met in the bar to discuss the possibility of entering a third Junior Football team, which would give players an opportunity to represent the Club who, for various reasons, had put their football careers on hold.

The "Dream Team" as it is affectionately known, was the brainchild of James Durkan and Anto Gilleran. James and Anto had previously played Junior Football for the Club, but in the intervening years had taken to discussing the game in the bar rather than participating in the playing fields. It was as a result of these late night discussions that they discovered there was a number of like minded individuals who were interested in playing football but didn't want to give the necessary commitment required to play on the existing Junior teams in the Club.

Before approaching the Adult Games Committee, they had to make sure that there were enough players interested to make it worth the Club's while entering the team. So James and Anto canvassed players who had played on the Junior B team under Christy Kilcoyne in the mid 90's but had stopped playing. Players like Paul 'Dougal' Byrne, Barry Lawlor, Mick Tobin, Declan O'Reilly, Eamonn Hartnett and Pat O'Brien had been on those teams and relished the opportunity to make a comeback. A number of hurlers also agreed to get involved, such as Gerry Ryan, Seán Fallon, Barry Heraty, Colm Ryan and Alan Kennedy. Brian Woods, who was active in the juvenile section of the Club, was also persuaded to come out of retirement. The rest of the panel was made up of younger players in the Club who were interested in the Dream Team's vision that football is to be enjoyed. Players like Dave Carroll, Ronnie O'Brien, Gareth Evans, Clint Storey, Neville, Mervyn and Carl O'Boyle and Paddy Evoy.

The 2002 season was not a particularly memorable one for the Dream Team as they struggled to find their feet in the early stages of the league. The few years away from playing football was obvious at the beginning of the season but as the year progressed, there was a gradual improvement.

Although the league was not going to be won in the first season, a respectable finish was achieved before concentrating on the Junior D Championship. Despite training very hard for the first round, they were defeated by Oliver Plunketts/Eoghan Ruadh and the panel then had the winter months to reflect on what might have been.

As the panel returned to training in early 2003, it was obvious that things were going to be different. The panel had grown considerably in size. Newcomers to the Dreams were John Walsh, Derek McGrath, Keith McDonald, Jimmy Harlow, Conor O'Riordan, Alan Linnane, Kevin Hayes and Tomas and Eoin Mangan, who had recently returned from Australia. The Dream Team now had an international dimension with the addition of Matt Brennan, Craig Higgins, Kevin and Bruce while the management team has been joined by Mervyn O'Boyle.

Training was stepped up from the previous year and performances have improved drastically as a result. At the time of writing, the Dream Team are riding high in the league and have genuine ambitions of an extended championship run.

Dream Team 2003
Back row: Karl Friel, Anto Gilleran, Seán Fallon, Keith McDonald, Kevin Webb (England), Gerry Ryan, Neville O'Boyle, Craig Higgins (Australia), Gareth Evans, Barry Lawlor, Paddy Evoy, David Carroll, Jimmy Harlow, David Kane, Derek McGrath, Pat O'Brien. Front: Mervyn O'Boyle, Matt Brennan (New Zealand), Paul Byrne (Pakistan), Tomás Mangan, Brian Woods, John Walsh, Eamon Hartnett, Eoghan Mangan, Declan O'Reilly, Ronnie O'Brien, James Durkan (manager).

HuRLiNG… The GReaTesT GaMe

Finbarr Casey

URLING is the greatest game in the world. My love of hurling traces back to my grandfather, Jack Casey from Ballyhea in north Cork. I'm sure you have all heard of Ballyhea by now. If not, you are one of the few club members who has yet to meet Declan Feore. Anytime I visited my relations in Ballyhea I was told many stories of my grandfather's legendary exploits on the hurling field. He also played hurling with Nemo Rangers in Cork city. How this came about was he was moved into Cork city with his job on the railway in 1927. His feet had only touched the station platform in Cork when he was asked to play for Nemo, his reputation had preceded him. He played junior hurling with Nemo in 1927 and duly won the championship. In 1928 he won the intermediate championship. In 1929 he played senior. He was transferred back in 1930 and played junior with Ballyhea and again won the championship. He played intermediate in 1931 and won the championship and was back playing senior in 1932. My father also played with Ballyhea before he moved to Dublin where he played with Young Irelands and won a Dublin junior championship. I played with An Caislean where my claim to fame was winning a minor hurling league medal. I also won a Dublin colleges hurling medal.

I joined St Judes club a few years ago so that my daughter Sinéad and son Niall could play our national games and carry on the family tradition. I would support their respective team as often as possible and I would say that I only missed a handful of their matches. Early on this year I was asked by Peter Lucey and Seán Breheny to take over the management of the Junior A camogie team with Ann Ryan, as this would leave them free to concentrate on the senior team. As Sinéad played with this team plus the fact that they are a lovely group of girls and a credit to the club, I had no hesitation in taking up this task.

We had a mixed year but we started well with a couple of wins in the Cup competition. Then as the year went into the summer we found it harder to field a team as players went on holidays and some went to work abroad. We had to supplement the team with players from the Under 16s, most notable of these being Vanessa Whelan, Niamh O'Sullivan, Fiona Monaghan, Aisling Lehane and Aisling Maher. Myself and Ann are most grateful to these girls for turning out to play with us when called upon. We won our first championship match after a replay against Thomas Davis.

We were beaten in the next round by the eventual winners of the competition Ballinteer St Johns. We gave a good account of ourselves but we didn't take some of our chances and Ballinteer did. This was the difference between the two teams. We managed a few wins in the league and that kept us away from the relegation zone. Our best results were in the cup competition. We beat Ballinteer and went on to meet and beat St Vincents in the semi final with a magnificent performance. We met Vincents in their own ground and as they had already beaten us in this competition they thought that they were going to do the same again. But St Judes were having none of it and with a tremendous hard working display they left "Vinny's" shell shocked. We now face Ballinteer in the final and I have no doubt that the St Judes girls will rise to the challenge.

St McDaras Hurling Champions 1986/87 – Back row (l-r): Brendan Byrne, Peter Keogh, –, David Duggan, Robert Goodwin, Dara Murphy, Ken Halpin, Ciarán Fitzpatrick, Raymond Moore, Bernard Daly, Gerard Garry, Eoghan Ryan, Aonghas Banks. Front: Fergal McCarthy, Michael Byrne, Ted Russell, Eamonn Walsh, Aidan Quigley, Barry Jeffries, Fiachra Feore, Andrew Corr.

Camogie

Marie O'Brien

WHEN THE girls of St Judes come together to play camogie, they may not realise that they are continuing a tradition that was started in 1903 by the girls of Keatings Branch of Conradh na Gaeilge. The first official camogie game took place in Pairc Tailteann, Navan in 1904. As Cumann Camogaiochta na nGael is about to celebrate its centenary – St Judes is celebrating its first twenty-five years. Cumann Camogaiochta na nGael was founded in 1904. The game was played with twelve-a-side teams, three substitutes allowed and twenty-five minutes each half. The pitch was much smaller then with smaller goalposts. The long hobble skirt was the uniform in the early days. Players ran with great difficulty and stopping the ball with the skirt was deemed a foul.

Our "chicks with sticks" today wear a different outfit. Skorts are now the latest fashion. Modern gear has helped to make the game faster and more enjoyable. Nowadays our "chicks" need to be as fit and skilful as their male counterparts.

Camogie changed radically in 2000 to fifteen-a-side teams with five substitutes allowed and thirty minutes per half. This enabled camogie to be played on standard sized GAA pitches with standard GAA goalposts. Cumann Camogíochta na nGael is a totally independent organisation. It is not affiliated to or part of the GAA. It has its own constitution and Uachtarán. Work is progressing on a Pilot Integration Project with the GAA. Two counties from each province are at present involved in the Pilot Project – Wexford, Laois, Roscommon, Galway, Limerick, Tipperary, Tyrone and Down. Committees are in place and work on strategies for integration is ongoing. It is hoped to have recommendations in place for Congress 2004. It is a tribute to St Judes GAA club that the camogie section is fully integrated and an integral part of the club. Whether it be the provision of pitches or the building of ladies dressing rooms, the club always supports camogie to the "hilt" (maybe that should be kilt).

In 1982 a camogie section was established in St Judes. Coaching sessions began on Thursday nights in Tymon Park. An Under 12 camogie league was set up. The purchasing of hurleys and helmets was made available through Bishop Galvin NS. By 1983 up to thirty girls were training for camogie under the watchful eye of Kay Hughes. Camogie novices were being coached by Carmel Reen and Nora Farrell.

In 1984 the first St Judes camogie team took part in the Community Games. Training continued on Thursday nights until the clock changed and then on Sunday mornings.

Catherine Kelleher registered eighteen Under 14 camogie players with Cumann Camógaíochta na Gael, Coiste Atha Cliath. They would need proper playing outfits and a regulation sized pitch before being sanctioned to play in leagues. These "chicks with sticks" were Lisa Morgan, Deirdre Feore (wonder whose daughter she is?) Ethna Murphy, Carol-Lynn Sweetman, Orla Williams, Amanda Murphy, Paula McDermott, Vivienne Cribbs, Martina Keaty, Lorraine Moore, Aileen Donoghue, Cathy Reen, Roisin O' Loughlin, Brenda Creaney and Áine Cahill. Where are you now girls?? You will always be welcome in St Judes!

By the end of 1985 camogie teams at Under 11 and 13 were well established. Several beginners were also being coached and a Junior team was formed for adults. Catherine Moore and Mary Devins joined the club this year and gave great help. A team took part in the Féile competition and also in the Community Games.

In 1986 Ann Dennehy, Mary Farrell, Rita Moran, Bob Carty and Ruth Carty joined the camogie section as mentors/trainers. Some of our camogie mentors attended a Camogie Coaching course in Ballyboden.

The provision of a camogie pitch in Tymon Park was warmly welcomed, but there was some concern at the siting of the posts so near the ditches. The Camogie Board did not pass the pitch, as it did not comply with the required dimensions. After some healthy discussion and movement of goal posts the matter was resolved. Nowadays this problem does not arise as camogie is played on standard size pitches.

The Junior B team won their first game in May 1986. In September of that year five camogie teams were registered with the County Camogie Board, four Juveniles and one adult.

By 1990 camogie was flourishing in St Judes. Our Under 11 team managed by Ruth and Frank Carty won the league and championship. A fantastic achievement for all concerned. The girls on this team were Lorraine Carty, Barbara O'Connor, Ellen Bone, Rosin Fitzpatrick, Sheila Loughman, Eimear Ryan, Joanne Hartnett, Gillian Barry, Niamh Farrell, Helen McGrath, Ciara Skelly, Isobel Russell, Denise McGeough, Andrea Hartnett, Fiona Guckian & Claire Walsh. Things augured well for camogie in St Judes. New and experienced mentors were helping out in the camogie section. Joan Molamphy, Tadhg Dennehy, Seamus Massey, Marie O'Brien, Seán Breheny, Billy O'Frighil and Philip Clarke were now giving assistance to the "chicks with sticks".

In 1991 our Under 11 team managed by Ann Dennehy and Seamus Massey won both league and championship.

The team of players were Joanne Reynolds, Ruth Breheny, Sarah Massey, Isobel Russell, Ciara Skelly, Aoife Kelly, Ellen Bone, Claire Walsh, Caroline Scanlon, Susan Quigley, Ruth Gordon, Cathy Dickens, Aisling Rafferty & Deirdre O'Connor.

In 1992 our Under 11 team managed by Seamus Massey and Marie O'Brien won the championship. The players were Lorna Cowzer, Sarah Hughes, Lisa Sheehan, Jacinta Bradshaw, Aoife Farrell, AnneMarie O'Brien, Deirdre Ryan, Ruth Maguire, Elaine Sherry, Niamh Cunningham, Caroline Scanlon, Michelle Carey, Elaine Clarke, Imelda Molloy, Sarah Massey, Aoife Kelly, Ailish Reid and Fiona O'Frighil. This team went on to win the League at Under 12 the following year and to reach the championship final again in 1994. They won the league in 1995 and were unlucky to be defeated by Naomh Mearnog in the championship final. One of our young players Marie Durkan died in 1993. Ar dheis Dé go raibh a h-anam. Her family presented a cup to the club and asked that a tournament be played in her honour. It was decided to hold the Marie Durkan Cup tournament annually. The first year of this tournament was 1994. In a closely contested final St Marks narrowly defeated St Judes.

In 1994 our Under 11 team managed by Ann Dennehy, Betty Collard and Ann Kelly won the Championship. The panel of players was Sheena McDonnell, Helena O'Brien, Roisin Eighan, Blaithin Keane, Jennifer Hartnett, Maeve Ward, Sinead O'Frighil, Siobhan Reid, Toni Cowzer, Niamh McGann, Karen Byrne, Claire Dennehy, Claire Mangan, Brona Maher, Suzanne Waine and Niamh Skelly.

Our Under 12 and Under 13 teams reached championship finals.

Our Under 14 team won the Dublin Féile and had the honour of representing Dublin in the National Féile in Limerick. The players were Elaine Sherry, Ailbhe Colgan, Caroline Scanlon, Sarah Massey, Deirdre O'Connor, Aisling Rafferty, Joanne Reynolds, Jennifer O'Reilly, Deirdre Joyce, Ruth Breheny, Fiona Egan, Cathy Dickens, Claire Walsh & Alice Ryan. Joan Molamphy, Rita Gallagher and Seamus Massey managed this team. Fiona Guckian was selected for the Dublin Under 16 panel. Olwynn Butler, Ellen Bone, Kathy Dickens and Sarah Massey were selected for the Dublin Under 14 panel.

In 1995 our Under 12 team were championship winners.The team was managed by Geraldine Mangan and Rita Gallagher. The players were Roisin Nolan, Claire Dennehy, Maeve Ward, Niamh McGann, Karen Byrne, Aoife Rafferty, Blaithin Keane, Sheena McDonnell, Helena O'Brien, Jennifer Hartnett, Brona Maher, Claire Mangan, Suzanne Waine, Niamh Skelly, Siobhan Reid and Sinead O'Frighil.

1997 saw our Junior A team promoted to Intermediate status. This team also won the Marie Durkan Cup. Sarah Massey, Aoife Kelly and Deirdre O'Connor played on the Dublin Minor team who were Leinster champions this year. The team was managed by Seamus Massey and Marie O'Brien.

Claire Mangan, Claire Dennehy, Suzanne Waine and Brona Maher were selected for the Dublin Under 14 team. Sarah Breheny and Fiona Guckian were selected for the Dublin Junior team.

1998 was a tremendous year for camogie in St Judes. We had teams playing at Under11, Under 12, Under 13, Under 15, Junior B and Intermediate levels. October was a month to remember. First there was that great day in O'Toole Park when the Junior B team beat Good Counsel in the championship final. This was the first adult camogie championship for the club. Just twenty-four hours earlier the Intermediate girls had drawn their championship decider with Portobello in Russell Park in an absolutely classic encounter. The replay a week later in O'Toole Park saw the St Judes girls hammer out a two point victory. A very proud moment indeed for the entire panel of players and mentors, under the guidance of Seamus Massey, Marie O'Brien, Bryan Duggan and Peter Ryan.The celebrations in the club went on for two weeks.

The Junior team players were, Ailish Reid, Suzanne Waine, Imelda Molloy, Deirdre Massey, Elaine Clarke, Andrea Hartnett, Sarah Hughes, Martina McGrath, Lisa Rohan, Brona Maher, Claire Mangan, Mary Howlett, Helena O'Brien, Jade McGurn, Lisa Kavanagh, Jacinta Bradshaw, Karen Walsh, Fiona O'Frighil and Lorraine Keane.

The Intermediate team players were, Elaine Sherry, Marina Reynolds, Sarah Breheny, Sarah Massey, Ailbhe Colgan, Fiona Guckian, Ruth Breheny, Tracey Culhane, Aoife Kelly, Deirdre O'Connor, Caroline Scanlon, Lisa Rohan, Suzanne Moore, Rachel Byrne, Emma Reynolds, Martina McGrath, Brona Maher, Sarah Hughes, Imelda Molloy and Claire Mangan. This win ensured St Judes had a Senior camogie team for the first time in 1999.

In 2000 the Senior B team won the Dublin championship, by defeating St Vincents in O'Toole Park in a close encounter. This win brought the first Senior championship title in any code to the club. Back to St Judes to celebrate this momentous occasion went mentors, Marie O'Brien, Geraldine Mangan, Bryan Duggan, Seamus Massey and the all important team of "chicks". They were Ailbhe Colgan, Ruth Breheny, Brona Maher, Caroline Scanlon, Suzanne Waine, Tracey Culhane, Siobhan Reid, Sinead O'Frighil, Elaine Sherry, Sarah Breheny, Jennifer Hartnett, Roisin Fitzpatrick, Emma Reynolds, Sarah Massey, Fiona Guckian, Niamh Skelly, Aoife Kelly, Ann O'Gara and Claire Mangan. The Marie Durkan Cup tournament was also won this year by St Judes. This was the last year that the Marie Durkan Cup tournament was held. The Cup was presented to the Dublin Camogie County Board as the Senior B Championship Trophy.

2001 saw the St Judes "chicks with sticks" win the Senior B championship again. This was a memorable evening in O'Toole Park. The girls played with great heart. Their skill and fitness out-classed a very good and competitive O'Tooles team. This win for St Judes meant Senior A status. It was appropriate that the St Judes team was presented with the Marie Durkan Cup as their winning trophy by Seamus Massey, Chairman of the County Board, who was also a mentor of the St Judes team.

In 2002 the Senior A team retained its status under the managerial eye of Peter Lucey, with Seán Breheny and Geraldine Mangan, by finishing mid table in the league and reaching quarter-final in the championship. The Junior B side won their league and were runners-up in the Cup. As a result they gained promotion to Junior A and are currently managed by Finbarr Casey and Ann Ryan. At Juvenile level – we have Under 11s managed by Irene Dunne, Under 12s managed by Mary McDonagh, Under 13s managed by Patricia Cahill, Under 14s managed by Concepta Ryan, Under 16s managed by Mary Monaghan, Mary Joyce and Philip Clarke.

St Judes had two players on the Dublin Under 14 team, which reached the Leinster final this year. They were Róisín Murray and Helena Ryan.

The camogie tradition continues.
Long live the St Judes "Chicks with Sticks".

Under 13 Camogie team, 1987 – Back row: Sinéad Hughes, Niamh Delaney, Emer Fitzpatrick, Louise McKeon, Deirdre Carty, Catherine Keeley, Felicity Lindopp, Caroline Doran. Front: Vivienne Lough, Fionnuala Crennan, Suzanne Moore, Marina Reynolds, Elaine Mackey, Aoife Hurley.

A memorable shinty weekend

Declan Feore

U NFORTUNATELY, in 1999, Ballyboden St Endas Clubhouse was destroyed accidentally by fire. In common with other clubhouses in the area we offered them the use of our facilities for meetings or functions. As they put in temporary portacabins in their grounds they did not need to avail of our offer. However, in the spring of 2000 they approached us for help. For many years Ballyboden St Endas had hosted shinty teams from Scotland. This year two development squads were due. We agreed to co-host the visitors, arranging accommodation for the weekend and providing them with sandwiches and light refreshments on their arrival on Thursday evening, before assigning them to their host families. A competitive match was organised for the following evening in Tymon Park. (The homeside was made up of Judes and Ballyboden players.)

The shinty squads (all under 18) had come from a week long training camp in Scotland. Two of them were the brothers Somhairle and Aonghas(Nui) MacDonald grandsons of the Scots Gaelic poet, Somhairle MacLean. They were accompanied by Garry Reid, National Development Officer, and Ronald Ross, regarded as the best shinty player ever. He was a member of the famous Kingussi Club and had the record for being the highest scorer in any season. He was to shinty what Christy Ring and DJ Carey were to hurling. His status as a shinty player was affirmed to me by Donnie Grant, President of the Camanachd Association, whom I met when we were invited to represent Ireland with Ballyboden St Endas and Ballycastle of Down, at the Linn-Gu-Linn (Century to Century) Festival in Dunoon later in the year.

In 1990, Ronald Ross scored three goals, when he made his International debut in Inverness. The following year, I had the privilege with my son Fiachra of seeing Ross, when he was 17 years of age, play his first game for Scotland in Ireland. They played an Under 21 inter-county selection at the Gaelic Grounds in Limerick. It was the curtain raiser to the 1991 All-Ireland Junior Championship Final between Tipperary and Kilkenny. I met Martin Molamphy, from Portroe, at these games. His nephew, Gerry O'Brien, was captain of the victorious Tipperary team that day.

Various members of St Judes and Ballyboden St Endas agreed to provide accommodation for the shinty visitors.

Stewart MacKenzie, a reporter with the Oban Times was assigned to our house. He brought with him a friendship Quaich. Ronald Ross was assigned to the family of Conal Keaney, who was being mentioned in despatches as having a great future as a Dublin hurler. Ross was looking forward to meeting him. Unfortunately, someone forgot to tell the Keaneys about the arrangement. So on the Friday night he, also, was accommodated in the Feore household.

Ronald Ross was also an International tennis player as was his girlfriend who was away on a Tournament that weekend. We, in Ireland, had not been introduced as yet to mobile text messaging. Ronald spent a great deal of time between drinking pints of Guinness, texting his girlfriend. We thought when we saw him playing with his phone and laughing uproariously, being unaware of text messaging, that the Guinness was getting to him.

A trip to Kilkenny was organised for Saturday. The players would be driven there by coach. It was agreed that they would all meet at Ballyboden. It was a beautiful morning and as we arrived at Ballyboden the sun could be seen glistening from the portacabins. Everybody was in bouyant mood. The sense of occasion was palpable. The Oban Times reporter commented out loudly on the great rapport that seemed to exist between ourselves and Ballyboden St Endas. Local clubman, Conor Sheehan, of good West Limerick stock, replied, "Don't be fooled by this apparant camaraderie – as soon as this weekend is over we will be back to our old rivalry again". "Och, I don't know", said MacKenzie, "the boys in Judes have great admiration for you people. They say you have the finest caravans in South Dublin".

On the Sunday afternoon a team made up mostly of Judes and Ballyboden Minors together with a few of us token players took on the shinty team led by Ronald Ross and Garry Reid. Naturally the result was a draw. The referee was Aodhán MacSuibhne, later to use his experience in many an inter-county battle.

St Judes hosted a party for all in the back lounge that night. Ciaran O'Brien, the very talented Minor hurler, and a gifted traditional musician, together with his musician friends provided the entertainment. It was regarded as one of the best performances of traditional music in the clubhouse. The shinty players also performed that night, ending their party piece with a "group mooner" much to the annoyance of their mentors, but to the great delight of our beautiful camogie players.

Gifts were exchanged between opposing organisers. For my part, I was fortunate enough to be the recipient of a fine bottle of Speyside single malt. I would now have a quality drink for my Quaich.

It was a memorable and thoroughly enjoyable weekend. We were eagerly looking forward to our trip to Dunoon.

A bRief hisTORy of ShinTy

Jimmy O'Dwyer

THE GAME of shinty goes back to the roots of Gaelic Scotland and the even earlier heritage of the Celtic race. Its demands of skill, speed, stamina and courage make camanachd, the sport of the curved stick, the perfect exercise of a warrior people. The qualities of body and mind it developed clearly contributed to the just fame of the Highlander in battle, not only those long ago but up until the last two World Wars. During the period of these two universal conflicts, organized shinty was discontinued and many of the playing generations then were lost to campaigns far distant from the pitches where they had followed this deeply-loved recreation of their ancestors.

Within the rivalries of the game, clan against clan, parish against parish and brae against strath, there developed a social comradeship in the world of camanachd and this continues to the present day.

In common with other sports, shinty moved out of a long previous history of unwritten rules and widely differing local variations in the last quarter of the nineteenth century.

In 1879 the Glasgow Celtic Society instituted a cup competition and established rules of play. About the same time the celebrated Captain Chisholm of Glassburn drew up "The Constitution, Rules and Regulations of the Strathglass Shinty Club" which were published in 1880.

On 13th February 1887, a famous game was played at Inverness between Strathglass and Glenurquhart when the field measured over 300 yards long by 200 yards wide, with twenty two players a side. Even with two adjoining glens, in this case, the variations in their codes of play needed discussion to get common rules agreed. By 1888, when the return match took place, revised Strathglass rules were produced and these came to be the accepted ones among clubs in the north while those in the south playing area of Scotland followed the Celtic Society rules.

In April 1893, another memorable game was played at the Dell in Kingussie between the home club and Glasgow Cowal, the latter winning by one hail to nil. The teams were fourteen a side and the occasion clearly showed the need for one authority to control the playing of shinty.

On 10th October of the same year, there was a great meeting of enthusiasts in Kingussie and the Camanachd Association was formed with the then Lord

Lovat as President and, for a long period, he remained a very influential leader in the game. The Camanachd Cup Trophy competition was instituted in 1895 and the first final was contested at Inverness on 5 April 1896 when Kingussie beat Glasgow Cowal by two hails to nil.

Over the long intervening years this has remained the overall championship competition for all Scotland and the Camanachd Cup Final, at a cycle of venues, is the outstanding occasion in the annual shinty calendar.

In 1922 the Sir William Sutherland Cup competition was instituted as the Scottish Junior Championship. The Glasgow Celtic Society has continued to operate the oldest competition of all in the South Clubs with the MacTavish Cup, established in 1898, as the equivalent for North clubs. The MacAulay Association, since 1947, has organised an open senior competition centred on Oban. From 1985 the Balliemore Cup has been competed for as the Scottish Intermediate Championship. At lesser grades, other trophy competitions have been developed including those run by the Schools Camanachd Association. There has been league competitions, initially administered by separate North and South Associations. After major reorganisation in 1981 all individual bodies agreed to work under the central administration. The league system remained in the North and South areas with a National League Final between respective Division 1 Champions. In the 1995/96 Season a new overall eight team Premier League was introduced. Also introduced was a representative district team competition integrated with Under-21 and Senior selection for the Shinty Hurling Internationals against Ireland.

The initial object of the Association was "to foster and develop the national game of shinty and it works to carry on a game which has been handed down to us by our forebears and of which, in turn, hand on, a game which knows no social distinctions, with, on the field of play, all men equal and the greatest of all, the most expert and finest wielder of the caman".

The Camanachd Association and the Gaelic Athletic Association of Ireland meet each year in International competition between the hurlers of Ireland and the shinty players of Scotland under a set of composite rules.

The earliest games in the series were played only at Under 21 level and saw Ireland winning regularly, but more recently the Scots have begun to record victories at this level. At senior level the Scots were undefeated until October last year. The International at Croke Park, Dublin on 15th October 2000 was won by Ireland, 57 points to 32. The game was played before a very large crowd and preceded the Ireland v Australia Gaelic/Aussie rules football match. A rule change which introduced 1 point for a 'wide' helped the Irish big hitters to secure the victory this time in a game which spectators found to be a thrilling spectacle.

The composite rules lead to a highly entertaining blend of both codes, which produces a fast and exciting game contrasting the ground skills of the shinty player with the aerial prowess of the hurler. In essence, the secret of victory for the Scots is to keep the ball on the ground, whilst for the Irish, the aim is to keep it airborne, where their broad-bladed sticks have a considerable advantage. The net effect is an end-to-end game which is absorbing to watch.

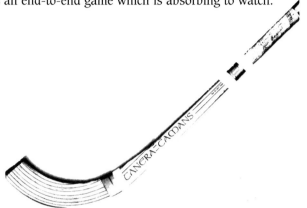

Shinty hurling exchange ... pictured in Croke Park exchanging gifts on the occasion of the visit of the children of Alba Comanachd to Dublin were (l-r): Lee Charnley, Donella Crawford (President, Alba Camanachd), Jimmy O'Dwyer, Sandra Skinner and John McFarlane.

I ꝼell aт Dunoon

Garrett Edge

ANY FANS of the Beautiful Game may be at least vaguely familiar with a sister game played by our Celtic cousins across from our northern shores. Indeed, recent years have provided followers of our games opportunities to attend hurling-shinty exhibitions in neighbouring Ballyboden St Endas. The involvement of a St Judes hurling team in Scotland's Linn Gu Linn festival in October 2000 was something of a landmark occasion for Albanaigh and Gaeil alike. Described by the Oban Times as the "largest festival of Celtic Sports ever organised", this feast of sporting and cultural events was held in misty Dunoon.

The St Judes contingent consisted mostly of recently successful Minors, with a stiffening of experienced players in the form of Barry McGann and Ronan Colgan. A number of pre-tournament sessions were organised by tour managers Declan Feore and Donie Cummins, while Garrett Edge was drafted in to act as official interpreter for these eminent sons of Cork.

TAXI – PLANE – COACH - FERRY

At lunchtime on Friday 6th October 2000, we left in a fleet of taxis for Dublin Airport bound for Scotland. When we landed in Prestwick, we were met by a luxury coach, which was assigned exclusively to us for the weekend, courtesy of The Mod Festival Company. We were driven on the two hour journey up to Gourock.

On the way we passed Largs, home of the famous "Hastie's Store", which has a reputation as the west of Scotland's premier malt whisky retailer. It boasts over 350 malt whiskies in store at any one time. We stopped off here on the way back for a couple of bottles of Macallan., while the lads were having a good feed of "fish 'n' chips".

We crossed from Gourock by Ferry to Dunoon, where we got a Civic Reception, hosted by the Argyll and Bute Council. We were formally welcomed by Hamish Campbell, Convenor of the Linn Gu Linn Festival and by Robin Banks, Chairman of The Mod Company. Dick Walsh, a Dublinman, was the Festival Administrator.

Following a few "wee drams" we were driven up to our weekend picturesque home in the mountains (about an hours drive).

On Saturday morning all participating teams marched from the town centre to the Stadium, where the Linn Gu Linn Festival was officially opened by Waterfordman Daniel Mulhearn, the Irish Consul General.

In addition to hurling and shinty, the festival boasted cultural, musical and dramatic activities. The coterie of Irish camogie and hurling teams was supplemented by two camogie teams from Glasgow and it was a matter of no small pride to our mentors to witness the single-minded determination with which the pride of St Judes embraced the native populace, making extraordinary efforts to integrate with the maidens of the locality. This selflessness transferred to the fields of play. In what was arguably the wettest weekend in Scottish history, our hurlers competed in mud and rain, the likes of which had not been encountered since the Somme. That casualties were light and all ranks were present for the grand finale, the Gala dinner which was downright miraculous. Disembarking Monday night 9th October , from the coach in the safety of the car-park in St Judes, the entire party seemed to share some invisible bond, forged in the face of mighty challenges on fields of play, sporting and otherwise. Brave Scots once proclaimed with pride, "I stood at Bannockburn". But few can say, "I fell at Dunoon!"

Shinty Minor team, 2000 shinty trip to Dunoon – Back Row (l-r): John Conlon, Donnacha Ryan, Neil Roche, Paul Molamphy, Mark Molloy, John Waldron, Michael Lyons, Shane Guckian, Fergal Grimes, Barry McGann. Front: Kevin Edge, Seán Breheny, Seamus Ryan, Tomas Mangan, Vincent Kelly, Dave O'Hara. In addition to these Ronan Colgan, Donagh O'Dwyer, Kevin Coghlan, Fintan O'Brien, Barry Lyons and Trevor Dickns also travelled.

Coaching

Niamh Leahy, Director of Coaching

THE IDEA of coaching is nothing new as it has been around for decades, but in recent years it has taken on a new lease of life. In the early nineties the Coaching and Games Development Department in Croke Park organised a year long full time coaching course. The participants on this course went on to work with various county boards around the country, four working with Dublin County Board.

The main emphasis in the beginning was coaching Gaelic Games in primary schools, but it was soon obvious that there was a great need to develop a strong link between GAA Clubs and their local schools. It was with this in mind that a number of the larger Dublin clubs, St Judes included, undertook to employ full-time coaches. The Coaching and Games Development side of GAA Clubs has become a vital area as there are so many different attractions vying for people's time nowadays.

With St Judes now fielding over fifty teams from juvenile to adult level, the role of the full-time coach covers a wide variety of areas including; coaching juvenile and adult teams, coach education, coaching in local primary and secondary schools, organising Summer camps and recruiting players.

As we are now fielding two teams at each age group right through the juvenile ranks, the next step is to improve the standard of the teams through mentor training. The majority of mentors now have Foundation Level Coaching Certificates and a number have Level One but in order to help teams progress it is vital that mentors keep up to date with new training methods and ideas. The best way to do this is to attend coaching courses and work your way up the coaching ladder.

There are six main feeder primary schools and one secondary school in the St Judes area. The club is extremely lucky to have teachers in Bishop Galvin and Bishop Shanahan who are also very involved in the club. They put a tremendous amount of work into promoting Gaelic Football, Hurling and Camogie (or "Hurmogie" as it's called in Mr. B's class!!) in school and always encourage the children to join St Judes. There is such a strong link between the club and these schools that it can't but be beneficial to St Judes in the future. The other primary schools, which are receiving regular coaching, are Scoil Mologa, Scoil Bhride, St Peter's and St Kilian's.

The teachers are extremely appreciative of the help provided to them by St Judes and the growing number of children joining the club from these schools proves how worthwhile it is to have regular contact.

The majority of players on St Mac Dara's teams are St Judes players. This is very positive as during the school playing season players get to practice their skills on a daily basis which benefits both club and school. It is also now plain to see the link from Bishop Shanahan to Bishop Galvin to St Mac Dara's to St Judes. It is the same children that are playing their way along this trail, ending up playing for our club.

Summer Camps have become a regular fixture on the club calendar. They began in the early nineties when Leinster Council organised and ran them and an average of fifty children participated in each camp. In 2001, we began running our own camps which gave us the opportunity to stamp our own identity on them by providing children with St Judes crested t-shirts, sliotars, bags and gloves rather than Leinster Council items. This has helped to improve the profile of the club in the community. There are now between 160 and 190 children attending each camp and is an excellent recruiting ground for new players. This summer we extended our camps to include secondary school students, for whom very little is provided during the summer months. These Advanced Coaching Camps included coaching sessions from county footballers and hurlers. We hope that this will help to keep players playing Gaelic Games at this vital age and will also improve the standards of the club teams at Under 13, 14 and 15 levels.

Clearly there are many aspects to the area of Coaching and Games Development and thanks to the foresight, hard work and positive attitude of many people, St Judes has come along way in its first twenty-five years of existence. We have some of the best facilities in the country and these along with the strong juvenile section of the club will continue to grow well into the next twenty-five years.

"Juvenalia"

I N 1991 Seán Breheny took over the Under 11 team, which had been coached at Under 10 by Bobby Carty. This team won the Corrigan Cup in football, beating St Killian's. The following year, they were beaten finalists in the Hanrahan Cup. When this team played Under 12, they held their own in the top half of the football league. At the same time, they were also successful in the Lucan Bank of Ireland Under 12 football tournament comprising 10 invited teams, beating Lucan Sarsfields in a very hard fought final. Full back Seán Breheny was voted Player of the Tournament. Success at Under 13 kept St Judes near the top of the table. Four of this team, Micheál Lyons, Brendan McManamon, Barry Faulkner and Seán Breheny represented Dublin South in the Garda sponsored Tournament in Westmanstown at Under 14, helping Dublin South to come out eventual winners. Between 1996 and 1997, the Under 14 footballers maintained their status near the top of the league table and they also won the McCarthy Cup, beating holders Corofin. This game was most notable, however, for being the first match in which John Waldron played for St Judes. The following season at Under 15 saw the team maintaining a respectable position in the top half of the table. They fell early on in the Juvenile Championship. They did not fare any better in hurling. They continued to show great promise up to Minor, when Bartle Faulkner took over as Minor Football Manager and Declan Feore as hurling manager.

FROM TEN TO NINE
Paul McGann

The year 1996 was the first in which the Juvenile section of the club decided to enter a team at Under 9 for competitive league football. Until then, our youngest players had started out on their football careers at Under 10. Because of the great increase in numbers in that year, thanks to the close cooperation of the local schools Bishop Shanahan and Bishop Galvin, it was clear that we had more than enough players to compete at the youngest possible age. As well as recruiting most of the players, Bobby Carty and Joe Mc Donnell had also earmarked and browbeat an unsuspecting parent, Paul Mc Gann to manage the team. The recruitment that year was so successful that the number of players totalled 45. This panel was later to form the basis of two Under 9 teams, and an

Under 10 team the following season. The list of players available for selection contained many names who would go on to have a significant impact on the success of their teams over the coming years. These included Martin Hartnett, Chris Guckian, Neal Mangan, David Browne, Shane Gallagher, Conor Finnerty, Ciaran Conroy, Colm Kilcoyne, Aengus O'Rourke, Gerard Fehily, Brian Malee, Gearoid Gilmore, Stephen and Peter Larkin - to name a few. Many of these excellent players were to go on at Under 14 and have double Féile success under the management of John Browne, Seamus Conroy and Tommy Hartnett.

The first day of the season saw a nervous team and mentor flag and net the camogie pitch to take on Ballinteer St Johns, on the 21st of September 1996. However with so many stars of the future on show it soon became obvious that St Judes were far too strong for the opposition. The score line of 6-12 to 0-1 confirmed that the team had great potential and the top scorer on the day, who continues to excel, was the captain, Shane Gallagher with 2-9. The team continued to perform well and lost just once to St Brigids of Blessington, to whom they finished league runners-up.

Because there were so many players it wasn't unusual to have almost a completely different team take the field in the second half of many games throughout the season and numbers continued to rise.

At the beginning of the following season the list of players had grown to 75 names. As many of the players continued to qualify to play Under 9, two teams were formed, with Pat Cosgrove taking responsibility for the Under 9 Bs. This was the first time for several years that we fielded two teams at the same age level. Little did we realise at the time that this was the start of a positive trend, which continues to this day.

The start of the 1997/98 season saw a rivalry commence between St Judes Under 9 and our near neighbours, Templeogue. An early season game, although only a challenge, was contested like a championship decider with many of the players knowing each other. The fact that Shane Gallagher, our leading marksman, attended St Josephs in Terenure added spice to an already interesting contest. The match was a typical 'end to end' encounter and no quarter was asked nor given. Scenes of great celebration by the St Judes team greeted the final whistle as they ran out 8-7 to 5-4 winners. Shane again delivered with a personal tally of 6-5. The season proved successful for the team, winning Division 2, with wins against St James Gaels, St Annes, Kilmacud Crokes (B), Cuala, Good Counsel, St Kevin's, Thomas Davis and Round Towers. On their way to the Shield final a couple of new players were beginning to make an impact including one who would be a corner stone of the team well into the future, Pronsias Mac Fhlannchadha.

He fought his way on to a very competitive team and made the centre back berth his own with defensive displays, which were inspirational. Having only beaten Good Counsel by 5-10 to 5-5 the team considered their chances in the final to be no better than 50/50. The final against St Kevin's and Kilian's, on their own patch in Kingswood, was a difficult affair with the opposition mentors getting very excited. The match was played in front of a huge crowd and was tightly contested, but in the end our lads triumphed on a score line of 4-9 to 2-2, with David Mc Gann delivering 2-7 of the total.

At Under 11, the team excelled once more, getting to the Championship decider in O'Toole Park. Along the way they had some fine wins but best of all was their victory over Ballyboden. However, on the day we were narrowly edged out by a Kilmacud team, which had never been beaten and continued its successful run for a couple of more years. It was to be 2002 before this St Judes team now at Under 14, who had suffered at the hands of Kilmacud since Under 9, eventually turned the tables in their last outing in Deerpark. Trailing by 10 points with a few minutes left in the first half we ran out winners by no less than 11 points. This victory over Kilmacud, who were the League champions, was yet another milestone in this young team's progress.

Over the next couple of years the panel continued to strengthen with excellent players being added, including Robert McGrath, Niall Kenny, Stephen McKenna, Shane Gaynor, Barry Keeney, Kevin McLoughlin, Moss Landman, Conor Ryan and Conor O'Doherty. The team also received a great boost with Micheál Mac Fhlannchadha and Nick Finnerty joining up as mentors, which has added a depth of knowledge and experience and has had a major impact on the team's development.

The 2000/2001 season at Under 12 was a watershed for the team. They needed to finish in the top 4 in South Dublin Division 1 to qualify for All Dublin Division 1 status the following season. Playing against the perennial heavy hitters such as Ballyboden, Cuala, Kilmacud, Templeogue, Ballinteer St Johns etc. made it a tall order and amazingly it all came down to the last game of the season - a home tie against Ballinteer. The players knew if Ballinteer won they would go Division One. We needed a win or even a draw.

The match was played in an intense atmosphere, with one score being cancelled by the next. St Judes held a slight edge almost to the end when Ballinteer landed an excellent point. The teams were deadlocked and the last few minutes were contested with a passion few would believe possible of those so young. The final whistle came amid scenes of uncontrolled joy for the players and mentors.

A draw - we were there.

This was also the year that the Easter tournament was hosted by St Judes. The South Dublin v North Dublin competition was run with the Southsiders going for three victories in a row. Six St Judes players, more than any other club on the South side made the three panels; Shane Gaynor, Shane Gallagher, David Mc Gann, Gearoid Gilmore, Kevin Mc Loughlin and Robert Mc Grath. The managers of the A team were Gerry Anderson (St Annes), Michael Carolan (Kilmacud), Shay Hayes (Cuala) and St Judes' Paul Mc Gann and they were delighted when their team lifted the trophy for the third time. Three St Judes players were on the winning team and David Mc Gann was the tournament's leading scorer with 4-3.

The season 2001/2002 was a year of consolidation in Division 1 of the league for the team. Meeting the Northside teams, the likes of Na Fianna, St Peregrines and St Vincents it was always going to be difficult. As it turned out the season ended with us needing two wins in the last two matches to be sure of survival. Sure to form the boys did the business finishing off the season with a great win away to Na Fianna. Despite turning around level at half time and having to play into a near gale force wind they again showed the heart that is their hallmark and won the day by four points leaving a disbelieving Na Fianna side behind them to play in Division 2 the following year.

Gerry Anderson and Paul Mc Gann were called upon once more to look after the South side team – this time for the Garda tournament at Under 13. Again a number of St Judes boys were recruited to the team and this time Pronsias MacFhlannchadha, Shane Gallagher and David Mc Gann represented the club. The trophy had not been South side since 1987 (before the lads were even born) and the task was a huge one. However the team put in a magnificent performance and the St Judes trio played a major part in returning the cup to the South side. The Garda Trophy sits proudly in our trophy cabinet today.

TRIP TO BRUSSELS

In May 2003 this Under 14 team travelled on an historic weekend trip to Brussels and played what were the first games played by any St Judes team outside the 'home countries', in the twenty five year history of the club. The trip, which was set up through a contact of Nick Finnerty in the European Commission, got off to a very wobbly start when it was discovered at boarding time that there was one more passenger in the group than the number of boarding passes.

However, the lads hadn't spent all those long hours on the training field without learning a little in the art of the side step, the Ryanair staff at the boarding gate proving no match for the St Judes young guns and soon the group of twenty one players, two girls and seven adults were on their way.

On arrival in Brussels on the Friday evening, when the children were sent packing to their host families for the weekend and as the elders began to relax over a pint (or two), they were lulled into thinking that they weren't totally crazy to have taken on such an ordeal. Over the following two days, two very entertaining football matches were played and though the Judes lads proved too strong for their hosts, new friendships were being made and the experience of winning an international cap in the St Judes shirt is one that will live long in the memory of all the boys.

The Saturday night in the Irish Club as guests of the Brussels GAA Club was definitely the highlight of the weekend for the adults, while on the Sunday the trip to the Six Flags Theme Park at Wavre even surpassed the thrill of gaining their first two international caps for the young St Judes stars. A stop off at the historic site of the battle of Waterloo on the way to the airport on Monday in an attempt to appeal to the culture which is undoubtedly lurking (somewhere) in the minds of the Judes lads certainly didn't seem to cut nearly as much ice.

The group arrived back in Dublin on Monday night and though Nick and Paul breathed a huge sigh of relief when all the lads were reunited with their mammies, the trip had been a memorable one for everyone.

Under 14 Football team trip to Brussels, 23-26 May, 2003 – Back row: Paul McGann, Pronsias Mac Fhlannchadha, Barry Keeney, David McGann, Niall Kenny, Conor Ryan, Gearoid Gilmore, Shane Gaynor, Peter Larkin, Warren Dempsey, Niall Cox, Nick Finnerty. Front: Shane Gallagher, Cormac Molloy, Conor O'Doherty, Stephen McKenna, Robert McGrath, Kevin McLoughlin, Conor Finnerty, Cormac Grogan, Michael McGrath, James Speers, Niall Tedford.

For the record the group of players that travelled on that historic trip were Conor Finnerty, David McGann, Pronsias Mac Fhlannchadha, Niall Cox, Conor O'Doherty, Robert McGrath, Michael McGrath, Niall Kenny, Stephen McKenna, Peter Larkin, Warren Dempsey, Shane Gallagher, Shane Gaynor, Gearoid Gilmore, Cormac Grogan, Barry Keeney, Kevin McLoughlin, Cormac Molloy, Conor Ryan, James Speers and Niall Tedford. The seven gallant adults who braved the trip were, Nick and Clodagh Finnerty, Paul and Bernie McGann, Mike and Joan McGrath and Martin Speers, with Katie Finnerty and Lisa McGann being the two courageous girls on board.

The team, in the current season, still competes at the highest level in the county and has aspirations to win a championship. The commitment and the passion displayed by this group of lads is typical of St Judes teams and is what the club fosters and takes great pride in. There is no doubt that these qualities will continue into the next 25 years … and beyond.

The rapid and successful development on the camogie front was highlighted by the achievements of players and mentors alike. The season in which the Under 14 camogie team won their league also saw the appointment of Seamus Massey and Marie O'Brien as selectors on the Dublin Minor panel, which included three St Judes players, Sarah Massey, Deirdre O'Connor and Aoife Kelly.

When Irene Dunne started like other parents bringing her children to Orwell Green little did she know that Mary Joyce would ask her to help out with the Under 11 camogie team. When Mary moved on with the older girls Irene stayed behind with the younger girls and with the help of Ann O'Gara brought the team all the way to the championship final in 1999. Unfortunately the young St Judes girls had to give way to a strong St Vincents side on the day. However, it was a great experience for the girls and most of them are still wearing the St Judes colours with pride and indeed two of this team, Roisin Murray and Helena Ryan went on to represent Dublin at Under 14 level. Team: Laura Faulkner, Ciara Mc Donald, Emer Lowe, Fiona Dunne, Ellen O'Neill, Ciara Tyrell, Sarah Curran, Emer Maher, Roisin Murray, Maeobh Kavanagh, Oonagh Mangan, Orla Dunne, Elizabeth Hurley, Rachel Cahill, Davina Lally, Aoife Dunne.

In 2002, again with Irene Dunne at the helm and with great help and encouragement from Aodhán Mac Suibhne, John Corcoran and Darragh Cahill, the Under 11 camogie girls won Division 1 of their league. The panel of players who represented the club on their marvellous run of 15 wins out of 16 games played were: Niamh Mc Donagh, Aoife Burke, Orla Dunne, Aisling Kilcoyne, Niamh Naughton, Aisling Lally, Laura Reynolds, Caoimhe O'Brien, Ciara Ni Mhannain, Sarah Reed, Lorna Gardner, Miriam Davis, Kirsty Kelly, Sarah Meehan, Emma Farrell, Ailis McBrien, Naoise Mc Allney, Aoife Dunne, Miriam

Fehily, Sarah Lucas, Teresa Dunne. The camogie season ended on a high with the Under 15 team winning the Championship.

As Ladies' Football developed gradually from its commencement in 1997 in the Juvenile Section, Gerry Barry was very much the driving force behind its success with great support from Áine Nhic Suibhne. Della Grogan began her club career a year later as manager of the Under 10 team and with Bernie Murray made great strides with the panel.

The Under 10 A girls football team was set up from scratch in September 2001 with the girls aged seven and eight. There were no remaining players from the then Under 10 team so we were all new to the job. Even then some girls had already mastered the basics from being coached in school by Niamh leahy especially Sally Jones, Helena Staunton, Zoe Brennan-Whitmore, Claire Ryan, Susan McGinnell, Emily Nicholson. We stayed out of the league that year just playing friendly matches. All the time the girls were improving, we had Niamh Kelly, Deirdre Maher, Sorcha O'Brien, Ciara Mongey, Aisling and Jenny Sheils, Amy Corcoran, Aoife Corcoran, Aoife Bass and our goalkeeper from the start has been Eilis McManus who has done some brilliant goalkeeping for us. The 2002 season began with a glorious win over Foxrock then another win and then some lean times. There was still commitment from the girls for training and games, with birthday parties being missed, and other arrangements being made to get to the Saturday evening match. All the hard work has paid off as we have just had a great win in the Shield with extra time being played. With continuous support from the club this team has great prospects for the future.

Joe McDonnell's "nursery" on Orwell Green attracted many enthusiastic and aspiring Dublin footballers! Meanwhile our juvenile teams competed in their respective leagues. Seán Breheny's Under 14 hurlers, many of whom now play at the highest levels in the club also added the PJ Troy Cup to its league win. In this same year, veteran club member Tommy Hartnett was appointed County Under 14 selector.

St Judes has successfully fostered excellent relationships with many schools in the surrounding areas. St Mac Daras and Bishop Galvin schools enjoyed considerable success with the formers senior camogie team and the latter's hurlers winning their respective Dublin competitions. Mac Dara's Under 16 footballers were narrowly beaten in the Leinster School Finals.

Initiatives to encourage involvement at the juvenile level included the development of recruitment policies of boys and girls, while the "Player of the Month" awards continued to foster excellence and sportsmanship. The attainment of senior status for our hurlers added a much-needed boost to the endeavours of our Juveniles.

The proposal for the appointment of a Club Development Officer was a successful response to the shortage of qualified coaches in all codes.

From its earliest days the club developed friendships with clubs at home and abroad. Towards the end of the season our Under 14 hurlers played friendlies in Carlow and Kilkenny. The AGM in June 1999 saw long serving Chairman and Secretary, Aodán MacSuibhne and Marie O'Brien, carry their enthusiasm to senior hurling inter county refereeing, and county camogie Secretary, respectively. Paul McGann became Chairman and Della Grogan began her tenure as Secretary of the Juvenile Section of the Club.

As the planet partied towards the Millennium, Jimmy O'Dwyer and Seán Breheny returned to the hurling nursery on "The Green". This work was supplemented by the massive involvement of the staff of Bishop Galvin's school in coaching one hundred and eighty eager boys and girls. A social and sporting highlight of the juvenile season came with the visit of twenty-five members of Fintan Lawlor's GAA Club of London. Reports of other mentors from the following year's reciprocal visit suggest a fun filled and memorable visit across the water. Kilmurray from Clare and Sarsfields of Laois were hosted by our families on their end of season stay in the capital. Even though twenty-four juvenile teams played their hearts out for their club, silverware was scarce at the end of the season. However, it was a source of pride to all when Helen Cosgrave represented her county at Under 14 football and Fiona Faulkner starred at Under 14 camogie. The work of schools and club bore fruit this year with Bishop Galvin's win in the Under 12 schools camogie final in Croke Park.

At the first AGM of the Millennium, the recruitment and development efforts of previous years were reflected in the significant increase in the numbers of hurlers especially, a growing part of twenty five teams competing in Dublin leagues. By September plans were well advanced for our new club games' coach to promote games in local schools, a welcome and necessary source of support to teachers. By Christmas of that wet and miserable year it was noted that medical expenses were running at an alarmingly high rate. There was considerable uncertainty as to the cause of this mini-financial crisis, and opinion varied from sodden pitches to over enthusiastic juveniles! The minutes of the March 2001 meeting reflected the frustration of the nation as it struggled with the threat of foot and mouth disease. "All matches and training are off", was wearily pronounced, while much ink was expended on items such as "expenditure" and the development of the "all-weather pitch". Discos had been arranged to provide for the growing numbers of juveniles and these proved to be incredibly popular and successful. The brightest news by summer was that Niamh Leahy, our first and much needed coach, had commenced operations. As we approached our twenty-fifth year, Niamh Leahy's work rate and positive impact on the juvenile players and their coaches is evident in the secretary's minutes, with fewer references to administrative matters and a rapid increase in planning for coaching and support. Nick Finnerty has taken over the reins as Juvenile Chairman and Mary Monaghan has just joined him to begin her term as Secretary.

By our twenty-fifth year the dedication of our Juvenile Games Committee in fostering participation and enjoyment of camogie, hurling and football, allied with the sheer enthusiasm, skill and heart of all of our young players, has ensured that the ranks of our senior and adult teams will continue to produce excellent players. The future of our distinctive and beloved blue jersey is assured. "Mol an oige agus tiocfaidh sí".

ST JUDES JUVENILE FOOTBALL TEAM FROM U10A (1990/91) TO U16A (1996/1997)

This overview covers the progress of the St Judes 1990/91 Under 10A football team from Under 10 (1990/91) to Under 16 (1996/97). The team had quite a successful run during this six year period winning two Division 1 titles, one Division 1 runners up and four third places in Division 1. They also reached the final of the Under 16A football championship in 1996/97. During this period the team competed in the highest division at each age level. Most the players on this panel came through the Green Nursery of Joe McDonnell & Co and many of the players had played in the previous years Under 10 competitions with Bobby Carty when they were Under 9s. Bobby Carty remained with the team for the first competitive year at Under 10A in 1990/91 and was joined by Don Lehane in that year who remained with both football and hurling squads up to their final minor year in 1998/99. Over the period mentors involved with Don Lehane in this football squad included Michael Glover from Under 11 to Under 15 and Tommy Hartnett from Under 15 to Minor. This particular team was probably one of the most successful dual football and hurling squads to come through the club since its inception and the teams operated almost exclusively at Division 1 level throughout this period. The team was very much a parish team built up almost exclusively from local players which very much accounted for the large numbers of players from these age groups who went on to play Under 21 and adult football and hurling in the club in later years. For championship games the team was supplemented by players from Seán Breheny's squad who were a year behind. A number of players from these panels played representative football for Dublin at some level during this period including Kevin Hayes, Andrew Glover, Ger Hartnett, Paul Goodall, Declan McCabe, Aidan Lalor, Seán Breheny, Michael Lyons, Brendan McManamon and John Waldron.

1990/91 Football Season (U10A): The Under 10A football team competed in Division 1 of the South-East League and finished third in a league which included St Judes, Ballyboden St Endas, Kilmacud Croke's, Templeogue, Cuala, De La Salle and Ballinteer St Johns. In the eleven matches played St Judes won seven and lost four. The league was won by Ballyboden St Endas with Ballinteer St Johns second and St Judes third. The four losses were the home/away fixtures against Ballyboden and Ballinteer, which gave St Judes a good target for improvement the following year. The team subsequently never finished out of the top three in either football or hurling as they progressed from Under 10A to minor level. The team scored 51 goals and 75 points in their first season in eleven games and conceded 14 goals and 23 points. With the exception of the Ballyboden and Ballinteer games St Judes had big wins against all other teams in the group. They defeated Kilmacud Crokes by 43 points at home (16-02 to 2-01) and by 15 points away (6-02 to 2-01). They also had home and away wins against De La Salle (5-5 to 1-1 and W/O), Templeogue (7-06 to 1-01 and 4-0 to 2-01), Cuala (8-02 to 2-01 and 11-02 to 4.-04). They had home and away defeats to Ballyboden St Endas (3-0 to 3-05 and 2-02 to 2-03) and Ballinteer St Johns (1-0 to 5-04 and 6-02 to 8-03).

1991/1992 Football Season (U11A): The Under 11A team competed in Division 1 of the South-East league and finished league winners in a league, which included St Judes, Ballyboden St Endas, Kilmacud Croke's, Ballinteer St Johns, St Olafs and Blessington. Features of the year were big wins against winners and runners up of the Under 10 league the previous year with a 31 point defeat of Ballyboden St Endas and a 28 point defeat of Ballinteer St Johns. In the ten matches played St Judes won ten and lost one and scored a total of 51 goals and 75 points and conceded 14 goals and 23 points. Results for the home and away fixtures were as follows with St Judes scores first: Kilmacud Croke's (10-11 to 2-02 and 7-09 to 0-01), Ballyboden St Endas (5-16 to 0-00 and 2-02 to 1-00), Ballinteer St Johns (8-07 to 1-00 and 3-07 to 2-09), Blessington (3-09 to 2-03 and 1-04 to 0-02), St Olafs (7-08 to 1-01 and 5-02 to 5-04 loss).

1992/1993 Football Season (U12A): The Under 12A team competed in Division 1 of the South-East League and finished league winners with thirteen wins and one loss. The team scored a total of 72 goals and 110 points to 17 goals and 34 points in fourteen games. A feature of the year were the big scores racked up by St Judes who averaged 25 points a game over the season and had an average winning margin of 19 points. Results for the home and away fixtures were as follows with St Judes scores first: Ballinteer St Johns (9.11 to 1.00 and 8.10 to 2.02), Blessington (5-07 to 0-03 and 11-05 to 0-00), Thomas Davis (5-

12 to 0-00 and 7-05 to 5-03), Ballyboden St Endas (W/O and 5-09 to 0-05), St Killians (5-11 to 1-05 and 3-07 to 1-02), Blessington (5-07 to 0-03 and 11-05 to 0-00), Lucan Sarsfields (6-14 to 1-01 and 3-07 to 2-05). The team played eight friendly football games throughout the year including a 23 point defeat of the St Judes Under 13A team (7-06 to 1-01) which was played instead of a league game against Ballyboden St Endas who decided not to travel to St Judes for the their away league fixture. St Judes also won the Under 12A Division 1 hurling league in 1991/1992 to complete a Division 1 football and hurling league double, which to our knowledge is a unique achievement in the club's history. Trophies and medals were presented to the players on an enjoyable night in the clubhouse with Paul Bealin (St Kevins/Dublin) doing the presentation.

1993/1994 Football season (U13A): The Under 13A team played in Division 1 of the All-Dublin Premier league in 1993/1994 and finished in the top three with six wins from 11 matches in a league dominated by St Brigids and Craobh Chiarain. They had league wins against Raheny (away), Ballymun Kickhams (home), St Vincents (home), Erins Isle (home), Raheny (home) and Ballymun Kickhams (away) and losses to St Brigids (away), Craobh Chiarain (home), St Brigids (home), St Vincents (away), Craobh Chiarain (away). The best performance of the year was the 7-14 to 1-03 away league win against Raheny. The team also played a number of cup and friendly games and finished the season with ten wins and two draws from their eighteen matches.

1994/1995 Football season (U14A): The Under 14A team played in Division 1 of the All-Dublin Premier league in 1994/1995 and finished in the top three. The team played a total of eleven games in the season with seven wins and one abandoned league match against St Vincents with St Judes in a winning position.

1995/1996 Football Season (U15A): The Under 15A team played in Division 1 of the league and finished runners-up with eight wins, three draws, two losses from thirteen games. St Judes recorded wins against Ballinteer St Johns (home), Thomas Davis (home and away), Kilmacud Crokes (home and away), Round Towers (home and away), Lucan Sarsfields (home). They drew matches against Templeogue (home and away) and St Marks and lost two games to St Marks (away) and Lucan Sarsfields (away). Despite beating Kilmacud Crokes both home and away St Judes were pipped for the league title by Kilmacud Crokes by a single point. St Judes were beaten by St Marks in the Under 15 football championship on a scoreline of 2-07 to 1-13 on a cold and windy day at St Marks. This was one of the shocks of the first round as St Judes started the year as one of the favourites for the juvenile championship.

1996/1997 Football season (U16A): This was a tremendous year for the St Judes Under 16 hurling and football squad culminating in the first ever underage hurling championship win for the club and only the second team in the club to reach a football championship final at any level. Between football and hurling a total of forty games were played between September 1996 and October 1997 covering league, championship, inter-county tournaments and friendly matches. Of the forty matches played thirty were won, two drawn, seven lost and one abandoned. St Judes scored a total of 98 goals and 291 points against 56 goals and 199 points during those games. The Under 16A team played in Division 1 of the league and finished third with five wins from their eight games. The team beat Raheny (2-08 to 1-10), Naomh Mearnog (11-13 to 1-02), Erin's Isle (2-07 to 1-06), Cuala (3-06 to 0-03), Ballymun Kickhams and lost to Kilmacud Crokes (0-04 to 1-11), St Brigids (0-05 to 3-07) and Craobh Chiarain (2-08 to 4-05). St Judes had a good league campaign but the Under 16 football championship run was the highlight of the football year. The championship started with a 2-09 to 1-03 first round victory over St Olafs at a windswept Newcastle on 22nd March 1997. The second round at Balgriffin on 26th April 1997 was against Skerries Harps who had already accounted for Ballyboden St Endas after three games and Thomas Davis after a replay plus extra time. The game resulted in a draw after extra time on a scoreline of 1-13 to 3-07 after a tremendous game of football. In the replay at Balgriffin on 3rd May 1997, St Judes played probably their best football of the year and ran out winners by 5-13 to 0-08 after a scintillating performance. Division 1 side O'Tooles provided the quarter final opposition in O'Toole Park on 7th June 1997 and after a hard fought battle St Judes emerged two point winners on a score of 1-08 to 0-09. This set up the prospect of an intriguing semi-final local derby clash between St Judes and Templeogue at O'Toole Park on 6th September 1997. This was a typical hard and close semi-final with the added bite of local rivalry. The game was however played in a good spirit despite the intense rivalry. St Judes ran out two point winners on a scoreline of 0-07 to 0-05 with all the Templeogue scores coming from frees. The county championship final on 4th October 1997 was against St Brigids in O'Toole Park with great Judes support in attendance. In an exciting game St Judes lost by a point after a tremendous performance against a very strong St Brigids side who had a great record in this championship over the preceding ten years. St Judes led by four points with ten minutes to go but conceded late scores to go four points down in the last minute. A brave comeback yielded a goal but Judes ran out of time and lost by a single point after a performance, which deserved a win but should have at least merited a draw. Nevertheless it was a great performance by a brave team who never know when they are beaten. St Judes were an imposing squad at Under 16 level with nineteen players from the panel measuring up at 5 foot 11 inches or taller including thirteen who were 6 foot plus. Under 16 Championship Final Team: Colm Sheehy, Eoghan O'Neill, Donagh O'Dwyer, Ciaran Coates, Ross McDermott, Ger Hartnett, Seán Breheny, Bart Lehane, Andrew Glover, Paul Goodall, Declan McCabe, Anthony O'Reilly, Donnacha Ryan, John Waldron, Kevin Hayes. Other Under 16 panel members: Fergal Daly, Brendan McManamon (holidays), Barry Faulkner, Paul Mahon, Eoghan Mangan, Colm McGovern, John McKinney, Seán McLoughlin, Paul Molamphy, Stephen Murray, John Walsh, Alex Meade-Wilson. Mentors: Don Lehane, Tommy Hartnett

ST JUDES JUVENILE HURLING TEAM FROM U10A (1990/91) TO U16 (1996/97)

This overview covers the progress of the St Judes 1990/91 Under 10A hurling team from Under 10A (1990/91) to Under 16A (1996/97). The team competed at Division 1 level for all but one year of this seven year period. During the period the team won two Division 1 hurling titles, one Division 2 winners or runners-up title (unfinished league) and two third places in Division 1. The combined football and hurling squad won four Division 1 titles, one Division 1 runners-up titles, one Division 2 winners/runners-up title, six third places in Division 1, one hurling championship and one football championship runners-up during this period. Prior to competitive leagues the players came through the Jimmy O'Dwyer School of Coaching and Jimmy together with Don Lehane ran the team at Under 10 level in 1990/91. Don Lehane managed the team for most of the period up to minor level with the assistance of Michael Glover from Under 11 to Under 14 and Joe Clavin, Tommy Hartnett and Seán Ward at Under 16 level. Tommy Hartnett and Seán Ward managed the team for most of the Under 15 hurling season in 1995/96. On an overall basis this was probably one of the more successful hurling squads in the club's history to date and in years to come a significant number of players from this panel went on to play adult hurling for St Judes. A number of players from these panels played representative hurling for Dublin at some level including Anthony Reilly, Ger Hartnett, Bart Lehane, Donagh O'Dwyer, Donnacha Ryan, Seán McLoughlin, David Ryan, Ciaran O'Brien and Colm McGovern.

1990/91 Hurling Season (U10A): The 1990/91 Under 10A hurling team started their competitive hurling life in Division 1 with a resounding 32 point defeat of St Olafs on the 19th April 1991 in Tymon on a scoreline of 11-04 to 1-02. They went on to win the league by decisively winning all their seven matches scoring 53 goals and 12 points in the process against 12 goals and 3 points and finishing up with an average winning margin of 20 points. Up until this point in the clubs history the underage football had enjoyed greater success than the hurling but this particular squad had their sights set on achieving success at Division 1 level in both hurling and football. This was partly to debunk the theory that it was impossible to run successful football and hurling teams with the same players but also to attempt to overcome the psychological stranglehold that Ballyboden St Endas exerted over underage hurling at that point. The vast quantity of raw material available to Ballyboden via a myriad of schools and estates determined that this was a battle to be won by quality rather than quantity and the St Judes team set about the task of developing the skill level and tactics of the team. St Judes started the campaign with a big win against St Olafs (11-04 to 1-02) and followed this up with wins against Clanna Gael (6-00 to 2-00) and Crumlin (8-00 to 1-00). The benchmark test against the unbeaten Ballyboden St Endas team arrived on 24th May 1991 with the game fixed for Tymon North. St Judes put in an outstanding display of hurling for this age level to totally outclass a bemused Ballyboden side that found themselves at the wrong end of a 26 point defeat (10-02 to 2-00). This was the first time that a St Judes Under 10A team had beaten a Ballyboden St Endas A team at this level and the team lined up as follows: Ger Hartnett, Brian O'Brien, Ronan Potts, Paul Molamphy, Alex Meade-Wilson, Donal Ward, Mark Carty, Bart Lehane, Andrew Glover, Conaire Fitzpatrick, David Ryan, Colm McGovern, Niall Dunne, Donagh Dwyer, Eoghan Mangan. Subs: Fergal Daly, Michael Lyons, Tomas Mangan, Bobby Neff, Killian Blake, Ciaran Coates (inj). Other panel members Seán McLoughlin, Aidan Russell and Mark O'Brien were unavailable for this game. St Judes went on to beat St Olafs (4-02 to 2-02) and Clanna Gael (7-02 to 2-00) in the next two games. They wrapped up the Division 1 league title in style with a sixteen point defeat (7-02 to 2-01) of a Ballyboden team gunning for revenge in the away fixture at Cherryfield.

1991/92 Hurling Season (U11A): In 1991/92 St Judes Under 11A hurling team competed in the All-Dublin Under 11 Premier league and finished third behind Craobh Chiarain and St Vincents. This was a highly competitive league with some tremendous games. This particular age group in Dublin went on to produce a number of outstanding county minor, Under 21 and senior hurlers in years to come. St Judes finished the season with seven wins from ten games and a scoring total of 35 goals and 17 points to 27 goals and 19 points. St Judes had home and away wins against Good Counsel (10-04 to 0-00 and W/O), Erins Isle (5-02 to 0-01 and 3-02 to 2-01) and Ballyboden St Endas (4-01 to 4-00 and 6-01 to 3-03). They had a home win and an away loss against Craobh Chiarain (3-

01 to 2-02 and 3-01 to 7-04) and home and away losses to St Vincents (0-03 to 3-04 and 1-02 to 0-6).

1992/93 Hurling Season (U12A): In 1992/93 St Judes again competed in Division 1 and ran out league winners with eleven wins from twelve games scoring a total of 54 goals and 37 points against 11 goals and 11 points. St Judes therefore completed probably a unique club record in winning Division 1 football and hurling titles in the same year. This temporarily at least silenced the critics who maintained that it was virtually impossible to achieve dual success with basically the same players as almost all the players in this squad played both football and hurling under the same team management of Don Lehane and Michael Glover. The only loss in the year was a one point home loss to Kilmacud Crokes (1-06 to 2-04), which the team later avenged in style by defeating Kilmacud by 21 points in the away fixture on a scoreline of 7-04 to 1-01. St Judes recorded home and away wins against the following teams: Good Counsel (10-01 to 0-00 and W/O), Crumlin (W/O and 11-06 to 2-01), Ballyboden St Endas (8-06 to 1-00 and 4-09 to 3-01), Clanna Gael (W/O and 7-02 to 2-03) and St Killians (6-03 to 0-01 and W/O). The Under 12A panel included the following players: Ronan Potts, Bart Lehane, Brian O'Brien, Mark O'Brien, Aidan Russell, Donagh O'Dwyer, Seán McLoughlin, Anthony O'Reilly, Eoghan Mangan, Tomas Mangan, Andrew Glover, David Ryan, Alex Meade-Wilson, Ross McDermott, Ger Hartnett, Ciaran Coates, Colm McGovern, Kevin Hayes, Donal Ward, Fergal Daly, Eoghan O'Neill, Conaire Fitzpatrick, Paul Molamphy, Stephen Murray.

1993/94 Hurling Season (U13A): In 1993/94 St Judes Under 13A team competed in Division 1 of an All Dublin league and finished up in third place in a league in which all the fixtures were not completed. They also won Division 1 of the Special Summer league with six wins from six games. In the Division 1 league St Judes started their campaign with a 51 point win against Whitehall Colmcilles on a scoreline of 14-10 to 0-01. They went on to record wins against Ballyboden (3-03 to 1-01) and St Vincents (8-04 to 4-01) and were defeated by Erin's Isle (4-03 to 3-07) and Craobh Chiarain (0-01 to 6-13). In the Special Summer hurling league St Judes ran out Division 1 winners with wins against Na Fianna (7-10 to 0-00), Ballinteer St Johns (9-05 to 3-06), St Kevins (8-03 to 1-08), Thomas Davis (7-05 to 2-01), Ballyboden St Endas (6-03 to 2-01) and St Killians (10-04 to 4-01).

1994/95 Hurling Season (U14A): St Judes again competed in Division 1 of a league in which a number of games were not played by the end of the season. St

Judes recorded wins against Crumlin (8-07 to 2-04) and St Vincents (5-04 to 0-02) and losses to Erins Isle (3-00 to 6-07), Craobh Chiarain (4-01 to 4-04), Ballyboden St Endas (1-04 to 2-04) and Kilmacud Crokes (2-08 to 3-07).

1995/96 Hurling Season (U15A): St Judes competed in Division 1 of the league and had a poor season by their standards recording one win and a draw from their five games with a win against Naomh Mearnog (3.02 to 1.00), a draw against Kilmacud Crokes (2-02 to 2-02) and losses against St Vincents (0-07 to 4-07), Craobh Chiarain (1-03 to 5-05) and Ballyboden St Endas (3-02 to 3-05). The championship was run in a league format that season and St Judes were knocked out after defeats to Ballyboden St Endas, Erins Isle and Craobh Chiarain.

1996/97 Hurling Season (U16A): This was the first year that St Judes played outside Division 1 level in hurling after a poor 1995/96 season by their standards. The league was not finished in this year and at the end of the league season St Judes had only played four games with wins against Naomh Mearnog (4-09 to 1-02), St Peregrines (8-04 to 6-05) and Cuala (3-06 to 3-03) and a loss against Crumlin (2-01 to 6-04). If the competition had been concluded they would have been in competition for the Division 2 title. St Judes had a tremendous run in the Under 16B hurling championship culminating in a one point victory against St Peregrines in the county final at Parnell Park on the 7th June 1997. This brought St Judes their first underage hurling championship success since the founding of the club. The championship started with a 21 point win over Whitehall Colmcilles on the 4th April 1997. They followed this up on the 10th May with an eight point victory over Ballinteer St Johns (4-02 to 0-06) at Wedgewood. In the semi-final at O'Toole Park on the 17th May 1997 St Judes had a facile 11 point victory over Clanna Gael (2-09 to 0-04). The championship final against St Peregrines was played on the 24th May 1997 in Parnell Park. St Judes started the game in fine style with some great outfield points. St Judes were rarely out of the Peregrines half with Anthony O'Reilly and Bart Lehane dominating midfield. Up front the ever dangerous Donnacha Ryan got great assistance from Alex Wilson, Seán Breheny and the tigerish Tomas Mangan in the corner. Judes defence was rarely troubled during this period and when the pressure came Paul Molamphy, Ciaran O'Brien, Ciaran Coates and company responded with some great defensive hurling and a lack of respect for good ash. Judes raced into an eight point lead with points from Donnacha Ryan, Donagh O'Dwyer, Alex Wilson, Seán Breheny and Michael Lyons. A St Peregrines goal against the run of play just before the break left the half-time scores St Judes 0-12 to Peregrines 1-02. St Peregrines improved their performance in the second half playing with a deceptively strong breeze. They began to eat into the Judes lead despite good defensive performances from James Dennehy, Ciaran O'Brien and Ger Hartnett. St Peregrines took the lead with a goal with ten minutes to go after a defensive error. To their credit St Judes responded with their best spell of hurling in the second half and eventually forced a goal when a rasping shot from Donnacha Ryan rattled the Peregrines net to put Judes a point up. This was to be the final score of the game and St Judes brought the first juvenile championship trophy back to the clubhouse.

Under 16 Hurling Championship Final Team: James Dennehy, Paul Molamphy, Ger Hartnett, Donal Ward, Eoghan Mangan, Ciaran Coates, Ciaran O'Brien, Anthony O'Reilly, Bart Lehane, Seán Breheny, Donagh O'Dwyer, Alex Wilson, Michael Lyons, Donnacha Ryan, Tomas Mangan. Substitutes: Seán McLoughlin, Ross McDermott, Colm McGovern, Shane Hartney, Eoghan O'Neill, Brian Eighan, Gavin Duffy, Paul Goodall, Kevin Hayes, John McKinney and Vincent Wallace.

Mentors: Don Lehane, Joe Clavin, Tommy Hartnett and Seán Ward.

McCarthy Cup team 1994 – Back row (l-r): Darren McGann, Donal Harte, Dennis O'Frighil, Alan Cullen, Eamonn Kennedy, Alan McDonald, Arthur Williams, Neville O'Boyle, Neil Synnott, John Campbell. Front: Sean McLoughlin, Liam Lyons, Conor Moore, Gerard Quinn, Ronan Howard, Niall Butler, Colin Barry, Seamus O'Loinsigh, Eoghan O'Connor, Matthew Tisdall.

THE ROAD TO THE UNDER 9 O'REILLY CUP 2001
Seán O'Loughlin

O'Reilly Cup 2001 Under 9 – For the record the panel for the O'Reilly Cup 2001 was as follows: Paul O'Sullivan, Fergal Heavy, Robert Hardy, Alan O'Beirne, Seánie O'Loughlin, Mark Kennedy, Mark "Sparks" Hannon, Paul Maguire, Daniel Sutcliffe, Oisin Manning, Killian Barden, Enda Maher, Diarmuid Cox, Killian C. O'Hora, Joseph McManus, Ever Griffin, John B. Carthy, Niall Murray, Brian Dervan, Kieran Fallon, Kevin Rooney.

Sunday 13th April 2003
As the song goes "It's a long way from Clare to here" and so it is tonight. We are on the road home after this year's Under 11 team's visit to Clarecastle and Lissycasey. High jinks, even higher spirits, a good sing song – we're all whacked, and that's just the adults.

Tour leader, elder statesman, Martin Hayes is convinced we deserve medals, Jack Hardy agrees but reckons they should be miraculous medals – laughter, one-liners and good natured banter. At last count 22 out of 32 boys are asleep - the remainder are tying laces to chairs or together. Some things never change. As I drift in and out of sleep, I can recall similar days in Corca Duibhne – West Kerry of 30 years ago, similar to our journey to win the O'Reilly Cup Div. 1, Sth Dublin Champions 2001.

Sometime in 2001

It seems like an age since we played a match, or for that matter since we trained. The country is gripped in some sort of crisis - if it's not the weather, it's the mad cows with BSE/CJD or worse still, foot and mouth; I can't recall what the issue was, but its playing hell with the fixture list, and all of a sudden, we're drawn to play Kilmacud Crokes in the first found of the cup.

A few of the boys from both teams are in the same school - Scoil Bhride Ranelagh – and this match is the talk of the school that week. Stiofan Ó Muircheartaigh is playing for Crokes, a relation of the commentator Micháel, originally from Doonsheen, a few miles east of Dingle. My own dad was their local vet, and many a call to a cow calving at 4a.m. was made easier by a lively discussion on team selections, who's going well in training and who's not. It's Tuesday, I'm pacing the floorboards, we're not ready. Of course, it doesn't dawn on "mo dhuine" that foot and mouth or whatever wasn't exclusively a D6W issue and Crokes aren't in that great a shape either.

Next up in the Quarter Final is away to Ballinteer St Johns. These guys are a class act, a really skilful team. They mix the traditional "Beir agus Buail" – catch and kick with the short passing game. They play in a truly sporting manner and in all our games it generally comes down to the wire in the last 5 minutes. Fortunately we catch them on an off day, winning 5-1 to 1-2. They are gracious and sporting in defeat. Round Towers are given a Bye to the final which means we're up against the might of Ballyboden in the semi-final. Ah yes local rivalry – an encyclopaedia could be written on it.

The Palio horse race in Sienna, Italy, Celtic v Rangers, bullfights in Madrid, basketball courts in New York, Liverpool v Everton, it's what keeps the blood flowing through the veins. All the above pale into insignificance to a GAA local rivalry match, at any age. You can sense it when you meet Bobby Carty, Joe McDonnell and Padraic McManus, who started off on the Green with these boys.

West Kerry rivalry. Dingle the fourth town of Kerry, capital of West Kerry, the other parishes including Lispole, Annascaul to the east, Castlegregory below the hill and west to the townlands of Fionn Trá, Feoghnach, Dún Chaoin, Baile na nGall to name a few; how they are wanted to beat the townies at any age group, Trainers, whole families, Christian Brothers, Nuns and Priests, exhorting, extolling, coercing, scolding, ranting and raving. And yet a week later, as if a fairy godmother had waved a magic wand, those said same rival supporters joined in unison as the combined parishes of West Kerry took on the might of Kerry football, - Listowel Emmets, Austin Stacks, Dr. Crokes etc. Strange folks adults!!!.

A large crowd had gathered for the semi-final, no doubt wanting this generation to make up for past disappointments of a decade or longer before, and we scrape home by a point. The final was set for 13th May at O'Toole Park, Theatre of Dreams for this group of boys. Communions made, clothes changed, jerseys pressed, birth certs checked, I's dotted t's crossed, what was the song we used to sing at school.

"Ha Ha Ha buail buail
Suas an phairc insteach san chúl
Ha Ha Ha Cul Cul Cul
An craobh seo corn ag Daingean Ui Chuis"

After the tense start, we run out easy winners, Joy unbounded!!! Shake hands boys, the presentation made, a word from our Captain, three cheers for Round Towers. Back to the clubhouse, cars tooting, rounds of applause, coke, crisps and pizza. Go h'iontach.

For the record the panel for the O'Reilly Cup 2001 was as follows: Paul O'Sullivan, Fergal Heavy, Robert Hardy, Alan O'Beirne, Seánie O'Loughlin, Mark Kennedy, Mark "Sparks" Hannon, Paul Maguire, Daniel Sutcliffe, Oisin Manning, Killian Barden, Enda Maher, Diarmuid Cox, Killian C. O'Hora, Joseph McManus, Ever Griffin, John B. Carthy, Niall Murray, Brian Dervan, Kieran Fallon and Kevin Rooney.

1997 U16 Football finalists v St Brigids – Back row (l-r): Michael Lyons, Ross McDermott, John Waldron, Bart Lehane, Paul Molamphy, Feargal Daly, Seán Breheny, Ger Hartnett, Andrew Golver, Donnacha Ryan, Donagh O'Dwyer, John McKinney, Kevin Hayes, Barry Faulkner, John Walsh. Front: Declan McCabe, Colm McGovern, Anthony Reilly, Alex Meade-Wilson, Ciaran Coates, Brendan McManamon, Paul Goodall, Eoghan O'Neill, Paul Mahon, Eoghan Mangan, Colm Sheehy, Stephen Murray.

2002 - A MAGNIFICENT SEASON FOR THE UNDER 14 BOYS
John Browne

In 2002, the boys' Under 14 team achieved a notable double success for the club by winning both the football and hurling Féile (Division 2) competitions, which were organised by the Dublin Juvenile Football and Hurling Boards. While many club teams had competed in these competitions over the years, the club had never before won the football Féile competition not to mention winning both Féile competitions in the same season. This was a historic achievement for the players concerned and is a positive reflection of their hard work and dedication over the past number of years. Such achievements would not be possible without the support of their parents and the people who have been involved in coaching the players over the years both at club and school level.

Football Féile

This competition took place over the May bank holiday week-end and St Judes were drawn in Division 2 Section B with the following clubs – Trinity Gaels, Naomh Barróg and Thomas Davis. Having won two and lost one of their first round matches, St Judes finished runners up in their group and qualified to meet Parnells in the semi-final. Following a close and hard fought match, St Judes emerged victorious on a 1-09 to 1-05 scoreline and qualified to meet Ballinteer St Johns in the final. The football final took place in the Naomh Mearnóg club in Portmarnock and the St Judes team saved their best performance for the final match to build up a lead of 2-07 to 1-01 by half time. Despite having to withstand fierce pressure from their opponents in the early stages of the second half, the St Judes team finished strongly to finish on a 2-13 to 3-02 final score line. To the delight of their mentors, John Browne, Tommy Hartnett, Seamus Conroy, Liam Larkin, and their parents, history was made by the St Judes Under 14 football team and the Féile trophy was presented to their captain Chris Guckian by Cáit Ní Cheallaigh, Chairperson of the Dublin Juvenile Football Board.

Hurling Féile

The hurling competition took place over the week-end of the 24th to 26th May and St Judes were drawn in Division 2 Section A with the following clubs – Kilmacud Crokes, Clanna Gael/Fontenoy and St Oliver Plunkett/Eoghan Ruadh. Following two wins and a draw in the group stages, St Judes qualified to meet St Brigids in the semi final match. While the final score line of 2-08 to 0-01 in favour of St Judes might suggest an easy win, the match was hard fought and St Judes had to rely on all their skills and some lucky breaks to achieve their victory. The final match took place in Silverpark on Sunday 26th May and St Judes were

U15 Football team 2003 Co. finalists – Back: Tommy Hartnett, Andy McCawn, David Browne, Ciaran Conroy, Colm Murphy, Colm Kilcoyne, Chris Guckian, Brian Maher, Martin Hartnett, Peter Morgan, Seán Walshe, Shane Gallagher, Mark Colgan, Niall Dervan, John Browne, Seamus Conroy. Front: Gerard Hanhoe, Donal Grimes, Seán Walshe, Kris Greene, Neal Mangan, Prionios Mac Fhlannchadha, Gerard Fehily, Niall Tedford, Seán Ó Cuiv, Stephen Larkin, Matthew Lucas.

up against a physically strong Erin's Isle team. The first half exchanges were close and scores were hard to come by. However, St Judes managed to build up a 3-01 to 1-01 lead by half time. The second half was even tighter with both defences on top and both teams only managed to add 1-01 to their half time scores. The final score line favoured St Judes and the game finished 4-02 to 2-02 in favour of the team from Templeogue. The St Judes players and their supporters greeted the referee's final whistle with scenes of great joy. When order was restored, Con O'Donoghue, Chairman of the Dublin Juvenile Hurling Board, presented the trophy to the St Judas captain, Chris Guckian.

An achievement such as this double victory does not happen by accident and is the result of many years hard work on the part of the players concerned together with the support and encouragement of their parents. This success also owes much to the hard work of the teachers in the local primary school, Bishop Galvin NS, and the mentors in St Judes GAA club. A special thanks is also due to Liam and Bernie McMahon for their kind sponsorship of the team jerseys and to Paul and Geraldine Mangan for their kind hospitality after both competitions. Last but not least, the team management who have stood by the team through thick and thin and provided support and encouragement to the players over the past number of years. To John Browne, Tommy Hartnett, Seamus Conroy and Liam Larkin special thanks for their continued dedication and support for the team and long may it continue. To cap a magnificent season, the hurling team also won the Division 2 league competition in September. The St Judes football and hurling squads which took part in the Féile competitions are as follows: - David Browne, Mark Colgan, Ciaran Conroy, Niall Dervan, Gerard Fehily, Kris Green, Donal Grimes, Chris Guckian, Gerard Hanahoe, Martin Hartnett, Chris

Hilliard, Colm Kilcoyne, Stephen Larkin, Brian Malee, Neal Mangan, Andrew McCann, Seán McMahon, Peter Morgan, Colm Murphy, Shaun Ó Cuiv, Aengus O'Rourke, Seán Walsh, Seán Walsh, Pronsias MacFhlannchadha, David McGann, Kevin McLaughlin, Gearoid Gilmore, Conor Finnerty, Peter Larkin, Niall Kenny and Shane Gallagher.

ST JUDES UNDER 13S WIN PJ TROY HURLING IN 2003
Declan Doyle

On a beautiful sunny day on Sat. 21st June 2003 St. Judes and Faughs co-hosted Division 2 of the PJ Troy hurling tournament in Tymon Park. Nine teams in total participated in this division with St Judes emerging as winners of the gold medal. The Judes boys under mentors Declan Doyle and Cormac Egan adapted well early on to the combination of ground hurling and normal hurling rules that were in place for the tournament and served up a fantastic display of hurling skills winning all their four games. In the morning they had victories over St Peregrines and St. Pats (P) whilst in the afternoon section St Judes defeated Crumlin and Oliver Plunketts/Eoin Ruadh. A great achievement indeed for this team which was even more notable due to the fact that we currently play in Division 3A of the hurling league. There were notable performances in particular from Kieran Mangan playing right corner forward who scored a number of fine goals in each game. Others who excelled were Captain, Cormac Grogan, who led by example all day, Paul Maguire, Kieran Kelly, Barry O'Connor, Fiacra Fitzpatrick and Gerard McManus in goal to name but a few.

It is hoped that this victory will be the launching pad of even greater successes for this team in the years ahead.

PJ Troy Competition Division 2 winners 2003 – Back row (l-r): Declan Doyle jnr, Donal Ring, Robert McGrath, Niall Wynne, Robert Byrne, Paul Maguire, Cormac Grogan, Conor O'Donnell, Emmet Byrne, Stephen Ruddy, Killian Tuite, Fiacra Fitzpatrick, Gary Deegan, Kieran O'Shea, Daniel Sutcliffe. Front: Kieran Mangan, Michael Scanlon, Niall Egan, Barry O'Connor, Gerard McManus, Nathan Stamp, Kieran Kelly, John Woolhead, Seán O'Neill.

The Dick McCarthy Cup

UNDER-14 INTERPROVINCIAL COMPETITION – Tommy Hartnett

THE DICK McCarthy Memorial Cup is in memory of Dick McCarthy, a former Tipperary official and member of Arravale Rovers GAA Club. The cup was presented to St. Judes GAA Club by his son, Bill McCarthy. It was the wish of the late Dick McCarthy that a competition be arranged at juvenile level for the cup.

In the Millennium year 1988 Jim Coghlan and Danny Lynch were asked by Bill McCarthy, son of the late Dick McCarthy, if the club would run a competition in football for juveniles for a cup which his father had purchased many years before which had been lying unused in Bill's attic since his father's death. Tommy Hartnett was approached by Jim and Danny and he came up with the idea of an Under 14 Football Interprovincial competition to foster relations at a young age between Dublin and the country.

The first competition was organised in 1988 and the first teams to take part were Rostrevor (Co. Down), St. Michaels (Co. Roscommon), Maynooth who stood in at the last minute for Arravale Rovers and St Judes. After an exciting weekend of football Rostsrevor from Co. Down became the first winners of the McCarthy Cup. Tommy Hartnett, with the assistance of Máire McSherry, ran the McCarthy Cup for eight years before it was taken over by a committee in 1996.

This competition, while competitive, is mainly for good football, fun, and the making of new friends. The competition has been so successful over the years that all clubs who have taken part have looked to return in the future. Clubs are selected randomly to represent their province which gives both strong and weak clubs a chance to participate. Since 1988 we have had teams from Down, Derry, Fermanagh, Donegal, Cavan, Westmeath, Roscommon, Galway, Mayo, Limerick, Cork, Waterford, Kerry and Sligo. Many of our teams have been invited for return visits to these clubs and many exciting trips have ensued. The main beneficiaries of this competition are St Judes as this competition gives an opportunity for the Under 14 team, whether it is strong or weak, to play against teams with different styles and at different levels to themselves. It also gives them the opportunity to make new contacts outside of Dublin. It also benefits the Club in that if these country players eventually come to Dublin to study or work they have a contact club in St Judes. Hopefully this competition will continue long into the future as the experience gained by the players is invaluable.

The Millennium Year

Tommy Hartnett

IN 1988 Dublin celebrated the millennium of the city of Dublin. It was the intention of the city council that this be a year of celebration and that all organisations should take part. In line with this all Dublin GAA clubs were requested by the county board to take part in the millennium parade through the city to Croke Park and to organise one other event to commemorate the year.

St Judes GAA Club decided to take a full part in the parade and as requested by the county board a Club Banner, a Club Flag and a Dublin flag as well as a placard with the club name were organised. Each club was allowed between 25 and 33 participants and arrangements were made for those who were to march in the parade to represent the club. On 15th May 1988 the group assembled at the clubhouse and were photographed in full regalia before departing by coach to the assembly point at the Irish Life car park in Abbey Street.

At 12.50 the parade of 120 clubs and 20 marching bands set off from Abbey Street and paraded through the city up O'Connell street and past the review stand at the GPO to be reviewed by the lord mayor of Dublin Carmencita Hederman. The parade continued up O'Connell Street around Parnell Square down to Mountjoy Square, passing close to the old Dublin Board headquarters in Belvedere Place, on down Fitzgibbon Street and into Croke Park. In Croke Park an area had been allocated to each club and this area was cordoned off by club officials armed with crisps, sweets and lemonade for the participants. The club was complimented on their turnout for the parade

The day continued with three exhibition matches Senior Camogie – Dublin v Rest of Ireland, Senior Hurling – Dublin v Rest of Ireland and Senior Football – Dublin v Rest of Ireland. At the end of three very entertaining games the group made their way to the coach and headed home after a very enjoyable day.

To mark the occasion of the millennium, on the clubs part, Tommy Hartnett suggested that a millennium weekend be organised to arrange for as many teams as possible in the club to play a match against a visiting team. Tommy organised the weekend with assistance from Máire McSherry. A total of 17 teams played matches throughout the weekend starting on Saturday morning 2nd July 1988 and finishing on Sunday evening 3rd July 1988. Everybody who took part was presented with either a Millennium Medal or a Millennium Pin and were given a meal after their match.

On Saturday 2nd July we had a dance in the hall which was packed out and a great success. The funds raised from the dance and a raffle held at the dance helped to finance the weekend. One of the highlights of the night was when St Judes U21's and Portarlington Under 21s got on stage and sang together which was the spirit it was hoped that the weekend would generate.

On the evening of Sunday 3rd July two matches were held, the first between the over 35 mentors from the country and the mentors from Dublin. The team from Dublin was managed by Donncha Ó Liatháin while the team from the country was managed by Ernest Kenny. A fine display of all styles of football (if some of the styles could be called football) was on show on the night.

The ladies' match was just as fine a display with Essie O'Gara's boots hanging from the goal cross bar sending a warning to the opposition. A truly memorable evening was had by all who participated in both matches with tales of both often recalled in the club. The results at the end of the day showed that St Judes teams did themselves proud by winning 14 matches, drawing 1 match and losing 2 matches. The result of the over 35 mentors' match is still in dispute with both sides claiming victory. However, in the neutral observer's opinion the result is not in doubt, it was just a great laugh. The details of the teams and the timetable for the weekend was as follows:-

Day	Date	Time	Pitch	Team	Opponent	Official
Sat	2/7	11.30	6	U10F	Dunboyne	J O'Dwyer
Sat	2/7	11.30	4	U11F	Dunboyne	F McSweeney
Sat	2/7	12.30	Cam	U12C	Donard	B Collard
Sat	2/7	1.30	Cam	U13C	Donard	
Sat	2/7	2.30	4	U12H	Templemore	J O'Dwyer
Sat	2/7	2.30	2	U16H	Templemore	T Fitzpatrick
Sat	2/7	4.00	2	U13F	Dunshaughlin	T Bassett
Sat	2/7	5.00	2	U15F	Longford	J McDonnell
Sat	2/7	6.30	2	U21F	Portarlington	D Ó Liatháin
Sun	3/7	11.30	6	U16F	An Caislean	D Lehane
Sun	3/7	11.30	4	U11H	Celbridge	F Carty
Sun	3/7	2.00	2	U14F	Na Fianna	D Lehane
Sun	3/7	2.30	4	U12F	Thomas Davis	J Malone
Sun	3/7	4.00	2	MINOR	Thomas Davis	
Sun	3/7	4.00	7	U15H	Kilmacud	D Feore
Sun	3/7	6.00	2	Jun AF	Longford	
Sun	3/7	7.30	2		Mentors	D Ó Liatháin
					Mentors	E Kenny
Sun	3/7	8.00	Juv	Dublin	Country	

Corn an Earraigh

Colum Grogan

I T WAS only in the last few weeks that I realised it's now eight years on and still going strong. In November 1995 after consolidating our position in Intermediate 1, Peter Lucey and I thought it would be a good move to try and get some challenge fixtures in place before the start of the 1996 campaign. At that time Seán Treacy of the Prison Service, the former Galway All-Star full back and a fellow Portumna man, used to attend an odd training session and give Peter Lucey a hand-out to vary the sessions.

Conal Bonnar the former Tipperary All-Star, and a working colleague of mine, was a selector of the UCD Fitzgibbon team and Humphrey Kelleher of Bank of Ireland (our then incoming Sevens' sponsors) was heavily involved with the Bank of Ireland GAA Club.

All three individuals were contacted to see if there involvement with their respective hurling teams could influence their participation in a four team tournament involving and being hosted by St Judes.

In February 1996 the first Corn an Earraigh took place involving a Bank of Ireland selection, The Prison Service, UCD and of course St Judes with the winners being the students of UCD. Since then other participants were DIT (winners 2000), University of Maynooth and Leixlip GAA Club. St Judes won for the first time last year and retained the trophy by defeating the Dublin under 19 Development Squad in this year's final.

This tournament has become an important fixture in the St Judes senior hurling calendar and has undoubtedly made an important contribution to the development of adult hurling in the Club.

My serenade for you (two).

Growing a Community

Finbarr Murphy

THE 1978 Summer Project kick-started the club. Subsequent Summer Projects brought in mentors and players. These took place in the open, in the full light of day, at the geographical centre of the parish – Orwell Green. They were a public showpiece for the club and an excellent recruiting ground. Perhaps two weeks of showing off in the glorious sunshine of July may appeal to the Northern Psyche, but it certainly gets you noticed and as well, it got us players like Fiachra Feore and Brendan Byrne and mentors like Jimmy Lee, Marie Bell and Bobby Carty.

Orwell Green may also be considered the communal centre of the parish. Beside it you have the Church, the national schools and the shops. It was in the church in September 1978 that the holding of the first meeting of the club was announced. In the schools Jimmy O'Dwyer, Peter Lucey, Kathryn O'Connell, Sinead Curley, Lisa Farragher, Elaine Dromey, Blathnaid Clancy, Alan Dodd, Eamon Treacy, and Seán Breheny have fostered and promoted our national games since 1975. It was in the schools that we registered players for the Summer Project, held our meetings, had our ceilís. We met for matches in the car park at the side of the shops. (It was much quieter in those days). Our fund raising cake sales took place in Brady's butcher's shop and sponsorship from the local shops, still valued today, was of major importance in the early days. Notice of meetings and events were announced in the church and posted up in Brady's shop. Children were appraised of match fixtures in Bishop Galvin school each week.

It was on Orwell Green that we played the mentors of Thomas Davis led by perhaps the greatest friend our club has ever had, Davy Griffin. It was to here that Jimmy Turner brought the first visiting team from Thomas Davis. Here also, we triumphed in Tug-a-War on the scouts field day. Here we had our Fathers and Sons' matches.

Here we did our practice and our training. Here we played our Summer Project and so came into contact with Community Games. To here in autumn 1981 Jimmy O'Dwyer moved from the rocks in Osprey to begin, what Joe McDonnell and Bobby Carty continue to this day (what is probably the most important activity of our club), the non-competitive introduction of children to our Gaelic games.

GREEN BEGINNINGS

In the beginning was a green and the green was the centre of the parish. For me that is where it all began, back in the summer of seventy eight. There was another Greene and he is one of the unsung heroes of Cumann Luth-Chleas Gael Naomh Jude.

Fr. John Greene called to welcome my family to the Parish early in 1978. In November 1977 we had arrived from Cork where, as a vocational school teacher, I had promoted hurling in Clonakilty, (the birthplace of Don Lehane's mother). I expressed my surprise and regret that there was no GAA in the parish. Some time later Father Greene came back to say that things were happening or about to happen on the GAA front and asked me in the meantime to join the Summer Project committee.

At the first meeting of the Summer Project committee I met Ernest Kenny and for the next year bumped into Ernest every week. It is only now that I realise that I was part of the network that he was developing to launch GAA in the Parish. Launch is maybe not the right word since Seamus Durkan and Donnchadh Lehane were already taking teams to compete in Robert Emmets competitions, and Jimmy O'Dwyer (a native of Tipperary) was teaching football in Bishop Galvin, the local parish school. There were wonderful people on the Summer Project committee, most of whom later had children playing for the club and many of whom took an active role in the social and training activities of the club. A few names spring to mind - May Durkan, Marian Connolly, Marie Morgan, Maureen O'Connor, Kay Ingham, Rita Moran, Theresa Connolly. Theresa became the oldest lady to represent the club in Camogie. In later years we were joined by Tommy Mulready, Bernie O'Boyle, Michael O'Boyle and Marie Bell. Among the overall Summer Project co-ordinators were Joe Morrin Jnr. and Gerry Hatch.

Summer Project registration day came and I attended armed with notebook. Jimmy O'Dwyer was already sitting at the desk taking names. He had hardly left when Joe Morrin Snr. arrived. Then Donnchadh Lehane and Charles Moran arrived. Seamus Durkan and May came and registered James for the under 10's and Kieran for the under 8's. Charlie stayed until the end and then began to gather the entry sheets. I objected but luckily enough Ernest came along and assured me that that was alright - Charlie was taking charge.

It was a great success. Jimmy graded players and we selected captains and made out the teams. One little glitch - there was a visitor, Masterson from up the mountains whom Jimmy mixed up with a younger player Masterson-Power from Glendown. He was selected as the last man on one of the teams. At the end of the first day we had a strike. The other teams were about to withdraw. We had to scrap day one and redo the teams.

Joe and Ernest looked after the Under 8s with the help of Gerry Quinn. Oliver Connolly, Jimmy and myself looked after the Under 10s helped by John Gallen, Frank McSweeney, and Des Cullen. Charlie and Donnchadh looked after the Under 12s. Fr John Greene, Eamonn O'Reilly, Cyril Bates and Pat Finn helped out. This year Donnchadh's grandson, Conor, has joined the Green, Pat Finn's grandchild Gavin has graduated from the green to the Under 9 team. At Under 14 we had one match with Seamus O'Connor and Mick Barrett among those who played.

The Under 10 captains were James Durkan, Conor Lehane, Kevin Hogan and Michael Kavanagh. Gerry Quinn with his accordion led the finalists out onto the Field. Father Greene refereed the final. Michael Kavanagh's team beat James Durkan's team. Medals were sponsored by Shea Lynch of Irish Rubies and presented to the winners and runners-up. In later years the medal ceremony was moved to the school hall and the club invited various Dublin and Inter-county stars including Tony Hanahoe, Barney Rock, Tommy Drumm and Dermot Early to present the medals.

In 1979 Charlie added a mens seven-a-side to the fare. Templeogue Wood and Orwell entered teams. It was won by Glendown with the Teachers as runners-up. In 1980 the teachers won and great excitement greeted the meeting of these two sides in 1981. The teachers had recruited an unfit Jim Coghlan as goalkeeper. Jim made an awkward tackle and collided with a forward shooting at the goal. The young man was flattened and a melee broke out. The match was abandoned and the men's sevens petered out.

We had a rule that each team had to match the number of players on the opposing side. A team had a panel of 9 or 10 players but at most 7 could play at any one time. All players had to be substituted in turn. In 1981 James Durkan's team met Niall O'Murchu's team in the Under 12 final. Niall substituted himself in the first quarter and Lenny Fitzpatrick in the second. Seamus arrived just after the start of the third quarter to find that James still had to substitute himself and his second best player. He had words with Donnchadh who finally pointed out that he was chairman of the club and that, as co-ordinator of the GAA for the Summer Project, I was responsible. Seamus appealed to me. I looked at my son. 1 goal and 2 points down with the final quarter approaching, and declared that we had to stick to the rules. James came off and Niall won by a couple of points. James and Niall went on to play on the Intermediate team that won senior status for the club.

Father Greene called a meeting to start a parish GAA club in September 1978. I had committed to forming a parish Bridge Club and unfortunately, it met the same night. A year later Charlie informed me that there was an executive meeting taking place. I said I wasn't a member of the executive. Of course you are and I expect you to be there was the reply. That was how things were done.

People have expressed surprise that we do not remember what we did. It was very much an ad-hoc time. You did what you had to. We had no constitution and no formal structure. I was appointed as the club's co-ordinator to the Summer Project without having attended a meeting. In the latter years of the Summer Project the under 10 and under 12 competitions were sponsored by Leslie Percy.

GREEN RECRUITMENT

Communication is a great problem. In the words of the Chinese proverb 'One SEE is worth a thousand TELLs'. Not everyone reads posters, listens to announcements or notes the message.

At the Summer Project of 1982 a lady and an elderly gentleman approached me. Her son wished to play in the Summer Project but had not known it was on and so had not registered. We found a slot for the young man, Brendan Byrne, who later represented the club in both hurling and football with distinction for many years. Brendan's grandfather Jimmy Lee became a mentor. He was a well-known sight – puffing away at his pipe and became known as 'the Father of the Club'. Charlie Moran gave a very moving public oration at his graveside. Brendan's parents Ann and Dermot also became active members of the club. His siblings Alan and Rachel in their turn became playing members.

Not every encounter was as successful. In 1981 I made the mistake of recruiting a North Corkman – Declan Feore. A year or two later a young man by the name of Bobby Carty asked me a question. I introduced him to Ernest and according to Tommy Hartnett, Ernest presented him with jerseys. Bobby found himself a team manager and executive member before he left the green. I think Tommy exaggerates but it's possible. In 1980 I recruited Tommy Mulready who managed a team and served on the executive up to 1987.

In the early days mentors recruited on the green included Tom Fitzpatrick, Willie Nolan, Michael Ryan, Pat Quigley, Gus Barry, Tommy Hartnett and Seán Ward.

David Bell played in the Summer Project, liked it and joined the Club. He may have done that anyway but we met his mother Marie and she became the first female manager of boys' football in the club. Leslie Percy was recruited in the same way and he and Marie took over as Summer Project co-ordinators. He also sponsored it for a number of years. They handed over to Bernie Gallagher who still manages the link between the club and the Community Games. Joe Morrin continued to run the Under 8 team until he became ill. Ernest and Charlie did their bit until the club withdrew from running this excellent, worthwhile venture.

COMMUNITY GAMES

Tommy Mulready introduced Dan Cash to the Summer Project committee in 1979. Dan had been running athletics in WORK residents association and was now extending his involvement to cover community games for the parish. I didn't really do any more than attend the meetings and report back to Ernest. Donnchadh, Seamus and Charlie first entered a team in 1980. This team beat Round Towers in the Dublin semi-final and lost to Popintree in Croke Park. In 1981 Jim Coghlan took charge of the Community Games gaelic team. From 1982 on the managers of the teams involved were responsible for the entry of their teams in the games. As documented elsewhere we entered Boys and Girls Football, Camogie and Hurling. Our best success was in 1994 when our camogie team managed by Seamus Massey got to the Leinster final.

Our hardest luck was in 1984 when we were beaten by an extended Round Towers team in a penalty shoot-out in the Dublin final. The last shot Dara Murphy dived and deflected. The ball almost stopped and rolled towards the post. Agonisingly it just made the inside. Round Towers with a Parish team were hammered in the Dublin final. Included on this team, which had previously won All-Ireland honours in rugby and soccer, were Kieran Durkan, Fiachra Feore, Declan O'Boyle and Eoghan Ryan.

Marie Bell took over my role as club co-ordinator for the Community Games and was a lot more proactive. Bernie Gallagher extended the role to include managing teams if necessary.

Finally, for myself it has been a pleasure and a privilege to be associated with Cumann Luthcleas Gael Naomh Jude over the past 25 years. I am delighted to have had the opportunity to contribute to this commemorative book.

Summer Project on The Green.

One ꝼine ꝺacenт Dublinꝏan

A TRIBUTE TO FRANK McSWEENEY ON HIS RETIREMENT – Declan Feore

When he was born he gave them all a fright.
Thought he was a spaceman and not a little mite.
The nurse said "Missus, he will never have a fall
They are always lucky when they are born with a Caul".

And he'll be......
Chorus
One fine day-es-cent Dub-a-lin Man
Who'll love his pint but prefer a small wan

"Oh Holy James's" (St) his father did say
Is the only school where McSweeneys will stay
So they packed them off to Jambo for years and years
And when he left it they were all in tears.

Cos they knew he'd be......
Chorus

Now when he grew up to be a fine young man
He left Rialto and joined Monaghan
Over in New York where he earned quite a lot
And also married his Cavan mot

Cos she knew he was.......
Chorus

Well he smokes I'm told a Hamlet Cigar
Though his daughter says "they're worse than the Jar"
But if he's got Havanas or even Piquers
As sure as God you can count them yours.

Cos he's......
Chorus

Now he often plays golf with Seán Conway
Who's well known for leading dacent men astray
And when the game is over they always have one
Seán has "a sweetner" and Frank a small one.

Cos he's......
Chorus

Now that he is retiring from the ESB
Moriarty is planting a fine big tree
Down in the carpark where the cars used to be
Saying "it'll produce as much as Frank you'll see"

Cos he was......
One fine day-es-cent Dub-a-lin Man
Who loved his pint but preferred a small wan.

Adult Football history (1979-2003)

Don Lehane

PART 4 – THE SENIOR 1 YEARS (1996–2003)

1996/1997 SEASON

The season 1997/98 was always going to be a year of consolidation at Senior 1 level for the first time. Team management was again Tommy Bassett, Seamus Durkan and Luke Mooney. St Judes got off to a flyer in the league with seven points from the first four games starting with a draw against Na Fianna on 22nd September 1996 and then three successive wins against Round Towers, Parnells and Garda. These early successes were crucial to our survival in Division 1 as we only won one (Erin's Isle) and drew one (Fingallians) of our remaining eleven matches in the league. St Judes finished up with a total of ten points in fourteenth place and narrowly beat the drop. Parnells and Garda in 15th and 16th place were eventually relegated to Division 2 but it was a nerve wracking end of season with Judes finishing off with six losses and dependant on favours from other teams to stave off relegation. The final ignominy in the season was a seventeen point loss to St Vincents in our final game at home on 7th July 1997. The club had an anxious wait for Parnells to play their last two games, which would decide our fate. In the event Parnells were relegated together with Garda. It was a tremendous relief all round to maintain our Division 1 status and no doubt the team could now push on from here. The league campaign went as follows:

96/09/22	V Na Fianna (9)	Draw	0.14 to 3.05	Home
96/10/06	V Round Towers (13)	Win	1.09 to 2.04	Away
96/10/20	V Parnells (15)	Win	2.09 to 2.06	Home
96/11/03	V Garda (16)	Win	0.16 to 2.08	Away
96/12/15	V Ballyboden SE (2)	Loss	0.10 to 2.14	Away
97/01/26	V St Sylvesters (7)	Loss	0.06 to 3.12	Away
97/03/09	V Kilmacud Crokes (1)	Loss	0.05 to 1.14	Home
97/03/23	V Erins Isle (6)	Win	1.13 to 1.09	Home
97/04/13	V Fingallians (11)	Draw	2.10 to 1.13	Home
97/05/07	V Whitehall CC (12)	Loss	1.09 to 2.10	Away
97/05/11	St Annes (5)	Loss	0.11 to 1.14	Away
97/05/14	Thomas Davis (4)	Loss	2.09 to 2.13	Away

97/05/18	St Brigids (10)	Loss	1.04 to 1.08	Home
97/07/02	Clontarf (8)	Loss	1.07 to 1.14	Away
97/07/07	St Vincents (3)	Loss	0.06 to 3.14	Home

St Judes (14) Played 15 Won 4 Drew 2 Lost 9 Total 10 points Finished 14th

The leading scorer charts are incomplete but the following was the state of play after the bulk of the matches: James Halligan (0-40), Declan O'Boyle (2-11), Kieran Durkan (0-14), John O'Riordan (1-11), Peter Gilsenan (2-6), Enda Sheehy (0-7), Fergal Kilbane (1-3), Enda Crennan (0-4), Jamsie O'Dowd (0-4), Shane Gallen (0-2) and Ken Lenihan (0-1).

In the championship St Judes were beaten by an Anton McCaul and Declan Sheehan inspired Ballymun Kickhams side in the first round in Parnell Park.

1996/97 Junior A JFL 1: Mick O'Brien, Gary Kane, Ernest Kenny, Maura McSherry. The Junior A team maintained JFL 1 status and were beaten in the first round of the championship by Liffey Gaels,

1996/97 Junior B JFL5: Donnchadh Lehane, John Browne, Joe Fallon, Christy Kilcoyne. Our Junior B team finished 4th in their league and were beaten in the third round of the championship.

1996/97 Junior C JFL 6: Charles Moran, Frank Clabby, Paddy Russell. Our Junior C team finished 3rd in their league.

1996/97 Junior D JFL 8: Seán McBride, Neil Doyle. Our Junior D team entered competition for the first time and finished well up third in the Division 8 table.

The U21 team managed by Tony McGinley finished mid table in Division 1 league. They had a great championship run which started with a first round win against St Marys Saggart and was followed up with a one point win against St Vincents in Stillorgan. St Vincents were championship favourites and had won the minor championship three years before with basically the same team. St Judes were eventually beaten by a point in the quarter-final by a Keith Barr managed Erin's Isle side and finished the game with fourteen men after Gavin Russell was sent off.

AOB: Enda Sheehy on Dublin senior football panel, Martin McKivergan played senior hurling for Kerry and Ernest Kenny was picked as a selector on the Dublin Junior football team.

James Halligan had an inspired game against Garda in the league when he scored eleven points. Tommy Bassett stepped down as Senior Football manager in 1997 after a successful period in bringing St Judes from Intermediate to Senior 1 level. It was reported in club minutes that "A delegation sent to locate Lucan Tennis Club with a view to inspecting its all-weather surface were fruitless".

They failed to locate the tennis club but rumour has it they had no trouble finding a comfortable hostelry and they returned fruitless but not pintless. The delegation was instructed to take up membership of the Boy Scouts before they embark on their next fact finding or seek and destroy mission.

Coaching News

All clubs are now putting increased efforts into improving the standard of coaching and St Judes are no different. A number of Dublin clubs have decided that all teams within their club should have a Level 1 coach involved and are gearing their efforts towards this objective. Periodic coaching courses run by St Judes over the years have been very beneficial in raising the standard of Gaelic games coaching in the parish. The first rung on the coaching ladder is the Foundation Level and back in the late 1980's a large group of St Judes mentors/managers were put through their first football coaching course at this level.

The course involved a considerable amount of physical effort on the pitch including fielding, soloing, pickups, point scoring and a number of training drills which were quite obviously aimed at a younger and less physically challenged age group than the participants present for this particular course. It is a shame that the sessions were not put on video as they would have brightened many a dark winter's night in the years ahead.

The initial enthusiasm gradually deteriorated with tiredness into total chaos with footballs being propelled around Tymon in directions completely at variance with the wishes of the kicker. The exercise was eventually abandoned in deference to the local wildlife, which at this stage were exiting Tymon in large numbers via the Wellington Lane exit and heading for the safer environs of Bushy Park.

In later years another group of mentors attended a minor coaching level course at St Vincents GAA Club. This was another very physical training course involving laps and sprint training which was unfortunately a little bit outside the scope of a game but largely unfit contingent of St Judes mentors who left St Vincents in a state of total exhaustion. Very few people had failed to pass these coaching courses since the time of Cúchulainn but a number of very worried participants left St Vincents clubhouse that weekend. They were of course wide open for a desperate trick played on them by Michael Fortune and Pat Brien amongst others, who arranged to send headed letters to a number of participants including Seán McBride, Gus Barry and Paddy Russell indicating they had failed the Foundation Level course. The envelopes were correctly addressed to one of the participants but the internal letter indicating that the participant had failed the

Foundation Level course was addressed to another participant in an apparent mixup of letters and envelopes. The result of the exercise was that each participant knew of one other person who had apparently failed the course but were unaware how they had fared themselves.

It resulted in a couple of very interesting days and nights as mentors tried to discreetly establish if someone else had received their letter indicating pass or failure. At the same time each participant was in the difficult position of deciding if they should inform another participant that they had failed the course. We have no hesitation in naming names here for the first time so that those who suffered psychological damage can exact proper retribution and that closure can be brought to this whole sorry episode. All course participants eventually received their certificates but the damage was done at this stage.

1997/1998 SEASON

Dave Foran took over management of St Judes Senior Football team (SFL1) in the 1997/98 season with Tommy Bassett and Seamus Durkan as mentors. Declan O'Boyle was also heavily involved in team training. Tommy Bassett, Luke Mooney and Seamus Durkan had brought the team from Intermediate level in 1993 to Senior 1 level in 1997 after a couple of great years. Dave Foran (Thomas Davis) was to be the first external manager appointed by St Judes. He was an ex Dublin senior county footballer, who had also spent a period coaching the Wicklow senior football team – a role which would prepare you to overcome any obstacle you encountered in your future life or else confine you to a life in a straight jacket in a padded cell.

St Judes retained their Senior 1 status in the 1997/98 season and finished around mid table in the league. At the end of the season Dave Foran departed to manage his old club Thomas Davis who were having a difficult time in senior football at this point. Dave Foran had informed the players in the dressing room before the St Vincents championship game that he would be leaving the team before the end of the season. On the departure of Dave Foran St Judes still had three league games left and needed to win at least one of them to be sure of staying up. In the event they won two games and drew one against Naomh Mearnog, Round Towers and Ballyboden respectively and finished up mid-table. Kenny Lalor had an inspired game against Naomh Mearnog on their old pitch in Portmarnock and every ball he kicked seemed to go over the bar.

Team management was taken over by Brian Talty, Christy Kilcoyne and Declan O'Boyle for the last two games of the season. Judes then beat Round Towers by nine points to seven and drew with Ballyboden. One of the matches which remains etched in the memory from that season was the tempestuous game against St Annes. It was Paul Walsh's (ex Annes) first game for St Judes and Kenny Lalor of course had also played for St Annes. The match deteriorated into a bit of a battle with a couple of players sent off and one mentor shipping a heavy punch on the line as he tried to bring a bit of order to the proceedings.

SFC 98	Rnd1	v Trinity Gaels	Win	O'Toole Pk
SFC 98	Rnd2 98/06/27	V St Vincents	Draw 1.07 to 1.07	Parnell Park
SFC 98	Rnd2 98/07/04	V St Vincents (R)	Win	Parnell Pk
SFC 98	Qtr/F 98/	V Ballyboden St Endas	Loss 0.09 to 2.14	Parnell Pk

St Judes Intermediate team had a good run in the championship before being knocked out by Ballyboden in the quarter finals. The Junior B and Junior D footballers won their respective Division 5 and Division 8 leagues. The U21 team under Tony McGinley had another tremendous run in the championship. They beat Kevins/Killians in the first round and then went on to a good win against a strong Synge Street side at the VEC grounds. In the third round (quarter-final) they knocked out one of the championship favourites St Sylvesters. They were unfortunately well beaten by a very strong St Brigids side in the semi-final. Their performances in reaching the quarter-finals and semi-finals in successive years augurs well for the future of senior football in St Judes.

AOB: Dublin Senior football panels: Enda Sheehy Enda Crennan, Ciaran Voyles and Ken Lalor. Ciaran Voyles also gained a Blue Star award after a great season and an inspiring couple of games in the senior championship, particularly in the two games against St Vincents. In the first game he outplayed Senan Moylan who was about six feet taller than him when in the vertical position but about five feet smaller when lying horizontally on the ground. In the replay St Vincents moved Eamon Heery over to mark him but after the initial fiery introductions both players decided it might be better to concentrate on the ball for the remainder of the game.

Dublin Junior football panels: Warren Linnie, John O'Riordan. Ernest Kenny was again a mentor on Dublin Junior football panel. On 28th February 1998 the second members' lounge in St Judes was unofficially opened.

Three minor football teams entered in competitions by St Judes for the first time – the only club in Dublin putting out three minor teams in the current season. In March 1998 a request was made to the adult games committee that mirrors be installed in the dressing rooms. It was also noted that three sets of nets were now missing. Maybe we should have considered installing cameras instead of mirrors.

In May 1998 the Club Chairman and Secretary were requested to attend a Dublin Senior Board meeting on Monday 25th May in conjunction with the cancellation of a Senior Football league fixture against Round Towers as a result of damage to a goalpost on Pitch 4. One of the posts was damaged in what were described as "suspicious circumstances".

In November 1998 an unhappy Tony McGinley resigned from management of the U21 team. He would be a big loss as his enthusiasm and energy had been a key factor in good performances from St Judes U21 teams in the last few seasons.

The senior footballers had by all accounts a very enjoyable week-end trip to Waterford in January 1999.

Most of the details from these trips away will have to remain under wraps unfortunately but Liam Keogh and Damien Carroll should be able to fill in some of the details for anyone curious enough to find out.

1998/1999 SEASON

In 1998/1999 the management of St Judes Senior Football Team (SFL1) was taken over by Brian Talty assisted by Christy Kilcoyne and Declan O'Boyle. This was the start of another successful period for St Judes at senior level. Brian Talty was a highly successful and innovative coach who had previously brought senior championship success to Parnell's and St Sylvester's before arriving at St Judes at the end of the 1997/98 season. His football career originated with Tuam Stars and he went on to win an All-Ireland club title with Thomond in 1978. He also won successive Dublin senior championships as captain of Parnells. He played for the Galway senior football team for a total of fourteen years between 1975 and 1989 winning 6 Connaught championships and one All-Ireland runners-up medal against Dublin in 1983. He proved to be a highly popular coach with St Judes players and supporters and went on to bring the team to 2nd position in the Division 1 senior league in his first season before going on to win the league in 2000.

In 1998 Brian was serving a GAA suspension which was a condition he had become regularly acquainted with over the years as his undoubted passion for Gaelic football sometimes exceeded his ability to control it particularly when dealing with the men in black.

St Judes lost just three games in the season against Kilmacud Crokes, St Brigids and our old friends from Sandyford St Olafs.

The following team lined out for the first league game of the 1998/99 season against St Vincents which St Judes won by four points:

Date: 24/01/1999 Competition: Senior Football League Division 1
Result: St Judes (0-14) V St Vincents (2-04) at Tymon North

Kieran Durkan (0-4)	Ken Lalor (0-2,1F)	Peter Gilsenan (0-2)
John O'Keeffe	Tom Prendergast (0-5,2F)	Enda Crennan (0-1)
Mick Fallon		Enda Sheehy
Damien Carroll	Martin McKivergan	Ciaran Voyles
Gavin Russell	Liam Belton	Liam Keogh
	Terence Orr	

Subs: Ciaran McGovern for Damien Carroll.

This was a good first league outing for St Judes who started slowly but were still a point ahead after twenty minutes. A couple of good scores before half time set them up for a much improved second half performance with early points from Kieran Durkan and Tom Prendergast. St Judes conceded a poor goal, which brought Vincents back into the game but they finished strongly to win by four points. Best for St Judes were Kieran Durkan, Tom Prendergast, John O'Keeffe and Enda Sheehy.

St Judes followed up their win against St Vincents with a three point win away against St Sylvesters on a scoreline of 2-08 to 1-08. Judes played well in the first half and led by 2-04 to 0-04 at half time with goals from Enda Crennan and Kieran Durkan. Sylvesters put on a lot of pressure in the second half and got well on top in midfield but Judes withstood the pressure well and finished the game strongly. Best for St Judes were Liam Belton, Damien Carroll, Kieran Durkan (1-0) and Enda Crennan (1-02). Other scorers for St Judes were Tom Prendergast (0-3), Peter Gilsenan (0-1), Kenny Lalor (0-1) and Enda Sheehy (0-1).

St Judes obtained a well earned draw against Na Fianna in their next league game in Tymon on 24th Feb 1999. St Judes were twelve points down at half time (2-07 to 0-1) having played against a very strong wind. St Judes came back very strongly in the second half and went two points up with five minutes to go before eventually having to settle for a draw. Best for St Judes were Enda Sheehy, Liam Belton, Tom Prendergast and Damien Carroll. Scorers for St Judes were Tom Prendergast (0-4,3F), Enda Crennan (0-3), Ken Lalor (1-01), Aidan Lalor (1-0), Damien Carroll (0-1) and Martin McKivergan (0-1).

On 21st March 1999 St Judes recorded a six point win against Round Towers in Clondalkin in a tough, physical encounter. St Judes led by two points at half time (0-06 to 0-04) and upped their game in the second half with good performances from Ciaran McGovern, Ken Lalor (0-5,1F),Tom Prendergast (0-5,3F), and Peter Harlow (1-02). Other scorers for St Judes were Peter Gilsenan (0-1) and Martin McKivergan (0-1).

St Judes lost their first league game with a four point loss against Kilmacud Crokes in Tymon (1-06 to 1-10) on 31st March 1999. Kilmacud were on top for most of the game. Scorers for St Judes were Peter Gilsenan (0-1), Peter Harlow (0-1), Ken Lalor (1-1,1F), Kieran Durkan (0-1), Tom Prendergast (0-2, 1F). They drew the following game against Ballymun Kickhams away with the teams level at half-time (1-04 to 0-7). St Judes should have won the game but the forwards played poorly. Best for St Judes were Liam Belton, Damien Carroll and Ray Kenny. Scorers for St Judes were Enda Crennan (1-03), Tom Prendergast (0-3, 2F), Ken Lalor (0-2). During this period St Judes had their seasonal loss against St Olafs in a tempestuous game in Tymon and also recorded a win against St Annes.

St Judes continued their league campaign with a good seven point win against Clontarf in St Annes Park on a scoreline of 3-11 to 2-07. This was a good all round St Judes performance with all the forwards contributing to the scoreboard. Best for St Judes were Ciaran Voyles, John O'Riordan, Peter Gilsenan (2-01), Mick Fallon (0-1), and Enda Crennan (1-03). Other scorers for St Judes were Conor Lehane (0-3,3F), Tom Prendergast (0-1), Ciaran McGovern (0-1) and Peter Harlow (0-1). Their next game was a home draw against Naomh Mearnog in Tymon on 13th June 1999 on a scoreline of 1-06 to 0-09. Scorers for St Judes were Tom Prendergast (0-4, 2F), Peter Gilsenan (1-0), Liam Keogh (0-1) and Enda Crennan (0-1).

St Judes next game was an eight point defeat against St Brigids in Tymon in a high scoring game (1-13 to 2-18). St Brigids were well on top in midfield for most of the hour and ran out easy winners with the St Judes defence struggling for most of the game particularly in the full-back line, where Liam Keogh, Mick Fallon and Damien Carroll were up against a very fast Brigids full-forward line. Scorers for St Judes were Tom Prendergast ((0-6, 3F), Peter Harlow (0-1), Kieran Durkan (0-2), Enda Crennan (1-03), Ciaran Voyles (0-1). In September 1999 St Judes had a big win away to a poor Whitehall Columcilles on a scoreline of 4-15 to 1-09. Scorers for St Judes were Enda Sheehy (0-2), Ken Lalor (2-2), Aidan Lalor (2-2), Enda Crennan (0-2), Peter Harlow (0-2), Tom Prendergast (0-4, 4F) and Peter Gilsenan (0-1). Great performances from the Lalor brothers Ken and Aidan who scored 2-02 each. Other good performances from Peter Harlow, Dara Murphy, Ciaran McGovern, Mick Fallon and Warren Linnie in goals who has been very consistent in goals.

In October St Judes recorded two good away league wins against Lucan Sarsfields (5-11 o 3-15) and Ballyboden St Endas (3-11 to 0-10) respectively. St Judes are recording some great scores in this league with the Lalor brothers in particular having a great scoring record with good assistance from Enda Crennan and Tom Prendergast. Scorers against Ballyboden were Peter Harlow (1-0), Tom

Prendergast (1-04, 2F), Enda Crennan (1-02), Peter Gilsenan (0-1), Enda Sheehy (0-1), Ken Lalor (0-2), Gavin Russell (0-1).

St Judes finished off their league campaign with a home win against Erins Isle in December on scoreline of 1-12 to 2-07 and St Annes. Scorers in the win against Isles were Tom Prendergast (1-03), Ken Lalor (0-6, 3F), Stephen Cunningham (0-1) and Enda Crennan (0-2).

St Judes finished runners-up in the Senior Football league Division 1 (SFL1) in 1998/99 after a very good season. The team was unbeaten in the league away from home and ran up some impressive scorelines throughout the league. In addition to some good point scoring the team averaged two goals a game over the year. The following were league results for the year:

99/01/24	V St Vincents	Win	0.14 to 2.04	Home
99/02/07	V St Sylvesters	Win	2.08 to 1.08	Away
99/02/24	V Na Fianna	Draw	2.10 to 2.10	Home
99/03/21	V Round Towers	Win	1.14 to 1.08	Away
99/03/31	V Kilmacud Crokes	Loss	1.06 to 1.10	Home
99/04/18	V Ballymun Kickhams	Draw	1.08 to 0.11	Away
99/06/09	V Clontarf	Win	3.11 to 2.07	Away
99/06/13	V Naomh Mearnog	Draw	1.06 to 0.09	Home
99/06	V St Brigids	Loss	1.13 to 2.18	Home
99/09	V Whitehall Colmcille	Win	4.15 to 1.09	Away
99/10/10	V Lucan Sarsfields	Win	5.11 to 3.15	Away
99/10	V Ballyboden St Endas	Win	3.11 to 0.10	Away
99/12/05	Erins Isle	Win	1.12 to 2.07	Home
99/	St Annes	Win		Home
99/	St Olafs	Loss		Home

An injury stricken St Judes side were beaten by St Vincents in the first round of the championship in 1998/99 on a scoreline of 2-13 to 3-11. A number of players including Ciaran McGovern (broken jaw), Enda Sheehy and Paul Cunny (even though he did come on as a sub) were on the injured list and a few more players were not available on the day including Kenny Lalor who was in the US. In the event St Judes could have won the game with a late rally and if the match had continued for another few minutes St Judes would probably have come out on top. Martin McKivergan had an unusually subdued game with his opponent scoring 1.06. Paul Cunny came on as a substitute although injured and played very well. In fairness the whole team performed poorly in the early part of the game but gave a tremendous display in the second half to come close to snatching victory. The following was the starting lineup for St Judes: Terence Orr, John O'Riordan (0-1), Liam Belton, Damien Carroll, Ray Kenny,Martin McKivergan, Ciaran Voyles, Peter Gilsenan, Mick Fallon (0-1), Liam Keogh, Enda Crennan (1-01), Kieran Durkan, Peter Harlow, Tom Prendergast (1-02,1F), Ken Lalor (0-6, 4F). Subsitutes Warren Linnie, Gavin Russell, Dara Murphy, Ciaran McGovern, Anton Doyle, Conor Lehane, Stephen Cunningham, John Doherty (0-2) and Paul Cunny.

The Junior A team under Donnchadh Lehane and Tony Gilleran were runners-up in the league and gained promotion to Intermediate 2 level. They were beaten in the quarter final of the championship by the eventual winners Fingal Ravens. Junior B team finished mid table and were beaten in 3rd round of B championship. Junior C team finished mid-table but the Junior D team failed to complete their match program and were withdrawn before the end of the season. The U21 team had a poor year mainly due to lack of competition as the league was abandoned after only one round of games. At this time Dublin County Board seemed to show a lack of interest in U21 football which can only be to the detriment of Dublin football in the years ahead. The U21 team went out of the championship in the first round after a good performance against a very good St Peregrines team.

AOB: Dublin SF panel: Enda Sheehy, Enda Crennan. Ernest Kenny Dublin Junior football manager/mentor.

- June 1999: Another request was made to the Adult Games committee to put "small mirrors" in the men's dressing rooms. What exactly is going on in those dressing rooms that requires the presence of "small mirrors" is an issue that is taxing the minds of our most eminent members. The committee is anxiously awaiting a further request for a revolving circular bed and mirrors in the ceiling.

- September 1999: No sign of the mirrors for the men's dressing rooms.

- Yet another request to straighten the goal posts on pitch number four which have become a tourist attraction for those who cannot afford a trip to the Leaning Tower of Pisa. There were no complaints from any of the players who proved that they were capable of putting the ball wide regardless of the angle of the perpendicular.

- In the senior football league St Judes were losing by eleven points against Na Fianna on a windy day and came back in the second half to go two points up before eventually having to settle for a draw.

- In the St Judes V St Olafs league game in Tymon "Big John" McGovern was manning his usual umpire position at the "Leaning Tower" end of Pitch number 4 when he got involved in a heated exchange with the Olafs umpire over a disputed score. The Olafs umpire momentarily forgot that he was not in the safe sancture of Sandyford and having lost the verbal exchange on points decided to up the ante to a physical level and threw a right hook at Big John. This was a serious miscalculation on his part considering the circumstances and he was lucky to get out of Tymon with just a large bump on his head. As Big John was winding up for a rib crushing bear hug Ciaran "Aeroplane" McGovern arrived horizontally head first over his shoulder and left the beleagured Olafs umpire on the flat of his back admiring the blue skies over Tymon. Barry McGovern was poised to enter the battle zone but calculated that the the brother/father combo would have completed the seek and destroy mission before he arrived and rather than be left out of the proceedings entirely decided to get another row going on the line.

St Judes fielded three minor football teams for the first time in the club's history in 1998/99. They were the only club in Dublin fielding three minor football teams that year. Players from these squads went on to play a crucial role on St Judes adult football and hurling teams by the 2002/03 seasons even though they were all still U21 at this point and were of course part of the successful U21 squads in 2001/2002. Excluding U16 players playing at minor level, over thirty two players from 1998/99 minor squads went on to play adult football by 2002/2003 while still all at U21 age level. By 2002 around ten of these thirty players had played at senior football level, another ten had played at intermediate level with the rest at junior level. It is probable that a number of additional players from this period will move up from junior to intermediate and senior level as they gain experience. Around eighteen players from the same age groups also went on to play adult hurling by 2002/2003 including eight players who played at senior hurling level for the club and the remainder at junior level at this point. Whilst these numbers include a couple of dual hurlers and footballers it is still a remarkable statistic that around fifty players playing minor in 1998/99 went on to play adult football and hurling for St Judes by 2002. They form a core element of the nine St Judes adult football and hurling squads in 2003.

2000 SEASON

This was another milestone year in the club with St Judes winning Division 1 of the Senior Football League (SFL1) for the first time in the clubs history. The team was managed by Brian Talty with Christy Kilcoyne and Declan O'Boyle as mentors. Charlie Moran took over as mentor from Declan O'Boyle in the later stages of the season. The team went through the league campaign dropping only three points with a draw against Kilmacud Crokes and the only defeat predictably against our old bogey team St Olafs. Whilst only narrowly escaping relegation themselves, St Olafs nevertheless always seem to put up a battle against St Judes. St Judes started off their league campaign with a lucky one point win against St Annes in Tymon on a scoreline of 2-6 to 0-11. The starting team for our first league game of the 2000 season was as follows:

Date: 27/02/2000 Competition: Senior Football League Division 1
Result: St Judes (2-06) V St Annes (0-11) at Tymon

Ken Lalor (1-1)	Enda Sheehy (0-3,1F)	Aidan Lalor (0-1,1F)
Enda Crennan (0-1)	Tom Prendergast	Adrian Connell
Mick Fallon (1-0)		Peter Gilsenan
Gavin Russell	Tom Morley	Peter Harlow
Ciaran McGovern	Liam Belton	Damien Carroll
	Warren Linnie	

Subs: Ray Kenny for Adrian Connell, Stephen Cunningham for Enda Crennan, John Doherty for Enda Sheehy

Tom Morley made his league debut for St Judes in this game despite carrying an injury and looks a talented player who will tighten up our central defence as well as offering a strong threat going forward. St Judes full-back line of Damien Carroll, Liam Belton and Ciaran McGovern played very well. Peter Gilsenan played well in midfield and up front the Lalor brothers were busy as usual. St Judes drew their next league game against Whitehall Colmcilles in Tymon after a lacklustre performance. Conor Conneely started this game at right-half forward and scored two good points. He is a hard-running player who is keen to get on the ball at all times but needs to release the ball a bit quicker into the St Judes full-forward line in particular. Scorers for St Judes were Tom Prendergast (0-2,2F), Enda Crennan (0-1), Ken Lalor (0-4,1F), Aidan Lalor (0-1), Conor Conneely (0-2), Ray Kenny (0-1).

On the 26th March 2000 St Judes had their seasonal defeat against St Olafs with a five point home loss after a poor performance particularly up front. Scorers for St Judes were Adrian Connell (0-2), Enda Crennan (0-2), Aidan Lalor (0-1), Kieran Durkan (0-1), Ken Lalor (0-1), Mick Fallon (0-1). St Judes found the going difficult at midfield and the half-forward line were not doing sufficient work to help them out. In defence Tom Morley had another good game and is settling in well. On 16th April 2000 St Judes recorded a good five point win away against St Marys Saggart. St Judes went into a four point lead after fifteen minutes (0-6 to 0-2) but played poorly for the remainder of the first half and went in at the interval two points adrift (0-6 to 0-8). St Judes were playing into the breeze in the second half but improved their performance considerably to run out comfortable winners against a St Marys side who are always difficult to beat at home. Best for St Judes were Tom Morley, Enda Crennan, Ken Lalor, Paul Cunny, Liam Belton and Conor Conneely. Scorers for St Judes were Ken Lalor (0-8, 5F), Kieran Durkan (0-2), Enda Crennan (0-3), Peter Gilsenan (0-1), Tom Prendergast (0-1) and Aidan Lalor (0-1).

On 26th April St Judes recorded a very good away draw against Kilmacud Crokes on a scoreline of 1-07 each. Enda Sheehy and Ciaran Voyles were absent from an otherwise full strength St Judes team. Defender Ray Kenny filled an unusual role in the full-forward line with limited success but it was not a position he had much experience in. Judes overall were the more aggressive side and fully deserved the draw in a game dominated by defences. Kilmacud got an early goal by Mick O'Keeffe but St Judes settled into the game with two points apiece from Peter Harlow and Ken Lalor (frees). The Judes defence was well marshalled by Liam Belton and Tom Morley. Conor Conneely covered a lot of ground at midfield where honours were probably even. Up front Enda Crennan was best in a hard working forward line and scored a good goal to finish off the Judes scoring. In defence Paul Cunny played very well as indeed did all the defenders.

On 28th May St Judes came away from Portmarnock with a three point win against Naomh Mearnog. St Judes started brightly particularly up front. They were six points up at half time (1-09 to 1-03) with first half scores from Peter Harlow (1-01), Enda Sheehy (0-03), Enda Crennan (0-3) and Aidan Lalor (0-2) - all scored from play. Naomh Mearnog came back strongly in the second half but five additional points from Aidan Lalor (three frees) and a point from Ken Lalor was sufficient for a St Judes win.

In June 2000 St Judes recorded two home wins against Round Towers (0-13 to 0-7) and Ballymun Kickhams (2-13 to 2-08) respectively. Gerry O'Reilly played at full-back in both games instead of Liam Belton. In the game against Round Towers Conor Conneely and Mick Fallon played well at midfield and Enda Crennan and Peter Gilsenan were best of a lively St Judes forward line. Scores for St Judes against Round Towers were Peter Harlow (0-01), Conor Conneely (0-3), Enda Crennan (0-04,2F), Peter Gilsenan (0-02), Aidan Lalor (0-02,2F), Mick Fallon (0-01). In the game against Ballymun St Judes conceded an early goal but came back to lead at half time by five points (1-07 to 1-02) with Enda Crennan contributing 1-02. The second half was relatively even with each side scoring 1-06 but St Judes always looked likely winners. Scorers for St Judes were Ken Lalor (0-6,4F), Enda Crennan (1-03), Kieran Durkan (1-02), Peter Gilsenan (0-01) and Conor Conneely (0-01).

In July St Judes beat Na Fianna at Moibhi Road by ten points (1-16 to 0-09) with Kenny Lalor dominating the scoring with an impressive 1-07 of which 1-05 was from play. Other scorers for St Judes were Enda Crennan (0-03), Tom Prendergast (0-02), Peter Harlow (0-01), Conor Conneely (0-01), Seán Breheny (0-01) and Tom Morley (0-01). Na Fianna did not put up much resistance but it was a good Judes performance. Seán Breheny and John Waldron made their league debuts as substitutes for St Judes.

On 16th August St Judes recorded a facile 4-19 to 1-07 home win against a demoralised St Sylvesters side. Scorers for St Judes were Ken Lalor (1-03), Kieran Durkan (0-04), Enda Crennan (0-03), Tom Prendergast (0-03,3F), Peter Harlow (0-03), Liam Keogh (0-02), Ciaran Voyles (0-01), Enda Sheehy (1-00), Adrian O'Connell (1-00), Peter Gilsenan (1-00). Good performances all round from St Judes with all the forward line getting in on the scores. On 27th August St Judes beat Lucan Sarsfields at home by seven points on a 2-12 to 2-05 scoreline. Scorers for St Judes were Tom Prendergast (1-05,2F), Ken Lalor (1-01), Kieran Durkan (0-03), Enda Sheehy (0-02) and Ray Kenny (0-01).

On 10th September St Judes decisively beat St Brigids at Russell Park in a crucial game of the 2000 league campaign on a scoreline of 3-12 to 1-08. This was a key top of the table fixture for both sides and a win for either team would set them up as favourites for the 2000 Senior Division 1 title. In the event St Judes stormed through the game in one of their best performances of the season and eventually ran out ten points winners on a scoreline of 3-12 to 1-08. The team was as follows: Terence Orr, Paul Cunny, Gerry O'Reilly, Damien Carroll, Ciaran Voyles, Tom Morley, Stephen Cunningham (0-01), Conor Conneely, Enda Sheehy (0-02), Enda Crennan (0-01), Kieran Durkan, Peter Harlow (2-01), Tom Prendergast (0-03), Peter Gilsenan (1-00), Ken Lalor (0-04). Good performances all round the field but particularly Terry Orr, Stephen Cunningham, Tom Morley, Peter Harlow and Tom Prendergast.

On the 16th September St Judes recorded a tense one point away win against Ballyboden. St Judes were well on top in the first half and led by five points at half time (1-03 to 0-01) with the Judes defence of Orr, Cunny, Belton, Cunningham, Voyles, Morley and O'Reilly completely dominant. Ballyboden came back in the second half with a couple of points and a goal which brought them right back into the game but a Conor Conneely point saw Judes come away with a with an important win. Scorers for St Judes were Enda Crennan (0-04), Tom Prendergast (1-00), Peter Gilsenan (0-01), Peter Harlow (0-01) and Conor Conneely (0-01).

The final games of the 2000 league campaign were played in October with an away game against Erins Isle and the final home game against Trinity Gaels. St Judes beat Erins Isle away on a 2-09 to 0-05 scoreline with the kind of dominant performance, which we have come to expect from the side at this stage.

Scorers for St Judes were Kieran Durkan (1-02), Gerry O'Reilly (1-00), Enda Sheehy (0-02), Ken Lalor (0-02,1F), Stephen Cunningham (0-01), Tom Prendergast (0-01), Enda Crennan (0-01). On the 27th October 2000 St Judes played their final league game of the campaign against Trinity Gaels in Tymon and won by five points on a scoreline of 1-17 to 1-12. The following team lined out for St Judes: Terry Orr, Paul Cunny, Gerry O'Reilly, Ciaran McGovern, Ciaran Voyles, Tom Morley, Stephen Cunningham, Mick Fallon, Conor Conneely, Enda Crennan (1-08,3F), Kieran Durkan (0-01), Peter Harlow (0-03), Peter Gilsenan (0-01), Enda Sheehy (0-01), Tom Prendergast (0-02). Enda Crennan had an outstanding game at half forwarding scoring a goal and five points from play plus three pointed frees. He got good support from Peter Harlow, Tom Prendergast and Kieran Durkan. St Judes defence was on top for most of the game and only a late Trinity Gaels goal put an air of respectability on the scoreline.

When St Judes had finished their league campaign in October they had to await the results of the remaining two fixtures of Kilmacud Crokes before knowing whether they had won the league. Kilmacud Crokes needed to win their last two fixtures to force a playoff with St Judes for the Division 1 title. As it transpired Kilmacud Crokes were beaten by Naomh Mearnog in the first of those two games at Portmarnock and St Judes won the Division 1 title for the first time in their history and sparked great celebrations in Templeogue. The game did not mean much to Naomh Mearnog as they were out of contention in the league. Brian Talty, Charles Moran, Johnny O'Gara and Juno the dog attended the Naomh Mearnog V Kilmacud Crokes game and by all accounts confused the local Portmarnock supporters with their vocal encouragement of the local side – Brian Talty on one occasion shouting as only he could at a bemused Naomh Mearnog defender to get back and pick up his man !. Juno O'Gara also played a role with an aggressive diagonal run across the pitch in an attempt to intimidate the dangerous Crokes corner forward Mick O'Keeffe. At the final whistle the loudest cheer of the night came from Templeogue branch of the Naomh Mearnog Supporters Club.

The 2000 Division 1 league went as follows with final league positions in brackets:

00/02//27	V St Annes (11)	Win	2.06 to 0.11	Home
00/03/12	V Whitehall CC (16)	Draw	0.11 to 1.08	Home
00/03/26	V St Olafs (14)	Loss	0.08 to 1.12	Home
00/04/16	V St Marys (12)	Win	0.16 to 0.11	Away
00/04/26	V Kilmacud Crokes (3)	Draw	1.07 to 1.07	Away
00/05/28	V Naomh Mearnog (5)	Win	1.15 to 1.12	Away

00/06/16	V Round Towers (15)	Win	0.13 to 0.07	Home
00/06/18	V Ballymun Kickhams(4)	Win	2.13 to 2.08	Home
00/07/15	V Na Fianna (10)	Win	1.16 to 0.09	Away
00/08/16	V St Sylvesters (6)	Win	4.19 to 1.07	Home
00/08/27	V Lucan Sarsfields (8)	Win	2.12 to 2.05	Home
00/09/10	V St Brigids (2)	Win	3.12 to 1.08	Away
00/09/16	V Ballyboden St Endas (7)	Win	1.07 to 1.06	Home
00/10/15	V Erins Isle (9)	Win	2.09 to 0.05	Away
00/10/27	V Trinity Gaels (13)	Win	1.17 to 1.12	Home

St Judes (1) Played 15 Won 12 Drew 2 Lost 1 Total Points: 26 Winners Division 1 SFL1

St Judes won the Senior Division 1 league with St Brigids runners-up and Kilmacud Crokes third. The following players played Senior league football for St Judes in the 2000 season: Terence Orr, Warren Linnie, Damien Carroll, Liam Belton, Gavin Russell, Peter Harlow, Tom Morley, Ciaran McGovern, Peter Gilsenan, Stephen Cunningham, Paul Cunny, Mick Fallon, Conor Conneely, Tom Prendergast, Enda Crennan, Aidan Lalor, Ray Kenny, Kenny Lalor, Kieran Durkan, Adrian Connell, Conor Lehane, Gerry O'Reilly, Enda Sheehy, Ciaran Voyles, Antoin Doyle, Seán Breheny, John Waldron, John O'Riordan, Liam Keogh, Andrew Glover, Michael Lyons, David Reynolds, Eoin O'Neill, Gerry Quinn. This was undoubtedly the strongest adult football squad in the twenty-five year history of St Judes. Two years later around thirteen of these players were no longer playing at senior level for St Judes.

St Judes had a great run in the championship before being knocked out by Kilmacud Crokes in the semi-final. The first round was a comprehensive win over a poor Garda side with Judes running out twelve point winners with Enda Crennan and Kenny Lalor scoring seven points between them and Enda Sheehy chipping in with a good goal. The second round match against St Sylvesters resulted in another twelve point victory which was a major surprise all round. Kenny Lalor and Enda Crennan again dominated the scoring charts with nine points between them against the side managed by Brian Talty prior to his arrival at St Judes. Peter Gilsenan scored a goal and a point, Kieran Durkan also got a goal but this was very much an all round team performance with the Judes defence restricting Sylvesters to seven points.

The quarter final of the championship against St Vincents was an altogether tighter affair. St Judes led by five points at the interval but St Vincents came back strongly in the second half. St Judes always looked the likely winners however and ran out three point winners with Kieran Durkan top scorer on five points. The match ended with some heated discussions after the final whistle. Words and a football were exchanged between a couple of opposing players and within a few seconds it had developed into a potentially nasty scene with a number of players and mentors from both sides involved. However common sense soon prevailed and order was restored.

St Judes were beaten in the county semi-final against Kilmacud Crokes by three points after a poor enough encounter. St Judes defence of Terry Orr, Paul Cunny, Liam Belton, Ciaran McGovern, Ciaran Voyles, Tom Morley and Stephen Cunningham played well behind a midfield of Enda Sheehy and Gerry O'Reilly which struggled at times. However it was up front that St Judes really lost the game. Enda Crennan had an outstanding game down the right and scored a goal and three points, but the rest of the forward line of Conor Conneely, Kieran Durkan, Peter Harlow, Peter Gilsenan and Kenny Lalor failed to raise a flag of any description for an hour which was unfortunate as this really was probably one of the strongest championship sides that St Judes ever put on the pitch and certainly had the capability to bring off the league/championship double. Nevertheless is was the most successful year that St Judes had at senior level and great credit was due to a very committed group of players and mentors. Eight of the above side went on to get Blue Star nominations that year with Enda Crennan, Paul Cunny and Tom Morley getting deserved Blue Star awards.

SFC Rnd 1 2000/05/13	V Garda	Win 1.13 to 0.04	O'Toole Pk.
SFC Rnd 2 2000/	V St Sylvesters	Win 2.13 to 0.07	Parnell Pk
SFC Qtr/F 2000/	V St Vincents	Win 0.14 to 0.11	Parnell Pk
SFC Semi/F2000/10/01	V Kilmacud Crokes	Loss 1.05 to 1.08	Parnell Pk

The Intermediate team won the Joy Cup with some great results. They finished in the top four of the league and were knocked out of the championship in the second round. The Junior A team finished mid-table in the league and got to the quarter final of the championship, where they were beaten by a point by Kilmacud Crokes after two draws. The U21 footballers were also beaten in the quarter final of the championship by Kilmacud Crokes after earlier wins against St Olafs in Silverpark and a Keith Barr managed Erins Isle in O'Toole Park.

AOB: Dublin SF: Enda Sheehy, Enda Crennan. Dublin JF: Stephen Cunningham, Aidan Lalor. Dublin Blue Stars: Enda Crennan, Tom Morley and Paul Cunny gained Dublin Blue Stars awards in a year when Judes received eight Blue Star nominations in total, namely the above three winners plus Terence Orr, Ciaran McGovern, Enda Sheehy, Conor Conneely and Kieran Durkan.

Super Saints

Jude's celebrate league success with solid victory over Wicklow club Emmets

Niall
SCULLY

ST JUDE'S 1-17
BRAY EMMETS 0-14

THE new Dublin League champions were presented with their trophy in the rain-fall of the Iveagh Grounds last night.

And after the presentation, the Templeogue team would have been forgiven for taking the night off, or at least taking it easy in their Evening Herald Floodlit Cup assignment.

But not a bit of it. The game was not a minute old when Adrian Connell thumped the ball to the back of the Bray net. And the subsequent mood of the Tymon Terriers suggested that they'd like to add more silverware to that historic first League trophy.

Nothing less is demanded by the management team, Brian Talty, Charles Moran and Christy Kilcoyne, who saw their boys progress to the last eight of the competition.

Jude's have only been seven years in Senior Football, and three seasons in the first division. Their coach, Brian Talty, lives every moment of every match.

He came out with the quip of the night when

☐ CLOSE CALL: John O'Riordan of St Jude's retains possession from Bray Emmet's Daragh O'Hannaidh in the Evening Herald Floodlit Cup at the Iveagh Grounds.

Evening Herald, THURSDAY, NOVEMBER 16, 2000

still on a high

HEY, JUDE'S PROVE THEY'RE A SMASH HIT!

☐ **IN A LEAGUE OF THEIR OWN:** Acting Dublin chairman Terry Roche presents the Evening Herald Dublin Senior Football League to St Judes captain Ciaran McGovern before last night's Floodlit Cup clash at the Iveagh Grounds *Pic: Ray Cullen*

he felt an Emmets player was climbing all over one of his men. "Hey Jim (Turner), why don't you give him a saddle."

On the opposite sideline to Talts was Sean Doherty, the former Dublin defender who is now part of the Bray management team.

Bray are a young side that promise much, and, until the last chapter, they were in contention all through.

This season they reached the semi-final of the Wicklow Championship, and in free-taker, Conor Flannery, they have the master-craftsman.

WONDERFUL

Flannery sent over some wonderful frees, and three two-pointers from him ensured that Bray only trailed by a point at half-time, 1-6 to 0-8.

Jude's introduced Roscommon's Conor Connelly on the restart, and what a splendid footballer he is.

His impact was immediate as the Saints attacked the clubhouse end goal.

They began to move with more purpose and

EVENING HERALD FLOODLIT CUP

they scored three points on the bounce from an Enda Crennan free and two points from Connell.

Ciaran Voyles then added another Jude's point before Crennan notched three scores in succession, the second of which was the best of the evening.

The accomplished centre half-back, John O'Riordan, won possession and struck a lovely pass to Crennan, wide on the right, from where he found the target in admirable style.

Tom Prendergast's free extended the Jude's advantage even more, but Bray continued to show spirit to respond with three late scores from Oisin O Hannaidh, Flannery and John O'Keefe.

"I think the fitness caught us in the end, but we enjoyed the Floodlight experience," summed up Bray's Liam McGraynor.

Jude's, following a marvellous campaign in

which they also reached the semi-final of the Championship, can now put the feet up for a well-deserved rest.

That's if Talts lets them of course.

FLOODLIT CUP SCOREBOARD

SCORERS — St Jude's: A Connell 1-3, E Crennan 0-6 (2f), T Prendergast 0-4 (1f), C Durkin 0-2, C Voyles, P Harlow 0-1 each. **Bray Emmets:** C Flannery 0-11 (5f), J O'Keefe 0-2, O O Hannaidh 0- 1.

ST JUDE'S — T Orr; P Cunny, G O'Reilly, D Carroll; C Voyles, J O'Riordan, S Cunningham; T Morley, M Folion; E Crennan, C Durkin, A Connell; P Harlow, R Kenny, T Prendergast. **Subs:** C Connelly for Kenny; A Glover for Harlow; A Doyle for O'Reilly (inj).

BRAY EMMETS — P O'Keefe; L Connelly, T Denvir, R O'Brien; K Lamb, D Gaskin, L McGraynor; D O Hannaidh, B O'Keefe; R Lyng, F Devitt, J O'Keefe; O O Hannaidh, C Flannery, P Moynihan. **Subs:** S Broderick for Moynihan; G Ebbs for Gaskin; M Woulahan for Devitt.

Refs: T Clarke (Lucan Sarsfields); J Turner (Thomas Davis).

2001 SEASON

St Judes finished eighth in Senior Football League Division 1 after a less than inspiring season. The team was managed again by Brian Talty, Christy Kilcoyne and Charles Moran. There were a lot of injuries during the year of which the most serious was a cruciate injury to Tom Morley against Craobh Chiarain. Tom Morley had settled in well to the team and was an inspiring figure at centre-back at this stage so his injury had a serious effect on team morale and performance. As events transpired he never played for St Judes again and when he recovered from injury he had already moved back down to Mayo. Paul Cunny, who was in the army, departed for a four month stint in East Timor after the Erins Isle league game and Liam Belton also picked up a long term injury. Kenny and Aidan Lalor had departed to join the Johnny Lalor managed St James Gaels at the end of the previous season and their departure had taken a lot of the sting out of the St Judes full forward line. A couple of the younger club players, including Michael Lyons, Seán Breheny, Andrew Glover, Eoghan O'Neill, Brendan McManamon and John Waldron had made their way on to the senior panel but overall St Judes never really got out a settled side and with the early season losses the league was already probably out of reach by mid May. Although St Judes finished up in mid-table there was a point at the latter end of 2001 where they had to beat Trinity Gaels to be sure of not getting dragged into the relegation battle.

St Judes started their 2001 league campaign on the 1st April 2001 with a two point away loss against St Sylvesters on a 1-06 to 1-08 scoreline. The starting team for the first league game of the season was: Terence Orr, Declan Loye, Liam Belton, Ciaran McGovern, Ciaran Voyles, Tom Morley, Stephen Cunningham, Mick Fallon, Gerry O'Reilly, Enda Crennan (1-04,1F), Kieran Durkan, Adrian O'Connell, Tom Prendergast (0-02,1F), Peter Gilsenan, Peter Harlow; Subs: Fergal O'Reilly for O'Connell, Michael Lyons for Harlow. Over the following month St Judes lost two further league games with home losses against Kilmacud Crokes (0-06 to 0-11) and St Brigids (0-08 to 2-18). Three losses from the first three league games of the season effectively finished off any expectations that St Judes would retain their Devision 1 title. The early season losses were surprising in that St Judes still had the bulk of their 2000 squad with the exception of Paul Cunny (army service), Conor Conneely, Enda Sheehy (injured) plus the Lalor brothers. They went on to win their next two games against Erins Isles and Craobh Chiarain but the loss of Tom Morley with a cruciate injury in the Craobh Chiarain game was a big blow to the team. From here until the end of the season the form of St Judes was erratic with a win usually followed by a loss. We did however manage to record a good league win against St Olafs which has been fairly elusive over the years – St Olafs were eventually relegated to Division 2 with Craobh

Chiarain. Over the season our wins against Erins Isle, Craobh Chiarain, Na Fianna, Ballymun Kickhams, St Annes, St Olafs, Trinity Gaels plus a draw against Naomh Mearnog were balanced by seven losses against St Sylvesters, Kilmacud Crokes, St Brigids, Lucan Sarsfields, St Marys, Thomas Davis and Ballyboden St Endas.

The league results were as follows with league finishing positions in brackets:

01/04/01	V St Sylvesters (4)	Loss 1.06 to 1.08	Away
01/04/	V Kilmacud Crokes (13)	Loss 0.06 to 0.11	Home
01/05/06	V St Brigids (9)	Loss 0.08 to 2.18	Home
01/05/16	V Erins Isle (11)	Win 0.11 to 0.05	Home
01/05/30	V Craobh Chiarain (15)	Win 1.14 to 0.06	Away
01/06	V Lucan Sarsfields (2)	Loss 0.07 to 1.12	Away
01/07/02	V Na Fianna (14)	Win 0.14 to 0.12	Home
01/10/21	V St Marys (7)	Loss 1.06 to 1.07	
01/11/04	V B'mun Kickhams(10)	Win 1.09 to 0.06	Home
01/11/18	V Thomas Davis (1)	Loss 0.09 to 3.10	Away
SFL1/2001	V Ballyboden SE (3)	Loss	
SFL1/2001	V St Annes (5)	Win	
SFL1/2001	V St Olafs (16)	Win Hurrah !	
SFL1/2001	V Trinity Gaels (12)	Win	
SFL1/2001	V Naomh Mearnog (6)	Draw	

St Judes (8) Played 15 Won 7 Drew 1 Lost 7 Total 15 points 8th Position

St Judes were beaten in the quarter final of the championship by St Brigids after a replay. They had a twelve point win against Garristown in the first round at Swords with Enda Crennan scoring ten of the nineteen points and Kieran Durkan scoring five points and Adrian O'Connell (0.02) and Enda Sheehy (0.02) completing the scoring. The quarter final against St Brigids ended in a draw with St Judes performing well in a game which they should have won. They were leading going into the last five minutes but a poorly conceded St Brigids goal left them two points adrift with time running out. To their credit they fought back well and late points from Enda Crennan and Enda Sheehy earned them a well deserved draw.

In the replay St Judes never really got going particularly up front where they were again too reliant on Enda Crennan to get the scores with five of their nine points. The departure of the Lalor brothers from the full-forward line at the end of lthe previous season was really having a serious effect on St Judes scoring potential up front at this point. On the other hand Briody the blond corner forward from St Brigids led the Judes corner backs a merry dance and finished up with three points from play. St Brigids ran out comfortable five point winners winners against the following St Judes side: Terry Orr, Declan Loye, Gerry O'Reilly, Ciaran McGovern, Ciaran Voyles, Paraic Ryan, Stephen Cunningham, Conor Conneely, Fergus O'Reilly, Enda Sheehy, Kieran Durkan (sub Seán Breheny), Peter Harlow (sub Brendan McManamon), Enda Crennan, Peter Gilsenan (sub Bill O'Toole), Michael Lyons.

SFC Rnd 1 2001/04/27	V Garristown	Won 0.19 to 1.04	Swords
SFC Qtr/F 2001/08/19	V St Brigids	Draw 1.11 to 2.08	Parnell Pk
SFC Qtr/F 2001/09/07	V St Brigids	Loss 0.09 to 0.14	Parnell Pk

St Judes won Evening Herald Floodlit Cup, beating Kilmacud Crokes in the final. They beat Bray Emmets in the first game on 15th November 2000 on a scoreline of 1.17 to 0.14 at the Iveagh Grounds on the night St Judes were presented with the Senior Division 1 league trophy. They went on to beat Garda and Thomas Davis in subsequent games before beating Kilmacud Crokes in a very exciting final. This was probably the best team performance from St Judes senior team in 2001.

The Intermediate footballers won the Loving Cup, came third in the league and were beaten in the second round of the championship after beating Scoil Ui Chonaill in the first round on a scoreline of 1-16 to 1-04. They were in contention for promotion right through the season but a crucial top of the table loss effectively finished their promotion hopes in a league where a couple of teams dominated and any loss was going to have a serious effect on promotion prospects. The situation was not helped when the senior footballers were fixed to play at the same time as the Intermediate footballers and in retrospect these fixtures should not have been allowed to clash as it meant that there were even problems with the allocation of substitutes to both teams. The uneasy relationship between senior and intermediate team management did not help to iron out difficulties that arose as the season progressed.

The following St Judes team lined out in the Intermediate championship game against Scoil Ui Chonaill: Ian Bassett, Kevin Hayes, Declan Clabby, Gerry Quinn, Eoghan O'Neill, John O'Riordan, Antoin Doyle, Tom Quinn, Gareth Roche, Brendan McManamon, Declan Kelly, Michael Lyons, Seán Breheny, Dara Murphy, John Waldron Subs: Jeff Kane for Waldron, Andrew Glover for Lyons, Declan Molloy for Murphy.

The Junior A footballers won the Murphy Cup, came second in the league and reached the quarter final of the championship. The Junior C team finished second in the League and were beaten in the quarter-finals of the championship. They had a five man management team of Mick O'Brien, Paddy Keogh, Neil Doyle, John Foley and Joe McDonnell.

The Under 21 footballers were beaten by St Marks in the 2001 Under 21 Division 1 South league final on 23rd March 2002. In the U21 championship St Judes beat Naomh Mearnog in the first round. They were beaten by eventual county champions UCD in the quarter final by three points in Tymon after a tremendous performance. St Judes were really the only team to put up a real battle against UCD in the 2001 Under 21 championship. The game was up for grabs until the closing minutes when St Judes missed a couple of close in frees and UCD broke away to get a crucial point leaving three points between the sides. The Judes U21 B team beat St Finnians (Newcastle) and Good Counsel in the first two rounds of the B championship before bowing out to eventual B championship winners Parnells in the quarter-finals. A number of teams competing in the Under 21B championship should really be competing in the A championship but the presence of UCD seems to have discouraged some of the faint hearted from going into the A championship thus causing serious difficulties for genuine B championship contenders.

AOB: County representatives: Enda Sheehy (Dublin), Conor Conneely (Roscommon), Gerry O'Reilly (Armagh), Fergus O'Reilly (Cavan). Dublin Blue Stars: Enda Crennan and Conor Conneely gained Blue Stars awards and St Judes had five nominations (Terence Orr, Gerry O'Reilly, Ciaran Voyles plus two winners). Ernest Kenny was a selector on Dublin Junior football team.

The March 2000 adult games committee reported that "Ernest Kenny was missing". It was rumoured that he was last seen in the Garristown area of North County Dublin bordering Meath and was attempting to smuggle a number of Meath players across the border to bolster the Dublin Junior Football team.

Ciaran McGovern silenced Brian Talty with his poetic response to a half-time tongue lashing from the Galway man for an unusually subdued first half performance in a league game on an ideal day for football: "Long flowing locks, a beautiful day, poetry in motion" was Ciaran's artistic impression of his first half performance.

Peter Harlow disturbed a hornet's nest in a turbulent game against St Marys when he "got involved" with a spectator who had encroached on the pitch not realising that a number of the man's sons were playing in the game. This resulted in one of the more entertaining trivial pursuits of the year as the whole family attempted to catch up with the elusive Harlow who had decided that discretion was the better part of valour and had promptly legged it towards the gap in pitch number 4.

2002 SEASON

The 2002 season was always going to be a difficult season for St Judes at senior level. Team management was Charles Moran and Seamus Durkan with coaching input by Kieran Durkan and Ciaran McGovern. Brian Talty had left to go back to Parnells before the start of the season which was extremely disappointing to all those who had football at heart in St Judes. Relationships between the senior and intermediate management teams had deteriorated somewhat during the preceding season and this of course made it extremely difficult to run teams without full co-operation between the two squads. These difficulties were instrumental in the decision of Brian Talty to move back to Parnells. This it should be said is not an unusual occurrence between first and second teams in clubs as they both strive for success. St Judes seniors were coming off the back of a great season in 2000 but had hit a serious run of injuries which depleted their squad and made it difficult to field teams for some games in 2001. On the other hand the Intermediate team were in serious contention for promotion to Intermediate Division 1 in the 2001 season. Matters were not helped when crucial senior and top-of-the table intermediate games were scheduled to take place at the same time. There were no winners in this situation – the senior team finished up mid-table in the league and the Intermediate team missed out on promotion by one place when finishing third in the league. In retrospect the problems should have been resolved at a much earlier stage of the 2001 season. In addition it goes without saying that team managements in co-operation should decide which squad a player belongs to and that all players should aspire to and be encouraged to play at the highest level within a club and should treat this as an honour. Likewise players playing at the borders of senior level or nearing the end of their senior careers should, where eligible, be willing and encouraged to play at lower levels within the club.

The departure of Brian Talty before the start of the 2002 season was not planned and came as a surprise and a shock to most people in St Judes. He had made a tremendous contribution in the relatively short period he was at St Judes with the Division 1 senior league title in 2000, semi-final of the championship in 2000 and the Floodlit Cup also in 2000. He was without doubt an outstanding and innovative coach and trainer who had the respect of the senior players in St Judes and was going to be a hard act to follow. In addition a number of senior players were no longer available for the 2002 season due primarily to injuries or having departed the club and it was very much a case of rebuilding a team around the remainder of the senior squad and the Under 21 side. The following was the core of a much changed panel of players who played senior football for the club in 2002: Terence Orr, Gerry Quinn, Damien Carroll, Ciaran McGovern, Ciaran

Voyles, Stephen Cunningham, Seán Breheny, Peter Gilsenan, Enda Crennan, Stephen Earley, Declan Loye, Damien Rafferty, Michael Lyons, Kieran Durkan, Peter Harlow, John Waldron, Brendan McManamon, Andrew Glover, Conor Conneely, Enda Sheehy, Paul Copeland, Damien Keogh, Gerry O'Reilly (part season), Joey Donnelly, Mick Fallon, David Reynolds and Eamonn Murray.

The team finished twelfth in Senior Football League Division 1 and maintained Senior 1 status which was a great achievement in the circumstances. A relatively young St Judes side struggled for most of the year with wins against St Annes, Lucan Sarsfields, Raheny, St Sylvesters and Na Fianna. With three games to play St Judes had nine points and were very much in contention for a bottom four relegation play-off position. However a draw against Naomh Mearnog and great wins against St Sylvesters and Raheny meant St Judes finished on fourteen points and out of the danger area. The 2002 Senior Football League Division 1 (SFL1) was won by Kilmacud Crokes who beat Ballyboden St Endas in the Top Four Final. In the league the top four teams played off in a semi-final, final format to decide the eventual league winners. St Sylvesters and Naomh Mearnog from the northside were relegated to Division 2 to be replaced by two southside clubs St Olafs and Ballinteer St Johns.

In the senior championship St Judes had an easy win against Craobh Chiarain in the first round but were knocked out by Lucan Sarsfields after a disappointing performance in the second round. From the 1999 championship team against St Vincents only six players lined out in the 2002 championship against Lucan namely Terry Orr, Ciaran Voyles, Kieran Durkan, Peter Gilsenan, Enda Crennan, and Stephen Cunningham. Enda Sheehy was of course a senior player in that period but was injured for both the 1999 and 2002 championship games. Ciaran McGovern was also an ever present in that period but did not play in the 1999 championship due to a broken jaw received against Ballymun Kickhams.

The following was the starting St Judes team for the league game against Ballymun Kickhams in April 2002: Terence Orr, Declan Loye, Damien Carroll, Damien Rafferty, Seán Breheny, Stephen Cunningham, Ciaran Voyles (0-01), Enda Sheehy, Peter Gilsenan (0-02,1F), Enda Crennan (0-03), Kieran Durkan, Peter Harlow (0-02), Brendan McManamon, Gerry O'Reilly, John Waldron.

The league results were as follows with league finishing positions in brackets:

2002/04/07	V B'mun Kickhams (5)	Draw	0-08 to 0-08
2002/05/01	V St Brigids (9)	Draw	0-10 to 1-07
2002/05/05	V Na Fianna (10)	Win	2-12 to 1-09
2002/05/08	V Lucan Sarsfields (8)	Win	1-11 to 0-09
2002/06/05	V Ballyboden (2)	Loss	0-07 to 0-12

2002/06/09	V Erins Isle (11)	Draw	0-12 to 0-12
2002/06/12	V Kilmacud Crokes (1)	Loss	0-08 to 1-11
2002/06/19	V St Vincents (3)	Loss	2-09 to 2-13
2002/07/03	V Naomh Mearnog (14)	Draw	2-05 to 0-11
2002/07/07	V St Sylvesters (13)	Win	0-10 to 1-03
2002/07/15	V Raheny (6)	Win	1-14 to 1-12
2202/07/21	V Craobh Chiarain (16)	Loss	0-11 to 0-12
	V St Annes (15)	Win	
	V St Marys (4)	Loss	
	V Thomas Davis (7)	Loss	

Senior football championship

SFC Rnd 1 002/07/11   St Judes V Craobh Chiarain   Win   3-10 to 1-06

SFC Rnd 2 2002/07/28 St Judes V Lucan Sarsfields Loss 0-6 to 0-10

Our Intermediate team under Colm O'Brien and Declan O'Boyle came second in the league and got promotion to Adult Division 3 (this is the old Intermediate 1 division). They were beaten in the second round of the championship. The Junior A footballers under Tommy Hartnett, Bartle Faulkner, Ernest Kenny and Noel Lyons won the AFL6 league (old Junior 2 division) and gained promotion to AFL5 (old Junior 1 division). They also had a tremendous run in the Junior B championship and won their way to the championship final with wins against Liffey Gaels, Ballyfermot in the first two rounds. On 29th September 2002 they beat Ballymun Kickhams in the quarter final in Tymon on a scoreline of 0.08 to 0.07. They then went on to record a comprehensive win in the semi-final against Ballyboden St Endas in Balgriffin on a scoreline of 3.10 to 0.08 in probably their best performance of the year.

They were eventually beaten in the county final by St Olafs on the 20th October 2002 in O'Toole Park on a scoreline of 0.04 to 1.04 after a lacklustre performance. The following team lined out in the B championship final: Robbie Hyland, Ronan Howard, David Campbell, Kevin Hayes, Liam Coffey, Shane O'Brien, Geoffrey Kane, Peter McGlynn, Conor McBride, Eoghan O'Neill, Mark Kavanagh, Bart Lehane, Dermot Barry, Ross McDermott, Donnacha Ryan. Subs: Niall Lalor, Paraic Craig, Barry Faulkner, Dave McGlynn, Peter McGlynn, Paul Cunningham, Ciaran Coates, Dara Lowe, Dara Keane, Stephen Joyce, Brian Sommers, Conor Ryan, Conor Lehane, Paul Sweeney.

St Judes did not compete in the Junior A championship in 2002. The Junior B team were beaten in the 2nd round of the Junior C championship by St Brendans and the Junior D or Dream Team were beaten in the 1st round of the Junior D championship by St Oliver Plunketts after a disappointing performance.

lary 16, 2003

St Jude's U21s show their class
Templeogue boys lift Division One football crown

St Jude's celebrate after winning the Division One U21 League crown in Bohernabreena last Saturday.

ST JUDE'S under-21 footballers showed their true class as they lifted the league title in Bohernabreena last Saturday.

In collecting the Division One title for the first time, the Templeogue side produced a gritty display in a hardfought encounter with Parnells.

Jude's started brightly with Damien Keogh scoring a point before Brendan McMenamen combined with Ross McDermott to fire home the opening goal inside the first five minutes.

However, Parnells bounced back and enjoyed a spell of domination that saw Stephen Cluxton, Stephen Mills and Martin Whelan fire over three unanswered points.

And when Cormac Sugrue blasted home a cracking goal on 14 minutes it left the Coolock side four points up and looking very dangerous.

But this lead was quickly wiped out as Jude's responded with McMenamen, Joey Donnelly, Keogh and Waldron sending over points to leave the sides deadlocked at the interval.

Substitute Seamus Ryan made an immediate impact when he fired over two scores in the second half before Whelan responded to leave the sides level.

The turning point in the game arrived on 16 minutes when a long defensive clearance was met by Keogh who unleashed a powerful shot to Jason Morgan's net.

Parnells found it difficult to recover from this blow, but they were awarded a penalty which was wasted by Dublin under-21 player Stephen Mills.

St Jude's Bart Lehane was sent off in the closing stages along with Martin Whelan of Parnells as the game threatened to boil over.

Parnells pushed forward late in the game and were unlucky not to score a goal when Mark Fitzpatrick blasted a shot off the post before Ross McDermott kicked over the crucial point in injury-time to leave the final score St Jude's 2-8, Parnells 1-7.

St Jude's under-21 captain Andy Glover proudly displays the League trophy with mentors Tommy Hartnett, Bart Faulkner and Paddy Keogh in Bohernabreena.

ST JUDE'S: P Copeland, G Hartnett, S Brehony, K Hayes, L Coffey, A Glover, N O'Shea, S Earley, B Lehane, D Keogh (1-2), J Waldron (0-1), P Cunningham, J Donnelly (0-1), R McDermott (0-1), B McMenamen (1-1). Subs: S Lynch for Donnelly, S Ryan (0-2) for Cunningham, C McBride for Hartnett and S O'Brien for Hayes.

Mark's reach U21 hurling 'B' Final

Richie Neville and David O'Callaghan were in action for St Mark's under-21 hurlers in the C'ship.

ST MARK'S under-21s qualified for their second final in the space of a week when they reached the 'B' Championship Hurling decider in Rathcoole last Saturday.

Adrift by a point at the break, Mark's turned on the style after the break as they coasted to a 2-10 to 1-1 win over Na Fianna.

Mark's stepped up the pace in the second half, their forwards coming up trumps with some vital scores.

Barry Kennedy was Mark's top scorer with six points while David O'Callaghan, Fergal and Ciaran Rabbitte also split the posts with good scores.

Eddie Cooling grabbed Mark's opening goal while substitute Stephen Tynan added a second to complete a fine outing for the Springfield side.

St Mark's now play Ballinteer St John's in the final.

ST MARK'S: A Long, A Gildea, A Mullen, G Browne, J McNeill, Conal Rabbitte, T Tuffy, S McCann, Ciaran Rabbitte, B Kennedy, D O'Callaghan, F Rabbitte, D Cullen, D Flaherty, R Neville. **Subs:** B Sharkey for Tuffy, E Cooling for Neville, S Tynan for Flaherty.

The Dream Team had come into existence in 2002 under the management of James Durkan and Anto Gilleran assisted by Pat O'Brien and later Mervyn O'Boyle.

The Under 21 football team with Tommy Hartnett, Bartle Faulkner and Paddy Keogh at the helm had a tremendous year all round. This squad is based around the players who reached the Under 16 football and hurling championship finals in 1996/97 and a number of these players also played in the Junior B football championship final later in the year. Therefore a number of these players played in three of the four football championship finals played by St Judes in the first twenty five years of their history. A number of the same players would also have played in a couple of hurling championship finals in the same period.

They Under 21 team won the Division 1 South league after an unbeaten run in the competition recording wins against Lucan Sarsfields, Liffey Gaels, St Brigids, St James Gaels, Naomh Fionnbarra, Crumlin and Good Counsel. On 28th October 2002 they beat Ballymun Kickhams in Dolphin Park in the All-Dublin Under 21 semi-final. They then went on to record a great win against Northside league winners Parnells in the All Dublin Under 21 final at Bohernabreena on 11th January 2003.

The Under 21 A football team also had a tremendous run in the championship, with wins against Naomh Mearnog in Tymon on 28th September 2002 and O'Tooles in Tymon on 12th October 2002. They beat the Barry Cahill led St Brigids in the championship semi-final on a scoreline of 2.12 to 2.10 after a tremendous game on a poor pitch in Newcastle on the 25th January 2003. Crucial goals at key times in the game from Damien Keogh and Seamus Ryan set up St Judes for a great victory against favourites St Brigids. They were beaten in the county final in Parnell Park on 22nd February by a very strong Kilmacud Crokes side on a scoreline of 0.04 to 0.11. Kilmacud Crokes were the better team on the day in a game in which St Judes never really got going particularly in the second half when playing with the wind when they managed to score only a single point. Kilmacud Crokes fielded a very strong side with a number of Dublin senior and Under 21 county players including Darren Magee, Conor Murphy, Liam Og O Heineachain, Paul Griffin and Nathan Kane. The St Judes Under 21 team lined out as follows with Evening Herald match ratings in brackets: Paul Copeland (8), Ger Hartnett (6), Seán Breheny (6), Kevin Hayes (6), Niall O'Shea (6), Andrew Glover (6), Shane O'Brien (6), Stephen Early (7), Ross McDermott (7), Damien Keogh (6), John Waldron (6), Paul Cunningham (7), Michael Lyons (6), Seamus Ryan (7), Brendan McMenamon (8). Subs: Bart Lehane (7) for Stephen Early (42 mins), Liam Coffey (6) for Andrew Glover (45 mins), Stephen Lynch (6) for Paul Cunningham (48 mins).

The St Judes Under 21B football were beaten in the B championship by Parnells. The B championship again seems to have a number of teams who should be playing in the A championship which is very unfair on genuine B championship teams. AOB: County representatives: Enda Crennan (Dublin SF), Conor Conneely (Roscommon SF), Damien Rafferty (Down SF), Michael Lyons (Dublin U21). Ernest Kenny was a mentor on Dublin Junior football team.

Michael Lyons picked up a Leinster Under 21 football championship medal and an All-Ireland runners-up medal when Dublin were beaten by a fine Galway side in the All-Ireland Under 21 final. Enda Crennan collected a Leinster senior football final medal with Dublin on the 14th July 2002 when Dublin beat Kildare in the Leinster final. The St Judes teams of recent years have always had tremendous supporters but it was not always the case. In the early days St Judes was obviously mainly known as an underage club and support for the earlier adult teams was limited if we exclude people who were involved as mentors or players. Frank McSweeney of course has been a tremendous supporter right through the years and oversaw St Judes progress from junior to intermediate and on to senior. When St Judes played their first Intermediate game against Kilmacud Crokes on 6th November 1988 the St Judes support consisted of Frank McSweeney, Ger Tannam's father and the Tannam family dog. The support base swelled in the nineties with our progress to senior football. The hardcore supporter set during this period would have included Jack Lernihan, Seán Conway, John McGovern, Patsy Tyrrell, Luke Mooney, Joe McDonnell, Mick O'Brien, McBrides, Feores, Tommy Bassett, Bernie Gilsenan, Br Bert Buckley, Finbar Hanratty, Christy Kilcoyne, Bernie Gallagher, Paddy Russell, Crennans, Quinns, Coghlans, Guckians, O'Garas, Lehanes, Ryans, Ernest Kenny, Morans, Joyces, Durkans, Orrs, O'Boyles, Monaghans, Bradys, Donnchadh Lehane, Jack Tierney, Charlie McGovern, Molamphys, Brehenys, Noel Lyons, O'Riordans, Kanes, Cunninghams and many more.

The year 2002 was unique in St Judes club history in that at the end of the year St Judes were now competing in Division 1 leagues at the following levels from minor to senior: Senior 1 football, Senior 1 Hurling, Senior 1 camogie, Intermediate 1 football (now AFL 3), Junior 1 football (now AFL 5), Junior 1 hurling, Junior 1 camogie, Under 21A football, Under 21A hurling, Minor A football and Minor A Hurling. The only missing links in the division 1 stakes are the Intermediate hurling and camogie division 1 leagues. St Judes were therefore competing at division 1 level in 11 of the possible 13 divisions. Adult football has made tremendous progress in the relatively short twentyfive year history of the club. The age profile of most of our present adult teams is quite young and there are great expectations for further progress and success in the coming years.

THE NOOK
Don Lehane

Social Column: To the uninitiated the Nook is the location in St Judes clubhouse bar where all key club issues are discussed, decided and ratified – a sort of upper chamber if you like. We will call it "The Nook" for convenience as it is a little shorter than describing it as "the area of the St Judes bar backing on to the wall between the main entrance to the back bar and the left semi-circle of the bar counter encompassing the bar exit". From the time the new clubhouse opened in 1988 The Nook quickly became the favoured meeting point of club mentors, selected players and senior supporters who enjoyed a pint and discussions on hurling and football related topics. Membership of The Nook is fairly informal but a serious knowledge of GAA matters is a prerequisite for long-term acceptance. It can take years for new members to gain full acceptance in The Nook. However exceptions are made as in the recent case of Paddy Keogh who made the breakthrough in a relatively short period despite showing a startling lack of knowledge on hurling when he sat his aptitude test. Automatic membership is given to anyone who was present at the GPO in 1916 or attended the 1947 All-Ireland Final in the Polo Grounds or was a participant in the Joe McDonnell led Battle of Glencullen in the eighties. The Nook has survived a number of demolition attempts down through the years but refuses to go away and its long-term future as a St Judes institution seems destined to stay regardless of periodic efforts by various management committees to consign it to oblivion. It has outlasted the Wailing Wall, the Berlin Wall and with the help of An Taisce is destined to outstay the Confession Box and The Lake. The unfortunate location of a bar exit in the centre of The Nook has been the source of a number of difficulties over the years and has resulted in some of the more entertaining physical contests outside pitch number 4. The club social committee have now recognised the potential crowd pulling effect of these events and a number of mostly heavy weight contests are regularly arranged during slack periods of the season or to camoflauge a poor championship run. Top attractions in recent times have Big John v Cigarette Machine and Johnny v The Bull Bars. Early attempts at disrupting activities in The Nook were rather crude and consisted mainly of full frontal assaults and swinging ice buckets which was bread an butter to Nook residents who had played their early football with Achill, Nobber, Ballymore Eustace, the Nire or the Willies. The introduction of a cigarette machine to The Nook was the first sign of an escalation in hostilities. However the immediate effect of this course of action was to introduce a whole new set of passing traffic to the Nook and the experiment lasted only a few weeks before normality was restored and the cigarette machine was removed to the environs of the Confession Box. The most recent attempt at disruption has been the introduction of bull bars to The Nook in a further fruitless attempt to close down the upper chamber.

Don Lehane on Nook duty with Jim Coghlan riding shotgun.

Johnny and Essie O'Gara with Padraig and Maureen O'Riordan.

Saints top s in

CHAMPIONS!: The victorious St. Jude's under-21 footballers celebrate their victory over Parnells at Bohernabreena.

Jude's battle back to beat the odds and claim title

ST. JUDE'S.....................2-9
PARNELLS.......................1-8

ST. JUDE'S overcame all the odds to defeat Parnells in the Under-21 Football League final at Bohernabreena on Saturday afternoon.

Tommy Hartnett's Saints entered the contest without four key players due to exams at Tallaght IT, and they looked to be paying the price as Parnells raced into a four-point lead after 20 minutes (1-5 to 1-1).

But the Templeogue side recovered brilliantly to pull level at 1-5 apiece by the turn, as Stephen Earley and Bart Lehane came to the fore in midfield, and half-forward Damien Keogh began to torment the Parnells' defence.

Jude's then pulled clear with a Keogh goal midway through the second half, and never looked back thereafter as they defended superbly to run out deserving four-point victors.

The first half was a tale of two superb goals. Barely six minutes had elapsed when Brendan McManamon produced a sublime finish to the net after a flowing move that also involved Joey Donnelly and Ross McDermott, leaving Jude's 1-1 to 0-1 up.

But Parnells responded five minutes later when, after Stephen Cluxton had pointed for the northsiders, Cormac Sugrue spectacularly netted from 25 yards to hand his side a one-point advantage (1-2 to 1-1).

Jimmy O'Grady's Parnells outfit assumed control for the following ten minutes and, with Stephen Mills displaying some superb skills in the half-forward line, moved 1-5 to 1-1 ahead after impressive points from Martin Whelan and Mills (2) himself.

Parnells weren't to score again in the half, however, and Hartnett's troops, with Keogh leading the way, took advantage to level matters at

FROM PREVIOUS PAGE
week. Our thanks to St James Gaels on organising a tremendous tournament. Best wishes to Ian Coughlan as he recovers from his knee operation. Adult playing membership fee €50 now due. Non players €25

THOMAS DAVIS
THE Executive Committee wish to thank all the club members who assisted in the hosting of the Dublin v Wicklow O'Byrne Cup match on Sunday last. All Adult hurlers please note that training has recommenced on Monday and Wednesday nights. Football training on Tuesdays and Thursdays nights. Members should check the fixture lists for details of the U21 Football Championship replay v Parnells. All members please note that Annual subscriptions are now due.

TRINITY GAELS
THE U15s-16s are scheduled for games this weekend, check the fixtures for full details. Senior footballers are due to take part in the Innsfails Compromise tournament this Sunday, all support welcome. The club would like to wish a speedy recovery to Stephen Kavanagh who is recovering from a recent operation. Best wishes also to Jonathan Smith who suffered a knee injury at the weekend. Executive committee meeting takes place this Thursday at 8.30. All players, supporters etc. are reminded that club

membership is now due and is payable to Eamonn Clifford - €30 for players and €10 for social members and juveniles. All outstanding Lotto monies should be paid to Vincent Murphy Snr ASAP. Adult training continues every Tuesday and Thursday at 7.0, both footballers and hurlers are urged to attend. All members should note that the club AGM takes place on February 10. Lotto, no jackpot winner - Jackpot next week €3,200.

UCD
THE term is now in full swing and all our teams are back in full training. On Wednesday our Freshers hurlers and Seniors play NUI Galway on January 25 in Belfield. Both ladies football teams have qualified for the all-Ireland League play-offs. The handball ladder league is in progress.

WANDERERS
JUNIOR 1 training continues on Tuesdays and Thursdays at 8.0 in Kilvere. Any player who cannot attend please contact Bert ASAP. All new players are very welcome

and anyone interested in playing should contact info@ballyboderwanderers.com or 0879789843. Juvenile training resumes this week in Knocklyon school, Boys Tuesday 7.0 (Contact Leo 4931399); Girls Wednesday 8.0 (Contact Rhona: 0863300412). Club AGM has been rescheduled and will now take place on Thursday, January 23 at 8.0 at Frank Kelly Park. All motions and nominations must be submitted in writing and received by the Club Secretary, Brendan Heavey, Rowan Hill, Tibradden, Dublin 16 no later than Friday, January 17. The club would like to wish David Mannion a speedy recovery from his recent injury. Any member who wishes to have an item included in the club notes please contact info@ballyboderwanderers.com or any committee member no later than Sunday.

WHITEHALL C'CILLES
MEETING for all adult footballers and hurlers tomorrow evening in Castlemoate House (opposite Coachman's Inn) at 7.45. All Adult players are asked to attend. Training resumes in Cloghran on Thursday at 7.30. The Junior Footballers have one game to play from 2002 Season and this will be fixed for Sunday, January 26. Training has now resumed for all Juvenile teams and for the nursery. Juvenile football games have been fixed for next weekend. Membership fees for 2003 are now due and members are asked to pay early.

Under 21 decider

GOAL! Brendan McMenamin of St. Jude's blasts the ball past Parnells' 'keeper Jason Morgan for the opening goal during the U21 FL decider at Bohernabreena
(Pictures: Ray Cullen)

the interval.

The second half resumed in a score for score fashion, as Parnells registered on the scoreboard through two points from Whelan, while Jude's substitute Seamus Ryan made an immediate impact by splitting the posts twice to leave the teams locked on 1-7 apiece after 40 minutes.

The game's decisive moment arrived midway through the half, when Keogh displayed brilliant predatory instincts to find the net in glorious style and hand Jude's a three-point cushion with a quarter of an hour remaining.

And it got better for the Templeogue crew soon after, as Lehane pointed to hand his side a commanding advantage (2-8 to 1-7).

Parnells were thrown a much-needed lifeline when John Peyton was fouled in the area with ten minutes remaining, but the otherwise impressive Mills couldn't

BY ALAN BRADY

take advantage from the penalty spot and sent his effort to the right and wide.

Controversy ensued five minutes later, when Parnells' Jude's received their marching orders for an off-the-ball skirmish.

Parnells were now throwing everything at Jude's, but the Templeogue defence stood firm as O'Grady's men began to panic.

The Collinstown team's day was summed up four minutes into injury time, when Mark Fitzpatrick had a fantastic opportunity for a goal that would have left the minimum between the sides, but the centre-half back struck the post when clean through.

That proved to be Parnells' last opportunity, and the final whistle sounded seconds later to hand Jude's a deserved victory.

MATCHFILE

► **SCORERS: St. Jude's:** D Keogh 1-2, B McMenamin 1-1, S Ryan 0-2, S Earley, B Lehane, R McDermott, J Waldron (f) 0-1 each. **Parnells:** C Sugrue 1-0, M Whelan (2f), S Mills (1f) 0-3 each, S Cluxton, B Byrne (f) 0-1 each.
► **St. Jude's:** P Copeland 8; G Hartnett 7, B Brehony 8, K Hayes 7; L Coffey 8, A Glover 8, N O'Shea 8; S Earley 8, B Lehane 8; D Keogh 9, J Waldron 8, P Cunningham 7; J Donnelly 7, R McDermott 8, B McMenamin 9. **Subs:** S Ryan 9 for Cunningham, C McBride 7 for Hartnett, S O'Brien 7 for K Hayes, S Lynch 7 for Donnelly.
► **Parnells:** J Morgan 7; P Rigney 7, G Ryan 7, L Browne 7; W Henry 7, M Fitzpatrick 7, C Quinn 7; M Whelan 6, B Byrne 7; S Mills 8, C O'Reilly 6, C Sugrue 8; E Browne 6, S Cluxton 7, J Peyton 6. **Subs:** D Fitzpatrick 6 for Mills, P McClelland 6 for O'Reilly.
► **Referee:** S McAllister (Starlights).
► **Ratings:** Match: Hard-fought game — 8. St. Jude's: Deserved winners — 9. Parnells: Faded away — 7.
► **Conditions:** Dull but calm.
► **Mentors:** St. Jude's: Tommy Hartnett, Bart Faulkner, Paddy Keogh. Parnells: Jimmy O'Grady, Mark Farrell, Mick Phelan, Olly Ryan.
► **Wides:** St. Jude's 4 (3 in first half); Parnells 8 (2 in first half).
► **Player-of-the-Match:** Damien Keogh (St. Jude's).

St Judes 2000 Victory Song

(Air: Merry Ploughboy) Gerry Quinn

Now we are the boys from St Judes
And our colours are navy and blue
To do battle for the Dublin Senior Football League
Came our stalwarts staunch and true.
So let us join in chorus
We will make the rafters ring.
Our boys they were victorious
We salute this gallant team.
Chorus
And now we are League Champions
Our hearts are filled with pride
Ciaran McGovern's men they were going to win,
Here's to Christy, Charlie and Brian.

From number one to twenty five
Our lads were tried and true,
Throughout the year we had no fear,
They did honour to the navy and blue,
All the other teams they had their dreams,
Ballyboden, Kilmacud to name a few,
They were toppled from their lofty perch
By the boys from brave St Judes.

Chorus
The year two thousand we will remember,
You did not let us down,
They brought home the cup in glory
And fought hard in every round,
For they stood the test with Dublin's best
Never hearing of defeat,
We'll cheer them on to victory
No matter who they meet.
Chorus

Club executive officers

ST JUDES GAELIC FOOTBALL CLUB

1978 – President None; Chairman Fr John Greene; Vice Chairman Ernest Kenny; Secretary Cyril Bates; Assistant Secretary Eamon O'Reilly; Treasurer John Gallen; Registrar Cyril Bates; PRO None.

1979 – President None; Chairman Fr John Greene; Vice Chairman Ernest Kenny; Secretary Cyril Bates; Assistant Secretary Eamon O'Reilly; Treasurer John Gallen; Registrar Cyril Bates; PRO None.

1980 – President None; Chairman Fr. John Greene; Vice Chairman Ernest Kenny; Secretary Charles Moran; Assistant Secretary Eamon O'Reilly; Treasurer John Gallen; Registrar Charles Moran; PRO None.

CUMANN PEIL NAOMH JUDE

1981 – President None; Chairman Fr John Greene; Vice Chairman Ernest Kenny; Secretary Charles Moran; Assistant Secretary Eamon O'Reilly; Treasurer John Gallen; Registrar Charles Moran; PRO None.

1982 – Chairman Donnchadh Ó Liatháin; Vice Chairman Ernest Kenny; Secretary Charles Moran; Assistant Secretary Eamon O'Reilly; Treasurer John Gallen; Registrar Jimmy O'Dwyer; PRO None.

CUMANN LUTHCHLEAS GAEL NAOMH JUDE

1983 – President Joe Morrin; Chairman Donnchadh Ó Liatháin; Vice Chairman Eddie Walsh; Secretary Charles Moran; Assistant Secretary Eamon O'Reilly; Treasurer John Gallen; Registrar Jimmy O'Dwyer; PRO None

1984 – President Joe Morrin; Chairman Charles Moran; Vice Chairman Eddie Walsh; Secretary Donnchadh Ó Liatháin; Assistant Mick O'Brien; Treasurer John Gallen; Registrar Jimmy O'Dwyer; PRO None.

1985 – President Joe Morrin; Chairman Charles Moran; Vice Chairman Eddie Walsh; Secretary Donnchadh Ó Liatháin; Assistant Secretary Mick O'Brien; Treasurer John Gallen; Registrar Jimmy O'Dwyer; PRO None.

1986 – President Joe Morrin; Chairman Charles Moran; Vice Chairman Eddie Walsh; Secretary Donnchadh Ó Liatháin; Assistant Secretary Mick O'Brien; Treasurer John Gallen; Registrar Jimmy O'Dwyer; PRO Declan Feore.

1987 – President Joe Morrin; Chairman Charles Moran; Vice Chairman Mick

Hartnett; Secretary Donnchadh Ó Liatháin; Assistant Secretary Mick O'Brien; Treasurer John Gallen; Treasurer Jimmy O'Dwyer; PRO Declan Feore.

1988 – President Joe Morrin; Chairman Charles Moran; Vice Chairman Mick Hartnett; Secretary Donnchadh Ó Liatháin; Assistant Secretary Tommy Hartnett; Treasurer Mick O'Brien; Registrar Jimmy O'Dwyer; PRO Declan Feore.

1989 – President Joe Morrin; Chairman Charles Moran; Vice Chairman Mick Hartnett; Secretary Tommy Hartnett; Assistant Secretary Donnchadh Ó Liatháin; Treasurer Mick O'Brien; Registrar Pádraig O'Riordain; PRO Declan Feore.

1990 – President Joe Morrin; Chairman Charles Moran; Vice Chairman Joe McDonnell; Secretary Tommy Hartnett; Assistant Secretary Donnchadh Ó Liatháin; Treasurer Mick O'Brien; Registrar Pádraig O'Riordain; PRO Jimmy O'Dwyer.

1991 – President Ernest Kenny; Chairman Donnchadh Ó Liatháin; Vice Chairman Joe McDonnell; Secretary Tommy Hartnett; Assistant Secretary Máire McSherry; Treasurer Jim Coghlan; Registrar Padraig O' Riordain; PRO Jimmy O'Dwyer.

1992 – President Frank McSweeney; Chairman Donnchadh Ó Liatháin; Vice Chairman Joe McDonnell; Secretary Tommy Hartnett; Assistant Secretary Maire McSherry; Treasurer Jim Coghlan; Registrar Tony McGinley; PRO Garrett Edge.

1993 – President Frank McSweeney; Chairman Donnchadh Ó Liatháin; Vice Chairman Seán Breheny; Secretary Maire McSherry; Assistant Secretary Tommy Hartnett; Treasurer Jim Coghlan; Registrar Tony McGinley; PRO Martin McCabe

1994 – President Frank McSweeney; Chairman Seán Breheny; Vice Chairman Martin Molamphy; Secretary Máire McSherry; Assistant Secretary Seán Fallon; Treasurer Jack Lernihan; Registrar Pádraig O' Riordain; PRO Martin McCabe.

1995 – President Donnchadh Ó Liathain; Chairman Seán Breheny; Vice Chairman Martin Molamphy; Secretary Máire McSherry; Assistant Secretary Tony Gilleran; Treasurer Jack Lernihan; Registrar Pádraig O'Riordain; PRO Martin McCabe.

1996 – President Donnchadh Ó Liatháin; Chairman Seán Breheny; Vice Chairman Martin Molamphy; Secretary Joan Molamphy; Assistant Secretary Máire McSherry; Treasurer Jack Lernihan; Registrar James Durkan; PRO Michael Fortune.

1997 – President Donnchadh Ó Liatháin; Chairman Martin Molamphy; Vice Chairman Charles Moran; Secretary Joan Molamphy; Assistant Secretary Máire McSherry; Treasurer John Brady; Registrar Jack Lernihan; PRO Michael Fortune.

1998 – President Ernest Kenny; Chairman Martin Molamphy; Vice Chairman Charles Moran; Secretary Joan Molamphy; Assistant Secretary Betty Collard; Treasurer John Brady; Registrar Jack Lernihan; PRO Michael Fortune.

1999 – President Ernest Kenny; Chairman Martin Molamphy; Vice Chairman Charles Moran; Secretary Seán Breheny; Assistant Secretary Betty Collard; Treasurer John Brady; Registrar Jack Lernihan; PRO Colum Grogan.

2000 – President Ernest Kenny; Chairman Seán McBride; Vice Chairman John Brady; Secretary Seán Breheny; Assistant Secretary Betty Collard; Treasurer Charlie Hennessy; Registrar Peter Hanrahan; PRO Colum Grogan.

2001 – President Jack Lernihan; Chairman Seán McBride; Vice Chairman John Brady; Secretary Seán Breheny; Assistant Secretary Marie O'Brien; Treasurer Charlie Hennessy; Registrar Peter Hanrahan; PRO Colum Grogan.

2002 – President Jack Lernihan; Chairman Seán McBride; Vice Chairman John Brady; Secretary Colum Grogan; Assistant Secretary Marie O'Brien; Treasurer Charlie Hennessy; Registrar Peter Hanrahan; PRO Declan Doyle.

2003 – President Jack Lernihan; Chairman John Brady; Vice Chairman Paul McCann; Secretary Colum Grogan; Assistant Secretary Marie O'Brien; Treasurer Frank Mahon; Registrar Betty Collard; PRO Declan Doyle.

Roll of honour – adult football

Year	Level	League	Competition Result	Comment
1987	Junior A	JFL3	Winners Junior 3 (South)	Promoted Jun Div 1 (JFL1)
1987	Junior A	JFL3	Winners Junior 3 (All-Dublin)	Beat St Patricks
1988	Junior A	JFL1	Winners Junior 1 (South)	Promoted Intermediate (IFL)
1988	Junior B	JFL4	Winners Ó Broin Cup	First adult cup win
1991	Junior A	AIJ 7s	Runners up All-Ireland Jun 7's	Defeated by St Olafs
1992	Junior A	AIJ 7s	Winners All-Ireland Junior 7's	Beat An Spidéal in final
1993	Inter	IFL	Winners Intermediate League	Promoted Senior 2 (SFL2)
1993	Inter	Loving Cup	Winners Loving Cup	
1993	Junior A	AIJ 7's	Winners All-Ireland Junior 7's	Beat Kilcummin in final
1994	Junior B	JFL 8	Runners up Junior 8	Promoted Juni Div 7 (JFL7)
1995	Junior A	JFL4	Runners up Junior 4	Promoted Jun Div 3 (JFL3)
1995	Junior B	JFL7	Winners Junior 7	Promoted Jun Div 6 (JFL6)
1996	Senior 2	SFL2	Runners up Senior 2	Promoted Senior 1 (SFL1)
1996	Junior A	JFL3	Winners Junior 3	Promoted Junior 1 (JFL1)
1996	Junior B	JFL6	Winners Junior 6	Promoted Junior 5 (JFL5)
1996	Junior C	JFL8	Runners up Junior 8	Promoted Junior 6 (JFL6)
1998	Junior B	JFL 6	Winners Junior 6	Promoted Junior 5 (JFL5)
1998	Junior D	JFL 8	Winners Junior 8	Promoted Junior 7 (JFL7)
1999	Junior A	JFL 1	Runners up Junior 1	Promoted Intermediate 2
1999	Senior 1	SFL1	Runners up Senior 1	
2000	Senior 1	SFL1	Winners Senior 1	
2000	Inter	Joy Cup	Winners Joy Cup	
2000	Senior	Herald Cup	Winners E.Herald Floodlit Cup	
2001	Inter	Loving Cup	Winners Loving Cup	
2001	Junior A	Murphy Cup	Winners Murphy Cup	
2001	Junior A	JFL	Runners up Junior league	
2001	Junior C	JFL	Runners up Junior league	
2002	Inter	IFL2	Runners up Intermediate 2	Promoted Inter. 1 (AFL3)
2002	Junior A	JFL1	Runners up Junior B C'ship	Lost to Fingal Ravens
2002	U21	U21 Div1	Winners U21 League (South)	
2002	U21	U21 Div1	Winners U21 League (All Dublin)	Beat Parnells
2002	U21	U21 Div1	Runners up U21 C'ship	Lost Kilmacud Crokes

Roll of honour – adult hurling

1989	Junior A Championship
1994	Top 4 Winners: Promotion to Intermediate 2
1995	Junior A Championship Runners up
	Intermediate Div 2 Winners: Promotion to Div 1.
	Doyle Cup
	Junior D - Runners up Murphy Cup and Fletcher Shield
1996	Junior A Championship
	Junior D Championship
1997	Corn Ceitinn
	All-Ireland Junior Sevens Shield Winners
1998	Intermediate Premier Division - Promoted to Senior 2.
	Corn Fogarty Runners up
	Junior C Championship
	Junior C League
1999	Junior B League
	Miller Shield
2001	Seniors Promoted to Div 1.
2002	Junior B Championship
2003	Junior A Championship Runners up

Roll of honour – camogie

1990	Under 11 League and Championship winners.
1991	Under 11 League and Championship winners.
1992	Under 11 Championship winners.
1993	Under 12 League winners.
1994	Under 14 Feile Na nGael Dublin winners
	Under 11 Championship winners.
1995	Under 14 League winners
	Under 12 Championship winners.
1998	Intermediate Championship winners
	Junior B Championship winners.
2000	Senior B Championship winners.
2001	Senior B Championship winners.
2002	Junior B League winners.
	Under 11 League South winners.

Roll of honour – All Ireland junior sevens hurling

YEAR	WINNER	RUNNERS-UP
1990	Mullinahone (Tipperary)	Faythe Farriers (Wexford)
1991	Portumna, (Galway)	Na Piarsaigh, (Limerick)
1992	Na Piarsaigh, (Limerick)	Killavilla, (Offaly)
1993	Lattin-Cullen, (Tipperary)	Rahoon/Newcastle, (Galway)
1994	St. Mogue's (Wexford)	Blarney, (Cork)
1995	Killanena, (Clare)	Carrigtwohill, (Cork)
1996	Killeagh (Cork)	Killanena (Clare)
1997	Argideen Rangers (Cork)	Killeagh (Cork)
1998	Tullogher/Rosbercon (Kilkenny)	Castlelyons (Cork)
1999	Kiltormer (Galway)	(Cork)
2000	Bride Rovers (Cork)	Galtee Rovers (Tipperary)
2001	Kiltormer (Galway)	Bride Rovers (Cork)
2002	St. Thomas's (Galway)	Ballybacon/Grange (Tipp).
2003	Moycullen (Galway)	Fr. O'Neills (Cork)

Laoch An Lae

1990	John Leahy, (Mullinahone)
1991	Damien Coleman, (Portumna)
1992	Damien Quigley, (Na Piarsaigh)
1993	Ger Maguire, (Lattin-Cullen)
1994	Brian Sheehan, (Blarney)
1995	Liam McNamara, (Killanena)
1996	Joe Deane, (Killeagh)
1997	Brian Hennessy, (Argideen Rangers)
1998	John Barron, (Tullogher/Rosbercon)
1999	Seán McKeigue, (Kiltormer)
2000	Andrew O'Flynn, (Bride Rovers)
2001	Dermot Kelly, (Kiltormer)
2002	Enda Tannion, (St. Thomas's)
2003	Eric Fox (Moycullen)

Roll of honour – All Ireland junior sevens football

YEAR	WINNER	RUNNERS-UP
1991	St. Olafs (Dublin)	St. Judes (Dublin)
1992	St. Judes (Dublin)	An Spideal (Galway)
1993	St. Judes (Dublin	Kilcummin (Kerry)
1994	An Ghaeltacht (Kerry)	Kilmeena (Mayo)
1995	Killevan Sarsfields (Monaghan)	St. Judes (Dublin)
1996	An Ghaeltacht (Kerry)	Ballykinlar (Down)
1997	Tyholland (Monaghan)	Drumconrath (Meath)
1998	Parke (Mayo)	Sneem (Kerry)
1999	Sneem (Kerry)	Ballinora (Cork)
2000	Sneem (Kerry)	Glenville (Cork)
2001	St. Agnes's (Antrim)	St. Aidan's (Roscommon)
2002	Ilen Rovers (Cork)	Curraha (Meath)
2003	Nobber (Meath)	St. Judes (Dublin)

Laoch an Lae

1991	Declan McFeeley	Foreglen O'Brien
1992	Donal Ó Flatharta	An Spideal
1993	Donal Dwyer	Kilcummin
1994	Cathal Carowley	Dohenys
1995	Dermot Lynch	Killevan Sarsfields
1996	Ian Larmer	Killevan Sarsfields
1997	Ian Farren	Tyholland
1998	Stephen Cloherty	Parke
1999	Frank Hussey	Sneem
2000	Michael Hussey	Sneem
2001	Paul Jordan	Antrim
2002	Diarmuid Duggan	Ilen Rovers
2003	Brian Farrell	Nobber

Roll of honour – juvenile football

1979/80	U 11 League Division 1 Winners
1981/82	U 10 League Division 1 Winners
1982/83	U 10 League Division 1 Winners
	U 11 League Division 1 Winners
	U12 League Division 1 Winners, Winners Centenary Cup
1983/84	U 11 League Division 1 Winners
1984/85	U 12 League Division 1 Winners
	U 13 League Division 2 Winners
1985/86	U13 League Division 1Winners
1986/87	U 14 League Division 1 Winners
	U16 League Division 2 Winners
1987/88	U 10 League Division 1 Winners, Winners Corrigan Cup
	U12 League Division 1 Winners
	U 15 League Division 1 Winners, Beaten in Championship Cup Final
1988/89	U 11 League Division 1 Winners
	U14 League Division 2 Winners, Winners McCarthy Shield
	U16 League Division 1 Winners, Winners Championship Cup
1989/90	U 12 League Division 1 Winners, Winners Special Cup
	U 14 League Division 1 Winners, Winners McCarthy Cup
1990/91	U 10 League Winners
	U 13 League Winners
	U15 League Division 1 Winners
1991/92	U 11 League Division 1 Winners
1992/93	U 12 League Division 1 Winners, Winners McCarthy Shield
1993/94	U 12 League Division 1 Winners, Beaten in Championship Cup Final
	U 16 League Division 1 Winners
1996/97	U 16 Beaten in Championship Cup Final
1997/98	U 9 League Winners
	U 11 Winners Special League
1998/99	U 11 Winners Special League
2002	U 10 Winners Special League
	U 14 League Division 3 Winners
	U 14 Division 2 Feile Winners
2003	U 15 League Division 2 Winners

Roll of honour – juvenile hurling

1983	Under 11	Runners-Up Division 1 South Dublin League
1985	Under 10	Winners Division 1 South Dublin Leauge
1985	Under 10	Runners-Up All-Dublin League
1986	Under 13	Winners Division 2 South Dublin League
1986	Under 13	Winners Dublin County Board Hurling Trophy
1987	Under 12	Winners Division 2 South Dublin League
1988	Under 14	Winners Division 1 All-Dublin League
1988	Under 14	Cup Winners Dublin Féile na nGael
1988	Under 14	Shield Winners Leinster Féile na nGael
1990/91	Under 10	Division 1 Winners
1992/93	Under 12	Division 1 Winners
1996/97	Under 16	Division 2 Joint Winners
1996	Under 11	Division 2 and Camaint Winners
1997	Under 12	Division 1 Runner-Up
1999	Under 14	Division 2 Winners
1999	Under 14	Runners Up Division 2 Féile
2000	Under 15	Division 2 Winners
2000	Under 15	Division 2 Championship Winners
2001	Under 16	Division 1 League Winners
2002	Under 14	Féile na nGael Winners (Division 2)
2003	Under 13	PJ Troy Tournament Winners (Division 2)

Roll of honour
– Bishop Galvin NS

ROLL OF HONOUR IN CUMANN NA MBUNSCOL FINALS

1989	Corn Chuchulainn	Division 3	Camogie
1989	Corn Frank Cahill	Division 3	Junior Hurling
1993	Corn Ui Phuirseail	Division 1	Camogie
1994	Corn Marino	Division 2	Senior Hurling
1996	Corn Herald Special	Division 1	Senior Hurling
2000	Corn Royal Breffni	Division 1	Girls' Football
2001	Corn Ui Phuirseail	Sp. Division 1	Camogie
2003	Corn Oidechais	Division 1	Junior Hurling
2003	Corn Oideachais B	Division 1	Junior Hurling